"Todd Hains has written an outstanding book about Luther's regular use of the analogy of faith when interpreting Holy Scripture. I commend this project highly. It makes a timely contribution to our understanding of both Luther's biblical exegesis and Luther's catholic, or traditional, approach to inculcating the Christian faith."
Douglas A. Sweeney, dean of Beeson Divinity School, Samford University

"It is widely recognized that Martin Luther was a singularly important contributor to the development of Christian theology and biblical exegesis. Dissatisfied with allegorical approaches to Scripture, Luther insisted on reading Scripture according to the literal sense. A break with the Catholic exegetical tradition, right? At the same time, Luther leveled withering criticisms against the literalist exegesis of his fellow Reformers, most of whom surely thought they were simply following his lead. How to place Luther within the emerging streams of Protestant biblical interpretation? By attending to Luther's exegetical deployment of the *analogia fidei*, the 'rule of faith' given in the Apostles' Creed, Todd Hains's meticulous study sheds new light on these questions. Sampling Luther's sermons *in extenso*, Hains will surprise even the seasoned reader of Luther with this thorough demonstration of the prominence therein of the *analogia fidei*. The result helps us better understand how Luther found himself fighting an exegetical *Zweifrontenkrieg* against both Catholic allegorizing and Protestant literalizing. The lessons from Hains's study, moreover, extend well beyond this important historical point. The Luther we meet here will challenge all serious Christian readers of the Bible to rethink the place of the 'faith once given' for the exegetical task today."
Mickey L. Mattox, professor of historical theology at Marquette University

"Church history, it has been said, is basically one long interaction of the church with the Bible. If so, the bold and at-times brash words of the sixteenth-century German Reformer Martin Luther have been undoubtedly one of the major voices in this unique colloquy. In this brilliant new study, Todd Hains delineates the various ways that Luther spoke into this centuries-long ecclesial *conversazione*. His study reveals that the German author, in his use of the rule of faith as an interpretative key, had far more in common with preceding voices and echoes than is usually imagined. He was a truly a Catholic exegete. An important monograph."
Michael A. G. Haykin, chair and professor of church history at The Southern Baptist Theological Seminary

"Drawing on extensive research in Luther's copious writings, Todd Hains has not only unlocked Luther's hermeneutical method but also given contemporary Christians an excellent guide into the mysteries of God's Word. This book is a treasure trove for preachers looking for better ways to feed their flocks with good solid nutrition gleaned from the Scriptures. Luther's approach to reading Scripture remains cutting edge and essential for contemporary Christians. In Todd's words, 'The same old catechism shines new light on new questions.' I think he's right. No matter your theological tradition, this book will broaden your mind and warm your heart."
Harold L. Senkbeil, author of *The Care of Souls: Cultivating a Pastor's Heart*

"Martin Luther, the analogy of faith, and allegory are all often employed like wax noses in contemporary hermeneutical debates. 'Luther said this,' 'the analogy of faith is that,' and 'allegory says anything you want it to say' are common tropes employed by a variety of interpretive camps in support of their own particular brand of biblical exegesis. Todd Hains's *Martin Luther and the Rule of Faith* speaks into this interpretive void and brings clarity and insight into an otherwise chaotic hermeneutical landscape. Hains describes and explains Luther's own views on the *analogia fidei* and allegory judiciously, and his tour of Luther's homiletical practice sheds further light on the subject. This is a retrieval project of the highest quality; even while it summarizes Luther's catechetical technique, it also catechizes the reader to read Scripture in light of its own catechism—the Ten Commandments, the Creed, and the Our Father. I cannot recommend this work highly enough to all readers, and especially to those who want to read the Bible with the saints."

Matthew Y. Emerson, professor of religion at Oklahoma Baptist University and author of *"He Descended to the Dead": An Evangelical Theology of Holy Saturday*

"Todd Hains describes how Luther was not an innovator but a faithful transmitter of the Christian tradition of biblical interpretation that relied on the rule of faith as conceptual lens to interpret the Bible. Hains detracts from a common interpretation of Luther as protagonist of the literal text that allows the reader—any reader—to interpret the plain sense of the text according to its literal grammatical sense. *Martin Luther and the Rule of Faith* is an impressive contribution to the study of the 'Catholic Luther' with its claim that Luther interpreted the Bible through a communal lens that had been in place since that lens was formulated in the early church and through the medieval tradition."

Christine Helmer, Peter B. Ritzma Chair of Humanities and professor of German and religious studies at Northwestern University

"In this deeply researched and accessibly written book, Todd Hains provocatively argues that Martin Luther was a Catholic interpreter of Scripture. The father of Protestantism interpreted Scripture not according to personal whim, subjective impression, or any rule external to Scripture itself, as it sometimes claimed, but always according to the analogy of faith (Rom 12:6), that is, the catechism. Hains convincingly shows that Luther's understanding of the Ten Commandments, the Apostles' Creed, the Lord's Prayer, and the sacraments governed his exegesis of the Bible, informing his every interpretive move. Hains commends the same approach for biblical interpretation today."

Ronald K. Rittgers, professor of the history of Christianity and Duke Divinity School Chair in Lutheran Studies

"In this impressive work, Todd Hains convincingly demonstrates the central place that the analogy of faith (*analogia fidei*) occupied in Martin Luther's theology and exegesis, and the significant ways it shaped his ministries as pastor, professor, polemicist, and doctor of the church. Scholars and students who engage this important book will never read the German Reformer the same way again."

Scott M. Manetsch, professor of church history at Trinity Evangelical Divinity School and associate general editor of the Reformation Commentary on Scripture

"Where would Luther stand in today's debates over how to read the Bible? 'Here I stand,' yes, but where is 'here'? Todd Hains demolishes the caricature of Luther encouraging individuals to read the Bible for themselves. In its place is the real, flesh-and-blood Luther who insists on reading the Bible according to the Rule of Faith: the three-corded catechism consisting of the Ten Commandments, the Apostles' Creed, and the Lord's Prayer. Where should we stand? On Scripture alone, to be sure, when read according to a hermeneutics of catechized faith."

Kevin J. Vanhoozer, research professor of systematic theology at Trinity Evangelical Divinity School

"Like the mastery of phonics for literacy, proper instruction in the simple foundations of the Christian faith opens up a disciple of Jesus to its immense profundity. That was Luther's conviction as a preacher and teacher of the Bible. That is also what Todd Hains demonstrates in his helpful account of Luther's analogical use of the catechism christologically and pastorally as the key to unlock the riches of God's Word. In this excellent book, Hains examines Luther's sermons on five passages as test cases to show how he did this."

John W. Kleinig, lecturer emeritus of exegetical and pastoral theology, Australian Lutheran College/University of Divinity

"What a rich and rewarding book! Todd Hains has provided us with an energizing guide to reading the Bible precisely as Holy Scripture. He shows not only that Luther was profoundly trinitarian in his Bible reading, but more importantly how. And his insights cut to the bone, shedding light on Luther's reading of Scripture as rooted in familiarity with the Ten Commandments, the Apostles' Creed, and the Our Father. In doing this Hains reaches into our own reading of Holy Scripture with surprising immediacy. Prepare for some of your caricatures of Luther to be smashed, but also be prepared to be delighted and fed by a work dripping with theological wisdom and energy."

Chris Tilling, head of research and senior lecturer in New Testament Studies at St. Mellitus College, London

NEW EXPLORATIONS IN THEOLOGY

MARTIN LUTHER AND THE RULE OF FAITH

READING GOD'S WORD FOR GOD'S PEOPLE

TODD R. HAINS

Foreword by Robert Kolb

An imprint of InterVarsity Press
Downers Grove, Illinois

InterVarsity Press
P.O. Box 1400 | Downers Grove, IL 60515-1426
ivpress.com | email@ivpress.com

©2022 by Todd Roger Hains

All rights reserved. No part of this book may be reproduced in any form without written permission from InterVarsity Press.

InterVarsity Press® is the publishing division of InterVarsity Christian Fellowship/USA®. For more information, visit intervarsity.org.

All Scripture quotations, unless otherwise indicated, are the author's translation of Martin Luther's translation of the Bible.

The publisher cannot verify the accuracy or functionality of website URLs used in this book beyond the date of publication.

Cover design and image composite: David Fassett
Interior design: Daniel van Loon

ISBN 978-1-5140-0296-4 (print) | ISBN 978-1-5140-0297-1 (digital)

Printed in the United States of America ∞

Library of Congress Cataloging-in-Publication Data
A catalog record for this book is available from the Library of Congress.

26 25 24 23 22 | 6 5 4 3 2 1

JESUS.

TUUS EGO SUM.

SALUUM ME FAC.

PSALMUS 119:94

☦

Prayer to Receive God's Word

In the name of the Father and of the † Son and of the Holy Spirit. Amen.

My heart composes a fine song. I want to sing of a King.
    My tongue is the stylus of a skilled scribe. *Ps 45:1*
The Lord is my light and my salvation.
    Whom shall I fear? *Ps 27:1*
For you light my lamp.
    The Lord my God makes my darkness light. *Ps 18:28*
Your word is a lamp for my feet
    and a light on my path. *Ps 119:105*
For in you is the source of life,
    and in your light we see light. *Ps 36:9*
When your word is revealed,
    it brings joy and makes the simple wise. *Ps 119:130*
This is my comfort in my misery,
    for your word gives me life. *Ps 119:50*

Glory be to the Father and to the Son and to the Holy Spirit, as it was in the beginning, is now, and will be forever. Amen.

Almighty God, long ago, at many times and in many ways, you spoke to our fathers by the prophets, but in these last days you have spoken to us by your Son, whom you appointed the heir of all things and through whom you created the world. Grant us grace in all humility and meekness to receive your Word with hearty faith, to hear him and keep him, and so to be made one with your dear Son; who lives and reigns with you and the Holy Spirit, one God, now and forever. Amen.

Contents

Foreword by Robert Kolb — xiii

Acknowledgments — xvii

Abbreviations — xix

1. Scripture Against Scripture
   An Introduction — 1

2. The Ancient Catechism
   Defining the Rule of Faith — 28

3. The Childish Doctrine
   Explaining the Catechism — 55

4. The Resurrection of the Dead
   Reading the Law According to the Rule of Faith — 80

5. The Spoils of Death's Death
   Reading the Historical Books According to the Rule of Faith — 95

6. The Upside-Down King
   Reading the Wisdom Books According to the Rule of Faith — 102

7. The Great Light in Darkness
   Reading the Prophets According to the Rule of Faith — 117

8. The Light of the Word
   Reading the New Testament According to the Rule of Faith — 133

9. Scripture According to Scripture
   Five Theses on the Rule of Faith — 159

10. This Is Most Certainly True
    A Conclusion — 173

Table of Sources — 177

Bibliographies — 191

   Primary Sources — 191

   Translated Primary Sources — 192

Secondary Sources	193
Modern Biblical Studies Resources	205
Name Index	207
Subject Index	209
Scripture Index	215

Foreword

Robert Kolb

In recent years, Christians have increasingly searched for an adequate "rule of faith," a summary of the foundational elements of biblical teaching, to help clarify our understanding of what the prophets and apostles have to teach us. The turbulence of the public square of ideas in North America and other parts of the world have caused Christians to look for guides to lead people into the Holy Scriptures, thus bringing its message for specific situations back into public discussion. The rich flood flowing from the Bible can overwhelm believers when, perhaps steeped in one writer's language, they venture into the lines of another biblical author. Even more challenging, the blast of many winds of doctrine within the fellowship of the faithful, which blow out of various, often contradictory, readings of the Holy Scriptures, stir Christians to seek a clear lighthouse in the storms of the early twenty-first century. The ancient church quickly found that an *analogia* or *canon fidei* may be of only passing help, but its core has been repeated by believers time and time again throughout the ages. Each age, region, and movement has devised its own interpretation of standard rules of faith, such as the ancient creeds, but they have stood the test of time, even as those who use them freshen the message for their own circumstances.

So it was in the time of the Reformation. Theologians summarized their rule of faith according to the model Philipp Melanchthon set in place with the Augsburg Confession of 1530. It was followed by a host of other confessional documents, including England's Thirty-nine Articles, and the Second Helvetic Confession of 1566 was among the most prominent documents defining the Reformed rule of faith.

Throughout the Middle Ages, the early church's form of the catechism as a program for instruction in the foundations of Christian belief had provided something of a rule of faith for newly converted adults, and for children in Christian families. The "catechism" became a term for a printed handbook in the age of print, but in a population still largely unable to read, teachers of the church recognized the advisability of composing the catechism in a form that could be memorized. Memorization seems to have come easier for those who could not read and write than it does for us today, dependent on internet information as we are. Luther found such a form for his largely oral culture in his *Small Catechism*.

In this volume, Todd Hains offers us a model to use as we try to take seriously the individual contexts and situations of authors who were speaking the message of the one God—the God of Abraham, Isaac, and Jacob, who became incarnate as Jesus of Nazareth. He puts Martin Luther's Small Catechism into service as a rule of faith to accompany our reading of the prophets and apostles as we share their message in twenty-first century contexts. Hains leads readers to recognize the universal and unchanging presence of God as he speaks through the voices of the biblical writers to address the challenges, problems, and sinfulness that we encounter in ourselves and our world.

Hains's study considers vital questions regarding biblical interpretation and authority as they emerge in Luther's preaching and teaching, questions that have been highlighted by Luther scholars and, more generally, theologians of several Christian traditions with different points of orientation in recent years. Hains shares with Luther a recognition of the importance of genre—the form in which others are trying to communicate. In finding our way through the several genres employed in Scripture, Luther's Small Catechism offers a plot summary that teaches us what to look and listen for in the pages of the Bible. This study is sensitive to questions of genre not only in its concentration on sermons and biblical commentary but also in its assessment of how Luther's catechisms guide interpretation of passages treated in the sermons from several genres of Old and New Testament texts.

With his experience as a preacher on the catechism, Luther was sensitive to the potential of taking his handbook as a summary of the biblical text into the pulpit. Hains skillfully probes Luther's homiletical applications of the catechism as a rule of faith in delivering his message to his hearers in Wittenberg and the readers of his sermons in print far beyond. This study will certainly stimulate lively discussion among those working on the Reformation and the history of preaching as well as those assessing the role and function of the *analogia fidei* in the history of the church.

Acknowledgments

Our God is a God of gifts. Any writing project makes that clear. Over a decade this project has traveled with me from the Midwest to the Pacific Northwest. I began it as a newly wedded husband; I brought it to completion as a father of two dear sons. All along the way I was supported, challenged, and cheered on.

This book began as a dissertation. My dissertation committee—Scott M. Manetsch, Douglas A. Sweeney, Mickey L. Mattox, and Richard E. Averbeck—read the proposal and drafts with diligent patience, asking questions that forced me to be clearer than I otherwise would have been. These men answered questions about sources, random Luther quotes, and program bureaucracy. My adviser, dear Dr. Manetsch, has tended to my formation as a scholar and as a Christian since I first matriculated to Trinity Evangelical Divinity School (TEDS) in 2007: he's listened to worries, theories, and rants; he got me a job with the Reformation Commentary on Scripture; he's constantly goaded me to listen; and he has prayed for me and with me. I would not be where I am today or who I am today apart from Dr. Manetsch's guidance and friendship.

A number of friends have been a strong encouragement to me. My fellow travelers at TEDS—David Hooper, Dan Cole, Mary Willson, Matthew LaPine, Thomas Middlebrook, and Kessia Reyne Bennett—taught me how to pursue academics for the benefit of the church. My compatriots at Lexham—Brannon Ellis, Jesse Myers, Derek Brown, Elliot Ritzema, David Bomar, Doug Mangum, Mark Ward, Abigail Stocker, Scott Corbin, and Lindsay Kennedy—offered advice on writing and framing and put up with more than one too many Luther anecdotes. Several mentors in the faith—Hal Senkbeil, John Kleinig, Bob Kolb, and Christine Helmer—challenged me to engage the whole Luther as polemicist, philosopher, and pastor. (They also reminded me that a good book finished is better than a perfect book unfinished.) My Lutheran pandemic friends—John Hoyum and Caleb Keith—sounded out some translations and test material and pointed me to Luther's emphasis on God's word of promise. And my dear friend Ethan McCarthy regularly asked how things were going, read and edited drafts, and prodded me to read something other than Luther and Ratzinger (with minimal success).

My editor, David McNutt, has patiently endured the eccentricities of an author who is also an editor. He and his team at IVP Academic prepared my manuscript for publication with grace and skill.

The congregations of First Saint Paul's Evangelical Lutheran Church (Chicago, Illinois) and Christ the Servant Evangelical Lutheran Church (Bellingham, Washington) kindly endured and seemed to enjoy adult education hours about Luther and the analogy of faith. They gave me the opportunity to test out the practical implications of my research on Luther and the analogy of faith.

Mom and Dad started me on the mundane adventure of the Christian life. They modeled dedication to the local church, faithful teaching, and regular Bible reading. But they also talked about these things, not assuming I would just learn by example—with catechesis words are always necessary. And they first introduced me to the analogy of faith, though they didn't know it, often pointing me to Luther's *Small Catechism* when I had questions. The privilege of theological studies would have never been possible without Mom and Dad.

Most importantly, my own dear little family has encouraged me and endured me during this long process. This manuscript began when it was just Veronica and me. Then our Franklin Owen came along, and soon after our Milo William entered the world. They brought much needed order to my habits and patterns. They have served as a constant reminder of the true goal and importance of theological studies: to raise up the new church that grows up every day. Throughout this Veronica has made sacrifices and concessions—the least of which includes messy books and papers strewn around our home—so that I could work toward completing this project. She also reminded me of the things that really matter, like needing to eat and measuring my value not in the quality or success of my dissertation but in baptism. She has done it all in patient love. "Strength and honor are her clothing" (Prov 31:25).

Abbreviations

ACCS   Ancient Christian Commentary on Scripture. 29 vols. Edited by Thomas C. Oden. Downers Grove, IL: InterVarsity Press, 1998–2009.

ACW   Ancient Christian Writers: The Works of the Fathers in Translation. New York: Newman; Mahwah, NJ: Paulist, 1946–.

ANF   The Ante-Nicene Fathers. 10 vols. Edited by Alexander Roberts and James Donaldson. Buffalo, NY: Christian Literature, 1885–1896.

BoC 1959   *The Book of Concord: The Confessions of the Evangelical Lutheran Church.* Translated and edited by Theodore G. Tappert. Philadelphia: Fortress Press, 1959.

BSELK   *Die Bekenntnisschriften der evangelisch-lutherischen Kirche.* 12th ed. Göttingen: Vandenhoeck & Ruprecht, 1998.

DWB   *Deutsches Wörterbuch.* Jacob Grimm and Wilhelm Grimm. 16 vols. Leipzig: Hirzel, 1854–1971.

E^2 *Dr. Martin Luther's sämmtliche Werke.* 2nd ed. 26 vols. Frankfurt and Erlangen: Heyder & Zimmer, 1862–1885.

FC   The Fathers of the Church: A New Translation. Washington, DC: Catholic University of America Press, 1947–.

LW   *Luther's Works [American Edition].* 82 vols. projected. St. Louis: Concordia; Philadelphia: Fortress Press, 1955–1986, 2009–.

LWA   *Luthers Werke in Auswahl.* 8 vols. Edited by Otto Clemen et al. Berlin: Walter de Gruyter, 1912–1933.

NPNF   *A Select Library of the Nicene and Post-Nicene Fathers of the Christian Church.* 28 vols. in two series. Edited by Philip Schaff et al. Buffalo, NY: Christian Literature, 1887–1894.

PG	Patrologia cursus completeus. Series Graeca. 161 vols. Edited by J.-P. Migne. Paris: Migne, 1857–1866.
PL	Patrologia cursus completus. Series Latina. 221 vols. Edited by J.-P. Migne. Paris: Migne, 1844–1864.
PPS	Popular Patristics Series. Crestwood, NY: St. Vladimir's Seminary Press, 1996–.
RCS	Reformation Commentary on Scripture. 28 vols. projected. Edited by Timothy George and Scott M. Manetsch. Downers Grove, IL: IVP Academic, 2011–.
TAL	*The Annotated Luther*. 6 vols. Edited by Hans J. Hillerbrand, Kirsi I. Stjerna, and Timothy J. Wengert. Minneapolis: Fortress Press, 2015–2017.
WA	*D. Martin Luthers Werke, Kritische Gesamtausgabe: [Schriften]*. 73 vols. Weimar: Hermann Böhlaus Nachfolger, 1883–2009.
WABr	*D. Martin Luthers Werke, Kritische Gesamtausgabe: Briefwechsel*. 18 vols. Weimar: Hermann Böhlaus Nachfolger, 1930–1983.
WADB	*D. Martin Luthers Werke, Kritische Gesamtausgabe: Deutsche Bibel*. 12 vols. Weimar: Hermann Böhlaus Nachfolger, 1906–1961.
WATR	*D. Martin Luthers Werke, Kritische Gesamtausgabe: Tischreden*. 6 vols. Weimar: Hermann Böhlaus Nachfolger, 1912–1921.

1

Scripture Against Scripture

An Introduction

I**N THE FALL OF** 1511 or the spring of 1512, Martin Luther (1483–1546) received unwelcome news under the pear tree of the Black Cloister: he was to become a preacher and teacher of the Bible. In a panic he rattled off fifteen reasons why he couldn't do it. They all boiled down to this: he was unworthy of the high calling of speaking God's words. But the general of Luther's observant Augustinian order, Johann Staupitz (d. 1524), was unmoved. And so, desperate to escape the ministry of the word, Luther whimpered: "Lord Dr. Staupitz, you're going to kill me! I won't survive three months." Staupitz wasn't worried: "Well now, in God's name! The Lord our God has important matters to attend to; he could use some learned people in heaven, too!" Whether in life or death, the ministry of the word was Luther's vocation.[1]

Luther survived the three months—he lasted in the office of the word more than three decades. Day in and day out he confronted what he understood to be the most difficult battle: Scripture against Scripture. "I've often said it—and I'll keep saying it—the greatest and most difficult struggle is that we must struggle with Scripture against Scripture."[2] Luther was a

---

[1] WATR 3:187.27–29, 188.1–27 (macaronic witness), 188.30–42, 189.1–18 (German witness), no. 3143b; quoting p. 189.6–7 (compare with p. 188.16–17), p. 189.7–8 (compare with p. 188.18–19). See also WATR 3:187.4–25, no. 3143a; WATR 5:98.21–29, no. 5371; WATR 5:654.34–36, 655.1–8, no. 6422. See Martin Brecht, *Martin Luther*, 3 vols., trans. James L. Schaaf (Minneapolis: Fortress, 1985–1993), 1:125–26.

[2] The Gospel on the Eighth Sunday after Trinity (July 30, 1525), WA 17,1:364.24–26 (print witness). On the battle of Scripture against Scripture, see also Sermon on St. Martin's (1530),

veteran of this ongoing battle. Early in his life it was one he waged against himself.[3] Later he waged it against the hierarchy of the Roman Church.[4] Soon it became a war on two fronts—against the Roman Church and against others who also opposed the Roman Church.[5] The enemy combatants changed, but the battle trudged along. And there was no getting out of it. As a doctor of the Bible, Luther had been commissioned for just this.

The struggle of Scripture against Scripture is a civil war. Enemy combatants do not wear distinctive uniforms; they often look and sound like brothers in arms. "Guard yourselves against false prophets who come to you in sheep's clothing, but inwardly they are ravenous wolves" (Mt 7:15).[6] Doctors of the Bible must constantly assess their allies, lest they be enemies, and their enemies, lest they be allies.[7] Satan is a subtle master of deception: he uses God's name and word to deceive. "[The enemy] snatches the sword out of your hand and tries to slay you with your own sword. You must anticipate this. You must fend off the sword, take back what is yours and strike him down. But no one can do this unless he is enlightened by the Holy Spirit, so that he can see this rogue."[8] Ultimately, like Jesus in the wilderness, doctors of the Bible do not struggle against flesh and blood but against Satan.

Reason is the double agent of the civil war of Scripture against Scripture. Submitted to faith it is a heavenly comrade-in-arms, but without faith it is

---

WA 32:154.22-155.7; Gospel for the Eighth Sunday after Trinity (*Church Postil*, 1544), LW 78:286-90 (WA 17,1:362.29-366 with changes as indicated by WA 22:142-43; text original to the *Church Postil*, pp. 143.1-144.6.).

[3]On Luther's struggle with—even hatred of—Romans 1:17, see WATR 4:72.27-73.34, no. 4007 (LW 54:308-9); WATR 3:228.6-32, no. 3232a-c (LW 54:193-94); for a brief analysis and explanation, see Brecht, *Martin Luther*, 1:225-27.

[4]Here Roman Church is a technical term referring to the Roman Magisterium—the pope, his curia, and agents. For example, see Sermon on the Second Sunday after Epiphany (1545), WA 49:684.14-23, 685.3-4. On the church, see John M. Headley, *Luther's View of Church History* (New Haven and London: Yale University Press, 1963), 29-41.

[5]For example, on Andreas Bodenstein von Karlstadt (1486-1541) and the "heavenly prophets," *Against the Heavenly Prophets in the Matter of Images and Sacraments* (1525), see LW 40:73-223 (WA 18:62-125, 134-214); Brecht, *Martin Luther*, 2:157-72.

[6]WADB 6:37.

[7]Luther says these enemies pray often, go to church often, preach often, and read the Bible often. Their sheep's clothing is God's name and word. See The Gospel on the Eighth Sunday after Trinity (July 30, 1525), WA 17,1:362.31-363.25, here quoting lines 17-19.

[8]The Gospel on the Eighth Sunday after Trinity (July 30, 1525), WA 17,1:364.26-29 I have rendered one of the third person singular's as *you*, to clarify the contrast Luther draws here.

Scripture Against Scripture 3

a satanic enemy. For Luther the analogy of faith—interpreting Scripture according to the catechism of the Ten Commandments, the Apostles' Creed, and the Our Father—is the touchstone or shibboleth that reveals friend or foe in the battle for the word of God.[9]

FAITH KILLS REASON

Luther is infamous for allegedly rejecting reason.[10] He calls it "Lady Hulda," "Lady Jezebel," "the devil's bride," "the devil's whore"—even the devil's "archwhore"![11] But he also calls it "a part of the true light," "a beautiful, marvelous instrument and tool of God," "a kind of divine sun," "the greatest, inestimable gift of God."[12]

He's using reason in different ways in these lists of blame and praise. Luther distinguishes reason by its domain, temporal or spiritual, and by its state, unregenerate or regenerate. Luther praises unregenerate reason in temporal matters—ruling a state, building a house, cultivating crops. It's a common gift to all people, regardless of confession. And so he can speak highly of Cicero and even Aristotle's Ethics.[13] (Luther doesn't talk about regenerate reason in temporal matters, because it seems to be beside the point.)

But unregenerate reason in spiritual matters? That's what sticks in Luther's craw. It's dumb and blind but imagines that its darkness will bring light.

---

[9] Sermon on St. Michael's (1539), WA 47:857.26–27, "But through the touchstone. Therefore whatever depends on the Ten Commandments, etc."; Sermon on John 2:24 (1538), WA 46:780.15–17 (compare with LW 22:265), "Let us go to the touchstone, and let us measure with the true yardstick and see if it fits with the Our Father and the articles of the Christian faith"; WATR 1:489.22, no. 966, "the catechism must rule"; House Sermon on the Creed (1537), LW 57:244 (WA 45:12.7–8), "these are the three greatest sermons: the Our Father, the Creed, and the Ten Commandments."

[10] On Luther's view of reason, see B. A. Gerrish, *Grace and Reason: A Study in the Theology of Luther* (Oxford: Oxford University Press, 1962), esp. 10–27, 161–66, 168–71; Oswald Bayer, *Martin Luther's Theology: A Contemporary Interpretation*, trans. Thomas H. Trapp (Grand Rapids: Eerdmans, 2008), 158–62. See also Lectures on Galatians 3:6 (1535), LW 26:226–35.

[11] Sermon on January 17, 1546, LW 51:374 (WA 51:126.6–7); *Against the Heavenly Prophets* (1525), LW 40:174–75 (WA 18:164.24, 25–26); Gospel for New Year's Day (*Church Postil*, 1522, 1540), LW 76:39 (WA 10.1,1:505.4).

[12] The Gospel for the Third Sunday of Christmas (*Church Postil*, 1522, 1540), LW 75:290 (WA 10,1.1:203.8–9; E² 10:191); WATR 3:106.18–19; *Disputation Concerning Man* (1536), thesis 8, WA 39,1:175.18 (compare LW 34:137); Commentary on Isaiah Chapter 9 (1543–1544), WA 40,3:612.31.

[13] For example, see WATR 3:698.10–17, no. 3904; WATR 6:345.28–33, no. 7031; Commentary on Isaiah Chapter 9 (1543–1544), WA 40,3:608.11–24.

"When God speaks, reason, therefore, regards His Word as heresy and as the word of the devil; for it seems so absurd."[14] To read God's word or hear God's word preached by reason alone is no different from reading the Bible with your eyes shut or to listen with your fingers in your ears.

No amount of history and philosophy, linguistics and critical analysis can bootstrap human reason into discovering the gospel, Jesus Christ—true God and true man—given for you. "Faith comes from preaching, but preaching comes through the word of God" (Rom 10:17).[15] We must start with the gospel of Jesus Christ. And that always means to die. "Do you not know that all of us who were baptized into Jesus Christ were baptized into his death?" (Rom 6:3).[16]

"Thus all devout people . . . kill reason, and say: 'Reason, you are foolish. You do not understand the things that belong to God (Mt 16:23). Therefore do not speak against me, but keep quiet. Do not judge; but listen to the Word of God, and believe it.' Thus devout people, by their faith, kill a beast that is greater than the world; and so they offer a highly pleasing sacrifice and worship to God."[17]

To see the light in spiritual matters, reason must be put to death, and that's just what the Holy Spirit does by God's word. This death and resurrection is not a one-time event. Just as the Christian life is a daily baptism of death and resurrection, so it is with Christian reason. By the power of the Holy Spirit and God's word our reason has become a mighty instrument of God.[18] Once blind and dead in spiritual matters, now reason can see and breathe.

And so Luther praises regenerate reason in spiritual matters—hearing God's word, be it in preaching, baptizing, absolving, or communing. As our

---

[14]Lectures on Galatians 3:6, LW 26:228 (WA 40,1:362.12-13).
[15]WADB 7:61. Erasmus follows the Majority text here, giving ῥήματος θεου instead of ῥήματος Χριστοῦ. See "Epistolae Pauli Apostoli," *Novum Instrumentum omne*, ed. Desiderius Erasmus (Basel: Froben, 1516), 18; *Novum Testamentum omne*, ed. Desiderius Erasmus (Basel: Froben, 1519), 340. Here Luther's doctrine of the word is at work in translating: he renders ἀκοή ("hearing") as "preaching." This is unique to his German Bible translation, compare his correction of the Vulgate (1529), WADB 5:643.
[16]WADB 7:47.
[17]Lectures on Galatians 3:6 (1535), LW 26:228 (WA 40,1:362.23-27).
[18]"But in a believer—who now is reborn and illumined by the Holy Spirit through the word—there it is a beautiful, majestic instrument and tool of God." WATR 3:106.17-19, no. 2938b. "Reason illumined by faith receives life from faith, for it's been killed and brought back to life." WATR 3:106.22-23.

bodies will be glorified on the Last Day, so our reason is glorified when it submits to death and resurrection by God's word and Spirit. And just as our bodies will still be our bodies as God created them but with purity and power, so it is with regenerate reason. "It's like when cold iron becomes red hot, it's a different and hot iron. And that's the rebirth that happens by the Holy Spirit through the word."[19] As the psalmist says, "For in you is the source of life, and in your light we see light" (Ps 36:9).[20]

And so Christians—pastors and parishioners alike—need to test the spirits. Thankfully, Luther says, Scripture has given us the standard by which to do this. "Paul sets this limit: 'If anyone is a preacher and holds the office of teaching others what the word is, let him above all see to it that he preaches nothing which is not in accord with the faith.'"[21] Parishioners too should know the faith, comparing the preacher's sermon against it, so that they can say, "That fits very nicely with my faith."[22] If the sermon does not harmonize with the faith, it is not God's word.[23] Luther regularly holds up this rule as the rule of preaching. "It is good that one preaches only according to the analogy of faith. All preachers should accustom themselves to this simple manner of preaching."[24] Indeed by this measure, *according to the analogy of faith,* Luther judged the teaching of his opponents—Catholics, Reformed, and Radicals—finding them wanting.

WHATEVER INCULCATES CHRIST

The theological message Luther preached was simple, though not necessarily easy. "We cannot preach anything at all but Jesus Christ and faith. That's the general goal. . . . The poor Holy Spirit knows nothing else."[25] The person and work of Jesus of Nazareth as gift and example for all humans is the full form

---

[19]WATR 3:106.30–31, no. 2938b. See the whole discussion, WATR 3:104.24-38, 105.1-10, no. 2938a; WATR 3:105.11-29, 106.1-10 (macaronic witness), 106.11-40, 107.1-15 (German witness), no. 2938b.
[20]WADB 10,1:213.
[21]Sermon on the Second Sunday after Epiphany (1545), WA 49:682.5-7 (LW 58:216).
[22]Sermon on the Second Sunday after Epiphany (1545), WA 49:682.10 (LW 58:217).
[23]"If you have the gift of prophecy, be sure that it fits the faith. If not, say: 'That the devil preached!' The Holy Spirit says that he reveals himself this way: that it fits with the faith." Sermon on the Second Sunday after Epiphany (1531), WA 34,1:107.8-10.
[24]WATR 4:447.4-6, no. 4719.
[25]Sermon on Monday after Pentecost (1532), WA 36:180.10-11, 181.9-10.

and content of the Christian gospel.[26] All doctrinal and ethical considerations orbited around Luther's understanding of Christ. Thus, for Luther, to preach meant to proclaim Christ: who he is, what he has done, what he continues to do, and what his benefits are.

Many identify justification by faith alone as the center of Luther's Christocentricism.[27] But Ulrich Asendorf finds this distorting. He argues that Luther's hermeneutic is first and foremost trinitarian. Thus, Luther's understanding of Christ is inseparably connected to the Trinity, Baptism, the Sacrament of the Altar, Confession, Absolution, justification by faith, sanctification, and so on. Asendorf underscores that we do not understand Luther's concept of justification by faith alone unless we understand his Christology and emphasis on the believer's union with Christ.[28] Another popular filter that enriches Asendorf's claim is the law-gospel dynamic, itself a restatement of the gift-example distinction.[29] For Luther, all of Scripture contains these two words of God: the law—his *no*, what he demands from us; and the

---

[26] The distinguishable but inseparable character of gift and example is fundamental to Luther's theology, see "Short Instruction: What Should Be Sought and Expected in the Gospels" (1522, 1544), LW 75:7–12 (WA 10,1.1:8–18; E² 7:8–13; compare with LW 35:113–24).

[27] Otto Hof, "Luther's Exegetical Principle of the Analogy of Faith," *Concordia Theological Monthly* 38, no. 4 (1967), 242–57, esp. 248–50; Elmer Carl Kiessling, *The Early Sermons of Luther and Their Relation to the Pre-Reformation Sermon* (Grand Rapids: Zondervan, 1935; reprint, New York: AMS, 1971), 101–8. On Luther's doctrine of justification, see Paul Althaus, *The Theology of Martin Luther*, trans. Robert C. Shultz (Philadelphia: Fortress, 1966), 224–50; Marc Lienhard, *Luther: Witness to Jesus Christ*, trans. Edwin H. Robertson (Minneapolis: Augsburg, 1982), 269–305; A. Skevington Wood, *Captive to the Word: Martin Luther; Doctor of Sacred Scripture* (Grand Rapids: Eerdmans, 1969), 51–72; Dietrich Korsch, "Glaube und Rechtfertigung," in *Luther Handbuch*, ed. Albrecht Beutel (Tübingen: Mohr Siebeck, 2005), 372–81; Risto Saarinen, "Justification by Faith: The View of the Mannermaa School," in *The Oxford Handbook of Martin Luther's Theology*, ed. Robert Kolb, Irene Dingel, and L'ubomír Batka (New York: Oxford University Press, 2014), 254–63; Mark Mattes, "Luther on Justification as Forensic and Effective," in *The Oxford Handbook of Martin Luther's Theology*, ed. Robert Kolb, Irene Dingel, and L'ubomír Batka (New York: Oxford University Press, 2014), 264–73. For a constructive clarification of Luther's doctrine of justification, see Jack D. Kilcrease, *Justification by the Word: Restoring Sola Fide* (Bellingham, WA: Lexham Press, 2022).

[28] Ulrich Asendorf, *Die Theologie Martin Luthers nach seinen Predigten* (Göttingen: Vandenhoeck & Ruprecht, 1988), 418–24.

[29] See, for example, Mary Jane Haemig, "The Influence of the Genres of Exegetical Instruction, Preaching and Catechesis on Luther," in *The Oxford Handbook of Martin Luther's Theology*, ed. Robert Kolb, Irene Dingel and L'ubomír Batka (Oxford: Oxford University Press, 2014), 453; Sigurjón Árni Eyjólfsson, "Überblick über die Bewertung von Luthers Predigten in der Forschung," in *Luther Between Past and Present: Studies in Luther and Lutheranism*, ed. Ulrik Nissen, Anna Vind, Bo Holm, and Olli-Pekka Vainio (Helsinki: Luther-Agricola-Society, 2004), 17–25.

gospel—his *yes*, what he has done for us in Christ.³⁰ They must be differentiated but held together. Luther preached that the dialectic of law and gospel is a lifelong occupation that illuminates Scripture and our relationship with God.³¹

No one disputes that Luther practiced Christocentric exegesis.³² But how he applies his Christocentric method is a different matter. What are the implications for allegory, the literal sense, and history? Gerhard Ebeling showed that Luther redefined rather than abandoned allegorical interpretation—as Huldyrch Zwingli (1484-1531) also recognized, chiding Luther as "an inept allegorist."³³ Nevertheless, scholars continue to posit a clean break between Luther and his exegetical forebears—usually rather dramatically, something like "he freed himself from the shackles of medieval exegesis."³⁴

---

³⁰Luther illustrates this with the first commandment. On law-gospel, see Bayer, *Martin Luther's Theology*, 58-66, 74-77, 90-91; Gerhard Ebeling, *Luther: Einführung in sein Denken* (Tübingen: Mohr Siebeck, 2006), 120-36; Althaus, *Theology of Martin Luther*, 251-73; Jaroslav Pelikan, *Luther the Expositor: Introduction to the Reformer's Exegetical Writings* (St. Louis: Concordia, 1959), 65-66. For a short but careful statement of Luther's doctrine of law and gospel, see Gospel for the Third Sunday in Advent (*Church Postil*, 1522; 1540), LW 75:142-49 (WA 10,1.2:155-62; E² 10:92-101).

³¹See Sermon on the Eighteenth Sunday after Trinity (1533), WA 37:174.13-20. See Asendorf, *Theologie Martin Luthers*, 67-73.

³²See Helmut Zschoch, "Predigten," in *Luther Handbuch*, ed. Albrecht Beutel (Tübingen: Mohr Siebeck, 2005), 317-18; Fred W. Meuser, "Luther as Preacher of the Word of God," in *The Cambridge Companion to Martin Luther*, ed. Donald K. McKim (Cambridge: Cambridge University Press, 2003), 136-40 (compare with *Luther the Preacher* [Minneapolis: Augsburg, 1983], 16-25); Asendorf, *Theologie Martin Luthers*, 16-21, 418-24; Wood, *Captive to the Word*, 91-92; Althaus, *Theology of Martin Luther*, 72-102; Gerhard Ebeling, *Evangelische Evangelienauslegung: Eine Untersuchung zu Luthers Hermeneutik* (Munich: Albert Lempp, 1942; rev. ed., Darmstadt: Wissenschaftliche Buchgesellschaft, 1962), 270-71; Kiessling, *Early Sermons*, 147. See further, Mickey L. Mattox, "Luther's Interpretation of Scripture: Biblical Understanding in Trinitarian Shape," in *The Substance of Faith: Luther's Doctrinal Theology for Today*, ed. Paul R. Hinlicky (Minneapolis: Fortress, 2008), 14-22; Albrecht Beutel, "Theologie als Schriftauslegung," in *Luther Handbuch*, ed. Albrecht Beutel (Tübingen: Mohr Siebeck, 2005), 445-46; Mark D. Thompson, *A Sure Ground on Which to Stand: The Relation of Authority and Interpretive Method in Luther's Approach to Scripture* (Carlisle, Cumbria, UK: Paternoster, 2004), 185-88; Johann Anselm Steiger, "Martin Luthers allegorisch-figürliche Auslegung der Heiligen Schrift," *Zeitschrift für Kirchengeschichte* 110, no. 3 (1999): 331-51. Bernhard Lohse awkwardly tries to modernize Luther's Christocentricism, see Lohse, *Martin Luther's Theology: Its Historical and Systematic Development*, trans. and ed. Roy A. Harrisville (Minneapolis: Fortress, 2006), 189, 195.

³³Ebeling, *Evangelische Evangelienauslegung*, esp. 44-89, 274-358; WATR 2:487.27-28, no. 2493 (1532).

³⁴Wood, *Captive to the Word*, 78. Wood tones down this overstatement on p. 165. See also Beth Kreitzer, "The Lutheran Sermon," in *Preachers and People in the Reformations and Early Modern Period*, ed. Larissa Taylor (Leiden: Brill, 2001), 45. In contrast, Kiessling labels Luther's allegories as "medieval in tone and strained in their application" (*Early Sermons*, 133-34). Of course,

Luther did not reject all allegories but only certain ones, namely those that do not conform to the analogy of faith. He straightforwardly states this in his lengthy excursus on allegory in the Genesis lectures: "When we condemn allegories we are speaking of those that are fabricated by one's own intellect and ingenuity, without the authority of Scripture. Other allegories which are made to agree with the analogy of faith not only enrich doctrine but also console consciences."[35] Elsewhere Luther extensively treats the definition of the analogy of faith; however, in this excursus he simply glosses it as an interpretation that fits with "Christ, the church, faith, and the ministry of the Word."[36] Such allegories are not wholly subjective; they are ruled by Christ who is himself the substance and Lord of Scripture. And yet allegories cannot be used to establish doctrine or the meaning of a text. Allegories persuade and illustrate; they belong to rhetoric, not dialectic.[37] Luther does not neatly distinguish allegory, typology, and figural interpretation.

Luther taught his students to read the words of Scripture as they stood.[38] Still, by this he did not mean what most exegetes today mean by *literal*. Most modern biblical scholars define *literal* according to the grammatical, literary, and historical meaning of a text, what Luther would have considered the simple literal sense. But he understands *literal* in two ways: this simple literal sense and the spiritual literal sense, the meaning of the words according to the full form and content of Scripture.[39] The whole of Scripture, for Luther,

---

Luther harshly condemned allegory without always clarifying that certain allegories are acceptable. For example, "An allegory is like a beautiful harlot who fondles men in such a way that it is impossible for her not to be loved, especially by idle men who are free from trial" and "I hate allegories" (Genesis lectures, LW 5:347; WA 43:668.3-5, 13).

[35]Excursus on Allegory at Genesis 9:12–16, WA 42:367.37–368.2 (compare with LW 2:151), as translated in Herman J. Selderhuis, "Introduction to the Psalms," in *Psalms 1–72*, RCS OT 7 (Downers Grove, IL: IVP Academic, 2015), xlviii.

[36]Excursus on Allegory at Genesis 9:12–16, LW 2:164 (WA 42:377.21–22).

[37]Commentary on Galatians 4:21–31, LW 27:311 (WA 2:550.29–34). On dialectic and rhetoric in Luther, see B. A. Gerrish, *Grace and Reason: A Study in the Theology of Luther* (Oxford: Oxford University Press, 1962), 46–47.

[38]Pelikan, *Luther the Expositor*, 126–27; Wood, *Captive to the Word*, 166; Thompson, *A Sure Ground on Which to Stand*, 191–247; Ebeling, *Evangelische Evangelienauslegung*, 342–43. Pelikan gives three exceptions to this rule: (1) the text indicates it shouldn't be interpreted literally; (2) another passage shows it shouldn't be interpreted literally; and (3) the text as it stands contradicts an article of faith.

[39]Mattox, "Luther's Interpretation of Scripture," 22–27; Pelikan, *Luther the Expositor*, 107–8; Heinrich Bornkamm, *Luther und das Alte Testament* (Tübingen: Mohr Siebeck, 1948), 74–86.

is defined by its substance, which is Christ. "Christ is Lord, not servant; he is Lord of the Sabbath, the law, and everything. And Scripture is to be understood not against, but for Christ. Therefore it must either refer to him or not be considered true Scripture."⁴⁰ Luther studied resources like the *Glossa ordinaria*—expanded with the work of Nicholas of Lyra (1270–1349) and Paul of Burgos (c. 1351–1435); the grammars of Johannes Reuchlin (1455–1522), David Kimchi (1160–1235), and Moses Kimchi (1127–1190); Sebastian Münster's (1488–1552) digest of medieval rabbinical exegetical work; and Desiderius Erasmus's (1466–1536) critical edition of the New Testament as well as the latest editions of the Old Testament.⁴¹ But Luther submitted these resources to the lordship of the faith; they are aids to interpretation, not lords over it.⁴² "Indeed grammar is necessary for declining nouns, conjugating verbs, and construing syntax, but for the proclamation of the meaning

---

⁴⁰Bornkamm calls Luther's understanding the *sensus literalis propheticus*, which is similar to the spiritual literal sense. For a concise treatment of the literal sense in the Reformation, see Selderhuis, "Introduction to the Psalms," in RCS OT 7:xlvi–lii, here xlvii. Authorial intent is another way of distinguishing the simple and spiritual literal senses: the human author's intent corresponds to the simple literal sense; the Holy Spirit's intent, the spiritual literal sense. See also Kathryn Greene-McCreight, "Literal Sense," in *Dictionary for Theological Interpretation of the Bible*, ed. Kevin J. Vanhoozer (Grand Rapids: Baker Academic, 2005), 455–56; Kathryn Greene-McCreight, "Rule of Faith," in *Dictionary for Theological Interpretation of the Bible*, ed. Kevin J. Vanhoozer (Grand Rapids: Baker Academic, 2005), 703–4; Christopher Ocker, *Biblical Poetics Before Humanism and Reformation* (New York: Cambridge University Press, 2002).

⁴⁰Theses Concerning Faith (1535), WA 39,1:47.1–4 (LW 34:112). A few lines down Luther states that "If our opponents press Scripture against Christ, we must press Christ against Scripture" (p. 47.19–20; LW 34:112). Usually, depending on his audience or opponent, Luther intends this use of "inculcate Christ" positively: you can and should find Christ in all of Scripture. He would not want this principle to be used to doubt Scripture or only to accept something as Scripture once *you* find Christ in it.

⁴¹See Johannes Reuchlin, *De Rudimentis Hebraicis* (Pforzheim: Thomas Anselm, 1506); Sebastian Münster, *Miqdaš YHWH*, 2 vols. (Basel: Michael Isinginius and Henricus Petrus, 1534–1535, 1546); *Novum Testamentum omne*, ed. Erasmus; *Biblia Hebraica* (Brescia: Gershom Soncino, 1494); *Biblia Hebraica*, 2 vols. (Venice: Daniel Bomberg, 1511, 1518). For the *Glossa ordinaria*, see *Biblia Sacra cum Glossa ordinaria, novisque additionibus*, 6 vols. (Venice: Magna Societas, 1603). See also Luther's letter to Georg Spalatin (January 18, 1518) on resources for Bible reading, *Luther: Letters of Spiritual Counsel*, trans. and ed. Theodore G. Tappert, Library of Christian Classics 18 (Philadelphia: The Westminster Press, 1960; reprint, Vancouver, BC: Regent College Publishing, 2003), 111–13 (WABr 2:132–34). Luther said if he could relearn Hebrew all over again, he would only use the best grammarians, David Kimchi and Moses Kimchi, see WATR 1:525.37–39, no. 1040.

⁴²Mattox, "Luther's Interpretation of Scripture," 11–57, esp. 46–47; Thompson, *A Sure Ground on Which to Stand*, 116–17. For more on Hebraic resources in the Reformation, see Stephen G. Burnett, "The Strange Career of the *Biblia Rabbinica* Among Christian Hebraists, 1517–1620," in *Shaping the Bible in the Reformation: Books, Scholars and Their Readers in the Sixteenth Century*, ed. Bruce Gordon and Matthew McLean (Leiden: Brill, 2012), 63–84.

and the consideration of the subject matter, grammar is not needed. For grammar should not reign over the meaning."[43] The substance determines the meaning; grammar only restricts the possibilities of expression.[44]

History receives a similar redefinition from Luther. He often talks about the importance of rooting interpretation in history.[45] "Faith is built on history."[46] Thus, the historical sense can even be called normative for Luther.[47] But by *history* Luther means the sacred history narrated by the Apostles' Creed. "The Creed—the confession of our holy Christian faith—is the history of histories."[48] This history—God's history—contains the history of the church, of every individual, and of the world.[49] And so history is not only a list of facts of when, where, who, and how; it is *for us*.[50] Until one understands this, one has not understood Jesus' history correctly. All modes and methods must be servants to Christ, the Lord of the Scriptures. Luther used grammar, (secular) history, literary methods, and culture as aids to interpretation, but only in service to faith in Christ for the purpose of inculcating the double love of God and neighbor.

So, contrary to the historical-critical guild, Luther argues that Christian faith through word and Spirit takes logical priority to everything in biblical interpretation. Luther is emphatic: biblical interpretation is impossible apart from the ministry and guidance of the Holy Spirit. Trying to understand God's word apart from God's Spirit would be like a blind man trying to see

---

[43]WATR 3:619.28–30, no. 3794. See further Luther's discussion with his translation team about translating particular difficult verses in the Old Testament, WATR 5:218, no. 5533 (1542–1543); and see Luther's comments on Psalm 22:16, WA 5:633–34.

[44]On Luther's use and understanding of grammar, Gerrish's comparison between Luther and Erasmus is helpful. See Gerrish, *Grace and Reason*, 161–66.

[45]Bornkamm, *Luther und das Alte Testament*, 77–78; Ebeling, *Evangelische Evangelienauslegung*, 225–39, 417–24; Wood, *Captive to the Word*, 165–66.

[46]Lectures on Isaiah 37:31 (1527–1530) WA 31,2:242.24. Luther says that history is firmer than allegories, "unless we transform them metaphorically into another substance according to the rule of faith" (p. 242.25–26).

[47]Pelikan, *Luther the Expositor*, 259, compare with 89–90; WADB 9,1:xxxvi–xxxvii. Pelikan acknowledges that Luther operates with a different definition of history "which seems to modern eyes allegorical or at least typological" (90).

[48]WATR 5:581.36–37, no. 6288.

[49]Ebeling, Evangelische Evangelienauslegung, 418–19, 453.

[50]Ebeling, Evangelische Evangelienauslegung, 423–24; Jin Ho Kwon, *Christus Pro Nobis: Eine Untersuchung zu Luthers Passions- und Osterpredigtens bis zum Jahr 1530* (Münster: LIT Verlag, 2008). See further, Sermon on Fifth Sunday after Epiphany (1546), LW 58:453; WA 51:183.10–15.

the sun: it doesn't matter what scientific tools and knowledge the blind man has, he's fully incapable of sight. Yes, God's word is light, and humans in their fallen state are incapable of seeing this light until the Holy Spirit opens their eyes. Luther argues that without the Holy Spirit even the biblical authors themselves would not accept Jesus' interpretation of their words. For example, Luther said this about Isaiah if he read Luke's use of Isaiah 9:6:

> Who would have been able to say this? That Christ is signified everywhere in Scripture? If the prophets themselves had come to the manger, they would have hesitated, unless the Spirit of the Lord illumined them. For this reason, a new light was necessary; the angel announced it after he lead them into the Scripture. In this way, Christ is known through the gospel; he is revealed through the Holy Spirit. Following this sign, it is Scripture so long as we find nothing in Scripture other than what presents Christ.[51]

It is a foundational mistake to try to read the Bible only in its original historical setting.[52] That would be to ignore, even to defy, the Holy Spirit's assistance and friendship. "The word of God reveals, the Spirit of God believes, the world and flesh neither see nor believe."[53] The Bible is a book of faith.[54]

But isn't this entirely subjective? For many today Luther's insistence on Scripture *for us*, its Christocentric focus, and its Spirit-led interpretation seem to have authorized infinite schisms, establishing the individual interpreter as the final court of appeals.[55] Worse yet, Luther seems to see himself

---

[51] Sermon on the Feast of St. Stephen (December 26, 1523), WA 11:223.5–10.

[52] Luther also argues that it's a mistake to read the Bible apart from its historical setting. See *How Christians Should Read Moses* (1525), WA 16:363–93 (LW 35:161–74). Scripture should not be applied in such a wooden fashion that "If I were to take up and keep every word of God, then I better build an ark too just like Noah!" Sermons on Exodus 20 (1525), WA 16:438.13–14. All Scripture is indeed for us, but it's not always a command for us. Christians must make careful distinctions in Scripture. "They are hopeless morons and true swine who want to be great teachers, write great books and yet know no distinction of the word of God." Sermons on Exodus 20 (1525), WA 16:439.13–15.

[53] WATR 5:398, no. 5921. See also WATR 1:601, no. 1205; WATR 2:243.10–11, no. 1871; WATR 5:385, no. 5871.

[54] See Jeffrey G. Silcock, "Luther on the Holy Spirit and His Use of God's Word," in *The Oxford Handbook of Martin Luther's Theology*, ed. Robert Kolb, Irene Dingel, and L'ubomír Batka (New York: Oxford University Press, 2014), 294–309; Althaus, *Theology of Martin Luther*, 16–19, 35–42, 341–44; Regin Prenter, *Spiritus Creator: Luther's Concept of the Holy Spirit*, trans. John M. Jensen (Philadelphia: Muhlenberg Press, 1953).

[55] See Brad S. Gregory, *The Unintended Reformation: How a Religious Revolution Secularized Society* (Cambridge, MA: Belknap, 2012). The accusation is common among Protestants, too; for

as judge over other individual interpreters—harshly censuring Erasmus, Zwingli, and Radical opponents. What else did Luther expect when he said "Here I stand"? By understanding one of the most neglected aspects of Luther's theology, the analogy of faith, we can understand Luther better as pastor, preacher, professor, polemicist, and doctor of the church.

The Analogy of Faith

In 1958 Bengt Hägglund mourned that the rule of faith or analogy of faith is addressed seldom—if it is, "it happens quite accidentally"—and used even less.[56] It continues to languish in obscurity and misunderstanding.[57]

Since the Enlightenment, exegetes have disputed the meaning of Paul's phrase "the analogy of faith" in Romans 12:6.[58] Everyone agrees that Paul sets a rule here, but scholars disagree whether Paul means *faith* in the

---

example, see Kevin J. Vanhoozer, *Biblical Authority After Babel: Retrieving the Solas in the Spirit of Mere Protestant Christianity* (Grand Rapids: Brazos, 2016), esp. 1–34.

[56] Bengt Hägglund, "Die Bedeutung der *Regula fidei* als Grundlage theologischer Aussagen," *Studia theologica* 12, no. 1 (1958): 1–44, here 2. Hägglund thinks this neglect is because modern theologians tend to restrict faith to its subjective sense only (*fides qua creditur*). He states that the rule of faith embodies "the entire teaching of the church, the teaching that was proclaimed by the apostles and prophets and that is grounded in Scripture" (3–4, quoting p. 4). Therefore, development is an inappropriate term for talking about Christian doctrine; the substance of Christian faith remains unchanged, though applied through new leaders and expositors to new situations and cultures (37). Hägglund calls theologians and exegetes to judge new methodologies by their interpretive fruits: Do they fit with the faith (40)?

[57] There are signs of hope. Scholars like Peter Leithart, Kevin Vanhoozer, and Daniel Treier advocate and exemplify ruled readings of the Bible. See Leithart, *Deep Exegesis: The Mystery of Reading Scripture* (Waco, TX: Baylor University Press, 2009); Vanhoozer, *Hearers and Doers: A Pastor's Guide to Making Disciples Through Scripture and Doctrine* (Bellingham, WA: Lexham Press, 2019); Treier, *Introducing Theological Interpretation of Scripture: Recovering a Christian Practice* (Grand Rapids: Baker Academic, 2008). And there are groups of scholars and pastors like the Center for Baptist Renewal who are championing ruled and creedal readings for pastors and everyday Christians. For a brief overview of the rule of faith in history, see Everett Ferguson, *The Rule of Faith: A Guide* (Eugene, OR: Cascade, 2015). Best yet, see John Kleinig, *God's Word: A Guide to Holy Scripture*, Christian Essentials (Bellingham, WA: Lexham Press, 2022).

[58] Karl-Heinz Menke, "Analogia fidei," in *Lexikon für Theologie und Kirche*, 11 vols., 3rd ed., ed. Michael Buchberger, Walter Kasper, and Konrad Baumgartner (Freiburg: Herder, 1993–2001), 1:574–77. Menke states that the Eastern tradition took Paul's phrase as using the faith subjectively, while the Western tradition took it objectively. Basil of Caesarea, John Chrysostom, and Ambrosiaster seem to confirm Menke; Pseudo-Constantinius does not. See Gerald Bray, ed., *Romans*, ACCS NT 6 (Downers Grove, IL: InterVarsity Press, 1998), 311–12. Origen isn't quite clear what he understands Paul to mean here, see Origen, *Commentary on the Epistle to the Romans* 4.5.3; 9.3.2–4. Nevertheless Daniel P. Fuller traces the content of the analogy back to Origen, see Fuller, "Biblical Theology and the Analogy of Faith," in *Unity and Diversity in New Testament Theology: Essays in Honor of George E. Ladd*, ed. R. A. Guelich (Grand Rapids: Eerdmans, 1978), 198n13. (Walter C. Kaiser Jr. misunderstands Fuller as saying that the first use of the phrase "analogy of faith" is in Origen's

objective sense or the subjective sense. Faith in the objective sense (*fides quae creditur*) is the core teaching of the church as handed down by the prophets and apostles; faith in the subjective sense (*fides qua creditur*) is the faculty of faith as exercised by an individual.[59] Before the Enlightenment, exegetes understood Paul as referring to the objective faith of Christian teaching; after the Enlightenment, the vast majority of exegetes understand Paul as referring to subjective faith. Exegetes assume this conclusion more than argue it. But Ernst Käsemann points out that if Paul intends to lay down a rule for the use of spiritual gifts, it makes no sense to have that rule be a subjective one measured by the gifted individual rather than an external measure.[60]

Most modern Protestant scholars see the analogy of faith as twofold: reading the dark passages of the Bible by the light of the clear passages of the Bible and reading the Bible according to its full content.[61] Some scholars

---

De principiis 4.26; it is not. See Kaiser, "Evangelical Hermeneutics: Restatement, Advance or Retreat from the Reformation," *Concordia Theological Quarterly* 46, no. 2–3 [1982], 172n20, 179.)

[59]Richard A. Muller, *Dictionary of Latin and Greek Theological Terms: Drawn Principally from Protestant Theology*, 2nd ed. (Grand Rapids: Baker Academic, 2017), 123. It is now a commonplace of modern commentaries to discuss whether Paul means *faith* subjectively or objectively.

[60]Ernst Käsemann, *Commentary on Romans*, trans. Geoffrey W. Bromiley (Grand Rapids: Eerdmans, 1980), 341–42; see also Henri Blocher, "The 'Analogy of Faith' in the Study of Scripture: In Search of Justification and Guidelines," *Scottish Bulletin of Evangelical Theology* 5 (1987), 25–27; Joseph A. Fitzmyer, *Romans: A New Translation with Introduction and Commentary*, Anchor Bible 33 (New York: Doubleday, 1993), 647–48. In contrast, see C. E. B. Cranfield, *A Critical and Exegetical Commentary on the Epistle to the Romans*, 2 vols., International Critical Commentary (Edinburgh: T&T Clark, 1985), 2:619–21; Douglas J. Moo, *The Epistle to the Romans*, New International Commentary on the New Testament 38 (Grand Rapids: Eerdmans, 1996), 765–66.

[61]Compare Blocher "The 'Analogy of Faith' in the Study of Scripture," 18–24. For the analogy as interpreting dark passages by clear passages, see Daniel J. Treier, "Scripture, Unity of," in *Dictionary for Theological Interpretation of the Bible*, ed. Kevin J. Vanhoozer (Grand Rapids: Baker Academic; London: SPCK, 2005), 731–34; John F. Johnson, "*Analogia Fidei* as Hermeneutical Principle," *Springfielder* 36, no. 4 (1973): 249–59; Grant R. Osborne, "New Testament Theology," in *Evangelical Dictionary of Theology*, 3rd ed., ed. Daniel J. Treier and Walter A. Elwell (Grand Rapids: Baker Academic, 2017), 591–95; Grant R. Osborne, *Hermeneutical Spiral: A Comprehensive Introduction to Biblical Interpretation*, rev. ed. (Downers Grove, IL: IVP Academic, 2006), 28–29, 361–62; H. Wayne Johnson, "The 'Analogy of Faith' and Exegetical Methodology: A Preliminary Discussion on Relationships," *Journal of the Evangelical Theological Society* 31, no. 1 (1988): 69–80; Daniel A. Tappeiner, "Hermeneutics, the Analogy of Faith and New Testament Sacramental Realism," *The Evangelical Quarterly* 49, no. 1 (1977): 40–52; David P. Scaer, "The Theology of Robert David Preus and His Person: Making a Difference," *Concordia Theological Quaterly* 74, no. 1 (2010): 75–91, esp. 80–85; Martin W. Flor, "The Free Conferences of 1903–1906 and the Concept of *Analogia Fidei*," *Concordia Theological Monthly* 40, no. 4 (1969): 218–27; William F. Arndt, "Hermeneutics," in *Lutheran Cyclopedia*, ed. Erwin L. Lueker (St. Louis:

seem to use the phrase *the analogy of faith* as a general term for someone's governing idea, and so they emphasize its danger: foisting the human reader's ideas on the Bible, whether that's an artificial unity, a shallow Christological reading, or an arbitrary ranking of passages.[62]

There is disagreement about the relationship between the analogy of faith (*analogia fidei*), the analogy of Scripture (*analogia scripturae*), and the rule of faith (*regula fidei*). Many equate the analogy of faith and the analogy of Scripture but distinguish the analogy of faith and the rule of faith. For them, to read by the analogy of faith and Scripture is to read Scripture according to Scripture, but to read by the rule of faith is to read creedally.[63] But some even pit the analogy of faith against the rule of faith. For example, Walter Kaiser claims that the Reformers crafted the analogy of faith to combat the Roman Catholic rule of faith, which he thinks is the *Glossa ordinaria*.[64]

Concordia, 1954), 463–64. For the analogy as interpreting a passage according to the whole Bible, see Blocher, "The 'Analogy of Faith' in the Study of Scripture"; Henry M. Knapp, "Protestant Biblical Interpretation," in *Dictionary for Theological Interpretation of the Bible*, ed. Kevin J. Vanhoozer (Grand Rapids: Baker Academic; London: SPCK, 2005), 633–38; Hank Voss, "From 'Grammatical-historical Exegesis' to 'Theological Exegesis': Five Essential Practices," *Evangelical Review of Theology* 37, no. 2 (2013): 140–52; Iain Provan, *The Reformation and the Right Reading of Scripture* (Waco, TX: Baylor University Press, 2017), 10–11; D. A. Carson, "Unity and Diversity in the New Testament: The Possibility of Systematic Theology," in *Scripture and Truth*, ed. D. A. Carson and John D. Woodbridge (Grand Rapids: Baker, 1983), 65–95, esp. 90–93; D. A. Carson, "Theological Interpretation of Scripture: Yes, but . . . ," in *Theological Commentary: Evangelical Perspectives*, ed. R. Michael Allen (London: T&T Clark, 2011), 196–97; Vanhoozer, *Biblical Authority After Babel*, 127–29; Flor, "The Free Conferences of 1903–1906 and the Concept of Analogia Fidei," 222–27.

[62]See Osborne, *Hermeneutical Spiral*, 361–62; Osborne, "New Testament Theology," 593; Carson, "Unity and Diversity," 90–93; Calvin R. Schoonhoven, "The 'Analogy of Faith' and the Intent of Hebrews," in *Scripture, Tradition, and Interpretation: Essays Presented to Everett F. Harrison by His Students and Colleagues in Honor of His Seventy-fifth Birthday*, ed. W. Ward Gasque and William Sanford LaSor (Grand Rapids: Eerdmans, 1978), 92–110. J. P. Koehler also sees the analogy of faith as a great threat to exegesis. His argument is tightly tied up in the American Lutheran controversy over election in the late nineteenth- and early twentieth centuries. See J. P. Koehler, "The Analogy of Faith," in *The Wauwatosa Theology*, 3 vols., ed. Curtis A. John (Milwaukee: Northwestern Publishing House, 1997), 1:221–68. In contrast to Koehler, see Francis Pieper, *Christian Dogmatics*, 4 vols., trans. unnamed translator (St. Louis: Concordia, 1950–1957), 1:359–67. Pieper distinguishes two uses of the analogy of faith: (1) interpreting unclear passages by clear passages; (2) Schleiermacher's use of "the whole of Scripture (*das Schriftganze*)," which requires every passage to be interpreted by numerous passages.

[63]See Provan, *The Reformation and the Right Reading of Scripture*, 10–11; Treier, "Scripture, Unity of," 731–34; Osborne, "New Testament Theology," 593; Osborne, *The Hermeneutical Spiral*, 28; Voss, "From 'Grammatical-historical Exegesis' to 'Theological Exegesis,' " 146.

[64]Kaiser, "Evangelical Hermeneutics," 171, 173; Kaiser, *Toward an Exegetical Theology: Biblical Exegesis for Preaching and Teaching* (Grand Rapids: Baker Academic, 1981), 134–35; see also Osborne, *Hermeneutical Spiral*, 28.

Lutherans tend to be the ones who see the analogy of faith, analogy of Scripture, and the rule of faith as the same thing—even though they might not agree on its meaning: interpreting unclear passages by clear passages or by justification by faith alone or by law and gospel.[65]

While historians have traced the phrase *the analogy of faith* to the medieval theologian William of Saint-Thierry (d. 1148), they have demonstrated the strong Reformation claim on it.[66] The Reformation use of the analogy may have been set up by Jacques Lefèvre d'Étaples (d. 1536) when he corrected the Latin translation of Paul's phrase in Romans 12:6.[67] Many

---

[65] For the analogy of faith as clear passages, see Arndt, "Hermeneutics," 463–64; Flor, "The Free Conferences of 1903–1906 and the Concept of *Analogia Fidei*," 222–27; but also Vanhoozer, *Biblical Authority After Babel*, 127–29. For the analogy of faith as justification by faith alone, see Hof, "Luther's Exegetical Principle of the Analogy of Faith," 249–52; Johnson, "*Analogia Fidei*," 249–59 (key to the analogy but not the analogy); Willem Jan Kooiman, *Luther and the Bible*, trans. John Schmidt (Muhlenberg Press, 1961), 219–20; not a Lutheran, but see also, Gerrish, *Grace and Reason*, 150–51. For the analogy of faith as law and gospel, see Robert D. Preus, *The Theology of Post-Reformation Lutheranism: A Study of Theological Prolegomena* (St. Louis: Concordia, 1970), 97, 141, 223–24, 330–31. Carson understands the analogy of faith and the rule of faith to be the same, but he sees them both as extrabiblical, see "Theological Interpretation of Scripture: Yes, but . . . ," 196–97. Knapp distinguishes the analogy of faith from the analogy of Scripture: the analogy of faith is a corollary to the analogy of Scripture; the analogy of Scripture is to read dark passages by clear passages; the analogy of faith requires that a reading fit with the big picture of biblical faith. But he doesn't clearly address the rule of faith. See Knapp, "Protestant Biblical Interpretation," 633–38.

[66] William of Saint-Thierry, *Expositio in Epistolam ad Romanos* 12:6, PL 180:672–73. See Bernhard Gertz, "Was ist *analogia fidei*?: Klarstellungen zu einem Kontrovers-Thema," *Catholica* 26, no. 4 (1972): 309–24; Gertz, *Glaubenswelt als Analogia: Die theologische Analogie-Lehre Erich Przywaras und ihr Ort in der Auseinandersetzung um die analogia fidei* (Düsseldorf: Patmos, 1969); based on Gertz's work, see Menke, "Analogia fidei," 1:574–77; Thomas Marschler, "*Analogia fidei*: Anmerkungen zu einem Grundprinzip theologischer Schrifthermeneutik," *Theologie und Philosophie* 87, no. 2 (2012): 208–36. Marschler criticizes exegesis done with the analogy of faith as " 'dogmatically contaminated' interpretation of the Bible" (229–30). He affirms the bracketing of the analogy until the end of the exegetical process like Kaiser and Carson; see Kaiser, "Evangelical Hermeneutics," 176–77; Carson, "Unity and Diversity," 90–93. Marschler is responding to Joseph Ratzinger's condemnation of this two-step process, see Ratzinger, "Biblical Interpretation in Crisis: On the Question of the Foundations and Approaches of Exegesis Today," in *Biblical Interpretation in Crisis: The Ratzinger Conference on Bible and Church*, ed. Richard John Neuhaus (Grand Rapids: Eerdmans, 1989), 1–23; Ratzinger, "Handing on the Faith and the Sources of Faith," in *Handing on the Faith in an Age of Disbelief*, by Joseph Ratzinger et al., trans. Michael J. Miller (San Francisco: Ignatius, 2006), 13–40; Ignacio Carbajosa, *Faith, the Fount of Exegesis: The Interpretation of Scripture in Light of the History of Old Testament Research*, trans. Paul Stevenson (San Francisco: Ignatius, 2013).

[67] Lefèvre translated Paul's phrase as *secundum analogiam, id est rationem fidei* rather than merely *secundum rationem fidei*. Gertz, "Was ist *analogia fidei*?," 312; Jacques Lefèvre d'Étaples, *Epistola ad Rhomanos* (Paris: H. Stephanus, 1515), 9r; no comment on Romans 12:6, see p. 92v. Gertz claims that Erasmus also contributed, but Erasmus translated Romans 12:6 into Latin as *iuxta portionem fidei* instead of *secundum rationem fidei*. See "Epistolae Pauli Apostoli," in *Novum*

historians believe Luther defined the analogy of faith as justification by faith alone, and so his followers used the analogy of faith as a battle cry against their papal opponents.[68] The Reformers would have used it to ward off Roman Catholic teaching that presented church tradition as normative (for example, Purgatory and Masses for the dead). In contrast, they saw themselves as holding Scripture as the highest authority, which interprets itself by its own light.

Richard Muller is one of the few to recognize that many of the Reformers defined the analogy of faith more specifically: it meant that the Bible must be read according to the Ten Commandments, the Apostles' Creed, and the Lord's Prayer.[69] Even Robert Preus in his learned examination of Post-Reformation Lutheranism doesn't see this. "The analogy of faith, according to all the old Lutheran theologians," Preus writes, "was simply the articles of faith that could be summarized under the categories of Law and Gospel."[70] And yet all the Lutheran scholastics he cites state that the analogy of faith is

---

Instrumentum omne, ed. Erasmus, 21; *Novum Testamentum omne*, ed. Erasmus, 343. In contrast, Luther revised the Vulgate to *ut consentiat fidei* (WADB 5:645.12).

[68]Gertz, "Was ist *analogia fidei*?," 311–13; Marschler, "*Analogia fidei*," 220; Menke, "Analogia fidei," 575; Hof, "Luther's Exegetical Principle of the Analogy of Faith," 249–52. Gertz cites Melanchthon's commentary on Romans 12:6, see Philipp Melanchthon, *Enarratio Epistolae Pauli ad Romanos* (1556), in *Philippi Melanchthonis Opera quae supersunt omnia*, 28 vols., Corpus Reformatorum 1–28, ed. C. G. Bretschneider (Halle: C. A. Schwetschke, 1834–1860), 15:1009. Robert C. Fennell also sees justification as one of six parts of Luther's definition of the analogy of faith (Christocentricisim, justification, faith, the nature of God and human nature, the reality of Satan, and pneumatology). Fennell has a near miss with Luther's actual definition of the analogy of faith: the catechism. See Fennell, *The Rule of Faith and Biblical Interpretation: Reform, Resistance, and Renewal* (Eugene, OR: Cascade, 2018), 47n56, 49–59. Fennell limits himself to examining Luther's second Galatians lectures and the *On the Bondage of the Will*.

[69]Richard A. Muller, *Post-Reformation Reformed Dogmatics: The Rise and Development of Reformed Orthodoxy, ca. 1520 to ca. 1725*, 4 vols., 2nd ed. (Grand Rapids: Baker Academic, 2003), 2:493–97, esp. 493. Muller cites Girolamo Zanchi (1516–1590), William Whitaker (1548–1595), Moïse Amyraut (1596–1664), Francis Roberts (1609–1675), and William Perkins (1558–1602). Francis Turretin (1623–1687) and Gulielmus Bucanus (d. 1603) also talk about the analogy of faith in these terms, see Turretin, *Institutes of Elenctic Theology*, 3 vols., trans. George Musgrave Giger, ed. James T. Dennison Jr. (Phillipsburg, NJ: P&R Publishing, 1992–1997), 1:53; 2.19.18); Gulielmus Bucanus, *Institutiones Theologicae, seu Locorum Communium Christianae Religionis* (Bern: Le Preux, 1605), 46; 4.23; English translation, William Bucanus, *Institutions of Christian Religion*, trans. Robert Hill (London: Snowdon, 1606), 44; 4.23. Although elsewhere Muller distinguishes between the analogy of faith and Scripture: the analogy of Scripture reads unclear passages by clear ones; the analogy of faith reads the Bible according to its basic meaning, and some people understand that in a ruled sense. See Muller, *Dictionary of Latin and Greek Theological Terms*, 25.

[70]Preus, *The Theology of Post-Reformation Lutheranism*, 330.

the Apostles' Creed (and some include the Ten Commandments).[71] Some historians, such as Derek Cooper, have misunderstood the analogy of faith as a post-Reformation development or as solely a Reformed hermeneutical tool.[72] Sujin Pak takes a mediating position: she recognizes that Luther uses the analogy of faith, but she mistakenly asserts that he doesn't tie it to the Apostles' Creed—that move, she claims, was made by second generation Reformers who needed to reassert clerical power.[73]

As a result of the Enlightenment turn, Protestant exegetes increasingly saw the analogy of faith as a logical fallacy (*petitio principii*, it assumes the conclusion); they replaced it with the standards of historical criticism and reason.[74] In contrast, the Reformers would see the standards of

---

[71] Matthias Flacius Illyricus (1520–1575) and Salomo Glassius (1593–1656) explicitly cite the Creed and the Ten Commandments: "All interpretation of Scripture and all doctrine or dogma . . . should agree with the sum of faith or Christian teaching, which is already contained in the Ten Commandments, the gospel, the Creed or in the catechism." (Flacius, *Clavis Scripturae Sacrae*, 2 vols. [Frankfurt and Leipzig: Paulus, 1719], 1:36); "It's nothing other than the analogy or rule of faith, which is the sum of heavenly doctrine, gathered from the clearest passages of Scripture. There are two parts: first, of faith, whose principal topics are set forth especially in the Apostles' Creed; second, of love, whose sum the Ten Commandments show." (Glassius, *Philologia Sacra* [Leipzig: Gleditsch, 1713], 498). Johann Gerhard (1582–1637) and Abraham Calov (1612–1686) imply the Creed: "The articles of faith is what the apostle understands by *pistis* in this passage [Rom 12:6]" (Gerhard, *Loci Theologici*, 9 vols., ed. Eduard Preuss [Berlin: Schlawitz; Leipzig: Hinrichs, 1863–1876], 1:238); "The analogy of faith is the agreement of the doctrine of faith brilliantly shown forth in holy Scripture, which is in those passages especially, where each doctrine has its proper seat." (Calov, *Biblia Novi Testamenti Illustrata*, 2 vols. [Dresden and Leipzig: Zimmerman, 1719], 2:207). I was unable to access Leonhard Hutter's *Loci Communes Theologici* (1619). And I only located the phrase but not its definition in Balthasar Mentzer (1565–1627): "All true interpretation of the Scriptures comes from the analogy of faith, Romans 12:6" (Mentzer, *Disputationes Theologicae et Scholasticae XIV* [Marburg: Egenolphus, 1606], 76).

[72] Derek Cooper calls this ancient principle "a post-Luther approach to theology and exegesis" ("The Analogy of Faith in Puritan Exegesis: Scope and Salvation in James 2:14–26," *Stone-Campbell Journal* 12, no. 2 [2009], 249).

[73] Sujin Pak, "The Protestant Reformers and the *Analogia Fidei*," in *The Medieval Luther*, ed. Christine Helmer (Tübingen: Mohr Siebeck, 2020), 227–45. See also Sujin Pak, "Scripture, the Priesthood of All Believers, and Applications of 1 Corinthians 14," in *The People's Book: The Reformation and the Bible*, eds. Jennifer Powell McNutt and David Lauber (Downers Grove, IL: IVP Academic, 2017), 48–50. In a 2017 essay, Pak implies that the analogy of faith was solely a Reformed principle, tying the analogy of faith to John Calvin and his heirs in contrast to Philipp Melanchthon, but in a 2020 essay she revised these claims to say: Luther indeed used the analogy of faith (but without the Creed), and second generation reformers, especially among the Reformed, wielded the analogy to reassert clerical power. See Sujin Pak, "The Protestant Reformers and the *Analogia Fidei*," in *The Medieval Luther*, ed. Christine Helmer (Tubingen: Mohr Siebeck, 2020), 227–45. See also Sujin Pak, "Scripture, the Priesthood of All Believers, and Applications of 1 Corinthians 14," in *The People's Book: The Reformation and the Bible*, eds. Jennifer Powell McNutt and David Lauber (Downers Grove, IL: IVP Academic, 2017), 48–50.

[74] Gertz, "Was ist *analogia fidei*?," 313; Menke, "Analogia fidei," 1:575.

historical criticism and reason as circular reasoning that assumes its conclusions and does not understand the Bible as a book authored by the Holy Spirit. Vatican II's proclamation about the analogy of faith, ironically enough, would fit the Reformers' interpretive approach much better: "Holy Scripture must be read and interpreted in the sacred Spirit in which it was written."[75] Again, the default bias for historical criticism and reason surfaces in modern exegetical discussions of Romans 12:6 *and* modern historical-theological discussions of the analogy of faith. For example, Skevington Wood writes, "The use of this term [the analogy of faith] by Luther and the Reformers generally was in fact a misapplication of its original occurrence in Romans 12:6."[76] And Leland Ryken: "[The analogy of faith] is an awkward phrase, based on a misinterpretation of Romans 12:6."[77]

After Protestants consigned the analogy of faith to the trash heap, Roman Catholics picked it up. They generally understood the analogy of faith in a similar way to the Reformers (that the Bible is one harmonious book written by God, thus obscure passages are interpreted by clear passages) but with the added twist of Roman Catholic tradition.[78] Discussions of the analogy of faith have since been further confused by Karl Barth's (1886–1968) polemic against the analogy of being (*analogia entis*), related to his diatribe against natural theology.[79]

Concerning Luther's use of the analogy, Otto Hof offers the most substantive treatment.[80] Only examining Luther's sermons on Romans 12:6, Hof

---

[75] *Dei verbum* 12.3; *Catechism of the Catholic Church* 112–14. See also Joseph Ratzinger, *God's Word: Scripture—Tradition—Office*, ed. Peter Hünermann and Thomas Söding, trans. Henry Taylor (San Francisco: Ignatius, 2008), 58–67, 91–99; Ratzinger, "Foreword," in *Jesus of Nazareth: From the Baptism in the Jordan to the Transfiguration* by Joseph Ratzinger, trans. Adrian J. Walker (New York: Doubleday, 2007), xi–xxiv. For a helpful description and analysis of Ratzinger's doctrine of Scripture, see Kevin J. Vanhoozer, "Expounding the Word of the Lord: Joseph Ratzinger on Revelation, Tradition, and Biblical Interpretation," in *The Theology of Benedict XVI: A Protestant Appreciation*, ed. Tim Perry (Bellingham, WA: Lexham Press, 2019), 66–86.
[76] Wood, *Captive to the Word*, 163.
[77] Leland Ryken, *Worldly Saints: The Puritans as They Really Were* (Grand Rapids: Zondervan, 2010), 147.
[78] *Dei Verbum* 12.3; *Catechism of the Catholic Church* 112–14; Joseph Ratzinger, *The Transforming Power of Faith*, trans. L'Osservatore Romano (San Francisco: Ignatius, 2013), 10–11, 23; Marschler, "Analogia fidei," 222–29; Gertz, "Was ist *analogia fidei*?," 313–16; Menke, "Analogia fidei," 576.
[79] See Gertz, *Weltsglauben als Analogie*; Gertz, "Was ist *analogia fidei*?," 318–24; Gottlieb Söhngen, "The Analogy of Faith: Likeness to God from Faith Alone?," trans. Kenneth Oakes, *Pro Ecclesia* 21, no. 1 (2012): 56–76.
[80] Hof, "Luther's Exegetical Principle." David Starling also handles Luther's use of the analogy of faith, but misdefines Luther's understanding of prophecy as predicting the future. Nor does he

shows that Luther employs around a dozen different phrases when speaking about the analogy of faith—sometimes even just "the faith."[81] Outside of these sermons, Luther uses even more expressions for it. Hof recognizes that Luther uses faith here in the objective sense and subjective sense. He identifies the gospel of justification by faith as Luther's definition of faith.[82] But Hof is not quite right; Luther defines the analogy of faith as understanding Scripture according to the catechism, that is, the Ten Commandments, the Apostles' Creed, the Our Father, and the sacraments—all of which he trusted as God's word. Moreover, Luther wanted this method to have a positive and negative function. Positively, we can only understand Scripture by the analogy of faith; negatively, it guards against heresy.[83] He commends learning the catechism as the task of a Christian, whether pastor or parishioner.

> Daily I find that there are now only a few preachers who truly and correctly understand the Our Father, the Creed, and the Ten Commandments and who are able to teach them for the poor common people. All the same, they dash into Daniel, Hosea, John's Apocalypse, and other such difficult books. The poor rabble are drawn in, listen to, and gawk at these jesters with great wonder. And when the year's through, they still can recite neither the Our Father nor the Creed nor the Ten Commandments. But it is these things

---

recognize that the tradition before the Reformers understood prophecy in three ways: (1) interpreting Scripture, (2) predicting the future, often associated with dreams, and (3) reading the stars. Starling "The Analogy of Faith in the Theology of Luther and Calvin," *Reformed Theological Review* 72, no. 1 (2013): 5–19; for a strong treatment of Calvin's use of the analogy of faith, see Peter Opitz, *Calvins theologische Hermeneutik* (Neukirchener-Vluyn: Neukirchener, 1994), 227–90. For passing references to Luther and the analogy of faith, see Steiger, "Martin Luthers allegorisch-figürliche Auslegung der Heiligen Schrift," 339; Wood, *Captive to the Word*, 163; Althaus, *Theology of Martin Luther*, 79, 96 n. 90, 340; Bornkamm, *Luther und das Alte Testament*, 79; Ebeling, *Evangelienauslegung*, 342–43, 346, 354. Mattox's article "Luther's Interpretation of Scripture" assumes the importance of the analogy of the faith for Luther, showing how worried he was about an unruled interpretive methodology.

[81] For example, "similar to the faith," "in accordance with the faith," "it must harmonize with the faith," "it must be in agreement with the faith," "it must be subject to the faith," "judged and directed by the faith," "must submit to the faith." Hof, "Luther's Exegetical Principle," 244, 248.

[82] Hof, "Luther's Exegetical Principle," 245–48.

[83] Hägglund recognizes this dual function in the tradition ("Die Bedeutung der *Regula fidei*," 38–40); Mary Jane Haemig intimates this for Luther and demonstrates it for his heirs ("The Living Voice of the Catechism: German Lutheran Catechetical Preaching, 1530–1580" [PhD diss., Harvard University 1996], 104). Mattox also points out the positive feature of the rule of faith, "Luther's Interpretation of Scripture," 56. Richard Muller points out the negative function, while intimating the positive role of the rule, see Muller, *Post-Reformation Reformed Dogmatics*, 2:493–97.

that are the ancient, true Christian catechism or common education for Christians![84]

There's a modern reluctance to state the rule or analogy of faith in a set formula. This tendency undercuts the historic use and goal of the analogy of faith: it is the Bible's own faithful guide to the Bible. To learn the analogy of faith, simple Christians—in particular, the illiterate majority of the church throughout the centuries—require a set formula. A set formula does not mean that there's only one way to state the analogy of faith. Luther, for example, is clear that there are many ways to say the same thing (*res*), but good pedagogy requires memorization. The Christian faith isn't something you know when you see it; the Christian faith is explicit and public, open to all by the inspiration of the Holy Spirit (and *only* by the inspiration of the Holy Spirit!).

That is how Luther understood the analogy of faith. He defined it as the catechism: the Ten Commandments, the Apostles' Creed, the Our Father, and the sacraments of Baptism, Communion, and Absolution. Martin Luther interpreted the Bible according to the analogy of faith.

ON SOURCES AND METHOD

The Weimar edition holds more than two thousand sermon transcripts, spanning all of Luther's preaching career from 1512, delivered to the Augustinian chapter in Erfurt, to 1546, in Eisleben days before his death.[85] Still,

---

[84] Preface to the *Commentary on Zechariah* (1527), WA 23:485.28–486.1. See further the Preface to the *Large Catechism* (1529), BoC 1959, 359–60; WA 30,1:126.4–127.20. Also: "The holy fathers or apostles arranged [the Ten Commandments, the Apostles' Creed, and the Our Father] this way, so that they would embrace the chief parts of Christian teaching for common people," Sermon on May 18, 1528, WA 30,1:2.21–23.

[85] Luther's first extant sermon could be from 1510; Erich Vogelsang seems to prefer that date himself, though he asserts that the date must remain an open question. Most scholars accept 1512, which avoids the awkward historical intimation that Luther began preaching before Johann Staupitz (c. 1460–1524) called him to do so in 1511 (Ulrich Asendorf, "Martin Luther als Prediger: Anmerkungen zur Bedeutung seiner Predigten im Rahmen seiner gesamten Theologie," in *Kirche in der Schule Luthers: Festschrift für D. Joachim Heubach*, ed. Bengt Hägglund and Gerhard Müller [Erlangen: Martin-Luther-Verlag, 1995], 11; Zschoch, "Predigten," 315). See Erich Vogelsang, "Zur Datierung der frühesten Lutherpredigten," *Zeitschrift für Kirchengeschichte* 50 (1931): 112–45, esp. 112–16. For the first extant sermon and the final sermon, see LW 51:5–13, 371–92 (WA 4:590–95; 51:123–34), respectively. For the number of extant sermons, see Kurt Aland, *Hilfsbuch zum Luther Studium*, 3rd ed. (Wittenberg: Luther-Verlag, 1970), 205–62.

scholars believe that we are missing about as many sermons as those contained in the Weimar edition—an enormous total, resulting from Luther's regular schedule of preaching two to three times a week.[86] "Often I preached four sermons in one day," Luther reminisced about his early preaching career.[87] After 1521 the record of extant sermons is more complete—approximately 90 percent—thanks to Luther's increased platform and the activity of faithful transcribers like Georg Rörer (1492–1557) and Johann Stolz (c. 1514–1556), among others.[88] Early in his career Luther would at times try to write down what he had preached after the fact, yet most of the records are from others' hands.[89]

Rörer has long been reputed as Luther's most accurate amanuensis.[90] His notes, as well as those of other clerks, are a hodgepodge of Latin and German. Despite Luther's slow manner of speaking, Rörer had to resort to a customized abbreviation system to capture even "the very bare bones" of Luther's sermons.[91] Rörer managed to capture Luther's very speech; however, he often elided words or phrases that he thought could be easily supplied—even entire sentences, especially proverbs, and biblical citations—and

---

[86] Asendorf, "Martin Luther als Prediger," 12; Fred W. Meuser, *Luther the Preacher* (Minneapolis: Augsburg, 1983), 18; Wood, *Captive to the Word*, 86; Ebeling, *Evangelische Evangelienauslegung*, 14-16. Meuser estimates that Luther preached about four thousand sermons, which seems reasonable. Two to three sermons a week over thirty-four years would give a range of 3,500–5,300 sermons.

[87] WATR 3:655.7–8, no. 3843 (LW 54:282).

[88] Ebeling, *Evangelische Evangelienauslegung*, 16; Kiessling, *Early Sermons*, 42. On Rörer and Stolz, see LW 58:xxiv–xxviii; Ebeling, *Evangelische Evangelienauslegung*, 18–21.

[89] Jonathan Mumme, *Die Präsenz Christi im Amt: Am Beispiel ausgewählter Predigten Martin Luthers, 1535-1546* (Göttingen: Vandenhoeck & Ruprecht, 2015), 41–45; Zschoch, "Predigten," 316; Wood, *Captive to the Word*, 88–89; Kiessling, *Early Sermons*, 55–56.

[90] See Bengt Löfstedt, "Notizen eines Latinisten zu Luthers Predigten," *Vetenskapssocieteten i Lund: Årsbok* (1985): 24–42. Löfstedt trusts Georg Buchwald's evaluation of Rörer's accuracy, while adding three reasons. First, Luther and Rörer are contemporaries with similar education and training. Second, Rörer admired Luther and likely could and would imitate Luther's speech. Third, Löfstedt finds that the style in Rörer's notes parallels Luther's letters and lectures (p. 37). For the bulk of the article Löfstedt explains the oddities of Rörer's Latin notes (27–40). See further Axel Wiemer, *"Mein Trost, Kampf und Sieg ist Christus": Martin Luthers eschatologische Theologie nach seinen Reihenpredigten über 1. Kor 15 (1532/33)* (Berlin: Walter de Gruyter, 2003), 19–23.

[91] Buchwald's introductory assessment of Luther's sermon series on 2 Peter and Jude, WA 14:2–3, quoting p. 2. Buchwald also finds the published version of these sermons "frequently toned down." Despite Luther's strong condemnation of using languages other than the vernacular, some of the Latin phrases and their German glosses are likely original to Luther, namely, technical terms and well-known proverbs (Löfstedt, "Notizen eines Latinisten zu Luthers Predigten," 26).

he suppresses transitions.[92] Luther talked about the analogy of faith and the catechism so often that his transcribers regularly patch over these references with a terse "u." (*und so weiter,* "and so on") or "etc.," or they abbreviate it by only naming one or some parts of the catechism.[93] Happily for us, Rörer taught his idiosyncratic system to Andreas Poach (1515–1585), who expanded the notes for publication for an early critical edition of Luther's works (Eisleben edition, 1564–1565).[94] Additionally, for many of the sermons we have other revised published versions, so we can compare Rörer's staccato versions of Luther's sermons against Poach's expansions and these other records.[95]

Luther's sermons will be the primary focus of this book. To show Luther's *teaching* on the analogy of faith, I will digest his sermons on Romans 12:6 (the reading for the Second Sunday after Epiphany), supplemented with other key sources. Luther is adamant that to read the Bible rightly is to read it according to the analogy of faith or the catechism. Before turning to Luther's use of the analogy of faith in interpretation, I will summarize Luther's explanation of the catechism. His explanation of the catechism is not limited to the *Small* and *Large Catechisms* (1529). I will especially focus on the records of Luther's quarterly catechetical sermon series—out of which the *Small* and *Large Catechisms* were born.

To show Luther's *use* of the analogy of faith, we will examine his exegesis of five passages from the five parts of the canon. Luther never exhaustively named and numbered the genres of the Bible. While he was sensitive to the Bible's literary nature, some scholars stretch his summary description of a

---

[92]Paul Pietsch's introductory comments to Luther's 1529 sermons, WA 29:xvi–xxx; see also WA 27:xix–xxiv. Pietsch also provides a table of Rörer's most common, non-Tironian abbreviations, WA 29:xx–xxiv.

[93]For example, Sermon on Pentecost Tuesday (1529), WA 29:376.15; Sermon on the Second Sunday after Epiphany (1536), WA 41:510.36–38, 511.1; Sermon on St. Michael's (1539), WA 47:857.26–27; Sermon on the Eighth Sunday after Trinity (1544), WA 49:533.22, 534.1–3; WATR 2:303.5–8, no. 2047.

[94]See LW 58:xxvi–xxvii; LW 69:136–40.

[95]See LW 58:xxvii. Clearly this complicated transmission history presents difficulties for text criticism. For an example of such careful text criticism, see Susanne Bei der Wieden, *Luthers Predigten des Jahres 1522: Untersuchungen zu ihrer Überlieferung* (Cologne: Böhlau Verlag, 1999). I do not intend to pursue explaining the text-critical nuances in my own work; the scholarship has shown that we can trust the ideas, if not the very words, as Luther's own.

book into its genre.⁹⁶ But he was attentive to canon. He published his German translation of the Bible by canon divisions: Law (1523), History (1523), Wisdom (1524), Prophets (1532), and New Testament (1522).⁹⁷ I have selected representative passages for each part of the canon: Genesis 22; Judges 14:14; Psalm 72; Isaiah 9:2-7; and Luke 24:13-49. These passages are well represented in Luther's teaching and preaching.⁹⁸ Altogether this book examines about 10 percent of Luther's sermons (185 out of 2,082 sermons) and 4 percent of Luther's postils (16 out of 412 postils), supplemented by lectures, tracts, and prefaces.⁹⁹ This will give us a full picture of Luther and the analogy of faith: the theory and the practice and whatever differences there might be between the two.

This book is not structured chronologically. Historians often have anxiety about such projects, and this is especially the case with historians of Luther and the Reformation. Luther was an occasional writer and speaker, and so his writing and speaking was heavily inflected by his current circumstances. This fact is often used to resist harmonization of Luther's views and statements over his lifetime. While Luther surely

---

⁹⁶For example, Proverbs is a book of good works; Ecclesiastes, a book of comfort; Song of Songs, a book of praise. See "Preface to the Books of Solomon" (1545), LW 35:258, 260 (WADB 10,1:7.3–4, 8.24–25); Robert Kolb, *Martin Luther and the Enduring Word of God: The Wittenberg School and Its Scripture-Centered Proclamation* (Grand Rapids: Baker Academic, 2016), 164–65.

⁹⁷And the Apocrypha was published in 1534. Luther accepted the Jewish canon delimitation instead of the Septuagint, but he followed the Septuagint's fourfold division of the Old Testament: the Law, History, Wisdom, and Prophets. See Rune Imberg, *Bibelläsaren som förändrade världen: Om Martin Luther som bibelteolog—bibelöversättare—bibelutgivare*, Församlingsfakultetens småskrifter 5 (Gothenburg: Församlingsförlaget, 2017), 48–49. (Thank you to Tomas Bokedal for sharing this article with me and summarizing it for me!) The *Glossa ordinaria* divides the Old Testament in the same way; *Glossa ordinaria*, 1:†5r. Luther rejected contemporary subdivisions of the New Testament (that paralleled the Old Testament subdivisions), see "Preface to the New Testament" (1522), LW 35:357–58 (WADB 6:2.14–21, compare with p. 3.16–21). Luther omitted this portion of the preface in complete editions of the Bible and all editions of the New Testament after 1537.

⁹⁸I also used the *Luther im WWW* database to locate relevant passages, searching key terms like *analoga fidei, secundum analogiam fidei*, Röm 12, 7, *iuxta praescriptum* Ro. 12., *iuxta analogiam fidei, so sollen sie dem Glauben ehnlich sein, das sie sich zum Glauben reimen, dem Glauben ehnlich, dem Glauben gemes, secundum fidei regulam, ad regulam Apostolis, ad regulam et normam fidei, reimt (reymt) sich mit dem glauben, reimt cum fide*. Also Luther tends to cluster other prooftexts around Romans 12:6, like Romans 12:3; 1 Corinthians 14:5; Galatians 1:8; 1 Thessalonians 5:21; 2 Peter 1:16-21; 1 John 4:1.

⁹⁹For the full list of sermons and postils, see Aland, *Hilfsbuch zum Luther Studium*, 205–62, 187–204, respectively.

developed and changed his mind, scholars tend to portray Luther as erratic and volatile, changing his mind willy-nilly. (Think of how the "older Luther" is treated—as if he wasn't still one of the sharpest theologians and philosophers of his era after 1521.[100]) Often this seems to result from confusing Luther's rhetoric for dialectic—as if the way he's trying to persuade his audience is the same as what he's trying to persuade them of.[101] To apply core concepts and doctrines in different settings requires verbal adornment fitted to the audience.

Luther talks about the importance of the catechism and the analogy of faith over his entire career. So much so that in a sermon in 1530, he excuses himself from explaining a catechetical topic: "You've often heard about this command in the catechism, and you know what it says: *Love God and neighbor*. Therefore I won't say a lot about it now."[102] He published on a part of the catechism (the Ten Commandments) as early as 1518 and on the entire catechism as early as 1520; he published multiple works on the catechism as a whole as well as each of its parts.[103] He doesn't use the catechism merely as an occasional solution. The catechism is the principled, animating logic to his theology. He gives no indication that he thought he had discovered the catechism. It's an ancient Christian tool that he knew by heart ever since he began school (just over the tender age of four).[104] Throughout his life he presents the catechism as the key to reading the Bible, whether one is a pastor, seminarian, or simple layperson. Of course, key experiences

---

[100] H. G. Haile shows the accusations of the elder Luther as senile for what they are: ridiculous. See H. G. Haile, *Luther: An Experiment in Biography* (New York: Doubleday, 1979), 31–43.

[101] For example, consider the reception of Luther's views of reason and allegory. (To be fair, Luther is particularly forceful with his rhetoric.) Gerrish shows that Luther distinguishes three types of reason: reason exercised in temporal matters, reason exercised in spiritual matters, and reason submitted to the word of God and faith. Luther only condemns reason exercised in spiritual matters. Because Luther doesn't give these three types different names, one must closely examine the context of his bombastic statements. See Gerrish, *Grace and Reason*, 10–27. Similarly Luther distinguishes two types of allegory: those ruled by reason and those ruled by the faith. He only rejects allegories ruled by reason.

[102] Sermon on the Eighteenth Sunday after Trinity (1530), WA 32:127.6–8.

[103] See *A Short Explanation of the Ten Commandments* (1518), WA 1:250–56; *A Short Form of the Ten Commandments, Creed, the Our Father* (1520), WA 7:204–29.

[104] See Brecht, *Luther*, 1:14–15; E. G. Schwiebert, *Luther and his Times: The Reformation from a New Perspective* (St. Louis: Concordia, 1950), 111; Johann Michael Reu, *Luther's German Bible: An Historical Presentation Together with a Collection of Sources* (Columbus, OH: The Lutheran Book Concern, 1934; reprint, St. Louis: Concordia, 1984), 76; James MacKinnon, *Luther and the Reformation*, 4 vols. (London: Longmans, Green, and Co., 1925–1930), 1:5, 4:318–23.

reinvigorated the intensity of Luther's advocacy of the catechism—particularly, the radicalization of Andreas Bodenstein von Karlstadt (1486–1541) and the shocking Church Visitations of 1528–1529.[105] And so, later in his career he can be especially clear: the catechism is the touchstone, the true cubit, the master, and the greatest sermon.[106] This isn't a development in dialectic but in rhetoric.

Because this book is not structured chronologically, it is much less repetitive than it otherwise would be, and it can focus on the inner logic of Luther's teaching.

On Translation and Terms

Translation always presents difficulties. Luther is no exception. Here I want to address Luther's spelling, the Bible version used, and some key words. Typical of his era, Luther's spelling is inconsistent and at times erratic. I have preserved his text according to the Weimar edition (and in some cases certain sixteenth-century editions). This includes unusual capitalization, which I have preserved in English translation only in one case: his use of *nomina sacra*.[107] Luther used capitalization to differentiate when *Herr* ("Lord") translated the Tetragrammaton (יהוה) or אֲדֹנָי: "HERR" for the Tetragrammaton; "HErr" for אֲדֹנָי. Luther applies this typographical solution across both testaments.[108]

---

[105] The Church Visitations were what drove Luther to reintroduce the catechism himself. Even after Karlstadt and the "heavenly prophets," Luther was still waiting for someone else to take up the task. See *The German Mass and Order of Service* (1526), LW 53:64–67 (WA 19:75.15–78.24). In contrast, see Preface to *The Small Catechism* (1529), TAL 4:212 (WA 30,1:264–65; BoC 1959, 338.

[106] Sermon on St. Michael's (1539), WA 47:857.26–27, "But through the touchstone. Therefore whatever depends on the Ten Commandments, etc."; Sermon on John 2:24 (1538), WA 46:780.15–17 (compare with LW 22:265), "Let us go to the touchstone, and let us measure with the true yardstick and see if it fits with the Our Father and the articles of the Christian faith"; WATR 1:489.22, no. 966, "the catechism must rule"; House Sermon on the Creed (1537), LW 57:244 (WA 45:12.7–8), "these are the three greatest sermons: the Our Father, the Creed, and the Ten Commandments."

[107] For examples, of Luther's unusual capitalization, see "DU aber nach deinem verstockten und unbusfertigen Hertzen"; "DEnn es ist kein ansehen der Person fur Gott"; "SIhe aber zu"; WADB 7:35 (Rom 2:5, 11, 17). This tends to happen at the beginning of a new thought.

[108] See "Preface to the Old Testament" (1523), LW 35:248–49 (WADB 8:30.20–28); Christine Helmer, "Luther's Trinitarian Hermeneutic and the Old Testament," *Modern Theology* 18, no. 1 (2002): 49–73; Heinrich Assel, "Gottesnamen und Kernstellen in Luthers Bibelübersetzung 1545: Eine systematisch-theologische Perspektive," in *"Was Dolmetschen für Kunst und Arbeit sei": Die Lutherbibel und andere deutsche Bibelübersetzungen*, ed. Melanie Lange and Martin Rösel (Leipzig: Deutsche Bibelgesellschaft and Evangelische Verlagsanstalt, 2014), 107–35.

Rather than use an English Bible version that approximates Luther's Bible translation, I have translated his version or have preserved his free rendering from the relevant sources. Luther had several editions of the Hebrew Bible on hand but used Gershon ben Moses Soncino's Brescia Biblia (1494) as his base text for the Old Testament.[109] Luther used Erasmus's critical edition of the New Testament as his base text for the New Testament, and in some passages Erasmus's base text differs from the modern critical editions (Erasmus only had seven incomplete manuscripts on hand, all from the Majority text tradition).[110] Where relevant, I've noted these differences and summarized modern discussions of the issue in the notes. Luther's Bible did not have verse numbers, though the Weimar editors have inserted the German versification, which is sometimes different from English versification; I have used English versification.

Some explanation is required for about half a dozen words in Luther's text. I have preserved the tone of Luther's labels for other groups. I have let their impoliteness remain not because I agree with these labels, but because it's accurate history. For example, *papistae* is consistently rendered "Papists," because Luther distinguished between Catholics like himself and Catholics who were ultimately—in his eyes—committed to the pope and his authority (hence, Luther's use of "Romanist"). *Anabaptistae* and *Widerteuffer* are rendered "Rebaptizers." Anabaptist has taken on a technical sense, but Luther in no way was trying to be fair; he meant the name as an insult. *Rotten* has been translated as "fanatic"; I used to do the same with *Schwärmer*, but Amy Nelson Burnett has changed my mind. She argues that *Schwärmer* should be left untranslated and un-disambiguated, because translating *Schwärmer* and disambiguating the various parties obfuscates the core reason Luther opposed these groups: they rejected—in his judgment—the ordained order of God. Modern scholars tend to understand *Schwärmer* as only referring to the

---

[109] A. Schleiff, "Theologisch-exegetische Einleitung," in WADB 9:xiii. Luther also had a copy of one of Daniel Bomberg's Bibles. See Stephen G. Burnett, "Luthers hebräische Bibel (Brescia, 1494)—Ihre Bedeutung für die Reformation," in *Meilensteine der Reformation: Schlüsseldokumente der frühen Wirksamkeit Martin Luthers*, ed. Irene Dingel and Henning P. Jürgens (Gütersloh: Gütersloher Verlagshaus, 2014), 62–69.

[110] William W. Combs, "Erasmus and the Textus Receptus," *Detroit Baptist Seminary Journal* 1, no. 1 (1996), 45–48

Radicals, but Luther often refers to the Reformed by this term.[111] And so I have left *Schwärmer* untranslated.

When referring to the Apostles' Creed, *symbolum* has consistently been translated "Creed." The chief Christian creeds—the Apostles', Nicene, and Athanasian Creeds—were often called "symbols" by the tradition, because these watchwords help us to distinguish true preaching from false preaching.[112] I use "analogy of faith" and "rule of faith" interchangeably. I do this for two reasons: (1) Luther uses them interchangeably (although he would prefer "analogy of faith" because of its biblical origins in Rom 12:6), and (2) "rule of faith" is now much more common than "analogy of faith," so I have tried to mix them together to minimize how foreign "analogy of faith" will sound to many. Finally, I have capitalized Baptism, Communion, and Absolution to indicate their status in the catechism. The word *sacrament* remains lowercased to distinguish the general use from the typical Lutheran use of "the Sacrament," meaning "the Sacrament of the Altar" or Holy Communion (Luther rarely uses the term "the Eucharist").

---

[111]See Amy Nelson Burnett, "Luther and the *Schwärmer*," in *The Oxford Handbook of Martin Luther's Theology*, ed. Robert Kolb, Irene Dingel, and Ľubomír Batka (New York: Oxford University Press, 2014), 511-13, 521.

[112]See Esther Chung-Kim and Todd R. Hains, *Acts*, RCS NT 6 (Downers Grove, IL: IVP Academic, 2014), 213n34.

2

The Ancient Catechism

Defining the Rule of Faith

Every year on the Second Sunday after Epiphany, Luther's congregation heard Paul's words to the Romans on spiritual gifts (Rom 12:3-8). While Luther did not always preach the Epistle reading on this Sunday, he usually used this opportunity to explain correct biblical interpretation. In this passage Paul lays down a hard and fast rule for interpretation: εἴτε προφητείαν κατὰ τὴν ἀναλογίαν τῆς πίστεως; "If someone has the gift of prophecy, let it be according to the faith."[1] According to Luther, this passage is essential for all exegesis, "for Paul sees that it's not enough to say, 'I have Scripture,' etc. Instead, you, lay person, look to the Creed and the Lord's Prayer. . . . Yes, just the catechism is enough for us to oppose false prophets."[2] Luther did not define the analogy of faith as merely interpreting Scripture with Scripture or with justification by faith alone or with just the Creed.[3]

---

[1] *Novum Testamentum omne*, ed. Erasmus, 343; WADB 7:67 (1546). Luther associated a cluster of verses with Romans 12:6, especially Romans 12:3; 1 Corinthians 14:5; Galatians 1:8; 1 Thessalonians 5:21; 2 Peter 1:16-21; 1 John 4:1.
[2] Sermon on the Second Sunday after Epiphany (1536), WA 41:511.28-29, 37-38.
[3] For example, Hof, "Luther's Exegetical Principle of the Analogy of Faith," 245-48; Kolb, *Martin Luther and the Enduring Word of God*, 99, 188-89. That Luther so often explained the analogy of faith clearly contradicts those who argue that the analogy of faith is a later innovation. For example, Cooper, "The Analogy of Faith in Puritan Exegesis," 240. In 2017 Sujin Pak implied that the analogy of faith was solely a Reformed principle; in 2020 she admits Luther used the analogy but mistakenly claims he didn't connect it with the Creed. See Pak, "Scripture, the Priesthood of All Believers, and Applications of 1 Corinthians 14," 48-50; Pak, "The Protestant Reformers and the *Analogia Fidei*," 227-45. On the various confessions' different presuppositions behind the analogy,

Instead he defined it as interpreting Scripture with the catechism.[4]

The analogy of faith is a special case of the analogy of Scripture—that Scripture is its own interpreter (*Scriptura sui ipsius interpres*). The analogy of Scripture compares passages to draw out their internal clarity; it does this by illumining passages that seem dark to humans with bright and clear passages. There's a general and special analogy of Scripture. The general analogy of Scripture takes one verse (or many) and compares it to another. The special analogy of Scripture is the analogy of faith: it takes the articles of faith as delivered in the catechism and puts them in conversation with any and every passage of the Bible. Luther determined clear passages by the catechism—how clearly they witnessed to Jesus the Lord of Scripture.[5]

To define the analogy of faith, this chapter will address four matters: (1) prophecy, (2) the catechism, (3) the office of the word, and (4) the audience of the ministry of this office. Luther's understanding of prophecy (general and special) sets up the question of truth and normativity in interpretation and proclamation. How do we know when prophecy comes from God and thus should be obeyed? Luther holds up the catechism—the Ten Commandments, the Apostles' Creed, the Our Father, and the sacraments—as the standard of prophecy. What fits the faith of the catechism is from God; what does not fit the faith of the catechism is not from God. While there is this shared standard of interpretation, God also orders his people. Some are ordained for the task of proclaiming God's word. These officeholders are not right and holy in themselves; they are right and holy in so far as they carry out their office according to the catechism. They are servants submitted to God's word and faith, otherwise they are liars and tyrants. God has given his prophetic word for the benefit of all his people, not just the learned elite. That's why God has given the church the catechism and analogy of faith. It is a "lay Bible."

---

see Selderhuis, "Introduction to the Psalms," in RCS OT 7:xlvi–lii; Philip D. W. Krey and Peter D. S. Krey, ed., *Romans 9–16*, RCS NT 8 (Downers Grove, IL: IVP Academic, 2016), 132–35.

[4]As we shall see, this is a special case of Scripture interpreting Scripture. In general, see Muller, *Post-Reformation Reformed Dogmatics*, 2:493–97.

[5]On the analogy of Scripture, see Wood, *Captive to the Word*, 161–63; Thompson, *A Sure Ground on Which to Stand*, 242–45; Althaus, *Theology of Martin Luther*, 79–81. On Jesus as the Lord of Scripture, see Luther's provocative *Theses Concerning Faith* (1535), theses 40–51, LW 34:112 (WA 39,1:47.1–24).

How Does Luther Understand Prophecy?

Luther recognized that most people wanted to hear new things, and they sought interpreters of Scripture who were willing to scratch their ears (2 Tim 4:3). "The impious bid [prophecies of Christ] farewell—they expect other prophecies from us about things to come, about the Turks and other contingencies." But faithful exegetes must refuse to quench this desire for speculation about temporal, earthly matters, instead responding: "We only have prophecies about Christ and his Word."[6] All prophecy is about Jesus—who he is and what he has done and what he will do—by his word and Spirit.

Luther distinguishes between special and general prophecy. Special prophecy is what the Old Testament prophets and New Testament apostles did by the Spirit's urging and guidance: they foretold future things about Christ and his word. General prophecy is to explain and apply Scripture for the life and faith of Christians.[7]

Like his contemporaries, Luther most often used *prophecy* in the general sense.[8] "'Prophecy' is the ability to explain and interpret Scripture correctly, and from it powerfully prove the teaching of faith and overthrow

---

[6] Afternoon Sermon on Pentecost Tuesday (1529), WA 29:377.26-28.

[7] WATR 1:15-16, no.45 (1531). See also WATR 1:545-46, no. 1079; 3:177, no. 121; Epistle on the Second Sunday after Epiphany (*Church Postil*, 1525), WA 17,2:38.25-39.4, LW 76:214-15; Afternoon Sermon on the Second Sunday after Epiphany (1531), WA 34,1:104.16-105.1; Sermon on Pentecost Tuesday (1535), WA 41:268.17-22. Compare Hieronymus Weller von Molsdorf's (1499-1572) comments on prophecy, Derek Cooper and Martin J. Lohrmann, ed., *1-2 Samuel, 1-2 Kings, 1-2 Chronicles*, RCS OT 5 (Downers Grove, IL: IVP Academic, 2016), 96-97.

[8] See Scott M. Manetsch, ed., *1 Corinthians*, RCS NT 9a (Downers Grove, IL: IVP Academic, 2017), 314-21; Pak, "Scripture, the Priesthood of All Believers, and Applications of 1 Corinthians 14," 50; Pak, "The Protestant Reformers and the *Analogia Fidei*," 232-33; in contrast, Starling, "The Analogy of Faith in the Theology of Luther and Calvin," 5-19. While Manetsch and Pak acknowledge that prophecy as interpretation of Scripture was uncontroversial among the Reformers (and their Catholic opponents), Starling claims that Luther alters his understanding of prophecy during his career: before the Peasants' War (1524-1526) he defines prophecy as forecasting the future; after the Peasant's War, prophecy is interpreting Scripture. Starling omits Luther's extended scholium on Romans 12:6, only citing the simple gloss on *prophecy* (see LW 25:106, 444-46; WA 56:119.9-11, 451.31-453.22). In Starling's telling Luther crafts the analogy of faith as a way to fight off the *Schwärmer*. Luther certainly used the analogy of faith against the *Schwärmer* (and Papists); however, even as early as his Romans Lectures (1515-1516), he makes clear this is the standard of true interpretation. For example, "One may prophesy new things, but not things that go beyond the bounds of the faith" (LW 25:446; WA 56:453.16-17). To be sure, in the extant glossa and scholia of the Romans Lectures, Luther assumes the twofold meaning of prophecy. For a caetena of Reformation commentators on prophecy, see RCS NT 9a:315-21; RCS NT 8:132-35; RCS OT 5:96-97.

false teaching."[9] While explicating the precise linguistic, grammatical, historical, and literary facets of the biblical text is necessary for certain modes of interpreting Scripture, Luther taught that the use of Scripture for the faithful was the sine qua non of exegesis.[10] The Spirit of God has given the gift of interpretation for two reasons: to approve and apply the Christian faith and to defend it from false faith. Prophets do not concern themselves with what humans demand but with what God demands. Therefore, prophets dedicate themselves to faithfully interpreting God's word for his people.[11]

Yet Luther recognizes the dilemma: "But how are we supposed to know what's true?"[12] There are various interpretations of the same texts of Scripture—variations that go beyond restating the same content in new words. Christians are confronted with competing claims of truth, but by what standard should they evaluate these claims? The authority of the person (for example, pope or priest)? The extraordinary means by which the claims were delivered (for example, ecstatic dreams)? Evaluating truth based on a person's authority or the extraordinariness of the means risks obscuring that God is the ultimate foundation of truth. God acts in various ways at various times for various reasons. So the standard of truth should not arbitrarily reject or accept certain authorities or means.[13]

---

[9] Epistle on the Tenth Sunday in Trinity (*Church Postil*, 1544), LW 78:340, WA 22:182.13–15.

[10] Kolb, *Martin Luther and the Enduring Word of God*, 98–208; Mattox, "Luther's Interpretation of Scripture"; Stephen G. Burnett, "Reassessing the 'Basel-Wittenberg Conflict': Dimensions of the Reformation-Era Discussion of Hebrew Scholarship," in *Hebraica Veritas?: Christian Hebraists and the Study of Judaism in Early Modern Europe*, ed. Allison Coudert and Jeffrey S. Shoulson (Philadelphia: University of Pennsylvania Press, 2004), 181–201; Todd R. Hains, "Career as Preacher at Wittenberg," in *Encyclopedia of Martin Luther and the Reformation*, ed. Mark A. Lamport (Lanham, MD: Rowman & Littlefield, 2017), 106–7. Regarding diverse methods for diverse modes of interpreting Scripture, see the criticism of Lewis Ayres and Stephen Fowl on the Pontifical Biblical Commission's document *The Interpretation of the Bible in the Church*, Ayres and Fowl, "(Mis)reading the Face of God: The Interpretation of the Bible in the Church," *Theological Studies* 60, no. 3 (1999): 513–28; Carbajosa, *Faith, the Fount of Exegesis*.

[11] Luther also associates visions and dreams with prophecy (Acts 2:17-18; Joel 2:28-29; Num 12:6), although he treats these special forms with suspicion. The human heart craves extraordinary means. Humans are prone to despise the ordinariness and simplicity of Scripture for visions and dreams. He sees the Radicals as prime examples. See Sermon on Pentecost Tuesday (1529), WA 29:376:1–6.

[12] Sermon on Pentecost Tuesday (1529), WA 29:376.10–11.

[13] Luther believed God could work through extraordinary means. However, he always emphasized that God has ordained ordinary means—worship in word and sacrament, the office of the word—and believers must not despise these means. Because the papal system still had these ordinary means, Luther affirmed their validity and efficacy, see Luther's response to Argument XIX in *Disputation on the Church* (1542), LW 73:307–8; WA 39,2:167–68.

Luther understood this problem of truth. And so he offered a clear and fast rule for evaluating truth: the analogy of faith. "The analogy of faith rules everything, so long as it corresponds to the word and faith. For Satan also is able to rouse Scriptures, visions, and dreams—but not according to the analogy of faith! In sum: all prophecy, visions, and dreams that come before you and are not according to the analogy of faith, reject them!"[14] In contrast, all prophecy, visions, and dreams that fit the analogy of faith, believers may embrace.

The analogy of faith is the standard of correct biblical interpretation. "All interpreters must take pains that their prophecy fit the faith; if it doesn't, it's not prophecy."[15] To explain Scripture according to the analogy of faith means to interpret Scripture in such a way that it corresponds to and does not contradict the catechism. "To see if the Spirit leads you, I will watch your mouth, and I will compare what you preach with the catechism. What fits with what the children pray, [that is God's word]."[16] The analogy of faith defines the center and boundary of prophecy.

There are many ways to state the analogy of faith, but there's only one analogy of faith. As with any message, there's the substance (*res*), and there's the words (*verba*): the what or the content and the how or the expression. The analogy of faith's substance—the trinitarian history, word, and work as given in the Bible—could be expressed in different ways. For example, Luther wouldn't have balked at using the Nicene Creed or Te Deum instead of the Apostles' Creed. He could also cite various Bible verses as the analogy of faith.[17] That's because for Luther, "Scripture can speak differently about

---

[14]Sermon on Pentecost Tuesday (1529), WA 29:376.10-15. One of the difficulties in unearthing Luther's use and explanation of the analogy of faith is the method and style of his sermon stenographers. Georg Rörer (1492-1557), the most prominent and historically trusted stenographer, abbreviated whole words, phrases, and lines of argument that he believed he could easily supply later with an unassuming "u." or "etc."—*und so weiter* and *et cetera*, respectively. See Hains, "Career as Preacher at Wittenberg," 106; Löfstedt, "Notizen eines Latinisten zu Luthers Predigten." See further Paul Pietsch's introductory comments to Luther's 1529 sermons, WA 29:xvi-xxx, and the 1528 sermons, WA 27:xix-xxiv. Pietsch provides a table of Rörer's most common, non-Tironian abbreviations, WA 29:xx-xxiv.

[15]Sermon on the Second Sunday after Epiphany (1536), WA 41:510.29-31.

[16]Sermon on the Eighth Sunday after Trinity (1544), WA 49:533.22, 534.1, compare with 533.39, 534.13-14. To complete the final two clauses, I have pulled up "das ist gottes wort" (533.14) from the alternate witness. See also Sermon on Saturday after Cantate (1531), WA 33:304.1-7 (LW 23:191); Sermon on St. Michael's (1539), WA 47:853.2-858.3.

[17]For example, Lectures on Genesis 22:12a (1539), WA 43:229.1-2; LW 4:129-30.

how we become saved, and nevertheless it's always the same sermon. It's stated with different words, and still it's the same substance."[18] And yet Luther often preferred to identify the analogy of faith with a particular set of words, namely the catechism. This was for pedagogical reasons. "The young and the unlettered people must be taught with a single, fixed text and version. Otherwise, if someone teaches one way now and another next year—even when desiring to make improvements—the people become quite easily confused, and all the time and effort will go to waste."[19] First, learn the very words, then learn their meaning, and then and only then can different words be used to express the same meaning. If the words are constantly being changed, how will any one learn them?[20]

What Is the Catechism?

The catechism is the church's ancient handbook for teaching all Christians its faith and doctrine.[21] It is comprised of the Ten Commandments, the Creed, and the Our Father—though the order of these chapters, as it were,

---

[18] Sermon on Cantate Sunday (May 7, 1531), WA 34,1:362.4–6.

[19] Preface to *The Small Catechism* (1529), TAL 4:213 (WA 30,1:268–69; BoC 1959, 339).

[20] This is why liturgy is so important—not just for children but for for adults too. And that's why you should get a prayerbook and pray God's words back to him as you read his word, sanctifying your daily life (1 Tim 4:5). See the orders of Morning Prayer and Evening Prayer in *Lutheran Service Book* (St. Louis: Concordia, 2006) or *The 1662 Book of Common Prayer: International Edition*, eds. Samuel L. Bray and Drew Nathaniel Keane (Downers Grove, IL: IVP Academic, 2021).

[21] Ferdinand Cohrs, *Die Evangelischen Katechismusversuche vor Luthers Enchiridion*, 5 vols. (Berlin: A. Hofmann, 1900–1907), 4:229–38; Robert James Bast, *Honor Your Fathers: Catechisms and the Emergence of a Patriarchal Ideology in Germany, 1400–1600* (Leiden: Brill, 1997), 1–52; Gottfried G. Krodel, "Luther's Work on the Catechism in the Context of Late Medieval Catechetical Literature," *Concordia Journal* 25, no. 4 (1999), 365; Albrecht Peters, *Commentary on Luther's Catechisms*, 5 vols., trans. Holger K. Sonntag, Thomas H. Trapp, and Daniel Thies (St. Louis: Concordia, 2009–2013), 1:17–19; Johannes Schilling, "Katechismen," in *Luther Handbuch*, ed. Albrecht Beutel (Tübingen: Mohr Siebeck, 2005), 306; Haemig, "The Living Voice of the Catechism"; Timothy J. Wengert, "Introduction to the *Small Catechism* (1529)" in TAL 4:201–2. Luther himself was well aware of this long-standing tradition. See, for example, his comments in the preface to *The German Mass and Order of Service* (1526): "This instruction or catechization I cannot put better or more plainly than has been done from the beginning of Christendom and retained till now, i.e., in these three parts, the Ten Commandments, the Creed, and the Our Father. These three plainly and briefly contain exactly everything that a Christian needs to know" (LW 53:65; WA 19:76.9–11). Luther uses the term Christendom—in opposition to modern usage—in place of church to guard against understanding church in a temporal and physical sense and to give a fuller sense of the communion of saints across all time and space. Sermon on the Creed (1523), WA 11:53.22–25. See Headley, *Luther's View of Church History*, 29–41.

varied from the early church to the Protestant Reformation.[22] The sacraments—Baptism, Communion, and Absolution—were often included, too. (As we will see in chapter three, Luther included the sacraments in the catechism.)

When Luther used the term *catechism*, he usually had this definition in mind.[23] Many—Lutheran or otherwise—tend to think of Luther's *Small* and *Large Catechisms* (1529) as *the* catechism.[24] However, those are best understood as commentaries on the catechism: one for children and one for adults and ministers of the word.

Jesus of Nazareth commissioned his church to disciple the nations of the earth in word and deed. "To me all power in heaven and earth has been given. And so go forth and teach all peoples and baptize them in the name of the Father and the Son and the Holy Spirit. And teach them to cling to everything I have commanded you" (Mt 28:18-20).[25] From the apostolic age, the catechism was used to prepare and confirm Christians in the basics of the faith for Baptism.

However, between the time of the Carolingians and the Reformation, the purpose of the catechism shifted from instruction in Christian basics to a tool for extracting a detailed and exhaustive confession of sins.[26] This was

---

[22]Krodel, "Luther's Work on the Catechism," 365-72; Bast, *Honor Your Fathers*, 6-10; Peters, *Commentary on Luther's Catechisms*, 1:40-51. Luther moved the Ten Commandments from final position to first position. Scholars argue that this fundamentally recast the shape of the catechism. The medieval shape of the catechism reflected this chain of logic: faith grounds prayer, prayer and faith ground obedience. This structure seems to follow Augustine's remarks in *Faith, Hope, and Love* built on 1 Corinthians 13:13. It is ironic that structuring the catechism as the Creed, the Our Father, and the Ten Commandments seems to have encouraged moralism. It seems to harmonize nicely with Luther's demand that love must flow from faith.

[23]For some examples, see WATR 1:489.22-26, no. 966; Sermon on the Eighteenth Sunday after Trinity (1530), WA 32:127.6-8, 131.3-25; Sermon on First Sunday in Advent (1530), WA 32:209.29-38, 210.13-19; Afternoon Sermon on the First Sunday in Advent (1530), WA 32:219.24-26, 220.12-16; House Sermon on the Creed (1537), WA 45:11.5-8, 12.7-9, LW 57:243, 244. See Peters, *Commentary on Luther's Catechisms*, 1:18-19; Peters identifies three other meanings for *catechism*: (1) training in the basics of the Christian life and doctrine; (2) special worship services for instruction in these basics; and (3) a type of book. See further Haemig, "The Influence of the Genres of Exegetical Instruction, Preaching, and Catechesis on Luther," 453-60; Kolb, *Martin Luther and the Enduring Word of God*, 99-100.

[24]BoC 1959, 338-56; TAL 4:212-52 (WA 30,1:239-474, 537-819) and BoC 1959, 358-461 (WA 30,1:125-238). On *The Annotated Luther*'s "updated" version of the *Large Catechism* (TAL 2:289-415), see chapter 3, note 3.

[25]WADB 6:133.

[26]Krodel, "Luther's Work on the Catechism," 365-72; David C. Steinmetz, *Luther in Context*, 2nd ed. (Grand Rapids: Baker Academic, 2002), 135-40; Schilling, "Katechismen," 306.

especially the case in the German-speaking world.[27] Lateran IV (1215) required that all faithful Catholic men and women receive annual Confession and Communion at Easter. And Confession had to be total, for only what was confessed could be absolved. The council exhorted the confessor to be diligent and deft in hearing Confession, so that "like a skilled physician he may pour wine and oil into the wounds of the injured."[28] New material was added to catechisms to help priest and penitent alike identify and treat each moral wound.[29]

Consider, for example, the first printed German catechism, Dietrich Kolde's (c. 1435–1515) *Fruitful Mirror* (1470, 1480).[30] This catechism has three parts: how to believe, how to live, and how to die. The first section includes the standard fare of the Apostles' Creed and the Ten Commandments, in addition to lists of sins, conditions for God's forgiveness, and signs that the believer stands in God's grace. In addition to the Our Father, the second section details numerous prayers: the Ave Maria, prayers for the canonical hours, prayers of preparation (for Communion and the Mass), daily prayers to Mary and other saints. But Kolde also gives codes of conduct: what to do at table, what to do at the sound of a bell, when to go to sleep, what to do when pregnant, how to raise children, how to use Mary for protection, and how to pray the Rosary. The second section also lists gifts of the Spirit,

---

[27] Anne T. Thayer, *Penitence, Preaching, and the Coming of the Reformation* (Aldershot, UK: Ashgate, 2002); Ronald K. Rittgers, *The Reformation of the Keys: Confession, Conscience, and Authority in Sixteenth-Century Germany* (Cambridge, MA: Harvard University Press, 2004).

[28] Canon 21, *Concilium Lateranense IV* (1215), in *Conciliorum Oecumenicorum Generaliumque Decreta*, 7 vols. projected, ed. Giuseppe Alberigo, Alberto Melloni, and Frederick Lauritzen (Turnhout: Brepols, 2007–2017), 2,1:178.521–22. Church Councils and regional Synods commanded catechesis—indeed preaching and teaching the catechism, according to Ferdinand Cohrs, "was again practiced most eagerly at the end of the Middle Ages" (*Evangelischen Katechismusversuche*, 4:234). Many parishes even posted placards around the sanctuary with parts of the catechism. See Bast, *Honor Your Fathers*, 18–20.

[29] Krodel emphasizes the abuse that happened from prescribing a thorough probe of the confessant's sin ("Luther's Work on the Catechism," 368, 372). Luther argued that while private confession was strong and healthy medicine, no one should be forced into it. Confession does not just mean listing sins; it is a time for the confessor to wield and apply the comfort and promise that the catechism teaches. See "Sendschreiben an die zu Frankfurt am Main" (1533), WA 30,3:565–71, esp. 566.29–567.2. See further Thomas N. Tentler, *Sin and Confession on the Eve of the Reformation* (Princeton, NJ: Princeton University Press, 1977), esp. 345–70.

[30] See Dietrich Kolde, *Mirror for Christians*, in *Three Reformation Catechisms: Catholic, Anabaptist, Lutheran*, ed. Denis Janz (New York: Edwin Mellen Press, 1982), 31–130; Krodel, "Luther's Work on the Catechism," 393–94n50; Steinmetz, *Luther in Context*, 136. Kolde's catechism began circulating in 1470; it was first published in 1480.

beatitudes, things to remember, and things that lead to sin. Finally the third section describes the good death, things that astonish the devil, and signs that someone is a good Christian.

During the Middle Ages, a great deal of additional material was added to the basics of the Ten Commandments, the Creed, and the Our Father. For Luther, this added material, no matter how well intentioned, moved the goal of the catechism from learning the essence of the Christian faith to naming and identifying bad behavior. Luther saw this shift from Christian faith to moralism—characteristic of catechisms like Kolde's—as a distortion of Christian faith.[31] "When I was twenty-one, I went to Mass three times a day. What kind of preaching did I hear? The kind that made a terror out of Christ and Moses' Pentecost out of the Holy Spirit's Pentecost. Yes, not so good. They stood on our own works."[32] By preaching Christ as an example for good works without first holding him up as a gift for us, parish priests interpreted the form through the shadow, rather than the shadow through the form. "It was a shadow of what was to come, but the body itself is in Christ" (Col 2:17).[33] Moses' Pentecost, when the law was written on stone tablets at Sinai, should be seen through the Spirit's Pentecost, when Christ's law was poured into human hearts at Jerusalem.

Luther lamented how damaging a catechism restricted to probing a person's life for sin could be.[34] To use the catechism only for defining and differentiating good and bad works is to rewrite salvation history, as if the gospel really just means live better like Jesus, and the law means if you live holy enough, then God will love you.[35] The people of God don't just need examples for how to live; they first need a guide to the gift of the forgiveness of sin and

---

[31] "Among the many harmful books and doctrines by which Christians are misled and deceived and countless false beliefs have arisen, I regard the little prayer books as by no means the least objectionable" (TAL 4:165; WA 10,2:375.1–3; compare with LW 43:11) See further *Little Prayer Book* (1522), WA 10,2:375–501; LW 43:11–45; TAL 4:165–200. Mary Jane Haemig details the works-focused distortion of the catechism in her introduction to the *Little Prayer Book*, TAL 4:159–65.

[32] Sermon on Pentecost Tuesday (1535), WA 41:268.8–11. On the Old Testament Pentecost and New Testament Pentecost, see the Epistle for Pentecost Sunday (*Church Postil*, 1544), WA 21:438; LW 77:325–26; RCS NT 6:19.

[33] WADB 6:231.

[34] For example, see the preface to *Prayer Book* (1522), WA 10,2:375.1–17, 376.1–10 (LW 43:11–12).

[35] On this anxiety, see Phillip Cary, *Good News for Anxious Christians: 10 Practical Things You Don't Have to Do* (Grand Rapids: Brazos, 2010).

true life. This required a catechism correctly preached. "In my youth and entire life, I haven't heard the Ten Commandments and Our Father preached."[36] When Luther complained that preaching was absent from the church of his youth, this is what he means: the gospel was preached as law, and the law was preached as gospel.[37] This results in either searing the conscience or weakening it to the point that it shudders at a leaf.[38] A person with a seared conscience believes that by his own good works, he might earn God's favor; a person with a terrified conscience believes that because of the gulf between his life and God's holy ways, he could never be loved by God. In contrast, Luther taught that because Christ is a gift for us, he can be an example for us.[39] Because God loves you, in Christ you live as God's child. Luther sought to remedy the state of medieval catechesis through preaching and writing.

Luther dedicated his career to teaching the catechism. At least as early as 1516, Luther preached on part of the catechism (the Ten Commandments). His home parish—St. Mary's in Wittenberg—revived the medieval practice of quarterly catechism sermons during Ember Days.[40] While Luther shared this burden with the pastors and deacons of St. Mary's—particularly Johannes Bugenhagen (1485–1558)—traces of his regular catechetical

---

[36] WATR 6:127.8–9, no. 6691.
[37] Some scholars remind students of the Reformation that too often the Reformers' propaganda is accepted at face value without considering rhetorical intent. For example, Bast highlights Justus Jonas's (1493–1555) exaggerations about the condition of the Ten Commandments before the Reformation; see *Honor Your Fathers*, 1–2. John Frymire also underscores this point about preaching; see *The Primacy of the Postils: Catholics, Protestants, and the Dissemination of Ideas in Early Modern Germany* (Leiden: Brill, 2010), 22–23.
[38] Luther often uses this imagery from Leviticus 26:36. For example, see, Lectures on Genesis 42:28b, 43:18, WA 44:504.17–30, 505.14–17, 543.25–26; LW 7:276, 277, 328.
[39] Luther taught the distinguishable but inseparable nature of Jesus as gift and example to be foundational to correct undstanding and application of the gospel, see "Short Instruction: What Should Be Sought and Expected in the Gospels" (1522, 1544), LW 75:7–12 (WA 10,1.1:8–18; E² 7:8–13; compare with LW 35:113–24).
[40] Luther regularly notes that St. Mary's holds quarterly catechetical sermon series, for example, see Sermon on First Sunday in Advent (1528), WA 27:444.3–5; Sermon on February 21, 1529, WA 28:510.9–10; Sermon on August 15, 1529, WA 28:595.10–11; Afternoon Sermon on Palm Sunday (1529), WA 29:146.11; Sermon on the First Sunday in Advent (1530), WA 32:209.29–30; Sermon on Fourteenth Sunday after Trinity (1531), WA 34,2:195.14. The Wittenberg Church Ordinance of 1533 prescribed the following times for the quarterly catechetical sermon series: the weeks of the Third and Fourth Sundays in Advent, the First Sunday in Lent, Holy Cross, and the middle of the hops harvest. Luther's great catechetical series in 1523 and 1528 were held at these times. See Wengert, "Introduction to the *Small Catechism*," in TAL 4:201–2, 204; Kolb, *Martin Luther and the Enduring Word of God*, 181–82; Bast, *Honor Your Fathers*, 4–6; Emil Sehling, *Die Evangelischen Kirchenordnungen des XVI. Jahrhunderts*, 19 vols. (Leipzig: Reisland, 1902–2010), 1:700–701.

preaching remain in the historical record. Most famously, he preached the entire catechism in three massive sermon series during Pentecost, Holy Cross, and Advent of 1528, which he used as the foundation for the *Small* and *Large Catechisms*.[41] He also gave an abbreviated series on the entire catechism (except for Baptism), with an appended sermon on the Ave Maria during Lent of 1523.[42] And, especially at the end of his life and career, Luther was responsible for preaching on Baptism during Epiphany.[43] In addition to these formal treatments of the catechism, Luther littered references to the content and meaning of the Ten Commandments, Creed, Our Father, and sacraments throughout his sermons—after 1529 he at times recites his commentary on the catechism verbatim.

Luther adapted the content and notes from his preaching for publication. He published two explanations on the Ten Commandments,[44] two on the Our Father,[45] one on the Creed,[46] and three on the catechism beside his *Small* and *Large Catechisms*.[47] He also published treatments of the

---

[41] In each of these three series, he preached through the Ten Commandments, the Apostles' Creed, the Our Father, and the sacraments of Baptism and Communion. For the Pentecost sermon series, see WA 30,1:2-27; for the Holy Cross sermon series, see WA 30,1:27-57; for the Advent sermon series, see WA 30,1:57-122.

[42] WA 11:30-62.

[43] Robert Kolb, " 'What Benefit Does the Soul Receive from a Handful of Water?': Luther's Preaching on Baptism, 1528-1539," *Concordia Journal* 25 (1999): 346-63; Martin Ferel, *Gepredigte Taufe: Eine homiletische Untersuchung zur Taufpredigt bei Luther* (Tübingen: Mohr Siebeck, 1969). The sermon on Maundy Thursday usually handled the Sacrament of the Altar. For a helpful collection of Luther's sermons on Baptism, see *Martin Luther on Holy Baptism: Sermons to the People (1525-39)*, ed. Benjamin T. G. Mayes (St. Louis: Concordia, 2018).

[44] Both are based on his 1516-1517 sermon series: *A Short Explanation of the Ten Commandments* (1518), WA 1:250-56; *The Ten Commandments Preached to the People of Wittenberg* (1518), WA 1:398-521.

[45] *German Explanation of the Our Father for Simple Lay People* (1519), WA 2:80-130 (LW 42:19-81); *A Short Form for Understanding and Praying the Our Father* (1519), WA 6:11-22. John Witvliet counts more than a dozen paraphrases of the Our Father, see John D. Witvliet, "The Interplay of Catechesis and Liturgy in the Sixteenth Century: Examples from Lutheran and Reformed Traditions," in *The People's Book: The Reformation and the Bible*, ed. Jennifer Powell McNutt and David Lauber (Downers Grove, IL: IVP Academic, 2017), 116.

[46] *The Three Symbols or Creeds of the Christian Faith* (1538), WA 50:262-83 (LW 34:201-29). But see also *Confession concerning Christ's Supper* (1528), LW 37:360-72 (WA 26:499-509); there is also an "updated" transaltion of this text in TAL 2:262-77. The editors have censored Luther's use of gendered pronouns for God—not as extremely as in their rendering of the *Large Catechism*. See further chapter 3, footnote 3.

[47] *A Short Form of the Ten Commandments, Creed, the Our Father* (1520), WA 7:204-29; *Little Prayer Book* (1522), WA 10,2:375-501 (LW 43:11-45; TAL 4:165-200); *A Simple Way to Pray for a Good Friend* (1535), WA 38:358-75 (LW 43:193-211; TAL 4:256-81).

sacraments of Absolution, Baptism, and the Sacrament of the Altar.[48] He augmented these works with hymnody, giving the illiterate and literate alike a more memorable version of the basics of the faith.[49] Each hymn blends paraphrase and interpretation, succinctly distilling and reshaping Luther's doctrinal theology into a poetic, devotional context.[50]

While Luther did not hold a formal lecture series on the catechism, he wove it into his lectures as a regular feature and emphasis. He understood the temptation for pastors to impress their parishes by regaling them with stories and rhetoric—after all many parishioners preferred it! "When we preach the article of justification, the people snore and cough, but their ears immediately perk up to stories."[51] "They say: 'Our pastor always harps on the same string! He always preaches the same sermon!' "[52] In addition, preaching before their eminent professors, young students might succumb to showing off: "They think when I'm in service, they want to teach me. No! Instruction must begin with the children in mind!"[53] The humility of the catechism was

---

[48] *The Sacrament of Penance* (1519), WA 2:714-23 (LW 35:3-22); *The Holy and Blessed Sacrament of Baptism* (1519), WA 2:727-37 (LW 35:29-43); *The Blessed Sacrament of the Holy and True Body of Christ* (1519), WA 2:742-58 (LW 35:45-73).

[49] Two hymns for the Ten Commandments, "These Are the Holy Ten Commands" (1524; LW 53:277-79; WA 35:426-28, 495-97) and "Man, Wouldst Thou Live All Blissfully" (1524; LW 53:280-81; WA 35:428-29, 497); one for the Creed, "In One True God We All Believe" (1524; LW 53:271-73; WA 35:451-52, 513); one for the Our Father, "Our Father in the Heaven Who Art" (1539; LW 53:295-98; WA 35:463-67, 527); one for Baptism, "To Jordan When Our Lord had Gone," (1541; LW 53:299-301; WA 35:468-70, 490-91); and one for Communion, "Jesus Christ, Our God and Savior" (1524; LW 53:249-51; WA 35:435-37, 500-501). See Ulrich Leupold, "Introduction to the Hymns," LW 53:191-210; Dorothea Wendebourg, "Introduction to Selected Hymns," TAL 4:115-16, 120-21; Christopher Boyd Brown, *Singing the Gospel: Lutheran Hymns and the Success of the Reformation* (Cambridge, MA: Harvard University Press, 2005), 10-11, 91-104; Robin A. Leaver, *Luther's Liturgical Music: Principles and Implications* (Minneapolis: Fortress Press, 2007), 107-69. Only Robin Leaver acknowledges a hymn related to Absolution ("From Trouble Deep I Cry to Thee [1523], LW 53:221-24; WA 35:419-20, 492-93), see Leaver, *Luther's Liturgical Music*, 111, 142-52.

[50] Christine Helmer has shown Luther's adept use of genre to present and apply (trinitarian) theology for different audiences, see *The Trinity and Martin Luther*, revised edition (Bellingham, WA: Lexham Press, 2017).

[51] WATR 2:454.5-6, no. 2408a; compare with no. 2408b.

[52] WATR 1:504.27-28, no. 1002; compare with WATR 2:522, no. 2554a-b.

[53] WATR 5:6.12-13, no. 5200. See also WATR 5:167, no. 5465; 396, no. 5903. Luther encouraged young preachers to ignore their teachers—Luther, Melanchthon, Bugenhagen—and consider only the small children. For particularly nervous novices, Luther suggested they think of the congregation as blocks of wood (WATR 4:447.23-26, no. 4719). See WATR 2:144, no. 1590; 3:115, no. 2954a; 4:446-47, no. 4719; 5:644, no. 6404; 6:196-97, no. 6798; 198, no. 6800. Luther often used Huldrych Zwingli (who apparently cited the Greek text in a sermon before the

a powerful and necessary antidote to pride. "It's best not to preach long, but instead to speak simply and childishly."[54] "To preach childishly is the greatest art."[55]

By bringing his students back to the catechism, Luther intended to show them that in the school of Christ, everyone is always a beginner. No Christian ever has total mastery of these basic doctrines in word and deed. Christian humility requires continually returning to the catechism, learning to speak of God as the children do.

> Although I'm an old doctor, nevertheless, I daily discipline myself—I must still recite the Ten Commandments, the Creed, and the Our Father with the children. And I always still get such great use and benefit out of it. Thus, no one should think that he's finished learning it, nor should he thus despise the word, because it's preached and pressed every day.[56]

Luther makes statements like this throughout his sermons, lectures, and printed works. Even this famous old, learned doctor of theology daily needed to nourish his soul, praying "Our Father, who art in heaven" and proclaiming to himself what this means.[57]

The Church Visitations of 1528–1529 showed Luther—with renewed urgency—that lay and clergy alike required remedial instruction in the doctrine and life of the church. "The deplorable, wretched deprivation that I recently encountered while I was a visitor has constrained and compelled me to prepare this catechism."[58] One anecdote from the Visitations is particularly enlightening. Having been asked about preaching the Ten Commandments, one parish pastor replied, "I don't have that book yet."[59]

Emperor!), Johannes Oecolampadius, and Johann Agricola as examples of showing off: WATR 3:571–73, no. 3729; 4:76, no. 4014; 446–47 no. 4719; 476–77, no. 4763.

[54] WATR 5:6.8–9, no. 5200.

[55] WATR 5:396.22, no. 5903.

[56] Afternoon Sermon on First Sunday in Advent (1530), WA 32:210.13–18. See also Sermon on First Sunday in Advent (1530), WA 32:209.36–38; Sermon on First Sunday in Advent (1531), WA 34,2:449.20–30; WATR 1:30.26–31.2, no. 81.

[57] On Luther's fame, see Haile, *Luther*.

[58] Preface to *The Small Catechism* (1529), TAL 4:212 (WA 30,1:264–65; BoC 1959, 338).

[59] Susan C. Karant-Nunn, *Luther's Pastors: The Reformation in the Ernestine Countryside* (Philadelphia: American Philosophical Society, 1979), 17. On the Visitations, see Karant-Nunn, *Luther's Pastors*, 17; Brecht, *Martin Luther*, 2:259–73. See also *Instruction by the Visitiors for the Parish Pastors of Electoral Saxony*, LW 40:263–320; WA 26:195–240. Gerald Strauss questions the success of Luther's ongoing catechetical program. See Strauss, *Luther's House of Learning: Indoctrination of the Young in the German Reformation* (Baltimore: The Johns Hopkins University Press,

The Office of the Word

For Luther the catechism is the objective measure of what is God's word and what is not.[60] He called it "the touchstone" and "the true cubit."[61] The Ten Commandments, the Apostles' Creed, and the Our Father are the true and genuine sense of all Scripture.[62] "In these three, all that Scripture has is simply encompassed."[63] The Bible, rightly understood, and the catechism share the same content.

This central content shapes the church and the people of God. And so Luther used this standard to argue against subjective individual readings of Scripture. "They say that holy Scripture has a wax nose—we can manipulate it however we want."[64] Because Scripture is so malleable, the pope and his allies argued that the church's Magisterium determine right readings of Scripture—"We're supposed to obey the Roman Church."[65] But Luther saw this as subjective interpretation: it enthrones the interpreter as the authority, rather than the words and voice of God. This fundamentally subverts the relationship

---

1978); in contrast, see James M. Kittelson, "Successes and Failures in the German Reformation: The Report from Strasbourg," *Archiv für Reformationsgeschichte* 73 (1982): 153–74. On Luther's progressive development of his commentary on the catechism, see Timothy J. Wengert, "Wittenberg's Earliest Catechism," *Lutheran Quarterly* 7, no. 3 (1999): 247–60. Wengert does not consider *Short Form* (1520) a proper forerunner to Luther's commentary on the catechism; in contrast, see Cohrs, *Evangelischen Katechismusversuche*, 2:241.

[60]On Luther's understanding of God's word, see Pelikan, *Luther the Expositor*, 48–70, 257; Bayer, *Martin Luther's Theology*, chs. 3–4; Phillip Cary, *The Meaning of Protestant Theology: Luther, Augustine, and the Gospel That Gives Us Christ* (Grand Rapids: Baker Academic, 2019), chs. 7–8; compare with Thompson, *A Sure Ground on Which to Stand*, 47–53; Wood, *Captive to the Word*, 134–38; Althaus, *Theology of Martin Luther*, 35–53. Barth's understanding of Scripture becoming or containing the word of God sometimes distracts scholars discussing Luther's view. Luther indeed affirmed that the Bible is the word of God; nevertheless, when Luther uses the phrase *the word of God*, he does not always mean the Bible. Luther could mean Scripture itself, the deeds of God (like the exodus and the sacraments), preaching, and Jesus Christ. Pelikan states that "ultimately, then, there was only one 'Word of God,' which came in various forms," always with the purpose of creating, redeeming, and revealing (*Luther the Expositor*, 70).

[61]For example, Sermon on Second Sunday after Epiphany (1545), WA 49:685.1; Sermon on St. Michael's (1539), WA 47:85.26–27; Sermon on John 2:24 (1538), WA 46:780.15–20 (LW 22:265).

[62]See Sermon on St. Martin's (1530), WA 32:150–58.

[63]Sermon on May 18, 1528, WA 30,1:2.20–21. Indeed Luther says that from the beginnings of the church these three were used as a summary of all Christian teaching for common people (2.21–23). See also *A Short Form of the Ten Commandments, Creed, the Our Father* (1520), WA 7:204.13–18; *Little Prayer Book* (1522), WA 10,2:375.16–17 (TAL 4:166; LW 43:12).

[64]Sermon on the Second Sunday after Epiphany (1545), WA 49:685.7–9.

[65]Sermon on the Second Sunday after Epiphany (1545), WA 49:685.3–4. Here Roman Church is a technical term referring to the Roman Magisterium—the pope, his curia, and agents. For example, Luther reminds his parishioners, "the Roman Church is a daughter of the Christian Church" (684.17–18). See further Sermon on the Second Sunday after Epiphany (1545), WA 49:684.14–23.

between God and his people. God's word—"the power of God" (Rom 1:16)—births the church; the church does not birth, grow, or construct God's word.[66] Holy Scripture is "the pillar and foundation of truth. Christ calls it a rock."[67]

Nevertheless, Scripture requires interpretation—not because it is dark, but because humans are. "And we see the miracle of how clear Scripture is in itself! The defect is in us, because we do not see. . . . Scripture is clear; our eyes aren't totally clear."[68]

Because God is a God of order and not chaos, he has distributed gifts and arranged his people to work together for one another's mutual benefit. Luther used Paul's words to the Corinthians to illustrate this (1 Cor 12). As the human body has many members—hands and feet, eyes and ears—so also Christ's body has many members; and still all these members compose one body. Apart from one another they are nothing.

> This is a wonderfully funny metaphor. . . . Consider your body. . . . If the members were at odds and they hack off your feet and say: "I want to walk on my hands!" And your feet want to make shoes and cultivate the earth—what kind of body will that be? . . . If your ears don't want to hear and your eyes don't want to see, but they want to make your hands do the hearing and seeing—how could you see?[69]

In the same way, God's people must work together under their one head, Christ Jesus. It would be ridiculous for the church's preachers to be silent and listen to the congregation preach.

---

[66]*De potestate leges ferendi in ecclesia* (1530), WA 30,2:681-90; see also Afternoon Sermon on the First Sunday after Epiphany (1529), WA 29:8-17. In this little tract, Luther demonstrates the hierarchical relationship between the gospel and the church: the gospel can exist without the church, but the church cannot exist without the gospel. Therefore the church cannot change the word of God (682.21-25). Elsewhere Luther says this positively: wherever the gospel is preached and believed, there the church is. In one passage Luther even says wherever the catechism is taught, used, and applied, there the church is (*On the Councils and the Church* [1539], WA 50:641.20-34; LW 41:164). In no way is Luther relativizing the importance of the church; instead he is arguing that the church's entire being is derivative, whenever this is forgotten, the church is derelict in her duties and offices.

[67]Sermon on the Second Sunday after Epiphany (1545), WA 49:685.9; citing Mt 7:24.

[68]Epistle for the Third Day of Christmas (*Church Postil*, 1540), WA 10,1.1:179.14-15, 180.3; E² 7:218; LW 76:276. In his dispute with Erasmus over the freedom of the will, Luther sets out his position on the clarity of Scripture. See Desiderius Erasmus and Martin Luther, *Luther and Erasmus: Salvation and Free Will*, trans. and ed. E. Gordon Rupp and Philip S. Watson, Library of Christian Classics 17 (Philadelphia: The Westminster Press, 1969).

[69]Sermon on the Second Sunday after Epiphany (1536), WA 41:509.4-5, 7-9, 11-12.

While it may be tempting, according to the eyes of reason, to assign greater honor to one member on account of their leadership role or less honor to another member on account of their lay role, all the baptized share equally in Christ's honor.

> Where Christ, the prophets, the patriarchs, all the apostles and saints are, there I am, too! The one who carries me, must take me with. And so, because we are members with the same head, who could be greater? If one member has a higher, more worthy office, he does not therefore have greater honor in the body. Although the foot treads through shit, nevertheless the foot is just as much a part of Christ as the eye.[70]

Yes, some offices are greater, even more honorable, but that does not mean that the person himself is greater or more honorable. Like the members of a body, each person has a task, each person benefits from others, each person needs others.

Christians must distinguish the person from the office.[71] "For there is no respect of the person before God" (Rom 2:11).[72] Someone does not somehow merit their office in the body of Christ. They have been called to and equipped for that office by God. He could just as well have called and equipped someone else for that same office. "But all these the very same

---

[70] Sermon on the Second Sunday after Epiphany (1536), WA 41:509.23-27. Luther often makes this point: every believer is just as much Christ's own, a child of God the Father, as whatever great saint you can imagine. See, for example, Afternoon Sermon on the Second Sunday after Epiphany (1531), WA 34,1:102.1-4, 104.4-8; Sermon on Pentecost Tuesday (1535), WA 41:266.24-29, 267.6-14; Sermon on the Third Sunday after Epiphany (1545), 690.2-11.

[71] Paul Althaus illuminates Luther's understanding of the person-office distinction by focusing on the secular government's enforcement of law—particularly regarding violence. For a magistrate to condemn a murderer to death or for the hangman to hang a murderer is not a sin; both exercise the office entrusted to them by God. Luther locates these offices under love of neighbor, because they are protecting society and curbing evil. (This teaching reflects God's own attribute of love, which, in a fallen world, is sometimes expressed as wrath.) When executing the law's wrath, officials should not be angry. They are speaking God's objective wrath toward sinful behavior. Thus, no one may object that these secular authorities are hypocrites or abusers of power. Like preachers, they speak a word from God that is dependent on their office not on their person. An interesting nuance related to secular justice is self-defense. When a person's life is in danger—not for anything related to the gospel—they may justly defend themselves. In this act they fulfill an extraordinary office: they stand in for the secular magistrates. See Althaus, *The Ethics of Martin Luther*, trans. Robert C. Shultz (Philadelphia: Fortress Press, 1972), 66-78. On office, see also Sermon on Shrove Tuesday (1540), WA 49:25-29; Afternoon Sermon on the Second Sunday after Epiphany (1531), WA 34,1:102-3.

[72] WADB 7:35.

Spirit works and distributes to each one, as he will" (1 Cor 12:11).[73] All offices and gifts are granted by the same Spirit. Therefore, Christians must not and cannot boast on account of their office. Likewise, Christ's people must be careful not to accept something as Christ's work and purpose, just because of a name—like Peter or Paul.

Luther illustrates this with extreme examples. Just because the pope or parish priest, Peter or Paul says this is what Scripture means, does not make it so. And just because Caiaphas or Judas says this is what Scripture means, does not mean he is wrong. All these people are called to the office of the word.[74] Still they must exercise diligence in their ministry; their words are not faithful automatically because they are ministers of the word. "Whether the Spirit directs you, I'll watch your mouth and compare what you preach with the catechism. What fits with what the children pray, there the Holy Spirit speaks—even if it's Caiaphas. On the other hand, if it doesn't fit [with what the children pray], there the Holy Spirit does not speak—even if it's Peter or Paul."[75] To determine whether Scripture was being interpreted correctly, Christians needed to distinguish the person from the office, carefully comparing the interpretation with the catechism. "But test everything, and retain the good" (1 Thess 5:21).[76]

Ignoring the person-office distinction resulted in one of two extremes.[77] One extreme collapses the person into the office; the other extreme collapses the office into the person. On the one hand, the office automatically baptizes and validates everything the person says and does; the person is collapsed into the office. In Luther's day this misconception was seen in the abuse of the papal and bishophric offices. On the other hand, a person with skill and talent assumes the office de facto without the church's confirmation; the office is seized by the person. In Luther's day this misconception was seen

---

[73] WADB 7:121.
[74] Sermon on Shrove Tuesday (1540), WA 49:29.2–6, 21–27.
[75] Sermon on the Eighth Sunday after Trinity (1544), WA 49:533.22, 534.1–3. See also Sermon on Saturday after Cantate Sunday (1531), WA 33:304.1–17; Epistle for the Tenth Sunday in Trinity (*Church Postil*, 1544), WA 22:183.7–10 (LW 78:341); Epistle for the Eighth Sunday in Trinity (*Church Postil*,1544), WA 22:153.9–18 (LW 78:299).
[76] WADB 7:249.
[77] According to Luther, Satan fears nothing more than the office of the word. And so, he does everything in his power to distort its truth and to disarm its power. See the Epistle for the Tenth Sunday in Trinity (*Church Postil*, 1544), WA 22:187.13–20; LW 78:345.

in the populism of the Radical movements.[78] Luther wielded the analogy of faith as a shield and sword against both extremes. These extremes are exemplified in Luther's three opponents: Papists, Radicals, and Sacramentarians. According to Luther, each group distorts the three sacraments according to works righteousness: the Papists mangle Absolution; the Radicals, Baptism; the Sacramentarians, the Sacrament of the Altar. Luther accuses them of taking these mysteries and works of God and making them works of humans. That's the natural consequence of ignoring the person-office distinction.

First, Luther addressed the false assumption that whatever pope or bishop says is true. Starting early in his career Luther showed how this failed according to the analogy of faith. He had several default examples: medieval Penance, pilgrimages, praying to the saints, Purgatory, and cloistered life. One of Luther's usual preaching strategies was imaginary dialogue.[79] (Most often he models how to respond to Satan in times of fear and doubt.[80]) He encouraged his congregation to interrogate the claims of church authorities, who said Penance and pilgrimages earn the forgiveness of sin.

> [The pope] says, "Doing good works, going on pilgrimages, and reproving oneself are good works and they purify." What prophecy does he get that from? It doesn't fit the faith, which says only believe in Jesus the Son of God, who etc. Through him I find the remission of sins and everything else. I don't find Christ on the Camino de Santiago! Instead he sits at the right hand [of the Father], and he is found everywhere.[81]

Forgiveness and true life are in Jesus Christ alone. People do not have to travel hundreds of miles to designated and approved holy places to achieve these free gifts found in the incarnate Creator of heaven and earth. To

---

[78] On the Radicals, see George H. Williams, *The Radical Reformation*, 3rd ed. (Kirksville, MO: Sixteenth Century Journal Publishers, 1992).

[79] Kolb, *Martin Luther and the Enduring Word of God*, 153–67, 195–207. Kolb expounds four facets of Luther's method of preaching: historical-grammatical, doctrinal-catechetical, narratival, and exhortative.

[80] For example, see Sermon on the Thirteenth Sunday after Trinity (1530), WA 32:102.34–103.4.

[81] Sermon on the Second Sunday after Epiphany (1536), WA 41:511.3–8. Luther interjects other questions, too: "Where's that prophecy?" (511.11); "What faith?" (511.13); "So how's that fit with the faith?" (511.16); "What? Are you crazy?" (511.32). See also Sermon on St. Martin's (1530), WA 32:153.2–6; Afternoon Sermon on the Second Sunday after Epiphany (1531), WA 34,1:106.3–12; Sermon on the Second Sunday after Epiphany (1537), WA 45:3.1–37, 4.1–17; Sermon on the Second Sunday after Epiphany (1538), WA 46:145–51; Sermon on the Second Sunday after Epiphany (1545), WA 49:682.26, 683.1–26, 684.1–23, 685.1–17.

suggest otherwise is to deny the teaching and command Jesus himself delivered to his apostles. "Here the pope and his men overstep the measure [of the faith], for they direct me to the devil . . . they direct me away from Christ toward Rome or Jerusalem."[82] So Luther instructed his parishioners not to accept such claims as God's own speech.

Second, Luther addressed the opinion that extraordinary experience validates whatever is said. After the arrival of the Zwickau prophets or "heavenly prophets"—one of the many snide nicknames he gave to Radicals—Luther began to use Radical preachers as another example of incorrect prophecy that fell afoul of the analogy of faith as well as the person-office distinction.[83] Often Luther was too exasperated with the Anabaptists to explain how their teaching does not hold up against the faith. (And he claimed he was not alone in this exasperation—"Even the devil can't get them to shut up!"[84]) Luther dismissed Anabaptists out of hand, because he saw them as fundamentally disordered and chaotic—a characteristic the devil loves.[85] They were preachers who could not preach but tried all the same.[86] They were ears who did not want to hear; instead they wanted to tear out the eyes and try to see for themselves.[87] "Today our *Schwärmer* cause all sorts of calamity in our way of life."[88] They were trying to dismantle and destroy the body.

Luther instructed his congregants to oppose these preachers, who prided themselves on their visions, with the analogy of faith.[89] "All prophecy, visions, and dreams that come before you and are not according to the analogy of faith, reject them!"[90] He used their teachings on suffering as an example of how the Radicals distorted Scripture. Some, particularly Thomas Müntzer (1489–1525), taught that Christians needed first to imitate Christ's life and

---

[82] Sermon on the Second Sunday after Epiphany (1537), WA 45:3.23-24.
[83] See Sermon on the Eighth Sunday after Trinity (1544), WA 49:525-34. On the early Radicals in Wittenberg, see Brecht, *Luther*, 2:146-94.
[84] Afternoon Sermon on the Second Sunday after Epiphany (1531), WA 34,1:100.7-8.
[85] Afternoon Sermon on the Second Sunday after Epiphany (1531), WA 34,1:101.4-10, 103.11-14, 104.1-3.
[86] Afternoon Sermon on the Second Sunday after Epiphany (1531), WA 34,1:100.6-7, 101.11-15.
[87] Afternoon Sermon on the Second Sunday after Epiphany (1531), WA 34,1:103.1-11.
[88] Afternoon Sermon on the Second Sunday after Epiphany (1531), WA 34,1:103.14, 104.1. Amy Nelson Burnett argues that *Schwärmer* should be left untranslated and un-dismabiguated, see "Luther and the *Schwärmer*," 511-13, 521.
[89] Sermon on Pentecost Tuesday (1529), WA 29:376.5-26.
[90] Sermon on Pentecost Tuesday (1529), WA 29:376.14-15.

suffering before they could receive him as a gift.[91] This was one way of interpreting Matthew 19:29: "And whoever abandons houses or brothers or sisters or father or mother or wife or children or land for my name's sake will receive a hundredfold and inherit eternal life."[92] Just as Christ abandoned family—and was abandoned by family—so also, according to such interpretations, must his people abandon this basic human bond. For Luther, this is works-based theology that smuggles in a denial of the fourth commandment, "Honor your father and your mother." So they are peddling suffering and abandonment, not the faith. "But the faith speaks in this way: Through your works you do not enter heaven, but through Christ's Baptism and blood."[93] In contrast to the Radicals, Luther explains Jesus' words in Matthew 19 as an extreme example of the loyalty and obedience Christ's people have to him. "If you are urged to deny the faith, etc., then it's time you say: 'Before I deny the faith, the gospel, and Baptism—I'd rather be strangled than abandon Christ!' "[94] According to the analogy of faith, this verse demands honor of father and mother, except when that honor comes at the cost of God's honor. Luther also unpacked Anabaptist baptismal theology in a way that showed it to teach dependence on human works.[95]

Luther included the Sacramentarians in this second group.[96] They constitute a special subset of the category *experience confirms office and teaching*: reason confirms office and teaching.[97] Luther did not oppose reason. As with so many things, Luther demanded that reason take its rightful place as servant not master—it is a handmaiden to faith. When servants like reason usurp the master's role, they become tyrants. Rightly ordered reason—informed, guided, and restrained by faith—Luther valued and wielded deftly.[98]

---

[91] For example, Thomas Müntzer, "Von dem getichten glawben," in *Schriften und Briefe: Kritische Gesamtausgabe*, ed. Paul Kirn and Günther Franz (Gütersloh: Gütersloher Verlagshaus Gerd Mohn, 1968), 217-24.
[92] WADB 6:89.
[93] Afternoon Sermon on the Second Sunday after Epiphany (1531), WA 34,1:105.14-15.
[94] Afternoon Sermon on the Second Sunday after Epiphany (1531), WA 34,1:105.16, 106.1-2.
[95] Sermon on Pentecost Tuesday (1529), WA 29:376.16-26.
[96] See Burnett, "Luther and the *Schwärmer*," 511-13, 521.
[97] Unrestrained by Luther's own categorization, we might better organize these abuses of the person-office distinction as great person, great experience, and great reason.
[98] See especially Gerrish, *Grace and Reason*, 10-27; Bayer, *Martin Luther's Theology*, 158-62. See further Graham White, *Luther as Nominalist: A Study of the Logical Methods Used in Martin Luther's Disputations in the Light of Their Medieval Background* (Helsinki: Luther-Agricola-Society, 1994); Notger Slenczka, "Luther's Anthropology," in *The Oxford Handbook of Martin Luther's*

However, he opposed reason unyoked from faith in eternal matters—a temptation too great for many people. For Luther the Zwinglian understanding of Holy Communion—"the Sacrament [of the Altar] is a sign of remembrance of our Lord with strong heartfelt love"—was a reason-driven denial of the Lord's teaching: "This is my body" (Mt 26:26).[99] Like the Anabaptist doctrine of Baptism and the Papist doctrine of Penance, the Sacramentarian doctrine of Holy Communion inappropriately made the Sacrament a matter of human works rather than faith.[100] Luther understood the Sacramentarians as unwitting proxies for Satan, sowing doubt and denying that Christ can be present with us: "But surely your faith says that Christ ascended into heaven? And is seated at the right hand of God? How then can you come to this idea that you believe his body is on the altar."[101] They subtly turned the Apostles' Creed against simple believers. And Luther taught his congregation to respond simply: "I will remain with the Lord; whatever he says, I will cling to."[102] God's word does not depend on our understanding. God does what he says without our consent, approval, and understanding. "Just because it's not comprehensible to me and you, does not mean it's untrue. Instead, it's this: God said it; how it happens, I'll let him worry about."[103] To confess God's word as true is to worship and adore the Lord our God; it's not merely a cognitive exercise.

At times Luther was so frustrated with the chaos introduced by the *Schwärmer* (Radicals and Sacramentarians), he simply dismissed them by demanding their preaching qualifications: they must show their license to

---

Theology, ed. Robert Kolb, Irene Dingel, and L'ubomír Batka (New York: Oxford University Press, 2014), 225–31; Eilert Herms, "Mensch," in *Luther Handbuch*, ed. Albrecht Beutel (Tübingen: Mohr Siebeck, 2005), 397–99; Dietrich Korsch, "Theologische Prinzipienfragen," in *Luther Handbuch*, ed. Albrecht Beutel (Tübingen: Mohr Siebeck, 2005), 359–61; Helmer, *The Trinity and Martin Luther*; Jennifer Hockenberry Dragseth, ed., *The Devil's Whore: Reason and Philosophy in the Lutheran Tradition* (Minneapolis: Fortress Press, 2011).

[99] Sermon on Pentecost Tuesday (1529), WA 29:376.18. For a modern treatment of Zwingli's understanding of Holy Communion, see W. P. Stephens, *The Theology of Huldrych Zwingli* (Oxford: Clarendon Press, 1986), 218–59.

[100] Sermon on Pentecost Tuesday (1529), WA 29:376.19. See Amy Nelson Burnett, *Karlstadt and the Origins of the Eucharistic Controversy: A Study in the Circulation of Ideas* (New York: Oxford University Press, 2011).

[101] See Sermon on St. Martin's (1530), WA 32:157.7–24, 158.1–20, here 157.7–9.

[102] Sermon on St. Martin's (1530), WA 32:157.14–15.

[103] Sermon on St. Martin's (1530), WA 32:158.8–11. Luther continues with the incomprehensibility of the resurrection of the dead.

preach (which he knew they didn't have) or perform a miracle (which he expected they couldn't do).

> Say to them: "Go and prove first that you have a commission to preach. If you are called by humans, then show letters and seals. If you are sent by God from heaven, then prove it with signs and wonders."
> They respond: "Why don't you want to listen us? We're more learned than your pastors."
> Respond to that: "That might be that you're more learned than our pastor, but what does that have to do with this? I'm not pleased that you refuse to use the common, ordinary means which God has ordained."[104]

Nevertheless, Luther usually directed his hearers to the catechism and the analogy of faith. "Let this be the sign and goal for you: to fit with the faith. 'Which faith?' Ask the children. 'I believe,' etc. along with Baptism, the Sacrament of the Altar, Absolution—that's the teaching it should fit with."[105] The officeholder does not serve himself, but God. And so the faith is the master of the church and her people.[106] Therefore, having an office or having confidence in what one teaches is not sufficient; instead one must carry out one's office faithfully, believing and doing what one teaches or is taught in confidence.[107]

A Simple Bible for Simple Folk

Preachers must be attentive to the situation of their congregations. To instill this in his students Luther talked about preaching as watering a garden.[108] The careful and caring gardener tends to each flower and plant, ensuring each one receives the basic nourishment necessary for growth and flourishing. If the gardener only attended to the needs of the more flamboyant and exotic flowers, all the other plants and flowers would wither and perish. "He would be a foolish gardener who in a huge garden prefers to tend just one flower."[109] So preachers must not be distracted by the learned of the congregation, trying to teach and entertain them with high concepts and

---

[104]Sermon on Easter Tuesday (1529), WA 28:473.34–40; compare with LW 69:363.
[105]Sermon on the Second Sunday after Epiphany (1536), WA 41:510.36–38, 511.1.
[106]Sermon on the Second Sunday after Epiphany (1545), WA 49:684.17–26, 685.1–14.
[107]Sermon on St. Martin's 1530, WA 32:154.12–16.
[108]WATR 3:310, no. 3421. See also WATR 4:446–47, no. 4719; WATR 6:126–27, no. 6691.
[109]WATR 3:310.12–14, no. 3421.

complicated phrasing. Instead, preachers must focus on the needs of the congregation as a whole—on watering all of the garden, as it were. Luther himself aimed his sermons at the young children—particularly his own children and foster children. By addressing and engaging these young ones, preachers also addressed and engaged all the congregation, from simple to learned. Fitting God's word with the catechism for the building up and correction of God's people never becomes unnecessary.[110] The catechism provides the basic contours of God's forgiveness and life for all contexts and congregations.

Pastors must always direct simple words to simple people. Luther had mastered Quintillian's rhetoric.[111] He carefully adapted classical rhetoric to the situation of his audience. But classical rhetoric demands that the complexity and grandeur of delivery complement the complexity and grandeur of the topic, Luther—agreeing with Augustine—believed this cannot be done with Scripture, for no one would be able to follow, removing the gospel from the grasp of the simple. And so he sought to present the gospel in the simplest manner possible. For example, he spoke of the gospel as the story of the smallest and most despised child.[112] Luther sought to give his people a lay Bible—the catechism and other brief, memorable summaries of Scripture's content.

Most of Luther's congregants could not read—between 70 and 96 percent.[113] So how on earth might they know whether the pastor's sermon

---

[110] As Steinmetz paraphrases Luther's own sentiment: "In matters catechetical, all Christians remain beginners. As one cannot grow beyond Christ, so one cannot grow beyond the catechism" (Steinmetz, *Luther in Context*, 138). See also Ben Myers, *The Apostles' Creed: A Guide to the Ancient Catechism*, Christian Essentials (Bellingham, WA: Lexham Press, 2018), 1–5.

[111] On Luther and rhetoric, see Birgit Stolt, *Martin Luthers Rhetorik des Herzens* (Tübingen: Mohr Siebeck, 2000); Ulrich Nembach, *Predigt des Evangeliums: Luther als Prediger, Pädagoge und Rhetor* (Neukirchen-Vluyn: Neuchkirchener Verlag, 1972); Neil Leroux, *Luther's Rhetoric: Strategies and Style from the Invocavit Sermons* (St. Louis: Concordia Academic Press, 2002).

[112] See Dedication of the Winter Part of the *Church Postil* (1522; 1544), LW 75:3–6 (WA 10,1.1:1–8; E² 7:1–5; compare with LW 52:3–6).

[113] Steven Ozment estimates around 4 percent of the general population of sixteenth-century Germany was literate in 1500; Mark Edwards, 5 percent (though in the cities it could be as high as 30 percent). See Steven Ozment, *Age of Reform, 1250–1550: An Intellectual and Religious History of Late Medieval and Reformation Europe* (New Haven, CT: Yale University Press, 1980), 201; Mark U. Edwards, Jr., "Luther's Polemical Controversies," in *The Cambridge Companion to Martin Luther*, ed. Donald K. McKim (Cambridge: Cambridge University Press, 2003), 193. On the mixture of oral and written culture, see Brian Stock, *Listening to the Text: On the Uses of the Past* (Baltimore: The Johns Hopkins University Press, 1990), 33–40. Luther acknowledged the use

fittingly and faithfully explains and applies the Bible? Well aware of his congregants' education, Luther masterfully adapts his sermons to his audience by regularly lifting up summary verses for them. He flags them by saying things like, this is a little Bible—"Now for you today in the city of David the Savior is born, who is Christ the LOrd" (Lk 2:11);[114] or this is what it means to be a Christian—"To call on the name of the Lord"[115] or "To be carried on Christ's shoulders" (Lk 15:5; Is 53:4-5).[116] Unsurprisingly Luther also refers to the catechism and Creed as one such summary, a little Bible or a lay Bible. "The catechism is a lay Bible. In it the entire content of Christian teaching is contained—what each and every Christian needs to know to be saved."[117] Simple Christians and children could and should use these powerfully distilled summaries of Scripture's content and meaning to orient themselves in life and doctrine.

---

and benefit of images for simple people and the illiterate. See the Passional section that was added to the *Little Prayer Book* in 1529, TAL 4:196-200 (compare with LW 43:42-45; WA 10,2:458-70). *The Annotated Luther* includes only four of the original fifty woodcuts; *Luther's Works* and the Weimar edition, none. I have been unable to track down a digitized copy of the first edition; however, see Martin Luther, *Ein Betbuchlin/ mit eim Calender und Passional/ hübsch zu gericht* (Wittenberg: Hans Lufft, 1538), c3r-i5r, available online via gateway-bayern.de. These woodcuts could be seen as a simplified *Biblia Pauperum*. The *Biblia Pauperum* depicted Old Testament parallels to or types of Jesus, helping readers see how the Old Testament is about Jesus. On the *Biblia Pauperum*, see Reu, *Luther's German Bible*, 294-96n32.

[114] WADB 6:217. Luther applied a *nomina sacra* system to his translation of the Bible, using "HERR" to refer to the Tetragrammaton and "HErr" to refer to the Second Person of the Trinity; concerning this typography, see "Preface to the Old Testament" (1523), LW 35:248-49 (WADB 8:30.20-28); Christine Helmer, "Luther's Trinitarian Hermeneutic and the Old Testament," *Modern Theology* 18, no. 1 (2002): 49-73. See Afternoon Sermon on Christmas Day (1533), WA 37:237.34; for a brief explanation of Luke 2:11 as miniature Bible, see Sermon on the Sunday after the Feast of the Circumcision (1545), WA 49:662.7-13, 662.16-663.5. Luther refers to Genesis 24:7 and even the entire Psalter as little Bibles, too. See Lectures on Genesis 24:5-7, WA 43:316.26-28 (LW 5:242); "Preface to the Psalms" (1528; 1545), WADB 10,1:98.20-100.2, 99.22-101.3 (LW 35:254); Albrecht Beutel, "Theologie als Schriftauslegung," in *Luther Handbuch*, ed. Albrecht Beutel (Tübingen: Mohr Siebeck, 2005), 446.

[115] Afternoon Sermon on Pentecost Tuesday (1529), WA 29:378.32-379.11.

[116] Afternoon Sermon on Christmas Day (1531), WA 34,2:513.19-25 (compare with Rörer's witness, lines 2-8).

[117] WATR 5:581.30-32, no. 6288. See further *A Short Form of the Ten Commandments, Creed, the Our Father* (1520), WA 7:204.13-18; *Little Prayer Book* (1522), WA 10,2:375.15-17 (TAL 4:166; LW 43:12); Sermon on the Ave Maria (March 11, 1523), WA 11:59.32-60.1; Sermon on September 14, 1528, WA 30,1:27.26; Sermon on September 25, 1528, WA 30,1:52.36-37; Sermon on November 30, 1528, WA 30,1:57.6-8, 58.14-15; A Sermon on Jesus Christ, Preached at Court in Torgau (1533), WA 37:55.12-16 (LW 57:118). See also Formula of Concord—though in reference to Luther's commentaries on the catechism—in BoC 1959, 465 (BSELK 1218.3-8).

In the catechism Luther gives simple Christians the central, foundational texts and teachings of the Bible: the Ten Commandments, the Creed, the Lord's Prayer, and the sacraments.[118] Today many balk at the idea that the Creed and sacraments are part of the Bible (obviously, the Ten Commandments and Our Father are), but this was standard for Luther's era—and foundational for Luther himself. Luther described the Creed as honey gathered from many different flowers of Scripture by the Bee—the Holy Spirit.[119] The Creed may not be one passage, but it is many passages woven together according to the inner logic of Scripture itself.[120] And while the Reformers vigorously debated what the sacraments meant and did, none of them would have challenged their clear and direct scriptural command: Matthew 28:19 and Mark 16:16 for Baptism; 1 Corinthians 11:23-26 (compare with Mt 26:26-28; Mk 14:22-24; Lk 22:19-20) for the Sacrament of the Altar; and John 20:22-23 (compare with Mt 18:18) for Absolution.[121]

---

[118]See Peters, *Luther's Commentary on the Catechisms*, 1:24, 24; Sermon on May 18, 1528, WA 30,1:2.20-23; WATR 2:482, no. 2482.

[119]Sermon on Trinity Sunday (1535), WA 41:275.29-34. Caspar Cruciger edited this sermon into a second postil on the Epistle reading for Trinity Sunday, see WA 21:522-24 (LW 78:17-29, here 23-24). See also Postil for the Gospel on Trinity Sunday (*House Postil*, 1544), WA 52:342.8-343.7. Luther also used this image of a bee gathering honey from many flowers to describe Sirach, see "Preface to the Book of Jesus Sirach" (1533), WADB 8:147.10-11; LW 35:348.

[120]See WATR 3:685.7-9, no. 3883; WATR 4:230, no. 4334. Even for modern literate people the Bible is too big and diverse a book to distill uncontroversial central premises—as if it were any other piece of literature. Regarding the rule of faith's dependence on Scripture, see Craig Farmer, "Introduction," *John 1–12*, RCS NT 4 (Downers Grove, IL: IVP Academic, 2014), li; Greene-McCreight, "Literal Sense," 455–56; Greene-McCreight, "Rule of Faith," 703–4; Tomas Bokedal, "The Rule of Faith: Tracing Its Origins," *Journal of Theological Interpretation* 7, no. 2 (2013), 233–55.

[121]While many Reformers didn't consider Absolution a sacrament, they clearly would have seen the forgiveness of sins as biblical. For Baptism's biblical command, see Sermon on May 28, 1528, WA 30,1:18.21-23; Sermon on September 24, 1528, WA 30,1:51.1-6; Sermon on December 17, 1528, WA 30,1:109.27-110.15; *Small Catechism* (1529); TAL 4:231 (WA 30,1:308.23-26, 310.1-3; BoC 1959, 348); *Large Catechism* (1529), BoC 1959, 437 (WA 30,1:212.13-21); WATR 2:301, no. 2041. For the Sacrament of the Altar's biblical command, see Sermon on May 29, 1528, WA 30,1:23.19-25; Sermon on September 25, 1528, WA 30,1:54.5; Sermon on December 19, 1528, WA 30,1:116.17, 117.5-6; *Small Catechism* (1529), TAL 4:235-36 (WA 30,1:314.21-30, 316.1-11; BoC 1959, 351); *Large Catechism* (1529), BoC 1959, 447 (WA 30,1:222.28-223.6). Luther usually cites the words of institution from memory, rather than these separate passages. For the words of institution, see *The German Mass and Order of Service* (1526), LW 53:80-81 (WA 19:97-99). For Absolution's biblical command, see *The Sacrament of Penance* (1519), LW 35:10-11, 22 (WA 2:715.10-20, 722.36-723.2); Sermon on December 15, 1528, WA 30,1:105.21-106.14; *Large Catechism* (1529), BoC 1959, 433 (WA 30,1:207.24-208.12); Epistle for the Sunday after Easter (*Church Postil*, 1544), LW 77:132-33, 133-45 (WA 49:144.29-32, 145.17-153.42); WATR 6:174, no. 6765.

For the sake of congregants—simple and learned—Luther exhorted pastors to remain rooted in this simple teaching, steadfastly preaching and teaching and applying the catechism day in and day out. Too many pastors give into the pressure and complaints of their parishioners. "Both nobles and peasants say: 'O, our pastor can't preach anything but the Ten Commandments, the Creed, and the Our Father! He always harps on the same string!' "[122] Pastors instead are tempted to preach esoteric matters ("lofty matters" they say). By doing this, they not only neglect the basics but distort and obscure the Christian faith—as if the difficult and dark passages of Daniel's prophecies and John's Apocalypse are the center of the words and deeds Jesus of Nazareth commanded to his disciples.[123]

Conclusion

Luther grounded his life and ministry in God's word. He wanted his congregants and students to do this, too. And this meant understanding God's word correctly. To be sure that the parishioners of St. Mary's and pupils of Wittenberg understood Scripture—preached and written—Luther taught them the rule of faith, which he most often called *the analogy of faith*. Scripture's interpretation must reflect the bones and heartbeat of Scripture: the catechism.

For the simple and learned alike Luther explained what the catechism is, what prophecy is, and what the office of the word is. The catechism is God's word as summarized in the Ten Commandments, the Creed, the Our Father, and the sacraments. Prophecy is the interpretation of Scripture (not temporal predictions about political intrigue!). The office of the word is ordained by God to speak the word of God to the people of God. God is no respecter of persons, and so his people must not be distracted by the officeholder's name and character. Instead, they must discern whether the speaker has indeed surrendered their tongue to God: Is God speaking?

For this reason, Luther understood Paul's words in Romans 12:6 to mean that it's not enough just to cite Scripture; Christians must use and

---

[122]WATR 2:522, no. 2554b; compare with WATR 2:522, no. 2554a; WATR 6:126–27, no. 6691. Here lines 26–28 (compare with 19–20).
[123]Preface to Commentary on Zechariah (1527), WA 23:485.28–486.3 (LW 20:156). Luther means that these passages are obscure from a human perspective.

understand Scripture according to the inner logic of Scripture. Without a key for how to put together the story of Scripture, lay people might well construct a false portrait of the Bible's author and main character.[124] Lay people require a key to Scripture's meaning and interpretation: the analogy of faith (the Bible's own key made from the Bible itself). "Yes, just the catechism is enough for us to oppose false prophets."[125]

---

[124] See Irenaeus, *Against Heresies* 1.8.1.
[125] "Sermon on the Second Sunday after Epiphany (1536)," WA 41:511.37–38. See also WATR 2:362, no. 2202b.

3

The Childish Doctrine

Explaining the Catechism

Daily Luther said the catechism aloud like a child. "Although I am indeed an old doctor, I never move on from the childish doctrine of the Ten Commandments and the Creed and the Lord's Prayer. But I still daily learn and pray them with my Hans and my little Lena."[1] He recommended the same discipline to his students and congregants. Lest the people of Wittenberg grow weary or cold in their practice, he and the city magistrates of Wittenberg also required attendance at the traditional quarterly catechetical sermon series—the last two weeks of Advent, the first week of Lent, the week of Holy Cross, and in the middle of the hops harvest. The Wittenberg Church Ordinance of 1533 enacted this as law.[2] Luther and his Wittenberg team of pastors and seminarians seized this opportunity to impress the meaning and import of the catechism on parishioners in a vivid but simple manner.

Luther did not always consistently gloss his definition of the catechism. He distinguished the Ten Commandments, the Creed, and the Our Father from the sacraments—explicitly in the *Large Catechism*, implicitly elsewhere. "We should be satisfied if they learned the three parts which have been the

---

[1] WATR 1:30.26-31.2. Hans (1526-1575) is Luther's eldest son; Lena or Magdalena (1529-1542) is his middle daughter.
[2] Sehling, *Die Evangelischen Kirchenordnungen des XVI. Jahrhunderts*, 1:700-701. See further Kolb, *Martin Luther and the Enduring Word of God*, 181-82.

heritage of Christendom from ancient times."[3] Clearly Luther understood the sacraments of Baptism, Communion, and Absolution to be essential to the Christian life, but for these precious communicants of grace to be understood and wielded most effectively, Christians need to know what kind of God they have. That's what the Ten Commandments, the Apostles' Creed, and the Our Father are for. "When these three parts are understood, we ought also to know what to say about the sacraments which Christ himself instituted."[4] The three foundational pillars of the catechism teach this knowledge.

At times the sacraments—besides Baptism—seem to have been an afterthought. For example, Luther addresses Absolution and Communion four days after he has completed the Lenten catechetical series of 1523.[5] In the *Large Catechism*, he only appended some thoughts about Confession and Absolution to the second edition; in 1531 he substituted a section on Absolution for a brief order of Confession in the *Small Catechism*.[6] And Luther regularly folded Confession and Absolution into his explanation of Baptism. "Our Lord and Master Jesus Christ, by saying 'Repent,' etc. willed all of Christian life to be repentance."[7] "And the Christian life is nothing other than a perpetual Baptism."[8]

We have seen that Luther deemed the ancient catechism to be the authoritative rule of faith. All Christians, worthy of the name, must know and cling to this rule, testing all things against it—especially the interpretation of

---

[3] Short Preface to *The Large Catechism* (1529), BoC 1959, 362 (WA 30,1:130.1-3). I will not interact with *The Annotated Luther's* "updated" version of the Large Catechism (TAL 2:289-415). The editors and translator have made Luther's text a wax nose for their own theological program, censoring Luther's use of masculine pronouns referring to God, translating *er* in reference to the Holy Spirit as "she," and calling the Our Father outdated and sexist, suggesting that people pray "Our Mother" or "Our Parent" instead. Kirsi Stjerna authorizes these decisions based on Luther's translating principles (TAL 2:288). These translation choices contradict Luther's interpretation of the second commandment. Luther holds to the principle that we learn to speak rightly of God by listening to how he speaks of himself in his word and by his Spirit. For example, see sermons on Exodus 32 (1526-1527), WA 16:612-39; Helmer, *Trinity and Martin Luther*, 235-42. Stjerna is welcome, of course, to make these arguments in her own writing; still it must be debated as true and faithful to God's word and faith. For an analysis of these sorts of theological moves, see Kathryn Greene-McCreight, *Feminist Reconstructions of Christian Doctrine: Narrative Analysis and Appraisal* (New York: Oxford University Press, 2000).
[4] Preface to *The Large Catechism* (1529), BoC 1959, 364 (WA 30,1:131.19-20).
[5] Afternoon Sermon on the Fourth Sunday in Lent (1523), WA 11:65-67.
[6] See BoC 1959, 349n5; TAL 4:232n54.
[7] *Disputation on the Power and Efficacy of Indulgences* (1517), WA 1:233.10-11 (LW 31:25; TAL 1:34); citing Matt 4:17.
[8] Sermon on May 29, 1528, WA 30,1:22.1.

Scripture. In this chapter we will examine Luther's exposition of the content and form of the catechism in relation to reading the Bible, so that we can identify his use of it more easily.

Broadly speaking, Luther agrees with the tradition: the Ten Commandments teach love, the Apostles' Creed teaches faith, and the Our Father teaches hope. (The sacraments bring Christ present along with his forgiveness, freedom, and life.[9]) While love, faith, and hope can be found in each part of the catechism—in fact Luther made a habit of weaving a fourfold garland out of the catechism: instruction, confession, thanksgiving, and prayer[10]—Luther keeps it simple for pedagogical purposes. In the same way, he teaches congregants to associate each article of the Creed with God's work of creation, redemption, and sanctification, respectively; nevertheless, he does not deny the unity of God's external works (*opera trinitatis ad extra indivisa sunt*).[11]

And while love may be the greatest of these, human love cannot be correctly ordered apart from right faith and right hope.[12] Together the catechism teaches how we should act, what God gives us, and how to pray.

The Ten Commandments: "The Teaching of Teachings"

The Ten Commandments are best ordered according to love of God and neighbor.[13] Luther numbers and divides the commandments in

---

[9]Peters, *Commentary on Luther's Catechisms*, 1:47. See below "The Sacraments: 'The Ceremonies of Ceremonies.'"

[10]*A Simple Way to Pray* (1535), WA 38:364.28-365.4 (LW 43:200, 209; TAL 4:267, 278).

[11]See A Sermon on Jesus Christ, Preached at Court in Torgau (1533), WA 37:41.2-5 (LW 57:101); Sermon on the Feast of St. Gallus in the Castle Church (1537), WA 45:181.9-182.30; *Treatise on the Last Words of David* (1543), WA 54:57.26-58.3 (LW 15:302). In *The Last Words of David*, Luther explicitly affirms the patristic principle: *opera trinitatis ad extra indivisa sunt* (the external works of the Trinity are indivisible). Some scholars have accused Luther of unorthodox views on the Trinity on account of his simple catechetical pedagogy. Christine Helmer has demonstrated how wrong this is and how unoriginal—a high commendation in Luther's eyes!—Luther is regarding the doctrine of the Trinity (Helmer, *The Trinity and Martin Luther*). See also Prenter, *Spiritus Creator*, 173-84, 238-46.

[12]Luther argues that Paul speaks quantitatively in 1 Corinthians 13: love continues after the Last Day. Faith and hope will no longer be necessary, because we will see what we believe and hope for (Rom 8:24-26). See WATR 1:373, no. 786; 2:371, no. 2232; 3:5, no. 2811; Epistle for Quinquagesima Sunday (*Church Postil*, 1540), LW 76:347-49 (E² 8:128-30; WA 17,2:170.29-172.21). These passages help clarify Luther's clunky marginal note on 1 Corinthians 13:13, WADB 7:123. On faith, hope, and love, see also Asendorf, *Theologie Martin Luthers*, 412-15.

[13]For the Ten Commandments as "the teaching of teachings," see WATR 1:34.3-4, no. 88; WATR 1:360.10, no. 757; WATR 3:183.20, no. 3134; WATR 5:581.33, no. 6288. On the Ten Commandments' positive and negative teachings, see WATR 1:542-43, no. 1067.

agreement with the medieval tradition: the first three commandments—the Lord God alone is God, honor his name, honor the Sabbath—comprise the first table; and the next seven—honor your parents, do not murder, do not commit adultery, do not steal, do not bear false witness, covet neither your neighbor's status nor relationships and possessions—comprise the second table.[14]

The first table teaches us how we should be oriented to God in our affections, thoughts, words, and actions. We love God by trusting his word, by acknowledging who he is according to his word, by speaking good of his name according to his word, and by reclining in his word like a small child on her parent's chest.[15] To pursue friendship with God outside of his word is the height of human arrogance and ignorance.[16] No matter the intention this is always idolatry. And yet this is the greatest and commonest temptation of humans: to seek and worship God according to our own thoughts, feelings, and desires. "What does it mean 'to make gods'? It's this: I take his name and word, and I interpret and twist it as I want."[17] And so Luther encourages his audience to ask questions—especially, "where's that written?"[18]

---

[14] See Peters, *Commentary on Luther's Catechisms*, 1:89–101. The Greek Orthodox and Reformed number the Ten Commandments differently than the Catholics and Lutherans (89–91). For Luther, the division between the ninth and tenth commandments was artifical, see Peters, *Commentary on Luther's Catechisms*, 1:90, 303–15. Of the three core chapters of the ancient catechism, Luther only changed the division of the Apostles' Creed. In practice he handled the Ten Commandments according to Origen's division, but he likely didn't renumber them because he didn't see the Latin tradition's division as a pedagogical hindrance (as opposed to the traditional twelve articles of the Apostles' Creed). On the number of the Ten Commandments, see Peter J. Leithart, *The Ten Commandments: A Guide to the Perfect Law of Liberty*, Christian Essentials (Bellingham, WA: Lexham Press, 2020), 11–18.

[15] For example, on trusting the word, see Sermon on the First and Second Commandments (1523), WA 11:36.4-28; on acknowledging his word, see Sermons on Exodus 20 (1525), WA 16:467.32-36; on speaking good of his name, see Sermons on Exodus 20 (1525), WA 16:464.27-30, 467.32-36, 470.38-471.8, 471.34-472.11; on reclining, see Sermon on the Third Commandment (1523), WA 11:38.12-15; Sermon on December 1, 1528, WA 30,1:64.16-19; Sermons on Exodus 20 (1525), WA 16:480.24-484.27.

[16] Luther's sermons on Exodus 32 (1526-1527) are especially illuminating, see WA 16:612-39; see also Sermons on Deuteronomy 5 (1529), WA 28:595-614, esp. 607-14.

[17] Sermons on Exodus 32 (1526), WA 16:620.12-13. Luther compared Aaron in the golden calf incident with the papacy. Aaron asks for the people's jewelry and he crafts a god from it. In the same way, the church asks for the people's good works—for example, virginity—for salvation. See Sermons on Exodus 32 (1526), WA 16:621.11-18, 622.1-21, 623.1-14. Luther encourages his congregation to respond to the teaching of *Schwärmer* and monks, saying: "It's a golden calf—that is, it's a dark mirror, in which we think we'll find God" (623.5-7).

[18] Sermon on the First and Second Commandments (1523), WA 11:36.22-28.

They must learn to test all things, keeping only what's good (1 Thess 5:21). The people of God need the catechism, lest they distort the word of God.

The second table instructs how we treat our neighbors in thought, word, and deed. We love our neighbor by honoring them—in their office, relationships, and possessions. We love our neighbor by giving them life, protecting and preserving their body, family, and reputation. Blessing is not a zero-sum game, as if only you can have a nice job and a beautiful family. When you see the rich blessing of God in other people's lives—work, skill, or family—you should be thankful and praise God for his kindness. To react with envy to blessing reveals how miserly you are—you want what others have and ignore the good you have been given.[19] "Above all, [God] wants our hearts to be pure, even though as long as we live here we cannot reach that ideal."[20]

In Luther's writing, a tripartite distinction of the law runs perpendicular to this twofold division: its civil, theological, and Christian uses. Luther affirms these three uses of the law.[21] The civil use of the law—primarily the second table—restrains evil (Rom 13:1-7). Without external punishment we would act on every wicked deed in our hearts.[22] "If we were to have space,

---

[19] Sermons on Exodus 20 (1525), WA 16:527.13-32.

[20] *Large Catechism* (1529), BoC 1959, 407 (WA 30,1:178.17-19).

[21] Harold Senkbeil summarizes the three functions of the law as to prescribe, proscribe, and describe; see *The Care of Souls: Cultivating a Pastoral Heart* (Bellingham, WA: Lexham Press, 2019), 170-73; see also *The Formula of Concord* (1577), Article 6. Luther never used the term "third use of the law," although he comes close in a disputed passage of the Antinomian Disputations, see *The Second Disputation against the Antinomians* (1538), LW 73:161 (WA 39,1:485.16-24). Jeffrey Silcock and Christopher Boyd Brown argue the passage is authentic. See "Introduction to the Antinomian Disputations (1537-1540)," in LW 73:3-43, particularly pp. 21-25 on the scholarly disputes of this passage. There's a rolling debate about Luther and the third use of the law. Some argue he denied it, for example see, Ebeling, *Luther*, 137-56; Lowell C. Green, "The 'Third Use of the Law' and Elert's Position," *Logia* 22, no. 2 (2013): 27-33. Some scholars who deny the Christian use of the law in Luther refer to his twofold distinction of the law in his Galatians lectures (WA 40,1:519.34-520.24; LW 26:337); however, Luther here handles the law explicitly as a prison, as something before Christ. Ebeling argues that the gospel must be the final word, implying there's no place for the law—even to be transformed through Christ's person and work. Others argue Luther affirmed the third use of the law, for example see Robert Kolb, "Luther's Hermeneutics of Distinctions: Law and Gospel, Two Kinds of Righteousness, Two Realms, Freedom and Bondage," in *The Oxford Handbook of Martin Luther's Theology*, ed. Robert Kolb, Irene Dingel, and L'ubomír Batka (New York: Oxford University Press, 2014), 172-75; Kolb, *Martin Luther and the Enduring Word of God*, 203-4; Peters, *Commentary on Luther's Catechisms*, 1:43, 49.

[22] Sermons on Exodus 20 (1525), WA 16:511.29-36. On the civil use of the law, see further Althaus, *Theology of Martin Luther*, 253-54.

time, place, and opportunity, we would all commit adultery."[23] The theological use of the law reveals our sin. The Ten Commandments are a mirror that show what humans really are, exposing our lack of love toward God and neighbor (Rom 3:20).[24] They strip away any pretension that we can measure up to what God asks of us, driving us to him for mercy. The Christian or third use of the law aids and guides us—never goads or motivates us—in the Christian life, so that we might carefully attend to how we live, rightly loving God and neighbor (Eph 5:15).[25] Human preachers faithfully preach the law, but the Holy Spirit alone wields and applies the use of the law to souls. Human preachers cannot choose which use they will apply in preaching or counseling.

The Ten Commandments reveal the fundamental posture required in reading and hearing the Bible. We approach it as servants not masters. God speaks authoritatively in his word to each person individually. No one can wonder, "Who knows, if he means me, too—it's directed only to the crowd."[26] God speaks as a father to his child: in the second person singular. Fallen humans are always tempted to think that the Lord their God is a passive-aggressive God, who speaks in the second person plural but really means a specific few. And so they pitch God's word into the wind, thinking it is for someone else. "I am the Lord your—your!—God. I mean you—yes, you!—and not someone else."[27] To strengthen those who struggle to believe God's promises really are for them, Luther encouraged them to think that all God's promises and consolation are just for them.[28] Luther does not want anyone to doubt that God speaks directly to them; this beautiful golden ring of the Ten Commandments is for you. "God does not speak with stones and trees,

---

[23]Sermons on Exodus 20 (1525), WA 16:511.19-20. See further WA 16:512.32-34. Luther alludes to the unimpedible nature of sexuality, *Large Catechism* (1529), BoC 1959, 393-94 (WA 30,1:162.17-21). He considered it a rare, special grace from God to be celibate; for example, see Sermon on the Second Sunday after Epiphany (1524), WA 15:417.25-418.31.

[24]Sermons on Exodus 20 (1525), WA 16:508.28-29, 509.26-31, 525.6-15. On the theological use of the law, see further Althaus, *Theology of Martin Luther*, 254-56.

[25]See, for example, Sermon on May 19 1528, WA 30,1:5.14-15; Afternoon Sermon on the Feast of the Circumcision (1532), WA 36:18.29-32; Sermon on the Twentieth Sunday after Trinity (1545), WA 51:65.4-8 (LW 58:300). On the third use of the law, see further Althaus, *Theology of Martin Luther*, 266-73; Peters, *Commentary on Luther's Catechisms*, 1:43, 49.

[26]Sermons on Exodus 20 (1525), WA 16:433.12-13. See also Sermons on Deuteronomy 5 (1529), WA 28:597.12-13.

[27]Sermons on Exodus 20 (1525), WA 16:433.18-19.

[28]Sermons on Exodus 20 (1525), WA 16:432.19-434.30.

but with you."[29] God's word norms our action toward God and neighbor, restraining us, convicting us, and directing us.

The Apostles' Creed: "The History of Histories"

We cannot keep the Ten Commandments by our own might.[30] While the Ten Commandments brutally reveal what we lack, "the faith gives the very thing we lack."[31] "The Creed is nothing other than an answer to this question: What kind of God is your God—the one who gave you the Ten Commandments?"[32] The Apostles' Creed tell us what kind of God we have and what he has done. The Apostles' Creed teaches faith.

Luther ordered the Creed according to the three divine persons and three divine works.[33] In contrast, the tradition taught that there were twelve articles—composed by the twelve apostles on Pentecost.[34] For simplicity's sake, Luther generally associated creation with the Father, redemption with the Son, and sanctification with the Spirit. "That's the most childish way of talking about the Creed."[35] Because its depths are unplumbable, preachers and parents need to ensure that their congregants and children know the foundational understanding of the Creed. So Luther strove to present the Creed in simplicity. But once people mastered this basic presentation, they

---

[29] Sermon on September 17, 1528, WA 30,1:35.2. See also Sermons on Exodus 20 (1525), WA 16:484.28–485.24

[30] Sermon on September 21, 1528, WA 30,1:46.1–4; *Large Catechism* (1529), BoC 1959, 411 (WA 30,1:182.18–31). For the Apostles' Creed as "the history of histories," see WATR 5:581.36–37, no. 6288; compare with WATR 1:34.4, no. 88; WATR 1:360.10–11, no. 757; WATR 3:183.20–21, no. 3134.

[31] Sermon on December 10, 1528, WA 30,1:94.21. Here *faith* refers to the Apostles' Creed.

[32] Sermon on May 23, 1528, WA 30,1:10.1–2. See also *Large Catechism* (1529), BoC 1959, 420 (WA 30,1:193.3–13).

[33] Sermon on May 23, 1528, WA 30,1:10.37–11.1; Sermon on September 21, 1528, WA 30,1:44.25–31; Sermon on December 10, 1528, WA 30,1:86.1–13; *Large Catechism* (1529), BoC 1959, 411, 412 (WA 30,1:182.32–183.11, 183.26–27). Luther divides the Creed into three articles the first time he writes on them, see *A Short Form of the Ten Commandments, Creed, the Lord's Prayer* (1520), WA 7:214.25–28.

[34] Rufinus states that the apostles drafted the Creed by committee (*A Commentary on the Apostles' Creed* 2, ACW 20:29–30; PL 21:337–39); sixth-century Pseudo-Augustine and Pirminius (c. 700–753) identify each article with a specific apostle, although their lists differ (Sermon 240.1, PL 39:2189; *De singulis libris canonicis scarapsus*, PL 89:1034). For a detailed explanation of this legend, see Henri de Lubac, *The Christian Faith: An Essay on the Structure and Use of the Apostles' Creed*, trans. Richard Arnandez (San Francisco: Ignatius, 1969), 32–53. On Luther and this legend, see Peters, *Commentary on Luther's Catechisms*, 2:8–10.

[35] Sermon on September 21, 1528, WA 30,1:45.19.

could generate a myriad of articles and applications: "Of course, if all the thoughts contained in the Scriptures and belonging to the Creed were gathered together, there would be many more articles, and they could not be expressed in so few words."[36] Luther's more streamlined pedagogy—in his estimation—was more wieldy for children and the unlearned.

Luther knows and affirms the unity of God's external operations—and at times he even points this out to his congregation. He especially brings this up when preaching on Baptism. "There's the whole Trinity."[37] Whatever the Father does, Jesus does, and the Spirit does. Because they share one divine essence, they are united in their work.[38] The divine persons are so united that only the processions distinguish them: "We know of no distinction to make except that the Father eternally begets and the Son is eternally begotten."[39] This is the best the tradition could do, following Paul's benediction in Romans (11:36): "From him and through him and in him are all things—to him be honor in eternity, AMEN!"[40] But Luther tries his best to accommodate his teaching and preaching to his audience.

The first article teaches about the Father and creation. Our Father is the Creator of heaven and earth. "That's my God first and foremost: the Father who created heaven and earth."[41] Nothing—from human life to the smallest insect, from the sun and moon to the depths of the sea—is outside of his sustaining power and care.[42] "You let out your Breath, so they are created, and you renew the form of the earth" (Ps 104:30).[43] And so all that is God's is ours, because we are his children.[44] Titles and possessions,

---

[36]*Large Catechism* (1529), BoC 1959, 411 (WA 30,1:182.33–183.1).
[37]Sermon on the Third Sunday after Epiphany (1534), WA 37:267.20–21. See also Sermon on the Feast of the Ascension (1531), WA 34,1:419.7–9.
[38]A Sermon on Jesus Christ, Preached at Court in Torgau (1533), WA 37:41.2–5 (LW 57:101); Sermon on the Feast of St. Gallus in the Castle Church (1537), WA 45:181.9–182.30; *Treatise on the Last Words of David* (1543), WA 54:57.26–58.3 (LW 15:302).
[39]A Sermon on Jesus Christ, Preached at Court in Torgau (1533), WA 37:41.15–16, also 41.19–21 (LW 57:101, 102). See also Sermon on March 4, 1523, WA 11:51.9–20.
[40]WADB 7:67. Sermon on the Feast of St. Gallus in the Castle Church (1537), WA 45:181.19–22.
[41]*Large Catechism* (1529), WA 30,1:183.23–24 (BoC 1959, 412).
[42]Sermon on March 4, 1523, WA 11:49.27–30; Afternoon Sermon on the Seventh Sunday after Trinity (1529), WA 29:473.11–26.
[43]WADB 10,1:445.
[44]Sermon on March 4, 1523, WA 11:50.30–32; Sermon on May 23, 1528, WA 30,1:10.18–20; A House Sermon on the Articles of the Creed (1537), WA 45:16.6–17.8 (LW 57:246–47).

status and relationships—none of these, in the eyes of faith, are earned or owned. "Look at your eyes, your hands, and all your members! They are God's gift. Consider your clothing and all your possessions with thanksgiving. Your cow, your goose, your sheep, your cattle—God gave them to you! Consider them with thanksgiving."[45] Even our very bodies—the most basic human possession—are not our own. Everything that we have is a gift from God.[46]

When you are afraid, remember who your Father is: the Creator of heaven and earth.[47] He holds total power and control over all things. Death, the devil, and his demons may rage on earth, but ultimately they are powerless.[48] To say "I believe in God the Father, Creator of heaven and earth" is to have full confidence and trust in God's grace.[49] Like any earthly father, God wants us to ask him for what we need. Not only should we ask for food and clothes, work and shelter, family and friends, but we should also ask for faith.[50] And yet we believe too little. We are numb to the miracles of life and healing.[51] "It's just as if we said: 'He gave me this great thing, but who knows if he can give me this small thing!' "[52]

The second article teaches about Jesus and redemption. "The whole gospel is contained in this article."[53] It is the heart of the catechism. This article succinctly and perfectly teaches about God's Son, so that children and the less educated can know the sum and substance of the Bible.[54] Only through Jesus—God's Word—can we know God.[55] "Who sees me sees the

---

[45] Afternoon Sermon on the Seventh Sunday after Trinity (1529), WA 29:473.1–4. See also Sermon on the Feast of the Ascension (1544), WA 49:421.23–26.

[46] Sermon on December 10, 1528, WA 30,1:87.15–16, 88.9–11; Afternoon Sermon on the Seventh Sunday after Trinity (1529), WA 29:472.31–34, 473.1–4; *Large Catechism* (1529), BoC 1959, 412 (WA 30,1:183.32–184.23).

[47] Sermon on March 4, 1523, WA 11:49.20–50.1.

[48] Sermon on May 23, 1528, WA 30,1:10.24–26.

[49] Sermon on March 4, 1523, WA 11:49.7–8.

[50] Sermon on March 4, 1523, WA 11:50.26–27.

[51] Sermon on March 4, 1523, WA 11:50.20–22.

[52] Sermon on March 4, 1523, WA 11:50.18–24, here 23–24.

[53] Sermon on December 10, 1528, WA 30,1:90.8–9.

[54] A House Sermon on the Articles of the Creed (1537), WA 45:18.14–16 (LW 57:248); A Sermon on Jesus Christ, Preached at Court in Torgau (1533), WA 37:71.20–27 (LW 57:137). See also, Sermon on December 10, 1528, WA 30,1:89.20–22; *Large Catechism* (1529), BoC 1959, 415 (WA 30,1:187.14–16).

[55] For example, see Epistle for Christmas Day (*Church Postil*, 1540), LW 75:202 (WA 10,1.1:48.11–18; E² 7:156).

Father" (Jn 14:9).[56] And Jesus is rightly seen by being rightly heard. Otherwise we strive after bare divinity (*nudus Deus, nuda divinitate*), and God is not to be sought outside of his word—as Luther makes quite clear in his treatment of the golden calf.[57]

The incident of the golden calf was an example of inappropriate worship of the one true God rather than bald idolatry of other gods. The people of Israel wanted to worship and glorify the Lord God who mightily, miraculously, and mercifully delivered them from slavery. But they tired of waiting for Moses to return from Mount Sinai, so they asked Aaron to help them worship the God who led them out of Egypt. Aaron obliges them by following the religious customs of the Egyptians: he crafts a golden calf. The Israelites see this calf as the Lord their God. They do not think that they are practicing idolatry or pursuing other gods. But what word from God do they have? Luther cites this as an example of Satan's devious work. "Where God builds a church, there Satan builds a chapel."[58] Satan subtly twists God's word and command, so that we might think that we are worshiping God, but we have inverted the relationship between master and servant.[59]

For Luther two phrases summarize the full scope, meaning, and benefit of the second article: "our Lord" and "for us." To say "Jesus is God's Son, our Lord" is to say that he has freed you from sin, death, hell, and every evil.[60] To confess Jesus as Lord is to move beyond acknowledging mere fact or history—as Satan and his minions do!—and to accept a gift.[61] It is one thing to say that Jesus was born of a virgin, is true God from true God, suffered, died, rose again, ascended, and will return to judge the world. It is quite another to say that all of this is for us. None of this Christ did for himself.[62]

---

[56] WADB 6:385.

[57] Sermon on March 5, 1523, WA 11:52.1–3, 7; A Sermon on Jesus Christ, Preached at Court in Torgau (1533), WA 37:38.13–39.22 (LW 57:97–99).

[58] Sermons on Exodus 32 (1526), WA 16:618.11–12.

[59] Good intentions alone do not satisfy God's requirements. Good intentions must be aligned with obedience to his word. Sermons on Exodus 32 (1526), WA 16:616.16–23, 617.1; Marginal comment on Exodus 32:5 (1545), WADB 8:301.

[60] Sermon on December 10, 1528, WA 30,1:89.8–10; *Large Catechism* (1529), BoC 1959, 414 (WA 30,1:186.9–187.10).

[61] See "Short Instruction: What Should Be Sought and Expected in the Gospels" (1522, 1544), LW 75:7–12 (WA 10,1.1:8–18; E² 7:8–13; compare with LW 35:113–24).

[62] A Sermon on Jesus Christ, Preached at Court in Torgau (1533), WA 37:67.14–19 (LW 57:133).

The Childish Doctrine 65

According to his divinity, Jesus is Lord over death, and through his resurrection he becomes Lord over death according to his humanity.[63] And so because all that is his is ours, through faith, we too become lords over death, dressed in his resurrection.[64] In sum, Christ has hallowed our humanity, and so wherever Christians are, that place is holy.[65]

We can only approach God through this baby. Wherever this child is, there God is! "Yes, this human is the true and proper God—apart from him there is no God. And wherever this little child lies in his cradle or in the arms and at the breasts of his mother, there God is substantially and personally."[66] While reason foolishly and arrogantly pursues God according to his majesty, God only reveals himself in weakness.[67] That is the kind of God we have. You need to remain with this child. Wherever he is, everything is subject to him.[68]

The third article teaches about the Holy Spirit and sanctification. If Christ's work and person remain hidden, what benefit is that? The Holy Spirit makes sure Christ's work and person do not remain hidden; he leads us to our liberating Lord and applies our Lord's benefits to us.[69] The Holy Spirit works—speaking and making holy—through the external offices of the church: preaching, Baptism, Communion, and Absolution.[70] "Where

---

[63] A Sermon on Jesus Christ, Preached at Court in Torgau (1533), WA 37:67.21-23 (LW 57:133). See further Sermon on the Thirteenth Sunday after Trinity (1530), WA 32:94.2-104.29.

[64] A Sermon on Jesus Christ, Preached at Court in Torgau (1533), WA 37:57.22-23, 67.28-31 (LW 57:121, 133).

[65] A Sermon on Jesus Christ, Preached at Court in Torgau (1533), WA 37:62.7-19 (LW 57:126-27).

[66] A Sermon on Jesus Christ, Preached at Court in Torgau (1533), WA 37:43.3-5 (LW 57:104). See also Sermon on March 5, 1523, WA 11:51.19, 27-28.

[67] A Sermon on Jesus Christ, Preached at Court in Torgau (1533), WA 37:43.6-25 (LW 57:104-5).

[68] Sermon on March 5, 1523, WA 11:51.30-52.4.

[69] Sermon on March 5, 1523, WA 11:51.14-15, 52.31-32; Sermon on March 6, 1523, WA 11:53.14-15; Sermon on May 23, 1528, WA 30,1:10.31-37; Sermon on September 21, 1528, WA 30,1:45.9-19; Sermon on December 11, 1528, WA 30,1:91.11-15; A House Sermon on the Articles of the Creed (1537), WA 45:22.6-23.1, 23.13-24.2 (LW 57:250, 251); *Large Catechism* (1529), BoC 1959, 415-16 (WA 30,1:188.6-17).

[70] Sermon on the Creed (March 6, 1523), WA 11:53.9-11; Sermon on December 11, 1528, WA 30,1:93.8-14; A House Sermon on the Articles of the Creed (1537), WA 45:23.1-12; LW 57:251. The Holy Spirit cannot and does not contradict Christ's word. See, for example, Epistle for the Tenth Sunday after Trinity (*Church Postil*, 1544), WA 22:176.30-177.4, 15-23; LW 78:335-36, compare with John 15:26. On the sacraments, see below "The Sacraments: 'The Ceremonies of Ceremonies.'"

Christ is not preached, there is no Holy Spirit to create, call, and gather the Christian church, and outside it no one can come to the Lord Christ."[71]

The Spirit sanctifies and gives life through three acts: he makes the church, he forgives sins, and he resurrects the dead.[72] The church is Christ's little flock gathered by the Holy Spirit. Luther understood "the communion of saints" to be a clarifying gloss of "the holy Christian church."[73] Christians are tempted to believe the church is a building, and this phrase clarifies that it is not. "If we're asked: Where do Christians gather? We answer: Not in some house, but in the word 'I believe' etc."[74] United in one faith and one Baptism these saints—despite appearances—are holy, because God gives them his holiness.[75] That the church remains is an article of faith; only God's power makes it possible.[76] By the power and wisdom of the Holy Spirit, the church proclaims God's word, birthing new Christians and nurturing them in God's forgiveness and life.[77] "The Christian church is

---

[71]*Large Catechism* (1529), BoC 1959, 416 (WA 30,1:189.1–3). On the ordered, coordinating work of the Word and Spirit, see Gospel for Pentecost Sunday (*Church Postil*, 1544), LW 77:354–55 (WA 21:468.35–469.11); Epistle for Septuagesima Sunday (*Church Postil*, 1540), LW 76:314 (E² 8:101; WA 17,2:135.21–23); *Schmalkaldic Articles* (1538) III.VIII, BoC 1959, 312–13 (BSELK 768.27–772.30; WA 50:245.1–247.4). Here Luther jabs at his opponents, saying "there was no Christian church" under the papacy, because people ignored the witness of the Spirit. This is clearly hyperbole; Luther acknowledges that the church under the pope still has Baptism, the Sacrament, and the Keys. For example, see WATR 1:408–9, no. 839; 2:201.20–202.20, no. 1745.

[72]Sermon on December 10, 1528, WA 30,1:91.3; *Large Catechism* (1529), BoC 1959, 415, 416 (WA 30,1:187.38–188.5, 188.19–23).

[73]Sermon on December 10, 1528, WA 30,1:92.4–18; *Large Catechism* (1529), BoC 1959, 415, 416–17 (WA 30,1:188.2, 189.6–190.17). Luther argues that "communion of saints" is a later addition to the Creed, highlighting that Rufinus (c. 345–411) did not include it in his commentary. See *Resolutio Lutheriana super propositione sua decima tertia de potestate papae* (1519), WA 2:190.21–25; Rufinus, *A Commentary on the Apostles' Creed* 39, ACW 20:74-76 (PL 21:375–77). Luther rendered *catholica* here as *Christlich*, because he saw it as the best German rendering. "We cannot translate *catholica* any better than *Christian*," *The Three Symbols or Creeds of the Christian Faith* (1538), WA 50:283.8–10, marginalia (compare with LW 34:229. Apparently Luther is following custom here, see Gudrun Neebe, *Apostolische Kirche: Grundunterscheidungen an Luthers Kirchenbegriff unter besonderer Berücksichtigung seiner Lehre von den notae ecclesiae* (Berlin: De Gruyter, 1997), 158n553. I'm indebted to Mickey L. Mattox for bringing this source to my attention. See also Luther's preference for *Gemeinde* over *Kirche*, *Large Catechism* (1529), BoC 1959, 416–17 (WA 30,1:189.6–190.3).

[74]Sermon on March 6, 1523, WA 11:54.22–23.

[75]Sermon on March 6, 1523, WA 11:53.21–27; Sermon on December 11, 1528, WA 30,1:92.3–18.

[76]A Sermon on Jesus Christ, Preached at Court in Torgau (1533), WA 37:50.27–39; LW 57:113–14; Sermon on Acts 15 (1524), WA 15:578–602 (compare with RCS NT 6:207, 208–9).

[77]On the church as mother, *Large Catechism* (1529), BoC 1959, 416 (WA 30,1:188.24–25); Sermon on March 6, 1523, WA 11:53.30–34. On the church as necessary for justification, Sermon on December 10, 1528, WA 30,1:94.1–2.

The Childish Doctrine 67

your mother, she births you through the word and carries you."[78] Baptism, Communion, and Absolution are sure signs of God's presence—yes, other signs are possible, but God ordained these signs.[79] The resurrection of the body is perhaps the most difficult of the Holy Spirit's works to understand. Luther cautions not to speculate about God's mechanics, but to cling to this truth.[80]

The Apostles' Creed reveals the joyous news that God is *for us*. We learn what kind of God we have, his name, and his work.[81] God—Father, Son, and Holy Spirit—accomplishes what we cannot. The entire gospel is contained in these few words of the Apostles' Creed.[82] One cannot be a Christian apart from these words. The Creed distinguishes Christians from all other faiths (though Jews and Muslims affirm the first article too).[83] Luther talks about two types of belief: "to believe of" and "to believe in" (his word choice). The first type of belief is a type of knowledge; the tradition calls it *fides quae fidetur*, "the faith that is believed." It is true whether I believe it or not. In this sense even the devil believes God. The second type of belief is trust; the tradition calls it *fides qua creditur*, "the faith by which it is believed." Both types of belief are necessary to be a Christian, but the second type is an especially Christian act. "That little word *in* is carefully chosen and should be pondered diligently, so that we don't say 'I believe God the Father' or 'of God the Father,' but 'in God the Father,' 'in Jesus Christ,' 'in the Holy Spirit.' "[84]

Christians do not merely know or believe these words, they believe *in* them. Even the devil believes these words, but he does not place his hope

---

[78] Sermon on December 10, 1528, WA 30,1:91.19-29.
[79] Sermon on March 6, 1523, WA 11:54.6-7; 30,1:19-21; *Large Catechism* (1529), BoC 1959, 419 (WA 30,1:191.28-36). Luther taught that the sacraments are necessary and exclusive—not just anything has been ordained for God's presence, that would erode all confidence. See Prenter, *Spiritus Creator*, 259-63.
[80] Sermon on March 6, 1523, WA 11:54.25-36; Sermon on December 11, 1528, WA 30,1:93.19-20. See also A Sermon on Jesus Christ, Preached at Court in Torgau (1533), WA 37:36.18-38 (LW 57:95-96). Luther gave similar advice regarding the mechanics of the Sacrament of the Altar, see Sermon on September 25, 1528, WA 30,1:54.7-30, 56.1-10. "I let [Jesus] worry about it; I should trust him. But how it happens? That he knows better than I" (WA 30,1:54.7-8).
[81] Sermon on May 23, 1528, WA 30,1:11.2-4.
[82] Sermon on March 4, 1523, WA 11:48.23-32; Sermon on March 6, 1523, WA 11:54.34-35.
[83] Sermon on May 23, 1528, WA 30,1:10.3-5, 9.26-30.
[84] *A Short Form of the Ten Commandments, Creed, the Lord's Prayer* (1520), WA 7:215.1-22, here lines 15-18; *Little Prayer Book* (1522), WA 10,2:389.1-22 (LW 43:24-25; TAL 4:178-79).

and trust in them; Christians do.⁸⁵ "Sure, many pray these words, but they don't know that the Creed is a dear little letter, as it were, that has the entire gospel."⁸⁶ Here, Luther says, is the entire gospel in brief; do not despise it! "If a person holds this in his heart as the words sound, he believes well."⁸⁷ In fact, Luther suggests that we add "for us" after every clause of the Apostles' Creed. "If you leave out 'for us,' then the entire sermon is for nothing."⁸⁸ God—Father, Son, and Holy Spirit—creates, redeems, and sanctifies *for us*.

The Our Father: "The Prayer of Prayers"

The Our Father teaches us how to pray.⁸⁹ By praying it in faith we most certainly receive what we request, for God is pleased with this prayer.⁹⁰ Christ himself gave these words.⁹¹ And in the second commandment God has commanded prayer.⁹² As the address of this prayer indicates, Christians approach God in the same spirit and attitude as a child approaches her father: in simple loving trust.⁹³ A Christian's prayer is holy not because of their person and works, but because of God's command.

Luther follows the traditional German wording of the Our Father as used liturgically in Wittenberg.⁹⁴ And he divides it into an address and seven

---

⁸⁵Sermon on March 5, 1523, WA 11:52.16-26; Sermon on March 4, 1523, WA 11:49.6-7.
⁸⁶Sermon on March 4, 1523, WA 11:48.24-26..
⁸⁷Sermon on May 23, 1528, WA 30,1:11.7.
⁸⁸Sermon on the First Day of Christmas (1529), WA 27:491-94, here 493.7-8. See also Afternoon Sermon on the First Day of Christmas (1531), WA 34,2:508.20-510.2; Sermon on the Sunday after the Feast of the Circumcision (1545), WA 49:662.7-663.5.
⁸⁹For the Our Father as "the prayer of prayers," see WATR 1:34.4-5, no .88; WATR 1:360.9, no. 757; WATR 3:183.19, no. 3134; WATR 5:582.1-2, no. 6288.
⁹⁰Sermon on the Our Father (March 9, 1523), WA 11:55.4-5; Sermon on May 28, 1528, WA 30,1:11.13-16, 36; Sermon on December 14, 1528, WA 30,1:98.10-16; Sermon on December 15, 1528, WA 30,1:108.24-26; *Large Catechism* (1529), BoC 1959, 420, 423-24 (WA 30,1:193.4-5, 11-13, 196.19-197.15); WATR 1:34.7-8, no. 88; WATR 1:360.11-12, no. 757; WATR 3:183.21, no. 3134; WATR 5:582.1-4, no. 6288.
⁹¹Sermon on May 28, 1528, WA 30,1:11.18-26; WATR 4:324, no. 4461.
⁹²Sermon on September 22, 1528, WA 47.22-24; Sermon on December 14, 1528, WA 30,1:95.6-11, 96.15-19, 99.7-15; *Large Catechism* (1529), BoC 1959, 420-21, 422 (WA 30,1:193.16-195.21).
⁹³Sermon on September 22, 1528, WA 30,1:46.37-47.1; Sermon on December 14, 1528, WA 30,1:95.23; *Small Catechism* (1529), BoC 1959, 346 (TAL 4:225; WA 30,1:251.1-14); Sermons on Matthew 5-7 (1532), WA 32:420.9-19.
⁹⁴Peters, *Commentary on Luther's Catechisms*, 3:4, TAL 2:225ne. Luther leaves out the doxology, because it was not included in the form used by the German parishes. The doxology gained renewed prominence in later generations of the Western church, because Erasmus includes it in his *Novum Instrumentum*. See *Novum Instrumentum omne*, ed. Erasmus, 11; *Novum*

The Childish Doctrine 69

petitions according to ancient church tradition.[95] This tradition teaches that the Our Father has two parts: the first three petitions address eternal requests; the last four petitions, temporal requests.[96]

The eternal petitions focus on our greatest needs: a life and doctrine according to God's word. God's name, kingdom, and will are the highest goods, which we should cherish and prize.[97] The world wants more possessions and status, but Christians want a certain character of life. The world says, we want material goods. That's like asking a king, who is ready to give you a great fortune, for some measly soup.[98] It asks too little of God. Christians say, we want eternal goods.[99] "Because God is the King of kings, nothing but the greatest should be asked of him."[100] The greatest we can ask for is the pure preaching and teaching of the word, right doctrine, and holy living.[101] Where God's word is, there he himself is, bringing pure justice, peace, and salvation.[102]

The temporal petitions focus on our needs in the flesh. We need bodily and spiritual sustenance, constant reminders of forgiveness, protection from

---

Testamentum omne, ed. Erasmus, 11 (although the Latin translation of the doxology is set in a smaller font size than the rest of the Latin text); Peters, *Commentary on Luther's Catechisms*, 3:6.

[95] See Augustine, *Faith, Hope, and Love* 30 (ACW 3:107-8; PL 40:286); Augustine, *Commentary on the Lord's Sermon on the Mount* 2.10 (FC 11:144-46; PL 34:1285-86); Augustine, Sermon 56.19 (FC 11:257; PL 38:386). Cyprian implies seven petitions, see Cyprian, *On the Lord's Prayer* 9-27 (PPS 29:70-85; PL 4:525-37); Tertullian—on whom Cyprian depends—agrees, although he more subtly intimates seven petitions, see Tertullian, *On Prayer* 2-8 (PPS 29:42-48; PL 1:1256-67); Origen, too, see *On Prayer* 24-30 (PPS 29:166-206). Luther himself cites Cyprian as his example, see *German Explanation of the Our Father for Simple Lay People* (1519), WA 2:86.30-87.2 (LW 42:27).

[96] See Sermons on Matthew 5-7 (1532), WA 32:420.18-21, 37-40. In contrast to Luther's own language, Peters discusses these as the "thy petitions" and "our petitions," following modern biblical studies. See Peters, *Commentary on Luther's Catechisms*, 3:10-11. For a modern discussion, see Ulrich Luz, *Matthew 1-7: A Commentary on Matthew 1-7*, trans. James E. Crouch, Hermeneia (Minneapolis: Fortress, 2007), 307-26. Some scholars do not separate "lead us not into temptation" from "deliver us from evil." Thus, they number six petitions in the Our Father, for example, see R. T. France, *The Gospel of Matthew*, New International Commentary on the New Testament (Grand Rapids: Eerdmans, 2007), 241-52.

[97] Sermon on May 26, 1528, WA 30,1:14.23-25; Sermons on Matthew 5-7 (1532), WA 32:420.20-38.

[98] Sermon on May 25, 1528, WA 30,1:13.16-19; *Large Catechism* (1529), BoC 1959, 427-28 (WA 30,1:201.1-25).

[99] Sermon on May 25, 1528, WA 30,1:13.2-9.

[100] Sermon on May 25, 1528, WA 30,1:13.18-19.

[101] Sermon on May 28, 1528, WA 30,1:12.17-18, 13.2-9, 13.22-24, 13.33-14.1; Sermon on September 22, 1528, WA 30,1:46.15-19, 32-36, 47.5-8, 33-34, 48.15-23; Sermon on December 14, 1528, WA 30,1:99.6-7, 14-15, 24-25.

[102] Sermon on September 22, 1528, WA 30,1:47.27-48.2; WATR 1:309.17-18, no. 659.

trials and sin, and a holy life and end.[103] In this life, temptation is certain to happen, whether it be of the flesh, of the world, or of the devil.[104] We too easily doubt that God gives all that our body and spirit need, that he forgives us, that he is able to make us stand, and that he will lead us from death into life. "All our protection stands in prayer."[105] The Our Father is our most powerful weapon against doubt and temptation.

The Our Father models how we are to speak to God. We do not need many words or repetition. Rote repetition ignores the situation of our lives and our real needs—plus words alone do not scare the devil.[106] Both indicate a cold, disinterested heart. God wants us to approach him like his children, not like blocks of wood.[107] And true prayer is the sigh of the heart.[108] Therefore Luther calls Christians to learn these words well; the Our Father is the most succinct prayer—it even summarizes all the prayers of the Psalms![109] Of course, it is not just these words that are pleasing to God. Christians should learn how to pray prayers with different words that nevertheless do not stray from the Our Father's content.[110] Only God by his word and Spirit teaches this: "Ah yes, the Lord Christ is the true master of [the Our Father]! He composed this prayer with such brevity and perspicuity as no human could. Indeed we're only able to obscure it with our explanations. So let's learn from the Lord Christ's mouth—he knows how to pray it."[111]

---

[103] Sermons on Matthew 5–7 (1532), WA 32:420.39–421.18.
[104] Sermon on March 9, 1523, WA 11:12.6–9; Sermon on May 27, 1528, WA 30,1:16.10–17.28, esp 27–28; Sermon on September 22, 1528, WA 30,1:46:19–26; Sermon on December 14, 1528, WA 30,1:102.8–9; Sermon on December 15, 1528, WA 30,1:106.18–107.15; *Large Catechism* (1529), BoC 1959, 424 (WA 30,1:197.16–32).
[105] Sermon on December 14, 1528, WA 30,1:98.2–3.
[106] Sermon on March 9, 1523, WA 11:55.17–18, 25–28; WATR 2:149, no 1603. Luther acknowledges the importance of repetition for learning the Our Father, although he does not call such repetition actual prayer. See *Large Catechism* (1529), BoC 1959, 421 (WA 30,1:193.29–33).
[107] Sermon on May 25, 1528, WA 30,1:12.4–5; Sermon on December 15, 1528, WA 30,1:108.15–18; *Large Catechism* (1529), BoC 1959, 424, 424–25 (WA 30,1:197.10–15, 33–37).
[108] Sermon on September 22, 1528, WA 30,1:46.19–22.
[109] Sermon on December 15, 1528, WA 30,1:107.18–20.
[110] Sermon on March 9, 1523, WA 11:55.12–14, 16–17; Sermon on May 25, 1528, WA 30,1:12.11–12. To help his audience with this, Luther often paraphrases the Our Father. Among many examples, see *A Simple Way to Pray* (1535), WA 38:360.13–363.16 (TAL 4:259–64; LW 43:195–98). See also Witvliet, "The Interplay of Catechesis and Liturgy," 115–18.
[111] WATR 4:324, no. 4461. See also Wesley Hill, *The Lord's Prayer: A Guide to Praying to Our Father*, Christian Essentials (Bellingham, WA: Lexham Press, 2019), 1–5.

The Childish Doctrine

The Our Father contains everything we need to ask for—whether we know it or not.[112] All of these petitions happen without our asking—God freely does what he wants. God's name is holy; his kingdom comes; his will is done. We are fed; our sins are forgiven; the flesh, the world, and the devil are defeated; and we are brought into freedom. But we ask that all these things happen in our lives and the lives of God's dear children and that we would acknowledge his abundant giving.[113] The Our Father is a most precious gift from the Lord, for "the Holy Spirit himself preaches here, and one word of his sermon is far better than a thousand of our prayers."[114] God himself speaks through our mouth and lips.

THE SACRAMENTS: "THE CEREMONIES OF CEREMONIES"

In the sacraments God the Father applies the person and work of Jesus Christ through the ministry of the Holy Spirit.[115] Those who believe the promises declared in the sacraments are forgiven, freed from sin, death, and the devil, and brought to true life.[116] The sacraments are God's word and work—nothing we do can change them. "Our faith must change, not God's word or work, which remains forever."[117] In this Luther stands firm against his Papal and Radical opponents: nothing needs to be added to the sacraments, and the sacraments are not based on our faith. Faith receives the perfect gift of the sacraments; it does not make them.[118] "Do you really think

---

[112]Sermon on December 15, 1528, WA 30,1:108.24-26; *Large Catechism* (1529), BoC 1959, 424 (WA 30,1:196.34-197.5); Sermons on Matthew 5-7 (1532), WA 32:421.18-20; WATR 5:582.1-4, no. 6288; see also Sermon on September 22, 1528, WA 30,1:46.27-29.

[113]This comes through most clearly in the sermons on December 14-15, 1528 and the *Small* and *Large Catechisms* (1529). In these petitions, Christians are united with all who pray it—across time and place. See Sermon on May 27, 1528, WA 30,1:17.30-31; WATR 1:340, no. 700; WATR 3:261, no. 3303; Peters, *Commentary on Luther's Catechisms*, 3:12-13.

[114]*A Simple Way to Pray* (1535), WA 38:363.13-15 (TAL 2:264; LW 43:198).

[115]On Luther and the category of sacrament, see Peters, *Commentary on Luther's Catechisms*, 4:1-72; Brian C. Brewer, "Sacramental Theology," in *Encyclopedia of Martin Luther and the Reformation*, ed. Mark A. Lamport (Lanham, MD: Rowman & Littlefield, 2017), 669-72; John T. Pless, "Sacraments," in *Dictionary of Luther and the Lutheran Traditions*, ed. Timothy J. Wengert (Grand Rapids: Baker Academic, 2017), 653-56; Althaus, *Theology of Martin Luther*, 345-52; Asendorf, *Theologie Martin Luthers*, 77-79, 273-86. For the sacraments as "the ceremonies of ceremonies," see WATR 5:582.5-6, no. 6288.

[116]See *Small Catechism* (1529), TAL 4:231, 232, 236 (WA 30,1:310-11, 316-17; BoC 1959, 348-49, 349-50, 352); Peters, *Commentary on Luther's Catechisms*, 4:65.

[117]WATR 2:315.14-15, no. 2083A.

[118]For example, WATR 6:170, no. 6761; *Large Catechism* (1529), BoC 1959, 440-41 (WA 30,1:216.6-217.14. To argue, as Brian Brewer does in *Martin Luther and the Seven Sacraments: A*

that God is so worried about our work and faith, that on account of them he would let his ordinance change?"[119] "A child hasn't believed, therefore is his Baptism worth nothing? That's like saying: I didn't believe the gospel twenty years ago, therefore the gospel was nothing."[120] Like the Ten Commandments, the Creed, and the Our Father, these words of God—the sacraments—are objective and unchanging, whether you believe or not, because they are God's work. Luther distinguished between essence and use. The sacraments' essence does not depend on the person; the sacraments are objective, defined by God, and undiminished by humans. The use of the sacraments depends on the person by the power and ministry of the Holy Spirit.[121]

Luther used a broader definition of sacrament than most of the medievals. Most medievals followed Hugh of St. Victor's (d. 1141) definition of a sacrament as a physical sign instituted by Christ. (In *The Babylonian Captivity of the Church* [1520], Luther admitted that there are only two sacraments according to this definition.[122]) Peter Lombard (d. 1160) extended the meaning of physical sign to ritual, justifying Absolution as a sacrament (as well as confirmation, marriage, ordination, and last rites). Luther accepted Lombard's extended meaning of physical sign, while holding tightly to Hugh of St. Victor's requirement of Christ's institution.[123] And so he rejected

---

Contemporary Protestant Reappraisal (Grand Rapids: Baker Academic, 2017), that faith must come first is to fundamentally misunderstand Luther. If one receives a sacrament without faith, it is not invalid—it need not be re-performed; instead, one must believe! See Sermon on May 28, 1528, WA 30,1:19.28–20.2; Sermon on December 17, 1528, WA 30,1:114.9–10; Sermon on December 19, 1528, WA 30,1:118.4–9; *Large Catechism* (1529), BoC 1959, 443–44 (BSELK 1124.8–36, 1126.1–34, 1128.1–2; WA 30,1:218.24–220.13). See Steinmetz, *Luther in Context*, 77–78. Luther's language about the sacraments as God's word seems to rub against his denial of *ex opere operato*. But E. Theodore Bachmann explains that Luther rejected the medieval debate of sacraments as something humans do; God performs the sacraments, see LW 35:64n39.

[119]*Large Catechism* (1529), WA 30,1:223.16–17 (BoC 1959, 447).
[120]WATR 2:316.3–5, no. 2083B. See also WATR 2:349–50, no. 2.178.
[121]Sermon on December 19, 1528, WA 30,1:116.12–16; WATR 2:315.14–25, no. 2083A. Luther often uses the example of an unbelieving Jew who receives Baptism, see, for example, Sermon on December 17, 1528, WA 30,1:114.12–15. He also makes vile comments about throwing such Jews into the Elbe, see WATR 1:124, no. 299; 2:217, no. 1795. On Luther's anti-judaism, see Thomas Kaufmann, *Luther's Jews: A Journey into Anti-Semitism*, trans. Lesley Sharpe and Jeremy Noakes (Oxford: Oxford University Press, 2017); for a succinct treatment of the Reformers' anti-judaism, see Selderhuis, "Introduction," in RCS OT 7:lii–liv.
[122]WA 6:501.33–38, 572.10–22 (LW 36:18, 124; TAL 3:21, 127).
[123]See further Peters, *Commentary on Luther's Catechisms*, 4:49–59. Peters argues that many scholars fail to understand Luther's different definition, and therefore they describe Luther (or

The Childish Doctrine 73

confirmation, marriage, ordination, and last rites as sacraments. Confirmation and marriage are described as "sacraments without the word"; last rites were not instituted by Christ; and ordination does not have a promise of forgiveness. Therefore, according to Luther, to call these sacraments is impiety and robbery. He was entirely unwilling to compromise God's word or promise attached to the rite.[124]

The sacraments are visible words. "My soul longs for your salvation, I hope in your word. My eyes yearn to see your word, and they say, When will you comfort me?" (Ps 119:81-82).[125] Luther regularly cited Augustine's phrase, "The word is added to the elemental substance, and it becomes a sacrament"; he held it as the best phrase of all of Augustine.[126] Our Lord bound his word of promise to common human things—water, bread, wine, human breath—in Baptism, Holy Communion, and Absolution. Baptism is worded water. Holy Communion is worded bread and wine. Absolution is worded breath. These words of life and forgiveness are not abstract and impersonal. That's made clear because they're bound to material. But we aren't to see these common materials with our eyes and reason but with God's logic—his word, which, spoken from all eternity, brings into existence what it says and sustains it (Ps 104:30; Rom 4:17; Col 1:16).[127] Hence Luther's common refrain is "as the words sound."[128] In

---

Melanchthon) as inexact or wavering on whether Absolution and preaching are sacraments—scholars almost always focus on the question of Absolution as sacrament (*Commentary on Luther's Catechisms*, 4:52). For examples of Peters's point, see Jonathan D. Trigg, "Luther on Baptism and Penance," *The Oxford Handbook of Martin Luther's Theology*, ed. Robert Kolb, Irene Dingel, and Ľubomír Batka (New York: Oxford University Press, 2014), 317; Brewer, "Sacramental Theology," 671; Ronald K. Rittgers, "Confession (Private) and the Confessional," in *Dictionary of Luther and the Lutheran Traditions*, ed. Timothy Wengert (Grand Rapids: Baker Academic, 2017), 158.

[124] *Against the Thirty-Two Articles of the Louvain Theologians* (1545), LW 34:354, 356, 357; WA 54:425.2-3, 427.21-22, 428.3-4, 7-8, 11-12). See further LW 34:354-60 (WA 54:425.1-430.18); *Defense of the Augsburg Confession* (1531) XIII, BoC 1959, 211-14; BSELK 510.25-518.23.

[125] WADB 10,1:509.

[126] Tractates on John 80.3, FC 4:116; Sermon on December 19, 1528, WA 30,1:117.15-16. Luther often uses this Augustine quote to establish the sine-qua-non nature of the word for a sacrament. For example, see WATR 1:321, no. 671; Sermon on May 29, 1528, WA 30,1:24.3-6; Sermon on September 25, 1528, WA 30,1:53.13; Sermon on December 19, 1528, WA 30,1:117.14-16; *Large Catechism* (1529), BoC 1959, 438 (WA 30,1:214.14-17).

[127] A promise does not describe or demand; a promise gives. Bayer, *Martin Luther's Theology*, 50-58.

[128] Afternoon Sermon on Laetare Sunday (1523), WA 11:66.12-13; Sermon on May 29, 1528, WA 30,1:23.30-31, 24.14; Sermon on May 30, 1528, WA 30,1:24.35-37, 26.21-22; Sermon on

hearing we see. "My eyes long for your salvation, and for the word of your righteousness" (Ps 119:123).[129]

In practice, Luther defined *sacrament* as something God alone does that Christ established with his promise of forgiveness and salvation.[130] On account of this, he blurred the number of sacraments. It can be argued that he held there to be only one sacrament—Jesus; two—Baptism and Communion; three—Baptism, Communion, and Absolution; or four—preaching, Baptism, Communion, and Absolution.[131] According to Albrecht Peters, what the Bible identifies with God's redemption Luther calls a sacrament; however, Luther never formalized this definition—or any definition for that matter.[132] "The Sacred Scriptures hold only one thing to be a sacrament: that's the Lord Christ himself."[133] And Jesus instituted certain actions or activities to bring himself present, namely, preaching, Baptism, Communion, and Absolution.[134] (Baptism, Communion, and Absolution are special cases of preaching; in each God proclaims his word of forgiveness and life.)

September 24, 1528, WA 30,1:51.13–14, 25; Sermon on September 25, 1528, WA 30,1:53.22, 31, 34–35, 54.10, 34, 55.8, 36; Sermon on December 17, 1528, WA 30,1:111.3–4, 21, 112.7–10, 113.2; Sermon on December 19, 1528, WA 30,1:117.4–5, 18, 22, 119.15–16; *Large Catechism* (1529), BoC 1959, 438–39 (WA 30,1:214.18–34); WATR 4:492–93, no. 4778.

[129] WADB 10,1:517.

[130] Luther groups the sacraments under the article of the forgiveness of sins, see Sermon on December 10, 1528, WA 30,1:92.18–93.3; again, this is part of the reason why he sometimes includes the sacraments as part of the catechism and sometimes does not. On the sacraments as God's action alone, in addition to the catechetical sermons, see, for example, WATR 3:671.1–672.15, no. 3868. See further, *Against the Thirty-Two Articles of the Louvain Theologians* (1545), LW 34:354–60 (WA 54:425.1–430.18).

[131] For one sacrament, see *Disputatio de fide infusa et acquisita* (1520), WA 6:86.7–8, 97.7–24. For two sacraments (the "major sacraments"), see *The Blessed Sacrament of the Holy and True Body of Christ* (1519), LW 35:67 (WA 2:754.1–8); *Confession concerning Christ's Supper* (1528), LW 37:370 (WA 26:508.25–29); Sermon on May 28, 1528, WA 30,1:18.18–19; Sermon on May 30, 1528, WA 30,1:27.21–23; Sermon on September 24, 1528, WA 30,1:50.29–30; Sermon on December 17, 1528, WA 30,1:109.25–27; *Large Catechism* (1529), BoC 1959, 436 (WA 30,1:212.5–6). For three sacraments, see Sermon on May 29, 1528, WA 30,1:22.22; *Against the Thirty-Two Articles of the Louvain Theologians* (1545), WA 54:427.26–28 (LW 34:357), 436.7–9. For four sacraments, see *Schmalkaldic Articles* (1538), BoC 1959, 310–13 (WA 50:240.27–247.4); Sermon on the Second Sunday after Epiphany (1538), WA 46:145.24, 146.4–5, 20–23; WATR 1:554–55, no. 1112.

[132] Peters, *Commentary on Luther's Catechisms*, 4:49. On Luther beginning with the Bible instead of a definition of sacrament, see Peters, *Commentary on Luther's Catechisms*, 4:56–57, 58; Pless, "Sacraments," 653.

[133] *Disputatio de fide infusa et acquisita* (1520), WA 6:86.7–8, 97.7–24. See Peters, *Commentary on Luther's Catechisms*, 4:23–24.

[134] WATR 1:435, no. 870; 1:577, no. 1168; 3:281, no. 3356. In the years after *The Babylonian Captivity of the Church* (1520), Luther, like Melanchthon, loosens what a visible sign is: a human act

The Childish Doctrine 75

Nevertheless, throughout the catechetical sermons Luther handles the major sacraments—as the tradition calls them—of Baptism and Communion, mentioning Absolution occasionally.[135]

In these sermons Luther explains what word of God establishes the sacrament, what it is, and what its benefits are. The Lord Christ instituted the sacraments with a promise and command from God. Baptism is water with God's name (Mt 28:19; Mk 16:16).[136] The Sacrament of the Altar is bread and wine with Christ's body and blood (Mt 26:26-28; Mk 14:22-24; Lk 22:19-20; 1 Cor 11:23-25).[137] Absolution is the sure proclamation of forgiveness (Mt 16:19; 18:18-19; Jn 20:22-23).[138] The sacraments bring forgiveness,

---

(WATR 1:435.11-12, no. 870; *Defense of the Augsburg Confession* [1531] XIII, BoC 1959, 211-12; BSELK 512.3-24).

[135]Regarding the connection between Baptism and Absolution, see, for example, Sermon on May 29, 1528, WA 30,1:21.22-31.

[136]For Baptism's definition, see Sermon on May 28, 1528, WA 30,1:19.25-27, 21.3-4; Sermon on September 24, 1528, WA 30,1:50.30-37, 51.36-38; Sermon on December 17, 1528, WA 30,1:110.18-19, 111.1-2, 112.3-6, 18-26; *Small Catechism* (1529), TAL 4:231 (WA 30,1:308.17-22; BoC 1959, 348); *Large Catechism* (1529), BoC 1959, 438 (WA 30,1:213.28-33). For the foundational Bible passages, see Sermon on May 28, 1528, WA 30,1:18.21-23; Sermon on September 24, 1528, WA 30,1:51.1-6; Sermon on December 17, 1528, WA 30,1:109.27-110.15; *Small Catechism* (1529); TAL 231 (WA 30,1:308.23-26, 310.1-3; BoC 1959, 348); *Large Catechism* (1529), BoC 1959, 437 (WA 30,1:212.13-21); WATR 2:301, no. 2041.

[137]For the Sacrament of the Altar's definition, see Sermon on May 29, 1528, WA 30,1:23.25-29, 24.13-24; Sermon on September 25, 1528, WA 30,1:53.9-22, 54.1-7; Sermon on December 19, 1528, WA 30,1:117.1-14, 119.14-26, 122.12-13; *Small Catechism* (1529), TAL 4:235 (WA 30,1:314.15-20; BoC 1959, 351); *Large Catechism* (1529), BoC 1959, 447 (WA 30,1:223.22-28). For the foundational Bible passages, see Sermon on May 29, 1528, WA 30,1:23.19-25; Sermon on September 25, 1528, WA 30,1:54.5; Sermon on December 19, 1528, WA 30,1:116.17, 117.5-6; *Small Catechism* (1529), TAL 4:235-36 (WA 30,1:314.21-30, 316.1-11; BoC 1959, 351); *Large Catechism* (1529), BoC 1959, 447 (WA 30,1:222.28-223.6). Luther usually cites the words of institution from memory, rather than these separate passages. For the words of institution, see *The German Mass and Order of Service* (1526), LW 53:80-81 (WA 19:97-99).

[138]For Absolution's definition, see *The Sacrament of Penance* (1519), LW 35:10-11, 22 (WA 2:715.10-20, 722.36-723.2); Sermon on December 15, 1528, WA 30,1:105.21-106.14; *Large Catechism* (1529), BoC 1959, 433 (WA 30,1:207.24-208.12); Epistle for the Sunday after Easter (*Church Postil*, 1544), LW 77:132-33, 133-45 (WA 49:144.29-32, 145.17-153.42); WATR 6:174, no. 6765. See Peters, *Commentary on Luther's Catechisms*, 5:48-50. While Jesus clearly commanded Absolution, its concrete sign is unclear according to the biblical record. Luther identifies a few external signs: the laying on of hands, the Christian who pronounces the Absolution, and that you have forgiven those who sinned against you. See Commentary on Isaiah Chapter 9 (1543-1544), WA 40,3:632.20-23; WATR 3:581-83, no. 3739; 5:447.29-36, 448.31-40; *Large Catechism* (1529), BoC 1959, 433 (WA 30,1:207.24-208.12). See Peters, *Commentary on Luther's Catechisms*, 4:38, especially n189. The sign of the cross would be another potential sign—surprisingly, I have not seen Luther mention it as such. He tends to present the sign of the cross as a special proclamation of Christ's victory. He especially recommends it as

freedom from sin, death, and the devil, and true life and salvation, because Christ is present with his word.[139] "Heaven has been given to me freely; it's my gift! And I have letters and seals to prove it: I'm baptized and go to the Sacrament of the Altar."[140] The sacraments nourish and strengthen faith, making the conscience joyful.

God alone establishes these words and works, not some human![141] Take away the word, and the sacrament and its benefits vanish. If we look at the sacraments with the eyes of reason, they are nothing. "If you take away the word, it's the same water the maid gives to the cow."[142] As the *Schwärmer* say, what can a handful of water do? A scrap of bread?[143] But Baptism is not mere

---

a consolation to those who are frightened. See, for example, The Third Sermon on the Gospel for the Easter Festival (*House Postil*, 1544), WA 52:261.1–8.

[139] For Baptism's benefits, see Sermon on May 28, 1528, WA 30,1:20.7–14, 21.15–16; Sermon on May 29, 1528, WA 30,1:23.9–15; Sermon on May 30, 1528, WA 30,1:25:4–5; Sermon on September 24, 1528, WA 30,1:51.14, 52.2; Sermon on September 25, 1528, WA 30,1:54.30–31; Sermon on December 17, 1528, WA 30,1:112.7–10, 113.2–6, 8–9; *Small Catechism* (1529), TAL 4:231 (WA 30,1:310.4–16; BoC 1959, 348–49); *Large Catechism* (1529), BoC 1959, 439 (WA 30,1:215.3–12). For the Sacrament of the Altar's benefits, see Sermon on May 30, 1528, WA 30,1:25.1–4,6–22, 26.7–12, 16–17, 27.6–7; Sermon on September 25, 1528, WA 30,1:52.39–53.1, 53.6–7, 54.33–34, 55.3–12; Sermon on December 19, 1528, WA 30,1:118.15–17, 119.16–18, 120.12–14, 121.12–17, 122.11–13; *Small Catechism* (1529), TAL 4:236 (WA 30,1:316.12–21; BoC 1959, 352); *Large Catechism* (1529), BoC 1959, 449 (WA 30,1:224.32–225.6). Peters highlights that on account of his polemics with the Reformed and the Radicals, Luther underemphasizes the unity brought through Holy Communion (Peters, *Commentary on Luther's Catechisms*, 4:43–48); still see *Blessed Sacrament of the Body of Christ* (1519), LW 35:51–52, 59–60 (WA 2:743.20–744.7, 748.27–749.22); Sermon on Sermon on May 30, 1528, WA 30,1:26.22–25, 27.17–18; WATR 4:27–28, no. 3947; 5:259–60, no. 5579. Luther does not systematically list the obvious benefits of Absolution—particularly, forgiveness—but here are some passages where he talks about the grace and mercy of receiving Absolution: *Large Catechism* (1529), BoC 1959, 457–61 (WA 30,1:233.20–238.15); WATR 4:260–61, no. 4362; 4:694, no. 5175; 5:281, no. 5632; see Ewald M. Plass, ed., *What Luther Says*, 3 vols. (St. Louis: Concordia, 1959), 1–9. See also Peters, *Commentary on Luther's Catechisms*, 4:65–68.

[140] WATR 6:166.28–30.

[141] Sermon on May 28, 1528, WA 30,1:19.10–12, 20.15–21; Sermon on May 29, 1528, WA 30,1:24.6–9; Sermon on September 24, 1528, WA 30,1:52.6–14; Sermon on September 25, 1528, WA 30,1:54.11–19; Sermon on December 17, 1528, WA 30,1:111.20–112.2, 114.18–21; *Large Catechism* (1529), BoC 1959, 437, 447 (WA 30,1:212.22–31, 213.12–17, 223.7–19); WATR 1:137–39, no. 342; 1:262–65, no. 574; 2:280.1–2, no. 1961; 4:411, no. 4634; 4:695, no. 5176; 5:439, no. 6016; 5:447–49, no. 6031 6:111–12, no. 6674; 6:170, no. 6761; 6:170–72, no. 6762; 6:178–79, no 6770.

[142] Sermon on December 17, 1528, WA 30,1:112.4–5.

[143] Luther regularly cites this objection of the Radicals, whom he sees as placing reason over faith, for example, see Sermon on May 29, 1528, WA 30,1:24.15–16; Sermon on May 30, 1528, WA 30,1:25.23–26.3; Sermon on September 24, 1528, WA 30,1:52.26–34. He also tells his congregation to leave these disputes to the doctors of the church; laity should simply cling to the word.

water, and the Sacrament of the Altar is not mere bread and wine! God has added his word to both, and that fundamentally defines the nature and reality of the sacraments. "Therefore, as far as I separate heaven from earth, so far I separate water from Baptism."[144] "Water is water, but when the institution is added, it's Baptism."[145] " 'This is my body.' These words make bread into the body of Christ given for us."[146] The word of God makes all the difference. So Christians must not look on the sacraments with the eyes of reason but with the eyes of faith, clinging to and trusting God's word. "I must listen to what my God says, not my reason."[147] Christians must not focus on the bare matter—water or bread and wine—but let Jesus explain what is happening: forgiveness, new life, and salvation.[148] "Don't look at him with your eyes, instead, stick your eyes in your ears."[149] And so Luther exhorted his congregation to consider the sacraments "as the words sound." This is the most characteristic piece of his teaching on the sacraments in the catechetical sermons.[150] "If you want to be a Christian, if you want to have the forgiveness of sins and life eternal, come forward! Here stands your God, who invites you to his body and blood, contained for you [in bread and wine]."[151] The word and command of God never changes.[152]

CONCLUSION

In his catechetical materials, Luther teaches the Christian essentials. Without knowledge of the Ten Commandments, the Apostles' Creed, the Lord's Prayer, and the sacraments, a person cannot be considered a

---

[144] Sermon on May 28, 1528, WA 30,1:19.17–18.
[145] Sermon on May 29, 1528, WA 30,1:23.27–28.
[146] Sermon on September 25, 1528, WA 30,1:53.23–24.
[147] Sermon on September 25, 1528, WA 30,1:53.34–35. If God wanted humans to be ruled by their reason, he would not have spoken his word.
[148] Sermon on September 25, 1528, WA 30,1:53.23–32.
[149] House Sermon on the First Sunday in Advent (1533), WA 37:202.15–16.
[150] Afternoon Sermon on Laetare Sunday (1523), WA 11:66.12–13; Sermon on May 29, 1528, WA 30,1:23.30–31, 24.14; Sermon on May 30, 1528, WA 30,1:24.35–37, 26.21–22; Sermon on September 24, 1528, WA 30,1:51.13–14, 25; Sermon on September 25, 1528, WA 30,1:53.22, 31, 34–35, 54.10, 34, 55.8, 36; Sermon on December 17, 1528, WA 30,1:111.3–4, 21, 112.7–10, 113.2; Sermon on December 19, 1528, WA 30,1:117.4–5, 18, 22, 119.15–16; *Large Catechism* (1529), BoC 1959, 438–39 (WA 30,1:214.18–34); WATR 4:492–93, no. 4778.
[151] Sermon on December 19, 1528, WA 30,1:120.12–14. At the end of this sermon, Luther addresses those who commune infrequently—particularly women and children, see WA 30,1:120.15–122.11.
[152] Sermon on December 19, 1528, WA 30,1:116.12–14.

Christian, and the Bible remains closed.[153] Yes, Luther commends interpreting Scripture with Scripture—that's what the rule of faith is after all. He even defines the clear passages by which Scripture is to be interpreted: the catechism. For Luther this is obviously appropriate and fitting, because each part of the catechism summarizes the Bible.[154] By the Spirit's ministry, these basics help a Christian to know what the Bible is about and what is an appropriate use and interpretation of the Bible. And this is more than enough to fill a lifetime![155] "I, Doctor Martin, a doctor and preacher, daily make myself pray and recite the words of the Ten Commandments and the Creed and the [Lord's] Prayer like the children. So don't be ashamed. Great fruit will follow."[156] So Christians—lay and learned, young and old—must approach Scripture with humility as servants not masters. "It is a disgraceful temptation that anyone imagines that he knows everything. It should be said: Indeed that's how the words sound, but I still haven't grasped them like I should."[157]

Luther is flexible in how he numbers the parts of the catechism. At times he defines three parts of the catechism—the Ten Commandments, the Apostles' Creed, and the Our Father; at others he outlines four parts of the catechism—the Ten Commandments, the Apostles' Creed, the Our Father, and the sacraments. Luther sees the sacraments as contained in the principal three parts of the catechism. The third article hold the sacraments of Baptism, Communion, and Absolution; in these words of God humans are embraced in the life of God, given true life and forgiveness.[158] When Luther draws out

---

[153] Sermon on May 18, 1528, WA 30,1:2.4-7; Sermon on September 15, 1528, WA 30,1:30.1-6; Afternoon Sermon on the Seventh Sunday after Trinity (1529), WA 29:471.21-24; *Psalm 68: On Easter, Ascension, and Pentecost* (1521), LW 13:17 (WA 8:17.2-4).

[154] Sermon on November 30, 1528, WA 30,1:61.11-12; Sermon on March 4, 1523, WA 11:48.23-32; Sermon on March 6, 1523, WA 11:54.34-35; Sermon on September 24, 1528, WA 30,1:50.19-22 (Psalms).

[155] Sermon on September 22, 1528, WA 30,1:46.27-29; Sermon on September 24, 1528, WA 30,1:51.15; *Large Catechism* (1529), BoC 1959, 441-42 (WA 30,1:216.15-19); A Sermon on Jesus Christ, Preached at Court in Torgau (1533), WA 37:47.11-14 (LW 57:109); A House Sermon on the Articles of the Creed (1537), WA 45:17.16 (LW 57:247).

[156] Sermon on the First Sunday in Advent (1530), WA 32:209.36-38.

[157] Sermon on the Eighteenth Sunday after Trinity (1530), WA 32:131.13-15. See also A Sermon on Jesus Christ, Preached at Court in Torgau (1533), WA 37:47.22-25 (LW 57:109); WATR 3:685, no. 3883.

[158] See, for example, Sermon on December 10, 1538, WA 30,1:92.18-93.3. No doubt Luther would also see a connection between the second article and the sacraments.

four parts of the catechism, he's emphasizing these physical words spoken, ordained, and commanded by our Lord Jesus Christ.

The catechism unfolds the inner logic of the Bible. And, for Luther, all the parts of the catechism can be folded into the first commandment: "I am the LORD your God" (Exod 20:2).[159] So much so that he despaired of the possibility of ever plumbing and mapping the depths of the Ten Commandments, the Apostles' Creed, the Our Father, and the sacraments. "I have often placed the Decalogue before myself to meditate on it diligently. And although I began with these words, *I am the Lord your God*, I spend most of my time with the word *I*, and I still can't understand enough! When could I ever get through the entire Decalogue in meditation?"[160] It is axiomatic for Luther that God's word is eternally generative. No matter someone's familiarity with Scripture, no matter their circumstances and context, God speaks. That's the lesson of the catechism, and we never finish learning it.

---

[159] WADB 8:261.
[160] WATR 2:407.36–39, no. 2287. On the generative character of God's word, see also A House Sermon on the Articles of the Creed (1537), WA 45:11.5–12.5 (LW 57:243–44).

4

The Resurrection of the Dead

Reading the Law According to the Rule of Faith

LUTHER READ ABRAHAM'S SACRIFICE of Isaac according to the catechism. He grounded this story in the first table of the law. Abraham was tempted not to trust God's word and to speak ill of him, but Abraham perseveres as a shining example of trust in God's word and character, although according to the eyes of reason God seems untrustworthy. Luther also assumed the Apostles' Creed. Taking a cue from the author of Hebrews, Luther insisted that Abraham confessed the resurrection of the dead. Luther also argued that Genesis 22:18 is the foundation of all of Scripture, containing the entire gospel in itself. Finally, Luther used the sacrifice of Isaac as a go-to example of allegory and typology: "We cannot resist taking histories and drawing out hidden interpretations from them, which Paul calls *mysteries*. To give a quick example. Isaac was sacrificed on the altar and yet remains alive, which means that Christ must die and rise again and be alive."[1] He constructed allegories out of this story according to the second article of the Creed.

To show Luther's use of the analogy of faith in Genesis 22, this chapter will focus on three issues: (1) how Abraham faces the temptation that God contradicts himself, (2) how Luther finds the crimson thread of the Bible in Genesis 22, and (3) how Luther allegorizes this passage. Abraham faces a temptation common to all: Is God a liar? First, God promised to make

---

[1] Sermons on Exodus 1 (1524), WA 16:68.11–15, quoting 1 Cor 14:2. See also RCS NT 9a:317.

Abraham a father of many nations; now he asks Abraham to sacrifice his only son. What sort of God is God? According to the catechism, God is a God who brings life out of death. For example, Luther shows how Genesis 22:18 succinctly and simply proclaims Jesus' birth, death, resurrection, and ascension. The catechism reveals the crimson thread of Christ running throughout the Bible. And that's why Luther finds certain sorts of allegories appropriate. Those allegories ruled by the faith help embellish—but do not establish—doctrine for the simple. Luther holds Abraham as a model for using the catechism to reason according to God's word.

How to Reason According to God's Word

Martin Luther presents the sacrifice of Isaac as a story of deep temptation. This temptation is suffered by all Christians—that God would contradict his promises. "He does at times test His own elect and appears as if He would act differently than He had before said. This happened to Abraham when he was commanded to sacrifice his son Isaac."[2] Thankfully "we have such a great crowd of witnesses around us" (Heb 12:1).[3] Luther teaches Abraham as a model for those in the midst of this temptation. Christians are to cling to God's promise—his first word.[4] "God plays with him like an apple, and yet [Abraham] stays still; he lets God do what he wants with him."[5] As the first table of the law teaches, we love and fear God by trusting his word and speaking and thinking well of him, no matter the circumstances.

How Abraham's fatherly heart must have ached! According to Luther's calculations, Abraham had waited twenty-five years until God fulfilled his promise to make Abraham a blessing to all the families of the earth (Gen 12:1-3).[6] And now that Isaac was entering manhood God commands Abraham to sacrifice this promised son?[7] "Abraham would have much rather perished with

---

[2]Gospel for the Second Day of Christmas (*Church Postil*, 1522, 1540), LW 75:249 (WA 10,1.1:130.18–20; E² 10:163).
[3]WADB 7:377.
[4]*In Genesin Declamationes* (1527), WA 24:391.15–16.
[5]*In Genesin Declamationes* (1527), WA 24:379.29–31.
[6]*Supputatio annorum mundi* (1541, 1545), WA 53:54, 55.
[7]Luther gives various ages for Isaac: twenty in the Lectures on Genesis 22:1–2 (1539; LW 4:91; WA 43:201.9) and the Genesis sermons (WA 14:299.14), twenty-five in the Lectures on Genesis

Sarah and all his goods."[8] "His heart had broken."[9] God had taken the most precious thing from Abraham.[10] Not only this, but Abraham himself has to kill his son and in a way that nothing will remain of him. And he has to wait three days. Perhaps worst of all: Isaac willingly bore the burden of wood, submitting to his father's will.[11] For Abraham, the laughter is gone; Isaac is already dead.[12]

Surely Abraham questioned the validity of God's word to him—even the validity of God's character! Is God capricious? "For God has commanded that we shall not murder, now he himself commands it—and Isaac's guilty of nothing!"[13] Moreover, the Lord God promised to make Abraham a father of many nations through this son.[14] "Here God becomes fickle and says the opposite: the son must now die. But why? What can reason say to this? It's totally beaten. It doesn't know a way out and must say, 'It's over now.'"[15] But Abraham does not respond according to reason. Shaped by trust in God's word and character, Abraham responds according to faith.[16] Rather than

---

22:6 (1539; LW 4:111; WA 43:215.7), and fifteen in the *Supputatio annorum mundi* (1541, 1545; WA 53:56). Nicholas of Lyra agrees with Josephus that Isaac was thirty-five (*Glossa ordinaria*, 1:266c; Josephus, *Antiquities of the Jews* 1.13). Sebastian Münster acknowledges disagreement about Isaac's age but settles on thirty (*Miqdaš YHWH*, 1:46). Luther seems to be swayed by Paul of Burgos's opinion on Isaac's age. Paul argues that Josephus is wrong about Isaac's age (forty-five—I'm not sure why this is different from what Nicholas cites), because the Bible does not call a man above the age of thirty a boy (v. 12), but also because this story is about Abraham's obedience not Isaac's (*Glossa ordinaria*, 1:270c–271d).

[8]Sermon on the Second Sunday of Advent (1523), WA 14:299.2. See also *In Genesin Declamationes* (1527), WA 24:381.10–11.

[9]Sermon on the Second Sunday of Advent (1523), WA 14:299.10.

[10]Sermon on the Second Sunday of Advent (1523), WA 14:298.16–17; *In Genesin Declamationes* (1527), WA 24:379.34–380.6.

[11]Sermon on the Second Sunday of Advent (1523), WA 14:299.2–9; *In Genesin Declamationes* (1527), WA 24:380.32–381.7, 22–25.

[12]*In Genesin Declamationes* (1527), WA 24:380.31–32, 382.11. Alcuin and Origen also emphasize how Abraham's heart must have ached, see *Glossa ordinaria*, 1:264, 264. (These are different columns, but because of a printing error they are numbered the same.)

[13]*In Genesin Declamationes* (1527), WA 24:382.14–15. Notice that Luther assumes the Ten Commandments here, even though this is before Moses. While Luther wouldn't likely be troubled by these sorts of modern chronological questions, he also says that all people know the Ten Commandments. They are the law of nature. "In nature all these commands are taught." Sermons on Exodus 20 (1525), WA 16:512.25–26.

[14]*In Genesin Declamationes* (1527), WA 24:382.15–17.

[15]*In Genesin Declamationes* (1527), WA 24:382.18–21.

[16]For Luther it would be fitting to say that Abraham's heart and mind have been shaped by the first table of the law. All people know these Ten Commandments, for they are the law of nature (Sermons on Exodus 20 [1525], WA 16:512.25–26). Luther ties knowledge of the law to the soul, jesting that "We would have to preach to a donkey, horse, ox, or bull for one hundred thousand years, before they get the law! Although they have ears, eyes, and a heart like humans

think that God is untrustworthy, Abraham chooses to believe what human reason cannot: the resurrection of the dead. "God is almighty and truthful. My son is already gone—I must let him go. But God still has such great power that if I and all the world were dead, he could raise him again—even over a hundred years later—and make him a father."[17]

God does not change. Therefore he wants his people to cling fiercely to his first word—always a word of promise—and let him interpret all second words.[18] God has a habit of testing his people's dependence and trust on him. Luther cites a strange passage from 1 Kings 13 as an example. God commands a prophet of Judah to eat no food and drink no drink at Bethel and to return home by a different way. An old prophet of Bethel comes and fetches the prophet, contradicting this earlier command because he spoke with an angel. The prophet of Judah obliges, but at table the old prophet proclaims that the prophet of Judah has disobeyed the word of the Lord and will die.[19] Just because someone says "God said it" or invokes some authority or even performs some sign or miracle does not mean you should obey. Everything must be tested against the word and promise of God. While the prophet of Judah may have wondered if God had tricked him, God would have rebuked him, "You should have trusted me over this man."[20]

Abraham does just that. He clasps God's promise to him so tightly that he overcomes his own feelings and confusion. "What an astonishingly great thing, that he could conquer his heart."[21] Even though their hearts doubt, Christians must hold firm to God's word and defeat God with his own word, just like Abraham. "Here God contradicts himself. That's a riddle that no one but the Holy Spirit can solve."[22] So leave it to God by his word and Spirit.

---

do—although they can listen, it doesn't penetrate their heart" (WA 16:447.29–31). See WA 16:447.27–39, 448.7–20.

[17] *In Genesin Declamationes* (1527), WA 24:382.25–28. See also Lectures on Genesis 22:1–2 (1539), LW 4:96 (WA 43:204.10–29).

[18] *In Genesin Declamationes* (1527), WA 24:383.20–25, 384.15–16, 384.30–385.15, 386.28–31. Luther cites Malachi 3:6 and Deuteronomy 13:1–3. For promise preceding law, see Sermon on the Third Sunday of Advent (1523), WA 14:304.2–9; *In Genesin Declamationes* (1527), WA 24:394.10–16.

[19] *In Genesin Declamationes* (1527), WA 24:385.16–30.

[20] *In Genesin Declamationes* (1527), WA 24:385.31–386.15, here 385.32–33. See also Sermon on the Second Sunday of Advent (1523), WA 14:300.14–19. Luther also gives the example of death-bed doubt, what if Jesus is not mine? See WA 24:382.33–383.23.

[21] *In Genesin Declamationes* (1527), WA 24:382.11–12.

[22] *In Genesin Declamationes* (1527), WA 24:382.12–14.

"Your heart says: 'Yes, but isn't this God's word too?' You answer: 'He will interpret it and do it as he means.' In this way, we must overcome him with his own word."[23] And let no one—not even God himself!—tear God's precious word from your heart. "Even if Moses or an angel or even Christ himself should come, nevertheless I'll hold to God's word, for it cannot lie."[24]

Sadly some Israelites mistook Abraham's example of faith as an example of works. Wanting to do something great for God so that they might be blessed, some people sacrificed their children to Molech.[25] (Luther seems to assume that the Israelites thought Molech to be a figure of the Lord God, just like the golden calf.) According to human reason, this seems far more glorious than what God has commanded for worship in his word. "Hey, if I'm to sacrifice something for our Lord God, I want to sacrifice something costly for him. What's it cost me to sacrifice a calf for him? I'll sacrifice my own son for him!"[26] Yes, it costs something to sacrifice a ram or sheep, but to sacrifice one's own child—that shows commitment.[27] According to Luther's historical sources, it surely would have required resolve: the temple of Molech was filled with the clang of bells and cymbals and the blast of horns to muffle the screams of children as their parents placed them on glowing coals in the metallic hands of a god made by human hands.[28] Some false prophets even preached this as a work pleasing to God; true prophets called it what it was: murder.[29]

The first table of the law teaches that God's people are to emulate the faith of the saints. (While the works of the saints are an example to the people of God, they are to be tested against the analogy of faith).[30] God had not sanctioned such offerings with his word. And that is the difference

---

[23] *In Genesin Declamationes* (1527), WA 24:386.21-23.
[24] *In Genesin Declamationes* (1527), WA 24:386.19-21; evoking Gal 1:8. See also WA 24:384.30-385.15; Sermon on the Second Sunday of Advent (1523), WA 14:300.20-23.
[25] Sermon on the Second Sunday of Advent (1523), WA 14:301.8-22; *In Genesin Declamationes* (1527), WA 24:387.18-388.11.
[26] WATR 6:58.32-34.
[27] WATR 6:57.22-30, no. 6586.
[28] WATR 6:58.19-29, no. 6586. Luther says that Nicholas is his source, see *Glossa ordinaria*, 1:1062; see also Münster, *Miqdaš YHWH*, 1:235.
[29] Sermon on the Second Sunday of Advent (1523), WA 14:301.12-13. Luther compares placing a child in a monastery to sacrificing him to Molech. Sermon on the Second Sunday in Advent (1523), WA 14:302.5-7; WATR 6:58.1-11, no. 6586; see also the marginalia on Leviticus 18:21, WADB 8:389.
[30] Sermon on Second Sunday of Advent (1523), WA 14:301.21-22; *In Genesin Declamationes* (1527), WA 24:389.11-390.2.

between Abraham's sacrifice of Isaac and these later Israelites. Abraham listened to God's word, which pleased the Lord; those like King Manasseh had no word from God (2 Kings 21:6).[31] And so Abraham obeyed the second commandment while these others did not. Luther points out that the human desire to follow the works of the saints persists. For example, some of Luther's contemporaries claimed that because Solomon was blessed for building a temple, anyone who finances a church will also be blessed.[32] "Not so! But if you're Solomon, then go ahead and build one. He had God's word for it; you have nothing and instead want to master God."[33] "Where his word is, there everything smells sumptuous."[34] Abraham models for us how to reason according to God's word.

The Promised Seed and the Second Article

Luther claims that the sacrifice of Isaac is also a story of great joy. Humans are justified by faith alone and not our own actions, because God will come in human form so that humans might be blessed.[35] These few words unlock this joyous news: "And through your Seed all the peoples of the earth will be blessed" (Gen 22:18).[36] Here is all of Christ's kingdom, all of his gospel, and all of Scripture.[37] "Even if we had no other word than this single passage, it would be enough."[38] Abraham and the prophets understood this passage's central importance. "And so all of Scripture is ordered according to it, so that it always pushes this verse. It's also the chief verse in all of Moses. It pertains to everything—what's before and after it."[39]

---

[31]Sermon on the Second Sunday of Advent (1523), WA 14:301.14–21; *In Genesin Declamationes* (1527), WA 24:388.12–27; marginalia on Leviticus 18:21, WADB 8:389.

[32]Sermon on the Second Sunday of Advent (1523), WA 14:301. 22–302.3; *In Genesin Declamationes* (1527), WA 24:388.28–389.10.

[33]*In Genesin Declamationes* (1527), WA 24:388.32–389.8. See also Sermons on Exodus 20 (1525), WA 16:437.13–439.15.

[34]Sermon on the Second Sunday of Advent (1523), WA 14:301.20.

[35]Lectures on Genesis 22:17–18 (1539), LW 4:170–71 (WA 43:258.41–259.21). Throughout his lectures on Genesis 22, Luther targets Papists and *Schwärmer* because, in his opinion, they divide word and Spirit and require human works.

[36]WADB 8:97.

[37]Sermon on the Third Sunday of Advent (1523), WA 14: 302.18–303.1, 306.12; *In Genesin Declamationes* (1527), WA 24:391.3–10, 394.31–33, 396.5–8.

[38]Sermon on the Third Sunday of Advent (1527), WA 14:302.201–21.

[39]*In Genesin Declamationes* (1527), WA 24:394.31–33. See also Sermon on the Third Sunday of Advent (1523), WA 14:306.12.

Luther argues that this single verse contains Christ's virgin birth, his death, resurrection, and ascension.[40] "Therefore, you have in this word the entire gospel."[41] The prophets based clearer prophecies about the Messiah—like Isaiah 7:14 and 2 Samuel 7:12—on this verse.[42] "These words are the subject matter and the gushing fountain, as it were, of many of the prophecies and addresses of Isaiah, David, and Paul."[43] The promise is mysterious, how can all the nations of the earth be blessed in this Seed? Everyone born of man and woman is cursed, and so those who claim the Seed's blessing as carnal are wrong.[44] To bring blessing, this promised Seed must not be cursed—in particular the Seed had to be divine. To share this blessing with humans, this promised Seed had to be human.[45] "The mother must not be pregnant by a man and yet she must be truly pregnant, so that she is called a true, natural mother and so that the child is her flesh and blood. So there's no other way than that without any unchastity the Seed be conceived by the Holy Spirit. Thus, it follows that the mother is a virgin and the child's mother truly

---

[40] Somewhat surprisingly Luther does not mention Christ's descent to hell here—although he seems to suggest it in Lectures on Genesis 22:17-18 (1539), LW 4:175; WA 43:262.11-17. While the *Glossa ordinaria* only makes allegorical connections to Christ's death and resurrection in Genesis 22, it makes a textual connection to Christ's descent. The interlinear gloss of "your seed will possess his enemies' gates" (v. 17) is "because Christ will descend to hell to plunder it." *Glossa ordinaria*, 1:268. For Luther on the descent, see A Sermon on Jesus Christ, Preached at Court in Torgau (1533), LW 57:127-38 (WA 37:62.22-72.11); A House Sermon on the Articles of the Creed (1537), WA 45:20.2-8 (LW 57:249). On the descent clause, see Matthew Y. Emerson, "He Descended to the Dead": An Evangelical Theology of Holy Saturday (Downers Grove, IL: IVP Academic, 2019); Joseph Ratzinger, *Introduction to Christianity*, rev. ed., trans. J R. Foster (San Francisco: Ignatius, 2004), 293–301.

[41] Sermon on the Third Sunday of Advent (1523), WA 14:306.8.

[42] Sermon on the Third Sunday of Advent (1523), WA 14:305.15–18; *In Genesin Declamationes* (1527), WA 24:396.24-29; Lectures on Genesis 22:17-18 (1539), LW 4:161 (WA 43:252.4-7). Luther sees 2 Samuel 7:12 as a prophecy of Christ's virgin birth, because the text says "son of your womb" (of the woman) rather than "son of the land" (of the man); see also WAB 9:317. See further "Preface to the New Testament" (1546), LW 35:359-60 (WADB 6:5.24-9.2).

[43] Lectures on Genesis 22:17-18 (1539), LW 4:151–52 (WA 43:245.10–11).

[44] On original sin, *In Genesin Declamationes* (1527), WA 24:391.19-27. On not a carnal blessing, Sermon on the Third Sunday of Advent (1523), WA 14:303.1, 306.8-9; Lectures on Genesis 22:17-18 (1539), LW 4:152-58 (WA 43:246.4-50.14). For the grammatical grounding of this point, Luther relies on Paul of Burgos's extended discussion of Hebrew grammar (*Glossa ordinaria*, 1:272–73). Nicholas also addresses this (*Glossa ordinaria*, 1:269); Münster indirectly rebukes rabbinic interpretations with an extended doxology of Jesus' name (*Miqdaš YHWH*, 1:46).

[45] See Sermon on the Third Sunday of Advent (1523), WA 14:305.11-306.8; *In Genesin Declamationes* (1527), WA 24:396.8-33.

and naturally."⁴⁶ Because the Seed is born without the curse brought by Adam and Eve, he is also free of sin and death.⁴⁷ The Seed is true God and true man.⁴⁸

All born of woman die. And so this Seed will be no exception; he too must die. But then how will he bless all people? As Abraham (and Isaac) believed, "God can indeed also raise him from the dead" (Heb 11:19).⁴⁹ Luther is baffled that Moses left out the dialogue between Abraham and Isaac about the resurrection of the dead before Abraham places Isaac on the altar. And so he improvises this dialogue.⁵⁰ Abraham and Isaac reconcile the promise of future blessing through Isaac and the demand to sacrifice Isaac according to faith: God will keep his promise even if Isaac is dead and gone.⁵¹ But Isaac only dies in his father's heart, and he is brought back to life in his father's heart when God provides a ram in Isaac's place. His apparent death and resurrection point to Jesus' death and resurrection. Jesus of Nazareth is the promised Seed—not Isaac or Jacob or some other holy man, although Jesus comes from their bloodline.⁵² No mere mortal can bless as this Seed blesses: "He brings the blessing; he conquers death along with sin and hell."⁵³ The promised Seed must rise from the dead.

---

⁴⁶*In Genesin Declamationes* (1527), WA 24:396.18–23. See also Lectures on Genesis 22:17–18 (1539), LW 4:160–61 (WA 43:251.36–252.3).

⁴⁷*In Genesin Declamationes* (1527), WA 24:396.31–32.

⁴⁸Luther draws out the Chalcedonian formula in new ways without resorting to its language. See Sermon on the Third Sunday of Advent (December 13, 1523), WA 14:305.20–306.7; *In Genesin Declamationes* (1527), WA 24:397.18–30; Lectures on Genesis 22:17–18 (1539), LW 4:160, 172 (WA 43:251.21–35, 259.25–32).

⁴⁹WADB 7:373. See *In Genesin Declamationes* (1527), WA 24:382.22–31; Lectures on Genesis 22:1–2 (1539), LW 4:96 (WA 43:204.10–19).

⁵⁰Lectures on Genesis 22:9 (1539), LW 4:112–13 (WA 43:216.15–31). Luther seems to christianize Josephus' version of the dialogue between Abraham and Isaac. According to Josephus, Abraham tells Isaac how he prayed for him, that the Lord must have found Isaac too good for this world, and that the Lord sought to spare Isaac from a brutal worldly death. Isaac willingly submitted. See Nicholas's comments on Genesis 22:9, *Glossa ordinaria*, 1:266–67; compare with Josephus, *Antiquities of the Jews*, 1.13. According to Louis Ginzberg, rabbis taught that Isaac's spirit actually left his body and returned. See Louis Ginzberg, *The Legends of the Jews*, 2 vols., trans. Henrietta Szold and Paul Radin, 2nd ed. (Philadelphia: The Jewish Publication Society, 2003), 1:225–31, here 229–30. Neither the *Glossa ordinaria* nor Münster mention this.

⁵¹Lectures on Genesis 22:9 (1539), LW 4:113 (WA 43:216.32–41). Luther believed that Abraham had taught Isaac about the resurrection of the dead and that except for Christ Isaac is the greatest example of obedience (LW 4:114; WA 43:217.22–36).

⁵²Sermon on the Third Sunday of Advent (1523), WA 14:305.1–8; *In Genesin Declamationes* (1527), WA 24:395.14–396.3.

⁵³*In Genesin Declamationes* (1527), WA 24:395.27–28.

Luther observes that a human body can only be in one place.[54] So a human king can only bless those in his immediate vicinity, where he holds court. If the Seed were an earthly king, he would be no different. But then how can he bless all people? He must rule in such a way that he is personally present with every person everywhere. He will reign in the human heart![55] "Therefore, he must rise again from the dead, ascend to heaven, and sit in the place, where he can see, fill, and hold in his hand all creatures—he receives power over all things, angels, and devils."[56] Christ descended deeper than any human can or has, and he ascended higher than any human can. He did this to redeem and gather all things to himself. The ascended Christ reigns and is present everywhere. He keeps sin, death, and hell bound and distributes gifts to his people.[57] For the promised Seed to bless all people, he had to ascend to heaven.[58]

With the help of the second article of the Apostles' Creed, Luther sorts out what Genesis 22:18 is all about: the birth, death, resurrection, and ascension of Jesus Christ. Grammar, history, and literary context alone do not reveal the meaning of this passage. Still Luther uses these tools as handmaidens of interpretation. In this passage, he especially uses Hebrew grammar, although more so to refute others' interpretations than to open up the passage's meaning. "Who could sum all this up with so few words, if the Holy Spirit himself is not speaking?"[59]

---

[54] Luther maintained three types of presence: local (like wine in a cask), definitive (or uncircumscribed like a spirit in a place or person), and repletive (supernatural like God's presence). Luther argued that while humans are only present in the local sense, Jesus, who is God and man, is present in all three modes. See *Confession concerning Christ's Supper* (1528), LW 37:210-19 (WA 26:321.19-333.25). The *Formula of Concord* affirmed this view in articles 7-8 on the Lord's Supper and the person of Christ. On the communication of attributes, see also *On the Councils and the Church* (1539), LW 41:95-119 (WA 50:582.15-604.9); *Disputation on the Divinity and Humanity of Christ* (1540), LW 73:254-80 (WA 39,2:92-121); Richard Cross, "Luther's Christology and the *Communicatio Idiomatum*," in *The Medieval Luther*, ed. Christine Helmer (Tübingen: Mohr Siebeck, 2019), 27-46. In the Genesis sermons of 1527 Luther uses an example that he later used in his debate with Zwingli on the Lord's Supper: even though an member of a person's body is hurt, we rightly say that the person is hurt (WA 24:399.10-20; compare with LW 37:211; WA 26:321.28-323.12).

[55] *In Genesin Declamationes* (1527), WA 24:397.12-14.

[56] *In Genesin Declamationes* (1527), WA 24:397.14-17.

[57] Sermon on the Feast of the Ascension (May 31, 1527), WA 23:703.4-705.13.

[58] See WATR 1:111-12, no. 267 (Beth Kreitzer, ed., *Luke*, RCS NT 3 [Downers Grove, IL: IVP Academic, 2015], 499); Sermon WA 49:418.35-422.13 (RCS NT 6:10-11).

[59] *In Genesin Declamationes* (1527), WA 24:397.31-32. Luther suggests these words be placed in golden letters because of their importance (WA 24:398.7).

Ruled Allegory

In his third and final sermon on Genesis 22, Luther focuses on drawing out the mystery of the sacrifice of Isaac, which Luther recognizes as Jesus' death and resurrection and the resurrection of the dead.[60] Of course, Luther has already touched on these theological truths, but now he frees himself to allegorize the text.

It's true that Luther worried that allegories could be fully unmoored from the text, steered by nothing more than the individual human interpreter's ideas, opinions, and feelings. That's the concern he's addressing with his harsh words against allegorizing.[61] But he did not object to allegory as a method. Any allegory is acceptable, if it fits the analogy of faith. Luther moored all biblical methods and resources to the quay of the Ten Commandments, the Apostles' Creed, and the Our Father.

Luther distinguished allegories that helped hearers understand (rhetoric) from allegories that constructed doctrine (misapplied dialectic). He rejected using allegory to build doctrine—even if the allegories were according to the analogy of faith. Allegory is only fit for rhetoric. "And if the words don't do it, still the story does—it's indicated from the words. Whoever wants to seek allegory in Scripture should strive for this: that everything refers to Christ."[62] Allegorizing according to Christ allows Luther to go back and underscore how the text presents Christ.[63]

Luther presents Isaac as an excellent type of Christ. Bound and ready for slaughter, Isaac is already dead in his father's heart and his own understanding. Abraham has every intention of killing his son; Isaac has every intention of dying. But Isaac lives, and a ram dies in his stead.[64] "So it is with Christ! He sure seems to die, but he doesn't really, instead a ram—that is, his human body—dies. So Isaac is a figure of Christ's divinity; the ram,

---

[60]Sermon on the Fourth Sunday of Advent (1523), WA 14:306.17–311.18; *In Genesin Declamationes* (1527), WA 24:398.23–404.16.

[61]For example, "An allegory is like a beautiful harlot who fondles men in such a way that it is impossible for her not to be loved, especially by idle men who are free from trial" and "I hate allegories" (Genesis lectures, LW 5:347; WA 43:668).

[62]Sermon on the Fourth Sunday of Advent (1523), WA 14:306.19–21. See also *In Genesin Declamationes* (1527), WA 24:398.23–31.

[63]Allegory is rhetoric for Luther, not dialectic. See further Ocker, *Biblical Poetics*.

[64]Sermon on the Fourth Sunday of Advent (1523), WA 14:307.7–10; *In Genesin Declamationes* (1527), WA 24:398.21–32.

his humanity."⁶⁵ Luther is clear that he is not talking about two Christs. "The Seed of Abraham is Christ—true God and true man."⁶⁶ As the church teaches, Jesus' two natures are united in his person without confusion, without change, without division, and without separation.⁶⁷ Luther is proclaiming the content of the Chalcedonian formula without explicitly using its verbiage. "We attribute all works to the entire person, even if only the body acts or suffers; for the two are united and made one. Although the man Christ has done and suffered everything, nevertheless because he is one person with the Godhead, we also say, 'God has suffered, died, and risen again.' "⁶⁸ God does not change, and so according to his divinity Jesus does not suffer, die, and rise again. All these things are done according to his humanity, but without dividing his personal integrity.⁶⁹

The resurrection of the dead is also wonderfully depicted here.⁷⁰ Again Luther builds on his earlier work. He has already established that Abraham holds two words from God together: he will be a father of many, and he must sacrifice his only son. They cannot both be true according to reason.⁷¹ And yet he believed. "Abraham understood the doctrine of the resurrection

---

⁶⁵Sermon on the Fourth Sunday of Advent (1523), WA 14:307.10-12. See also *In Genesin Declamationes* (1527), WA 24:399.21-32. Luther agrees with Nicholas of Lyra and Paul of Burgos (who quotes Origen) about this allegorical type, see *Glossa ordinaria*, 1:266-67, 271-72. Surprisingly Luther does not connect Isaac bearing the wood for his sacrifice with Jesus bearing his own cross.

⁶⁶Sermon on the Fourth Sunday of Advent (1523), WA 14:306.36. See also *In Genesin Declamationes* (1527), WA 24:398.33-34.

⁶⁷See "The Chalcedonian Definition of the Faith," in *Creeds, Councils and Controversies: Documents Illustrating the History of the Church, AD 337-461*, ed. J. Stevenson and W. H. C. Frend (London, SPCK, 1989), 353.

⁶⁸*In Genesin Declamationes* (1527), WA 24:399.15-19. Luther exemplifies the personal unity with a wound: if a person hurts their head, we say the person is hurt (not just their head). See WA 24:399.11-14; See also Sermon on the Fourth Sunday of Advent (1523), WA 14:307.3-5. While the phrase "der mensch Christus" is awkward, Luther is not dividing the natures and assigning actions to the nature rather than the person—his overarching point here is that Christ is one person. It seems he intentionally avoided the technical *secundum quid* qualifiers here—perhaps on account of audience.

⁶⁹*In Genesin Declamationes* (1527), WA 24:399.21-32. Some twentieth-century scholars argued that Luther indeed taught that Jesus suffered according to his divinity. They are contradicting Luther's explicit testimony and Chalcedonian faithfulness, see David J. Luy, *Dominus Mortis: Martin Luther on the Incorruptibility of God in Christ* (Minneapolis: Fortress, 2014). For an example of Luther's response to whether Christ suffered according to his divine nature, see WATR 6:67-70, no. 6600.

⁷⁰Sermon on the Fourth Sunday of Advent (1523), WA 14:307.12-308.5; *In Genesin Declamationes* (1527), WA 24:399.33-401.8.

⁷¹On the question of double truth and Luther, see Gerrish, *Grace and Reason*, 49-54.

of the dead."⁷² Now Luther points this to Christ. Just as Isaac seemed to die but lived, so also with Christ. "Thus in this figure the entire kingdom of Christ is summed up, for where the resurrection of the dead is, there is everything that concerns Christ's kingdom."⁷³ Still the apostles, unlike Abraham and Isaac, struggled to believe; they expected a king and kingdom of earthly glory. But a kingdom of earthly glory requires no faith. Christ's kingdom is a kingdom of faith. He reigns on earth in our hearts, giving every good gift.

The ram, donkey and servants, and Mount Moriah can fruitfully be allegorized about the preaching office (one of Luther's four sacraments).⁷⁴ The ram sacrificed in Isaac's stead is tangled in thorns, not roses and dianthuses. And this is the plight of preachers. They do not have an easy life: they are not respected by the world, but they faithfully combat the world's wisdom and piety.⁷⁵ Ministers of the word engage the godless (that is, the thorns) with their God-given office (that is, their horns), for human glory and power cannot be defeated with human glory and power but only with God's power, the gospel (Rom 1:16).⁷⁶ "As the ram butts with its horns, so also the preaching of the gospel buffets whatever is great—it can't suffer those who trust their smarts and piety."⁷⁷ Unsurprisingly these confrontations come at a price. Ministers of the word will be martyred like Christ and his apostles, because the horns of the gospel cannot give way.⁷⁸

Luther allegorizes the donkey and servants to show how the preaching office must distinguish between law and gospel.⁷⁹ The donkey is our flesh and blood; the servants are teachers of the law; Isaac is our conscience; Abraham

---

[72] Lectures on Genesis 22:1–2 (1539), LW 4:96 (WA 43:204.23).
[73] Sermon on the Fourth Sunday of Advent (1523), WA 14:308.4–5. See also *In Genesin Declamationes* (1527), WA 24:401.6–7.
[74] See chapter 3, "The Sacraments: 'The Ceremonies of Ceremonies.'"
[75] Sermon on the Fourth Sunday of Advent (1523), WA 14:308.5–10; *In Genesin Declamationes* (1527), WA 24:40.9–13.
[76] Sermon on the Fourth Sunday of Advent (1523), WA 14:308.10–16; *In Genesin Declamationes* (1527), WA 24:13–22. Luther generally understands horns as symbols of an office's power, see, for example, Luther's comments on Psalm 22:21b, Gloss on Psalm 22:21 (1513–1515), WA 3:137.39–40 (RCS OT 7:181n38).
[77] *In Genesin Declamationes* (1527), WA 24:401.14–16.
[78] Sermon on the Fourth Sunday of Advent (1523), WA 14:308.15–18; *In Genesin Declamationes* (1527), WA 24:401.17–28.
[79] Sermon on the Fourth Sunday of Advent (1523), WA 14:308.18–309.14.

is our faith.⁸⁰ Isaac is led only by his father, while the donkey and servants are left behind.⁸¹ In the same way our hearts and consciences are led by faith; our external works are not demanded. "With the gospel we do not lead our mouth or feet to God, but our heart. We can't keep it in our ears or in our mouth or on our tongue—no, it must live in our heart!"⁸² The gospel applies to human hearts and consciences; the law applies to human bodies and actions. To confuse this is to compromise the power of the gospel and the purpose of the law. Our bodies remain filled with sin during this life. The law helps us direct an honest life and restrain the old Adam. Our heart and soul must rest in the freedom that the Lord God is our Master. And so the gospel purifies and recreates our heart and conscience.⁸³ The preacher must attend to the whole person—both the old self and the new self. He must, therefore, apply law *and* gospel; he must handle the internal and external life.⁸⁴

Moriah is the church of God, the place where God's word is preached.⁸⁵ Humans do not choose where and how God will be worshiped; God does.

---

⁸⁰Sermon on the Fourth Sunday of Advent (1523), WA 14:308:22–309.1; *In Genesin Declamationes* (1527), WA 24:402.2–13. Luther only implies Isaac to be our conscience and Abraham to be our faith. In his sermon he contrasts this allegory with one not found in the *Glossa ordinaria*: the donkey and servants—our fleshly thoughts—must be left behind during worship, so that we might do good works. See Sermon on the Fourth Sunday of Advent (1523), WA 14:308.19–21; *In Genesin Declamationes* (1527), WA 24:401.29–402.7. Nicholas reports the rabbinic teaching that the two servants are Ishmael and Eliezer and allegorizes them as the law and prophets as well as Peter and John. See *Glossa ordinaria*, 1:264; compare with Lectures on Genesis 22:3 (1539), LW 4:108 (WA 43:213.10–12); *In Genesin Declamationes* (1527), WA 24:403.4–6.

⁸¹Sermon on the Fourth Sunday of Advent (1523), WA 14:309.9–12.

⁸²*In Genesin Declamationes* (1527), WA 24:402.13–15. See also Sermon on the Fourth Sunday of Advent (1523), WA 14:309.2–3.

⁸³*In Genesin Declamationes* (1527), WA 24:402.21–403.4.

⁸⁴In Genesin Declamationes (1527), WA 24:403.6–8.

⁸⁵Sermon on the Fourth Sunday of Advent (1523), WA 14:309.17–310.9; *In Genesin Declamationes* (1527), WA 24:403.9–404.11. In his lectures Luther allegorizes Moriah as the word of God and faith, because the word, faith in the word, and suffering on account of the word go together. See Lectures on Genesis 22:1–2 (1539), LW 4:101 (WA 43:208.18–23). Over his entire career, Luther was interested in the etymology of Moriah. He changed his mind about its etymology between his Genesis sermons and his Genesis lectures. In 1523 he teaches what the text implies (Gen 22:2, 14): Moriah means "the Lord's face" or "the Lord sees"; see Sermon on the Fourth Sunday of Advent (1523), WA 14:309.17–18; *In Genesin Declamationes* (1527), WA 24:403.15–17. In 1539 he teaches that the Vulgate's translation of Moriah ("vision," *visionis*) was universally rejected; see Lectures on Genesis 22:1–2 (1539), LW 4:99 (WA 43:206.25–27). See also his marginalia on Genesis 22:2, WADB 8:94–95. Paul of Burgos commended leaving the word untranslated to allow for several meanings at once: myrrh, instruction, and fear. (Paul also allowed for rendering it as *Maria*—a suggestion later editors squelched.) See *Glossa ordinaria*, 1:270, 273. Luther allows

If humans made these decisions, our mind and heart would define worship, and nothing would be certain. But worship retrains our heart and conscience in faith. "And so the word will strike down everything that isn't from God's word and from faith."[86] God's word is certain.

Conclusion

Luther interpreted the Torah according to the analogy of faith. According to reason these books are a jumble of stories and random laws, but according to faith these books teach faith and its fruits.[87] In the narrative of the sacrifice of Isaac, Abraham is an example of a person shaped by the analogy of faith. He honors and obeys God's word, even when it seems absurd and repugnant. Abraham was willing to sacrifice his only son because of God's promise: "And through your Seed all the peoples of the earth will be blessed" (Gen 22:18).[88] Here Moses crystallizes two things that the Torah teaches. First, God's word is all about Christ. "If you would interpret well and confidently, set Christ before you, for he is the man to whom it all applies, every bit of it."[89] And, second, God's word alone is to be obeyed. "He cannot and will not permit those who are his to undertake anything that he has not commanded, no matter how good it may be. For obedience, which depends

---

for Paul's three options: myrrh was plausible grammatically (although too focused on external forms of worship), instruction was fitting grammatically and theologically (although quite subtle linguistically), and fear was the most fitting. See LW 4:99–101 (WA 43:206.15–208.17). Münster rejects the Vulgate's translation as impossible on account of spelling. He considers two possible translations: myrrh and fear (and thus a place to worship). See Münster, *Miqdaš YHWH*, 1:46. The *Glossa ordinaria*, Luther, and Münster all mention that Solomon built the temple at Moriah (2 Chron 3:1), which made good sense on account of Moriah's long history as a place of worship (going back to Cain and Abel). Contemporary biblical scholars continue to debate whether Moriah is formed from ראה ("to see"), ירא ("to fear"), or ירה ("to teach"). See Victor P. Hamilton, *The Book of Genesis: Chapters 18–50*, New International Commentary on the Old Testament (Grand Rapids: Eerdmans, 1995), 102–3; Nahum M. Sarna, *Genesis*, The JPS Torah Commentary (Philadelphia: The Jewish Publication Society, 1989), 391–92. They also disagree whether the sacrifice happened at Moriah; some believe Moriah to be a later ideological insertion. See Gerhard von Rad, *Genesis: A Commentary*, rev. ed., trans. John H. Marks (Philadelphia: The Westminster Press, 1972), 240; Claus Westermann, *Genesis 12–36: A Contintental Commentary*, trans. John J. Scullion (Minneapolis: Fortress, 1995), 357; compare with Hamilton, *The Book of Genesis*, 102.

[86]*In Genesin Declamationes* (1527), WA 24:404.3–4. See also Sermon on the Fourth Sunday of Advent (1523), WA 14:310.6–7; marginalia on Isaiah 2:2, WADB 11,1:31.

[87]"Preface to the Old Testament" (1523; 1545), LW 35:237–39 (WADB 8:13.23–15.37).

[88]WADB 8:97.

[89]"Preface to the Old Testament (1523; 1545), LW 35:247; WADB 8:29.32–33.

on God's word, is of all works noblest and best."[90] No matter how well intentioned, humans cannot choose and create commands to please God. They must seek God where he has chosen to be found: in his word. And so Luther focused his interpretation of Moses' books, like his interpretation of all the Bible, on the second article of the Creed and the first commandment. Luther insists that the New Testament is only the Old Testament preached.[91] There's no difference in substance. "Even if Moses or an angel or even Christ himself should come, nevertheless I'll hold to God's word, for it cannot lie."[92]

---

[90]"Preface to the Old Testament (1523; 1545), LW 35:239; WADB 8:17.18-21.
[91]"Preface to the Old Testament" (1523; 1545), LW 35:235-51 (WADB 8:10-32), esp. pp. 235-36 (p. 11.13-21). See also "Preface to the New Testament" (1522; 1546), LW 35:357-62 (WADB 6:2-11); Gospel for Epiphany (*Church Postil*, 1544), LW 76:111-12 (WA 10,1.1:625.12-626.23; E² 10:387-88; compare with LW 52:205-6). The entire Bible flows from the fount of Moses—the historical books, Wisdom books, and Prophets are Moses preached. See "Preface to the Old Testament" (1523; 1545), LW 35:246-47 (WADB 8:29.13-31). Luther does a quick run through of key verses in "Preface to the New Testament" (1522; 1546), LW 35:359-60 (WADB 6:5.24-7.21). See further chapter 8, "The Word Illumines the Word."
[92]*In Genesin Declamationes* (1527), WA 24:386.19-21; evoking Gal 1:8.

5

The Spoils of Death's Death

Reading the Historical Books According to the Rule of Faith

LUTHER DID NOT PREACH or teach on the Historical Books very often. He only preached one sermon on a passage from the Historical Books: Judges 14:14 during Easter week of 1516. And he held an early, incomplete lecture series on Judges (1516–1518). Even then he read the Bible according to the analogy of faith. He saw Samson as a type of Christ.[1] Luther turned to an ancient church metaphor—the baited Leviathan—to draw out this typology. And he listened to what Scripture says about Scripture, allowing Hebrews 2:14 and 1 Samuel 2:6 to clarify Samson's riddle. Luther interpreted Judges 14:14 according to the second article of the Apostles' Creed.[2]

Because Luther treated the Historical Books on their own so rarely, this chapter will be different from the other chapters. First, we will focus on Luther's use of the analogy of faith in Judges 14:14. Luther uses the second article to find Christ's history in this riddle. Second, we will examine a preface Luther wrote for a commentary on 1 Samuel. Despite so little focused work on the Historical Books, Luther prescribes how they should be read: according to the analogy of faith.

---

[1] In Genesis 49:16-18, Jacob prophesies about Samson, who was such a powerful figure that Jacob had to add a warning that Samson is not the Christ but only a type of Christ (v. 18). See Lectures on Genesis 49:16-18 (1545), LW 8:280-87; WA 44:785.1-790.3; marginalia on Genesis 49:16, WADB 8:195.
[2] Elsewhere Luther also describes the characters in Judges as fitting examples of the first commandment, WATR 1:209.15-20, no. 475.

The Riddle of the Resurrection

Judges 14:14 is an unusual text for Easter. "Food came out of the eater, and sweetness out of the strong."[3] The riddle's answer seems to arise from the overall shape of the narrative—just a few verses earlier Samson has scooped honey out of the lion he struck down. But Luther does not share this detail, instead he drills deeper.[4] "It's full of wonder and contradiction."[5] It does not make sense for food to come out of the eater, unless it is vomit. But that's not really food; it has no nourishment. "We would die, if we had to eat like that!"[6] This whole riddle seems backward, as if heat came from cold or cold from heat! "Who has ever been warmed by snow or ice? Who has sat by a fire and ever felt cold emitting from it? In the same way, who has sucked out honey and oil from the very hardest rock? Who has drawn out water from the rock? Who has brought forth water by the jawbone of a donkey? But this is what we read in the Scriptures."[7] In this way it is unusual in the same way that Easter is: it is upside down from human expectations and experience.[8]

Human expectations and experience are confounded by the mystery of the second article.[9] Indeed the second article baffles even the devil. Luther

---

[3] WADB 9,1:139.
[4] The Weimar editors assume that monks were the audience of this sermon and Luther's lectures on Judges. Perhaps his fellow monks were familiar with the fuller context of Judges 14, but one wonders about the common Wittenberg faithful.
[5] Sermon on the Character of Christ's Resurrection (March 1516), WA 1:58.19.
[6] Sermon on the Character of Christ's Resurrection (March 1516), WA 1:58.24. Some modern biblical scholars argue that Samson adapted this riddle from one about vomit and semen to confuse his opponents. See James L. Crenshaw, "Riddles," in *The Anchor Bible Dictionary*, 6 vols., ed. David Noel Freedman (New York: Doubleday, 1992), 5:722; James L. Crenshaw, *Samson: A Secret Betrayed, A Vow Ignored* (Atlanta: John Knox Press, 1978), 112–18. See also Susan Niditch, *Judges: A Commentary*, Old Testament Library (Louisville: Westminster John Knox, 2008), 156–57. Still most modern commentators say little about this verse, simply taking it at face value. See Daniel I. Block, *Judges, Ruth*, New American Commentary 6 (Nashville: B&H, 1999), 432–33; Barry G. Webb, *The Book of Judges*, New International Commentary on the Old Testament (Grand Rapids: Eerdmans, 2012), 371–72.
[7] Sermon on the Character of Christ's Resurrection (March 1516), WA 1:58.28-30, 59.1-2; alluding to Deut 32:13; Exod 17:6; Judg 15:19.
[8] See "Short Instruction: What Should Be Sought and Expected in the Gospels" (1522, 1544), LW 75:7-12 (WA 10,1.1:8-18; E² 7:8-13; compare with LW 35:113-24).
[9] To prepare for this, Luther begins with an awkward allegory. The lion is the people who opposed Christ—those who followed the letter so closely that they could not see the whole or spirit of the text. The honey is Scripture, where the gospel is always found. Scripture's sweetest honey can never be found until such wooden literal interpretation is put to death. See Sermon on the Character of Christ's Resurrection (March 1516), WA 1:59.1-28. Here Luther seems to be influenced

described this with an ancient metaphor of the church: the baited Leviathan.[10] This metaphor is rooted in Job 41:1: "Can you catch Leviathan with a fishhook? And lash his tongue with a cord?"[11] Like a fisherman, God baits a hook with Christ to catch the devil: the bait is Jesus' human nature; the lure is Jesus' divine nature. Like a fish, the devil only sees the bait and gets caught on the fish hook of divinity. His tongue is lashed, because he can no longer accuse. Christ has taken away all human sin and borne it on the cross. If the devil wants to taunt someone about sin, he will have to talk with Jesus.[12] And so the eater is defeated in the eating. "Now because the children have flesh and blood, he participated in it in the same way, so that he through death could take the strength of the one who had power over death—that is the devil—and redeem those who through fear of death must be slaves to it their entire lives." (Heb 2:14-15).[13]

Luther recontextualized the baited Leviathan metaphor for Judges 14:14.[14] The riddle is about Christ's death and resurrection.[15] The lion represents the

---

by Jacques Lefèvre d'Étaples. See Heiko A. Oberman, *Forerunners of the Reformation: The Shape of Late Medieval Thought Illustrated by Key Documents* (New York: Holt, Rinehart, Winston, 1966), 281–96. Uwe Rieske-Braun draws this out as an allegory on law and gospel, *Duellum mirabile: Studien zum Kampfmotiv in Martin Luthers Theologie* (Göttingen: Vandenhoeck & Ruprecht, 1999), 125–28.

[10]On the baited Leviathan metaphor in the early church, see Rieske-Braun, *Duellum mirabile*, 171–88. While it's not clear how far back the baited Leviathan metaphor goes, at least as far back as Origen, Leviathan has been understood as the devil (Origen, *Selecta in Job*, PG 12:1047–50). See also Gregory of Nyssa, *Catechetical Orations* 24.4 (PPS 60:115); Cyril of Jerusalem, *Catechetical Lectures* 3.11-13 (FC 61:115); Rufinus, *A Commentary on the Apostles' Creed* 16–17 (ACW 20:50–52; PL 21:354–56).

[11]WADB 10,1:89.

[12]For example, see Sermon on the Thirteenth Sunday after Trinity (1530), WA 32:102.25–103.4.

[13]WADB 7:349.

[14]On Luther and the baited Leviathan metaphor, see Rieske-Braun, *Duellum mirabile*; Luy, *Dominus Mortis*, 184–86. Luther identifies Leviathan as a *Walfisch* (not necessarily a whale as we think of today, but a massive mysterious sea beast), but sees Job using this creature typologically for the devil (WADB 10,1:89). Nicholas connects Leviathan with the devil and the *balaena*, described in Pliny the Elder, *Natural History* 9.2, 5 (*Glossa ordinaria*, 3:390). Münster does not connect Leviathan with the devil; he merely points to Pliny's *balaena* (see *Miqdaš YHWH*, 2:1375). Johann Agricola adapted the baited Leviathan metaphor in an especially fun way: the mongoose versus the sea monster. See Graham Tomlin, *Philippians, Colossians*, RCS NT 11 (Downers Grove, IL: IVP Academic, 2013), 194.

[15]Sermon on the Character of Christ's Resurrection (March 1516), WA 1:59.29–60.7; *Praelectio in librum Iudicum* (1516), WA 4:584.14–22. The *Glossa ordinaria* also interprets this verse about Christ's resurrection. Nicholas simply points the riddle back to Samson discovering honey in a lion's corpse. He compares the Philistines pressing Samson's bride to Saul's conversion through Ananias. Just as the Philistines could not have solved Samson's riddle except with his bride's help, Saul could not have become a Christian except with the help of Christ's bride—the church.

enemies of humans: the devil and his retinue of sin, death, and hell. Samson represents Christ. The honey in the corpse of the lion represents Christ's benefits: the gospel—the preaching of the forgiveness of sins and true life. Christ is the food that comes out of the eater; his gospel is the sweetness that comes out of the strong. In trying to devour Samson, the lion is rent in two, and honey is found in its corpse. In the same way the devil tries to swallow Christ whole, but instead Christ marches out of the devil's mouth and becomes our bread from heaven, bringing us forgiveness and life. "Now by being killed he brings to life, as it is said: 'The Lord kills and brings to life, [he leads into hell and back out].' "[16] The underlying logic here is the same as the baited Leviathan metaphor. Christ is God and man in the unity of his person. The devil cannot destroy him but only destroys himself. And therefore humans can share Christ's benefits.

At the height of his career Luther also allegorized Judges 14 using the baited Leviathan metaphor—albeit slightly differently.[17] The lion is Jesus' human nature; Samson is Jesus' divine nature.[18] The honeycomb and bees born out of the jaws of the dead lion are the gospel and the church.[19] Here Luther says "jaws of the dead lion," although he translates the Hebrew appropriately as "in the corpse of the lion."[20] The gospel and its people are

---

See *Glossa ordinaria*, 2:247-48. Münster does not comment on these verses (*Miqdaš YHWH*, 1:495).

[16] WA 4:384.19-20; quoting 1 Sam 2:6. See WADB 9,1:189.

[17] WATR 5:394.1-5, no. 5895. The date of this table talk is unclear. The table talk were recorded from 1529 to 1546, so it's from the height of Luther's career and long after the methodological searching of his early career. The Weimar editors tried to sort the table talk chronologically; their placement intimates this table talk is from the 1540s. See WATR 1:XI; 3:XV-XVI; 5:XXXVII.

[18] This is similar to Luther's interpretation of Genesis 22: the ram is Jesus' human nature; Isaac is Jesus' divine nature.

[19] It is unclear whether Luther agreed with Pliny the Elder about the production of honey. Pliny stated that honey was the saliva of the heavens or juice of the stars, which bees gather and regurgitate in their hives (*Natural History* 11.12). Luther said that bees produce honey out of the nectar of flowers (WATR 6:368.16-20, no. 7071). Pliny's idea about honey would seem to be more fitting for Luther's allegory, for he would not say that the church *makes* the gospel. In a table talk of 1539, Luther again says that bees symbolize the church. The king bee without its sting—Pliny said the king bee has no sting—symbolizes Christ who binds his people together and does not abandon them. But just as the beehive loses all order and rule without the king bee, so also does the church without Christ. See WATR 4:413.5-11, no. 4639. The queen bee was held to be male until the sixteenth century. See Pliny the Elder, *Natural History* 11.4-23, here 16.

[20] Compare *faucibus mortui leonis* (WATR 5:394.3) with *in dem ass des Lewens* (WADB 9,1:139). In the table talk he must be quoting the Vulgate from memory, see *Glossa ordinaria*, 2:245-46. See also Niditch's note on the variety in the versions of Judges 14:8, Niditch, *Judges*, 147n.

brought to life out of death's jaws. That's the place where death thought it had surely won the battle but in the act of killing is killed by Life himself. When the church recites that Jesus died, descended to hell, and rose again, it proclaims that because Jesus returned from the deepest hell, joy is born out of suffering, and peace of conscience is born out of bodily persecution. The food produced from the eater sustains those who suffer and are oppressed.

Luther Redefines History

Luther read history in the Historical Books in a straightforward manner. He wrote prefaces for every canonical division of the Bible—including the Apocrypha—except the Historical Books.[21] Apparently Luther thought it was obvious how to read these books of the Bible: they should be read firmly trusting God and looking for his living promises.[22] But Luther understands history in a fundamentally different way than we do today. As Jaroslav Pelikan puts it, Luther's definition of history "seems to modern eyes allegorical or at least typological."[23] Luther even used the catechism to define history.

---

[21] See LW 35:235-411; the prefaces appear in canonical order before each book in WADB 6-12. See William M. Marsh's study of the prefaces, *Martin Luther on Reading the Bible as Christian Scripture: The Messiah in Luther's Biblical Hermeneutic and Theology* (Eugene, OR: Pickwick, 2017).

[22] Like most of his contemporaries, Luther calculated the timeline of world history based on the Bible; see *Supputatio annorum mundi* (1541; 1545), WA 53:22-82. While he understood years of reigns and ages straightforwardly, he was discerning regarding multiple witnesses and tensions in the biblical witness. On the Historical Books, for example, see WATR 1:364-65, no. 765; on the Gospels, for example, see Sermon on the Saturday after the Feast of Saint Dorothy (1538), LW 22:218-19; WA 46:726.11-727.28.

[23] Pelikan, *Luther the Expositor*, 90. Pelikan is here talking about Luther's description of his own exegesis as "historical." Several contemporary studies on Luther have sought to reclaim Luther's emphasis on the *historical* and *grammatical* aspects of exegesis. But many of them have insufficiently attended to Luther's "Christianized" definitions of history and grammar. And so sometimes they sound like they are arguing that Luther is the original historical-critical exegete. At other times they seem to contradict themselves, because they correctly flesh out Luther's strong use of the faith which is believed, particularly the second article. See, for example, Provan, *The Reformation and the Right Reading of Scripture*. On Luther's understanding of history, see Headley, *Luther's View of Church History*, esp. 1-55. See also Ebeling, *Evangelische Evangelienauslegung*, 423-24; Kwon, *Christus Pro Nobis*; Pelikan, *Luther the Expositor*, 259, compare with 89-90; WADB 9,1:XXXVI-XXXVII. "More important than grammar is history, which—seen from Luther's concept of the course of history—is here the Sacred History" (WADB 9,1:XXXVI). See further, Sermon on Fifth Sunday after Epiphany (1546), LW 58:453; WA 51:183.10-15.

By *history* Luther meant the never-ending sacred story narrated by the Apostles' Creed. "The Creed—the confession of our holy Christian faith—is the history of histories."[24] This history spans from the Trinity's first act of creation to our future new life with the Trinity in the new Jerusalem. It contains the history of the church, of every individual, and of the world.[25] Profane world history, however, must be distinguished from this history. Sacred history is not simply the enumeration of time-bound facts of human will and plans, like a king conquering another king; it is also God's judgment and will. It is *for us*.[26]

That's what we saw in Luther's early Easter sermon on Judges 14:14. Samson's riddle points beyond itself and Samson's current circumstances and experience; it points to the One who "is before all things, and it all fits together in him" (Col 1:17).[27] Unfortunately, we have no other sermons on the Historical Books. But Luther addresses what to do with this part of the Bible in a preface he wrote for a commentary on 1 Samuel by Justus Menius (1499–1558).[28]

The Historical Books teach faith in action.[29] And so these histories must be approached in faith. Without faith these histories are "dead things which are only useful to their own age."[30] Luther laments that even the great exegetes of the church approached these stories more interested in mere ethics.[31] But a Bible restricted to ethics is nothing more than a book of law and will only help as much as a book of law. (Plus even philosophers can teach ethics![32]) The church must teach the faith; to act otherwise is to forfeit the office Jesus

---

[24] WATR 5:581.36–37, no. 6288.
[25] Ebeling, *Evangelische Evangelienauslegung*, 418–19, 453. See WATR 5:581.36–43, no. 6288.
[26] Luther addressed history in an occasional manner; however, he endorsed Justus Menius's focused treatment, see "De sacrarum historiarum usu, prologus," in *In Samuelis Librum Priorem ennaratio* (Wittenberg: Johannes Lufft, 1532), 1r–5r.
[27] WADB 7:229.
[28] Martin Luther, "Praefatio," in *In Samuelis Librum Priorem ennaratio*, Justus Menius (Wittenberg: Johannes Lufft, 1532), unpaginated; WA 30,3:539–40 (LW 60:8–10). Justus Menius was a pastor who translated many of Luther's Latin works into German and helped Luther during certain controversies. After Luther's death, Menius entered a controversy about the relationship between good works and salvation; his view is rejected in *Formula of Concord* 4. See further RCS OT 5:710.
[29] "Praefatio" (1532), unpaginated; WA 30,3:539.11–14, 26–28; LW 60:8, 9.
[30] "Praefatio" (1532), unpaginated; WA 30,3:539.18 (LW 60:8).
[31] Here he cites Origen, but elsewhere he includes Jerome and Augustine. See Excursus on Allegory at Genesis 9:12–16, WA 43:368.16; LW 2:151.
[32] Excursus on Allegory at Genesis 9:12–16, WA 42:368.37–38; LW 2:152.

entrusted to it. Just as fallen humans are reborn through faith, these histories are also reborn through faith.[33] These stories of ancient peoples and ancient places are brought to life today. And that's why Christians need teachers like Menius to guide them through books of history like 1 Samuel: to show them how to correctly understand these stories and "how to handle them skillfully according to the analogy of faith (as Paul teaches)."[34] Reading the Historical Books according to the analogy of faith will help Christians to distinguish false knowledge that puffs up from true knowledge that builds up (1 Cor 8:1), useless allegories from useful allegories, and false teachers from true teachers.[35] The Historical Books—like the entire canon of Scripture—must be interpreted according to the analogy of faith.

---

[33] "Praefatio" (1532), unpaginated; WA 30,3:539.30–35 (LW 60:9).
[34] "Praefatio" (1532), unpaginated; LW 60:10 (WA 30,3:540.7–8); alluding to Rom 12:6.
[35] "Praefatio" (1532), unpaginated; WA 30,3:540.8–12; LW 60:10; alluding to 1 Tim 6:20.

6

The Upside-Down King

Reading the Wisdom Books According to the Rule of Faith

Luther considered Psalm 72 among the hardest passages of Scripture. "Psalm 72 and Psalm 73 are the most difficult of all the Psalms!"[1] Luther lectured once on Psalm 72 (in his first lecture series on the Psalms, 1513–1515); he preached on it twice: one Sunday in May of 1533 and a seven-part series in the late winter of 1540. Throughout his career Luther read the Psalms according to the analogy of faith—chiefly the second and third articles of the Creed, although in his *Summaries of the Psalms* (1531–1533), he said that nearly every psalm can be read according to the first table of the law and the first three petitions of the Our Father.[2] Luther understands Psalm 72 primarily to be about the Messiah and his kingdom. And so he interprets this psalm according to the second and third articles of the Creed.

To show Luther's use of the analogy of faith in Psalm 72, this chapter will focus on three issues: (1) how Luther interprets the king of Psalm 72 as the king described in the second article of the Apostles' Creed, (2) how Luther sees the church as described in the third article of the Apostles' Creed in Psalm 72, and (3) how Luther connects the Psalms to the Ten Commandments and the Our Father. Luther uses the catechism to clear up the strange speech of the psalmist. The psalm cannot be applied to temporal rulers. The

---

[1] WATR 1:177, no. 410. See also WATR 2:642, no. 2763a (RCS OT 7:487); WATR 2:642–43, no. 2763b.
[2] *Summarien vber die Psalmen, Und vrsachen des dolmetschens* (Wittenberg: Hans Lufft, 1531–1533), C6r-v; WA 38:27.28–28.11.

catechism reveals the logic of the Chalcedonian doctrine woven into the psalm. Like Christ the King, his people cannot be judged according to reason. According to reason they are weak, divided, and sinful; according to faith they are a strong, united, and holy people. The church is an article of faith. Finally, Luther's treatment of Psalm 72 will be complemented by his book *Summaries of the Psalms* (1531–1533). Luther sees every psalm as intimately connected to the Our Father and Ten Commandments.

THE KING OF THE SECOND ARTICLE

In his sermons on Psalm 72, Luther contrasts how reason and faith interpret this text. Reason sees that this psalm is about a great earthly king.[3] This is the great hope, according to Luther, of the Jews, Muslims, Anabaptists, and Papists. "The Jews dream that the Messiah will be a king like Solomon was—a king to whom all nations were bodily subjected. That's what the Turks hope—the Papists too. And that's what the rebaptizers think. And some fanatics still pursue it!"[4] Such people read Psalm 72 to be about a human king of a temporal kingdom, who brings bodily peace, justice, and blessing—like in the time of Solomon.[5]

"But the text doesn't allow it."[6] Any earthly king, like Solomon, will one day die. How can that fit with "We will fear you as long as the sun and moon endure—from generation to generation" (v. 5)?[7] The Jews thought this meant that the king would have a long dynasty.[8] But that's not what this text means, according to Luther: "He shall be only one person, and he shall be eternal;

---

[3]Following Hermann Gunkel's work, scholars categorize Psalm 72 as a royal psalm about the king of Israel. See Hans-Joachim Kraus, *Psalms 60–150*, trans. Hilton C. Oswald, Continental Commentary (Minneapolis: Fortress, 1993), 76–77, 80–81. Throughout his commentary on the Psalms, Kraus gently pushes biblical scholars toward a more Christological reading.
[4]Fourth Sermon on Psalm 72 (February 15, 1540), WA 49:30.12–14. Throughout this sermon series, Luther regularly mentions the Ottoman Turks. After the siege of Vienna in 1529, the Ottoman Turks continued to pressure the Holy Roman Empire; in 1541 the Ottoman Turks took control of Hungary. Luther's comment about fanatics refers to efforts by Radicals like those in the kingdom of Münster. After 1535, the Magisterial Reformers filtered all Anabaptists through the chaos of Münster. On the kingdom of Münster, see Williams, *The Radical Reformation*, 561–82.
[5]Second Sermon on Psalm 72 (January 6, 1540), WA 49:16.2–7. See also First Sermon on Psalm 72 (January 5, 1540), WA 49:12.10–15; Fourth Sermon on Psalm 72 (February 15, 1540), WA 49:31.8–26.
[6]Sermon on Psalm 72 (May 28, 1533), WA 37:83.9.
[7]WADB 10,1:331.
[8]Third Sermon on Psalm 72 (January 11, 1540), WA 49:21.18–20.

he will have no successors."[9] An earthly king also must rule from a specific place. How can that fit with "He will reign from one sea to the other and from the Water to the end of the world" (v. 8)?[10] Solomon ruled over a territory a third the size of Germany, according to Luther.[11] And no king—not even of the Romans or the Ottoman Turks—has ruled over the entire globe.[12] But this king rules over every tribe and nation, and he does not hold court in some earthly place—be it Rome, as the Papists think, or Jerusalem, as the Jews think. "He has his seat at the right hand of the Father."[13] According to God's power this king rules not merely over geography but human hearts. And what king "brings your people to righteousness and rescues your poor" (v. 2)?[14] Temporal rule is surely a gift—even if rare.[15] Still good temporal rule only curbs evil; it does not usher in righteousness. If a government keeps its citizens free from prison and safe from invading armies, if a government preserves one's property and protects one's family from the greed and appetite of others, "that's—on earth—a beautiful and glorious gift."[16] All the same, humans under such rule live enslaved to sin and death, and not even a good king can free us from these enemies.[17] For even the best rulers are filled with sin and oppression—worse, the best rulers are often God's enemies.[18] "The kings in the land rebel, and the lords take counsel together against the LORD and his anointed" (Ps 2:2).[19] In contrast the king of Psalm 72 metes out God's own justice and righteousness. He is God's equal.[20]

---

[9] Second Sermon on Psalm 72 (January 6, 1540), WA 49:20.3. See also Seventh Sermon on Psalm 72 (March 7, 1540), WA 49:46.4–14; Lectures on Psalm 72, LW 10:409 (WA 3:467.15–16).

[10] WADB 10,1:331. While Luther translates נָהָר as "the Water," he adds a marginal gloss in 1531: "that is, from the Jordan." It is unclear why Luther chose "the Water" instead of "the River." Reuchlin's Hebrew dictionary—a resource he knew well—shows that נָהָר means "river." See Reuchlin, *De rudimentis hebraicis*, 309, s.v. נָהָר.

[11] Sermon on Psalm 72 (May 28, 1533), WA 37:83.12–13.

[12] Fourth Sermon on Psalm 72 (February 15, 1540), WA 49:33.41–42

[13] Fourth Sermon on Psalm 72 (February 15, 1540), WA 49:34.5–10, here 9. See also First Sermon on Psalm 72 (January 5, 1540), WA 49:14.17–19, 24; Second Sermon on Psalm 72 (January 6, 1540), WA 49:16.32–35; Seventh Sermon on Psalm 72 (March 7, 1540), WA 49:47.40–48.6.

[14] WADB 10,1:331.

[15] First Sermon on Psalm 72 (January 5, 1540), WA 49:12.27–29, 13.35–38. Luther cites Saxony's own ruler as one such rarity.

[16] First Sermon on Psalm 72 (January 5, 1540), WA 49:14.1–4, quoting 3–4.

[17] First Sermon on Psalm 72 (January 5, 1540), WA 49:14.4–11, 15.2–4; Second Sermon on Psalm 72 (January 6, 1540), WA 49:17.17–21.

[18] First Sermon on Psalm 72 (January 5, 1540), WA 49:12.35–13.6.

[19] WADB 10,1:109.

[20] First Sermon on Psalm 72 (January 5, 1540), WA 49:13.32–35.

The Upside-Down King

This king did not come to create a kingdom free of any poor—as the Jews thought—but to establish a kingdom of the poor; this king comes to save the unrighteous.[21]

Faith understands that this psalm is about God's promised king. "And see, here is more than Solomon." (Mt 12:42).[22] Here is a king like no other: One begotten in eternity by the Father and in time by the power of the Holy Spirit in the Virgin Mary.[23] The King described in Psalm 72 is the King described in the second article—God's only Son, our Lord. Christians alone understand this.[24]

> Christ was—from the beginning—the crusher of the serpent, [as has been passed down] through the patriarchs and prophets. [Christ was] true God and true man. He came in the flesh not to begin a new earthly kingdom but first to found and establish and begin an eternal kingdom, where souls are freed from sin and death. This is the Christian faith, and this is the Messiah the prophets wrote about.[25]

Luther approaches Psalm 72 as he approaches any other passage of Scripture: armed with the faith of the church. He focuses especially on the Chalcedonian formula.

Luther agrees with the exegetical tradition before him. The very first verse of Psalm 72—"God, give your justice to the king, and your righteousness to the king's son"[26]—clearly teaches the truth that the Messiah is true God and

---

[21] First Sermon on Psalm 72 (January 5, 1540), WA 49.16.37–17.17.
[22] WADB 6:59.
[23] In his early lecture on Psalm 72, Luther follows Paul of Burgos's striking comment on יִנּוֹן in verse 17. Paul argues that it's best to render יִנּוֹן as "filiated"; thus here and in many other passages Scripture confirms the processions of the Trinity—in particularly the eternal generation of the Son. See Glossa on Psalm 72:17, WA 3:461.27–28. Later in his career Luther still understands יִנּוֹן to mean filiated but he takes it in a different sense: that Jesus' name will be born in our children and our children's children, so that his name is preached from generation to generation. Münster makes a similar comment. See Luther's marginal gloss on *reichen*, WADB 10,1:332–33; Seventh Sermon on Psalm 72 (March 7, 1540), WA 49:49.7–14; Münster, *Miqdaš YHWH*, 2:1218–19; Reuchlin, *De rudimentis hebraicis*, 322–23. The verb נִין can be rendered as "to produce shoots" or "to get descendants," see s.v. Ludwig Koehler and Walter Baumgartner, ed., *The Hebrew and Aramaic Lexicon of the Old Testament*, 5 vols., trans. and ed. M. E. J. Richardson (Leiden: Brill, 1994–2000), 2:696.
[24] First Sermon on Psalm 72 (January 5, 1540), WA 49:12.16–19; Second Sermon on Psalm 72 (January 6, 1540), WA 49:16.23.
[25] Second Sermon on Psalm 72 (January 6, 1540), WA 49:16.23–28.
[26] WADB 10,1:331. Luther capitalizes the first two letters of the first word of a psalm to distinguish it from the superscription. (Unless he's translating the Tetragrammaton, then he capitalizes the

true man.²⁷ "In this psalm the holy prophet sang and prophesied of the true King of all kings, that he shall be true man and true God in one person."²⁸ The words *king* and *king's son* indicate that David is talking about a man. "He calls him true man, who must be born of the line and seed of David."²⁹ The words *your justice* and *your righteousness* indicate that this king is no mere man; he is also God. While Magistrates have been given a code of law, it can only restrain the wicked and preserve the body and physical goods—and that only by God's help. "It's a kingdom, but it's beggarly."³⁰ God's word accomplishes his own justice and righteousness, which extends to body and soul. "This is God's judgment: he hangs death on the cross, he decapitates sin, and he drowns the flesh in Baptism."³¹ Through this judgment God makes us innocent before him, saves us, and gives us life.³² The psalmist asks that this king be given God's own justice and righteousness. This is to ask "let him be equal to you."³³ And because of God's word in the first commandment and Isaiah 42:8, this man must be true God—equal to God

---

whole word.) Typically Luther uses GOtt as a *nomina sacra*, referring to the Son, but here the capitalization is for literary purposes. On Luther's use of *nomina sacra*, see Helmer, "Luther's Trinitarian Hermeneutic and the Old Testament"; Assel, "Gottesnamen und Kernstellen in Luthers Bibelübersetzung 1545."

²⁷See the summary sentences at the beginning of the following sermons: Second Sermon on Psalm 72 (January 6, 1540), WA 49:15.26-29; Third Sermon on Psalm 72 (January 11, 1540), WA 49:21.2-6; Fifth Sermon on Psalm 72 (February 22, 1540), WA 49:35.30-32; Sixth Sermon on Psalm 72 (February 29, 1540), WA 49:40.24-27; Seventh Sermon on Psalm 72 (March 7, 1540), WA 49:45.26-29. See also Luther's allegorical interpretation of verse 5, Lectures on Psalm 72, LW 10:409-10 (WA 3:467.19-38). See *Glossa ordinaria*, 3:955-56. Münster does not explicitly touch on Jesus' two natures, but he does focus on Solomon as a type of Christ. See Münster, *Miqdaš YHWH*, 2:1219.

²⁸Second Sermon on Psalm 72 (January 6, 1540), WA 49:15.26-27.

²⁹Sermon on Psalm 72 (May 28, 1533), WA 37:84.4-5. See also Sermon on Psalm 72 (May 28, 1533), WA 37:83.21-85.4; First Sermon on Psalm 72 (January 5, 1540), WA 49:13.33-34, 36-37; Second Sermon on Psalm 72 (January 6, 1540), WA 49:16.32-35.

³⁰Sermon on Psalm 72 (May 28, 1533), WA 37:84.10-36, here 13.

³¹First Sermon on Psalm 72 (January 5, 1540), WA 49:14.11-13.

³²See Third Sermon on Psalm 72 (January 11, 1540), WA 49:21.6-8; Fourth Sermon on Psalm 72 (February 15, 1540), WA 49:31.38-39. In his early lectures on Psalm 72, Luther almost exclusively focuses on *judgment*. He explicitly uses the quadriga, although with his trademark: he establishes the quadriga on faith, not love. See David C. Steinmetz, *Luther and Staupitz: An Essay in the Intellectual Origins of the Protestant Reformation* (Durham, NC: Duke University Press, 1980), 55n123, 59-64. See WA 3:467.19-468.13; LW 10:409-10. Jesus is God's judgment and word (WA 3:466.6-7; LW 10:407). Also Luther emphasizes that God's word does what it says (WA 3:466.6-7; LW 10:407).

³³First Sermon on Psalm 72 (January 5, 1540), WA 49:13.34-35.

in eternity.[34] "Therefore he's God and man. And nevertheless he is not himself the Father, but a distinct person to whom [justice] is given."[35] The Chalcedonian formula leads to the doctrine of the Trinity.

This God-man is the king we need. "We seek such a King, who is true God with you and true man born of David, who dies for us and gives the Holy Spirit, who makes ready and joyous hearts."[36] All other kings have no power to lift us out of our poverty—our enslavement to sin, death, and the devil. "He will preserve his lowly people with justice and help the poor and annihilate the blasphemer" (Ps 72:4).[37] Although externally humans might seem rich and mighty, internally all humans are poor and weak. This acknowledgment is demanded by this King and his message. "He died not for saints but for sinners."[38] Before we become saints we must become nothing, for God only creates out of nothing (as the first article and third petition teach). "Christians do not become holy by their own power."[39] Luther paraphrases Jesus' invitation to holiness: "Whoever believes in me will no longer be called a sinner but will have his sins forgiven."[40] We need the power of God—poured into our hearts by the Holy Spirit (Rom 5:5).

The People of the Third Article

The beginning of Psalm 72 describes the King we seek; the end of Psalm 72 describes his kingdom.[41] Just as this King is like no other king, so his kingdom is like no other kingdom. "Therefore we must distinguish between worldly reign and the Christian church."[42] Here again the

---

[34]First Sermon on Psalm 72 (January 5, 1540), WA 49:14.23-35. See also Sermon on Psalm 72 (May 28, 1533), WA 37:85.4-27. WADB 11,1:129; Third Sermon on Psalm 72 (January 11, 1540), WA 49:21.18-25; Fourth Sermon on Psalm 72 (February 15, 1540), WA 49:31.19-22. Luther clarifies Psalm 72:1 with Isaiah 42:8 and Psalm 110, as well as as the first commandment. See Sermon on Psalm 72 (May 28, 1540), WA 37:85.20-32; First Sermon on Psalm 72 (January 5, 1540), WA 49:14.25-41.

[35]First Sermon on Psalm 72 (January 5, 1540), WA 49:14.25-41, here 40-41.

[36]Sermon on Psalm 72 (May 28, 1533), WA 37:86.33-35.

[37]WADB 10,1:331.

[38]Second Sermon on Psalm 72 (January 6, 1540), WA 49:18.34-35.

[39]Sermon on Psalm 72 (May 28, 1533), WA 37:86.21.

[40]Sermon on Psalm 72 (May 28, 1533), WA 37:86.18-19.

[41]Fourth Sermon on Psalm 72 (February 15, 1540), WA 49:30.2-8; Sermon on Psalm 72 (May 28, 1533), WA 37:85.33-86.14.

[42]Fourth Sermon on Psalm 72 (February 15, 1540), WA 49:30.8-9.

relationship between faith and reason is central to separating Christ's kingdom from all others. And so to correctly understand this psalm, it must also be read according to the analogy of faith, specifically the third article of the Creed: "I believe in the holy Christian church, the communion of saints."

Reason—unbridled by faith—wants to commingle the kingdom of the church with the kingdoms of the world.[43] In particular, clergy want to seize the sword and become kings, and kings want to govern clergy. Those in the magisterial estate have their work cut out for them, and it is good as far as it goes. "But it's nothing compared to Baptism."[44] In Baptism there is no distinction of persons, but the distinction of persons is basic to worldly government. Baptism deals with eternal realities; government only temporal ones. The devil wants nothing more than to confuse these kingdoms, so that the church would be ruled by reason and temporal power.[45] Luther cites the Jews, the Turks, and the Papists as examples of this confusion: the reasoned madness that restricts the Messiah's rule to the physical.[46]

But the church is a kingdom of faith. "This is the difference from the visible kingdom: it cannot be grasped by senses or reason; it is entirely above reason, etc."[47] According to the eyes of reason, the works of the church are mere human works. In Baptism a man pours mere water over a child. In the sacramental meal a man offers mere bread and wine to others. In Absolution a man speaks to another. But that's not the truth of the matter! The works of the church are the works of God. "There Christ is. You do not see him, nevertheless he works in you."[48] The eyes of faith see that in Baptism God gives

---

[43]Fourth Sermon on Psalm 72 (February 15, 1540), WA 49:30.14–31.26. Here Luther teaches about the three estates—church, government, and family—in order to help common Christians distinguish the kingdoms. The church is for eternal life; government is for temporal peace; family is for the growth and nourishment of the human family. Each estate's officeholders are tempted to coopt the works and purpose of the other estates—although here Luther makes this point only about church and government. The contrast between government and church tends to be the starkest for Luther, particularly because he sees government as the only estate ordained after the fall. Additionally Luther tends to draw the estates of church and family close together. For example, he talks about the family as a little church.

[44]Fourth Sermon on Psalm 72 (February 15, 1540), WA 49:30.30–31.

[45]Fourth Sermon on Psalm 72 (February 15, 1540), WA 49:30.10–12.

[46]Fourth Sermon on Psalm 72 (February 15, 1540), WA 49:30.13–14, 31.8–9, 31.18–22.

[47]Third Sermon on Psalm 72 (January 11, 1540), WA 49:21.29–30.

[48]Third Sermon on Psalm 72 (January 11, 1540), WA 49:25.10–11.

a child the laver of regeneration; in the sacramental meal God offers himself; in Absolution God forgives.[49]

The psalmist teaches this by saying, "He will fall like rain on the fleece" (Ps 72:6).[50] Following the tradition, Luther understands this verse to be a reference to the story of Gideon (Judg 6–7).[51] Gideon wants to be sure that the Lord God will give Israel victory over the Midianites, and so he asks God for a sign: first, that the morning dew only soaks a fleece, but the ground is dry; second, that the morning dew soaks the ground, but the fleece is dry. On the way to battle with Midian, the Lord God tests Gideon, winnowing Gideon's army from 32,000 men to 300 men. Gideon boldly displays his faith in God's victory by commanding his men to approach the Midianite camp not with weapons but with trumpets and empty jars.[52] This episode from the life of Gideon demonstrates how God's power and victory are not like human power and victory. Like the morning dew, no one knows whence the church or its King comes.[53] The church's King defeats the enemies of sin, death, and the devil with their own weapon: Christ's blood on the cross.[54]

---

[49] Third Sermon on Psalm 72 (January 11, 1540), WA 49:21.31–34. In this passage Luther only makes this point about Baptism, nevertheless, as chapter three has shown, Luther would say this about all the sacraments.

[50] WADB 10,1:331. In contrast to modern translations (and even the KJV!), Luther follows the Vulgate and renders גֵּז more literally as "fleece." (This is the usual meaning of this word and the related word גִּזָּה, see s.v. Koehler and Baumgartner, ed., *The Hebrew and Aramaic Lexicon of the Old Testament*, 1:185, 186). Modern commentators do not say much about this translation issue, except for Marvin E. Tate, *Psalms 51–100*, Word Biblical Commentary 20 (Dallas: Word, 1998), 220.

[51] Luther added a marginal reference to Judges 6 in 1531 (WADB 10,1:331). Luther interprets the allusion differently than the fathers. The fathers understood the dew-soaked fleece to typify the pregnant Virgin Mary. Luther calls this a "fine, friendly gloss," although he does not judge it to be entirely fitting with the text. Instead Luther interprets the dew-soaked fleece and dew-soaked ground as meaning that only the Holy Spirit makes Christians (whether Jews or Gentiles). Although Luther ends this sermon with a wink at the fathers' interpretation, saying that all Christians are made fruitful like Mary: by the dew of the word and Baptism (WA 49:25.21–23). See Third Sermon on Psalm 72 (January 11, 1540), WA 49:24.22–25.23; *Glossa ordinaria*, 3:958–59. Münster translates גֵּז as *tonsuram (graminis)*, that is, "mown (grass)." Nevertheless, he glosses it as a description of how abundantly Christ gives gifts. Münster, *Miqdaš YHWH*, 2:1218, 1219.

[52] Third Sermon on Psalm 72 (January 11, 1540), WA 49:22.27–23.35; WADB 9,1:108–13. In this sermon Luther only points out that Gideon's men are victorious; he does not draw out the upside-down nature of their victory.

[53] Third Sermon on Psalm 72 (January 11, 1540), WA 49:25.2–8.

[54] Third Sermon on Psalm 72 (January 11, 1540), WA 49:24.2–4.

Because their King has defeated death, Christians no longer fear death.[55] "And their blood will be valued as precious before him" (Ps 72:14).[56] Even though their King has won, Christians do not expect a life filled with temporal peace and victory. Their peace and victory is in Christ, but until Christ comes again, Christians should expect to suffer even unto death.[57] Luther recounts horrific accounts of martyrdom to underscore this point. In the Roman Empire, Christians were beheaded and tortured (their flesh was torn so that animals would mangle them further)—as many as 70,000 in a day, according to Luther.[58] During the sieges of the Ottoman Turks, Christians were ravaged and beheaded—young children's severed heads were displayed on pikes.[59] St. Agnes (291–304) and St. Agatha (c. 231–c. 251)—saints Luther often mentions in sermons—were brutalized and cast in prison.[60] St. Lucia (c. 283–304) was forced into prostitution.[61] These Christians bravely faced temporal death and shame. They are evidence of St. Vincent's (d. 304) quip: "Among Christians death is a game; prison and suffering are glory."[62] Because Christ has bound death's jaws and placed death on a leash (Job 41:1, 5), Christians face death without fear.[63] "No people can handle death and the devil like Christians can!"[64] They believe in the resurrection of the dead.

---

[55]They believe in the resurrection of the dead, as the third article teaches; Fourth Sermon on Psalm 72 (February 15, 1540), WA 49:33.1–14.

[56]WADB 10,1:333. The Sixth Sermon on Psalm 72 (February 29, 1540) focuses on this verse and martyrdom; WA 49:40.24–45.24.

[57]Sixth Sermon on Psalm 72 (February 29, 1540), WA 49:44.14–15.

[58]Sixth Sermon on Psalm 72 (February 29, 1540), WA 49:41.28–33.

[59]Sixth Sermon on Psalm 72 (February 29, 1540), WA 49:42.5–9, 42.37–43.1. The Ottoman Turkish army had a fearsome reputation—especially the 20 percent of soldiers who received no pay except the plunder of war. See Nina Berman, "Imperial Violence and the Limits of Tolerance: Reading Luther with Las Casas," in *Early Modern Constructions of Europe: Literature, Culture, History*, ed. Florian Kläger and Gerd Bayer (New York: Routledge, 2016), 141–43.

[60]Fourth Sermon on Psalm 72 (February 15, 1540), WA 49:32.20–23. See Ernst Schäfer, *Luther als Kirchenhistoriker: Ein Beitrag zur Geschichte der Wissenschaft* (Gütersloh: Bertelsmann, 1897), 233, 235.

[61]Sixth Sermon on Psalm 72 (February 29, 1540), WA 49:42.29–33. See Schäfer, *Luther als Kirchenhistoriker*, 236.

[62]Sixth Sermon on Psalm 72 (February 29, 1540), WA 49:44.31. See Schäfer, *Luther als Kirchenhistoriker*, 236–37.

[63]Sixth Sermon on Psalm 72 (February 29, 1540), WA 49:44.33–45.14; Fourth Sermon on Psalm 72 (February 15, 1540), WA 49:33.1–14. Luther subtly weaves in the baited Leviathan metaphor. This sermon of Luther's echoes the logic of Athanasius's *On the Incarnation* 29.

[64]Sixth Sermon on Psalm 72 (February 29, 1540), WA 49:44.26–27.

And so Psalm 72 also describes a kingdom like no other. This kingdom is constantly in the midst of suffering and death, yet it is peaceful and joyous, because its King is seated at the right hand of the Father with sin, death, and the devil under his feet.[65] The citizens of this kingdom are everywhere, thriving where nothing else can thrive, for their flourishing is no human work—it is the very work of God.[66] For now the existence of the church is an article of faith. "Whoever wants such a church where there's no disunity in doctrine (against the first table) and no crime and wickedness (against the second table) will not find it."[67] This side of Jesus' return, the church is imperfect in faith and love; it is mixed in with the ordinary lives and works of ordinary people who remain sinners but who are also holy. The church, like its individual members, is *simul justa et peccatrix*, simultaneously sinner and saint.

This kingdom we see by faith and not by sight or reason—at least for now. "Until the hour comes . . . until [Christ] brings us before the Father himself. Then God will be all in all, and it will no longer be necessary to baptize, to preach, to speak Absolution. We will not suffer persecution, and we won't need Scripture. For we will see with our eyes what we already believe in the word."[68] One day we will experience the kingdom of God as tangibly as we do the temporal world.

Connecting the Psalms to the Ten Commandments and the Our Father

Luther primarily reads Psalm 72 as he reads most of the Psalms: according to the second and third articles of the Creed.[69] (He also hints at the first

---

[65] Fourth Sermon on Psalm 72 (February 15, 1540), WA 49:32.22–23, 33.20–22; Sixth Sermon on Psalm 72 (February 29, 1540), WA 49:45.13–14.

[66] Seventh Sermon on Psalm 72 (March 7, 1540), WA 49:48.20–23; Lecture on Psalm 72, LW 10:414 (WA 3:471.12–21). In his early lecture on Psalm 72, Luther interprets verse 16 about the church. The church is like grass in two ways: it grows without any human work and it sprouts suddenly everywhere. See Lecture on Psalm 72, LW 10:414 (WA 3:471.12–21).

[67] Sixth Sermon on Psalm 72 (February 29, 1540), WA 49:41.20–22.

[68] Fourth Sermon on Psalm 72 (February 15, 1540), WA 49:33.22, 23–26; citing 1 Cor 15:28. See also Second Sermon on Psalm 72 (January 6, 1540), WA 49:20.26–30.

[69] See James Samuel Preus, *From Shadow to Promise: Old Testament Interpretation from Augustine to the Young Luther* (Cambridge, MA: Harvard University Press, 1969), 212–25; Scott H. Hendrix, Ecclesia in via: *Ecclesiological Developments in the Medieval Psalms Exegesis and the* Dictata Super Psalterium *(1513–1515) of Martin Luther* (Leiden: Brill, 1974), 155–283; Brian T. German,

article of the Creed, the Sacrament of the Altar, and the Ten Commandments.[70]) However, his *Summaries of the Psalms* (1531–1533) shows that Luther wanted the Psalms to be fruitfully interpreted with the Ten Commandments and the Our Father.[71] The Psalms are rich with meaning according to the analogy of faith.

Luther wrote the *Summaries of the Psalms* to help simple Christians understand the Psalms. The better they understand the Psalms, the better they can enter them and pray them as their own.[72] The Psalter has five themes: psalms about Christ and the church, psalms of doctrine, psalms of comfort, psalms of prayer, and psalms of thanksgiving. And these five themes are not mutually exclusive. "However, we should know that the Psalms and all their verses shouldn't be divided so neatly and precisely into these [five] parts."[73] Some psalms contain several, even all of these categories.

As an additional aid to the simple, Luther ended his summaries by connecting the psalm to the relevant commandments of the Ten Commandments and the relevant petitions of the Our Father. Luther wanted to be sure that Christians understood how thoroughly the Ten Commandments and the Our Father pervade the life and speech of the saints and prophets. "And

---

Psalms of the Faithful: Luther's Early Reading of the Psalter in Canonical Context (Bellingham, WA: Lexham Press, 2017).

[70]Luther emphasizes that everything is gift (as the first article of the Creed teaches), see Fifth Sermon on Psalm 72 (February 22, 1540), WA 49:36.31-34. In his early lecture on Psalm 72, Luther agreed with the *Glossa ordinaria* and applied verse 16 to the Sacrament of the Altar, see LW 10:413-14 (WA 3:470.25-11). Before delving into the stories of the martyrs, Luther briefly treats the lies of the devil: lies against the first table are lies against worship and faith; lies against the second table are lies against love. See Sixth Sermon on Psalm 72 (February 29, 1540), WA 49:41.1-25, esp. 8-9. And the entire final sermon of 1540 draws Psalm 72 and the first table together, see Seventh Sermon on Psalm 72 (March 7, 1540), WA 49:45.26-49.34.

[71]To complete this book required nearly four years and the help of Veit Dietrich and Justus Menius. Luther dictated summaries of the first twenty-five psalms to Dietrich during their time together at the castle Coburg in 1530. (Luther needed to be accessible during the discussions at the Diet of Augsburg, but could not safely enter the imperial city, because he remained under imperial ban. See Brecht, *Martin Luther*, 2:369-410.) As often happened with Luther's works, the printer began printing while Luther was still composing. The printer began in 1531 (as the title page shows) but did not finish until 1533 (as the last page shows). Upon completion of the project, Menius—also on behalf of Dietrich—wrote to Luther: "I give thanks that you have finally freed us from the summaries of the psalms." See the editors' introduction in the Weimar edition, WA 38:1-7.

[72]*Summarien vber die Psalmen* (1531–1533), B3r, B3v-B4r (WA 38:17.21-23, 18.11-14).

[73]*Summarien vber die Psalmen* (1531–1533), B3r-B4r (WA 38:17.21-18.14), here B3v (WA 38:18.7-8).

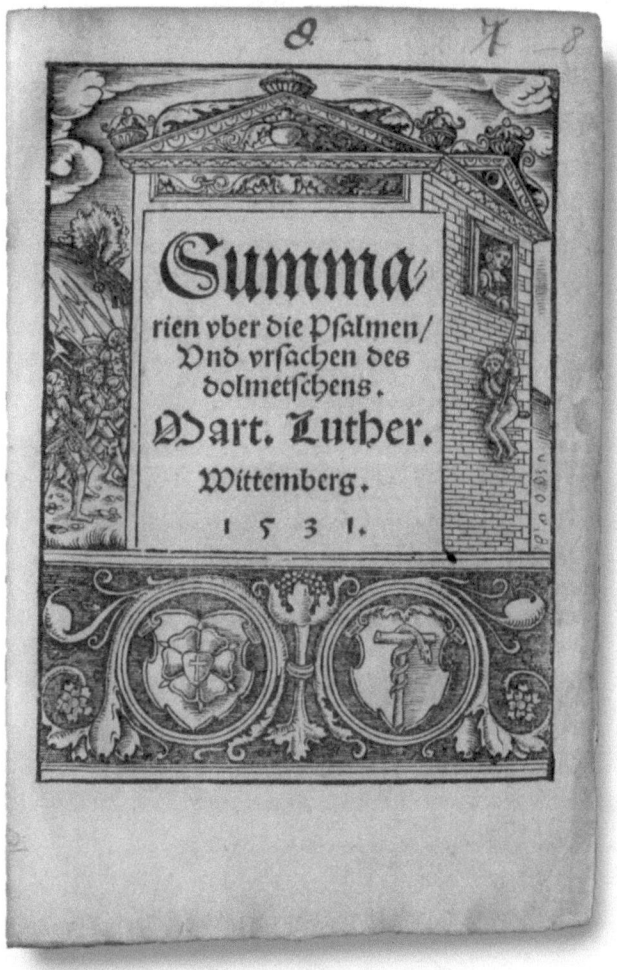

The title page of Luther's *Summaries of the Psalms* depicts Michal helping David escape from Saul and his soldiers (1 Sam 19:11-12)

they always treated it newly, and yet they never taught anything new. They never walked away from the tablets of Moses and the Our Father. Thus, we must grasp how all the writings and holy lives of the prophets flowed from the commandments of God. There they remained; they didn't stir up new teaching."[74] Luther mostly points out the connection between the Psalms and the first table and the first three petitions (though he mentions

---

[74]*Summarien vber die Psalmen* (1531–1533), C6v (WA 38.4-8).

the fourth petition once and the seventh petition three times).[75] The psalms of prayer belong with the second commandment and first petition. The psalms of doctrine, comfort, and thanksgiving belong to the second and third commandments and the first and third petitions.[76] The prophetic psalms about Christ and the church belong to the first and third commandments and the first and second petitions.[77] "And often many psalms belong to all three commandments and petitions."[78] Luther stopped doing this at Psalm 31. He apparently thought this application of the analogy of faith was so obvious that it was getting pedantic. "From the previous psalms we have enough examples, so that everyone can easily recognize to which [commandments and petitions] every psalm belongs."[79]

Conclusion

Luther taught that the Wisdom books—as represented by the Psalms—must be interpreted according to the analogy of faith.[80] Otherwise humans are tempted to read these books about temporal wisdom. "The Jews—on account of the veil over their eyes—make all Scripture about temporal justice and peace."[81] But the Bible does not tell of a King and kingdom like any other. The Bible proclaims the King and kingdom of the Creed: a King who is God and man, who has defeated sin, death, and the devil; a kingdom of every tribe and tongue of the earth, whose citizens are joyous in the midst of death,

---

[75] Luther connects Psalm 4 with the fourth petition and Psalms 3, 4, and 13 with the seventh petition. See *Summarien vber die Psalmen* (1531–1533), B5r-v, B8v (WA 38:19.8–10, 19.23–27, 22.18–19).

[76] *Summarien vber die Psalmen* (1531–1533), C6r-v (WA 38:27.31–35).

[77] Luther does not say this explicitly. He labels the ten prophetic psalms accordingly: eight have to do with the first commandment (Pss 2, 8–9, 14, 16, 21–22, 24); two, the second commandment (Pss 16, 24); five, the third commandment (Pss 14, 16, 19, 24, 29); four, the first petition (Pss 14, 16, 22, 24); nine, the second petition (Pss 2, 8–9, 14, 16, 21–22, 24, 29); one, the third petition (Ps 24). One psalm he does not identify the petition it belongs with (Ps 19).

[78] *Summarien vber die Psalmen* (1531–1533), C6v (WA 38:27.35–36).

[79] *Summarien vber die Psalmen* (1531–1533), C6r (WA 38:27.29–31).

[80] In the last sermon on Psalm 72, Luther focuses on the two offices of the Christian: to pray and to praise. The catechism is key to these offices, for example, "Abide and pray your Creed and the Our Father. Christ is always for you" (WA 49:47.37–38).

[81] Second Sermon on Psalm 72 (January 6, 1540), WA 49:16.28–29. "May Christ give us the grace to rightly understand this psalm as it was composed by the poet—not as the Turk, Pope, and Jews understand it (concerning bodily and worldly reign)," Seventh Sermon on Psalm 72 (March 7, 1540), WA 49:49.32–34.

SUMMARIES OF THE PSALMS (1531–1533)

PSALM	TEN COMMANDMENTS #	COMMANDMENT	OUR FATHER #	PETITION	TYPE
1	3	Honor the Sabbath	2, 3	Thy kingdom come; thy will be done	Comfort
2	1	I am the LORD your God	2	Thy kingdom come	Prophecy
3	1	I am the LORD your God	7	Deliver us from evil	Prayer
4	1	I am the LORD your God	3, 4, 7	Thy will be done; Give us daily bread; deliver us from evil	Comfort, Prayer, Doctrine
5	2, 3	Honor his name; honor the Sabbath	1, 2	Hallowed be thy name; thy kingdom come	Prayer
6	1, 2	I am the LORD your God; honor his name	1	Hallowed be thy name	Prayer
7	2	Honor his name	1	Hallowed be thy name	Prayer
8	1	I am the LORD your God	2	Thy kingdom come	Prophecy
9	1	I am the LORD your God	2	Thy kingdom come	Prophecy
10	2	Honor his name	1	Hallowed be thy name	Prayer
11	2	Honor his name	1	Hallowed be thy name	Prayer
12	2, 3	Honor his name; honor the Sabbath	1, 2	Hallowed be thy name; thy kingdom come	Prayer
13	2	Honor his name	1, 7	Hallowed be thy name; Deliver us from evil	Prayer
14	1, 3	I am the LORD your God; honor the Sabbath	1, 2	Hallowed be thy name; thy kingdom come	Prophecy, Doctrine
15	3	Honor the Sabbath	3	Thy will be done	Doctrine
16	1, 2, 3	I am the LORD your God; honor his name; honor the Sabbath	1, 2	Hallowed be thy name; thy kingdom come	Prophecy
17	2, 3	Honor his name; honor the Sabbath	1	Hallowed be thy name	Prayer
18	2	Honor his name	1	Hallowed be thy name	Thanksgiving
19	3	Honor the Sabbath			Prophecy
20	2	Honor his name	3	Thy will be done	Prayer
21	1	I am the LORD your God	2	Thy kingdom come	Prophecy
22	1	I am the LORD your God	1, 2	Hallowed be thy name; thy kingdom come	Prophecy
23	3	Honor the Sabbath	2	Thy kingdom come	Thanksgiving
24	1, 2, 3	I am the LORD your God; honor his name; honor the Sabbath	1, 2, 3	Hallowed be thy name; thy kingdom come; thy will be done	Prophecy
25	2	Honor his name	2	Thy kingdom come	Prayer
26	3	Honor the Sabbath	1, 2	Hallowed be thy name; thy kingdom come	Prayer
27	1, 2	I am the LORD your God; Honor his name	1, 2	Hallowed be thy name; thy kingdom come	Thanksgiving, Prayer, Comfort
28	1, 3	I am the LORD your God; Honor the Sabbath	1, 2	Hallowed be thy name; thy kingdom come	Prayer
29	3	Honor the Sabbath	2	Thy kingdom come	Prophecy
30	3	Honor the Sabbath	1	Hallowed be thy name	Thanksgiving
31	2, 3	Honor his name; honor the Sabbath	1, 3	Hallowed be thy name; thy will be done	Thanksgiving, Prayer, Comfort

because their King is Life himself.[82] The realities of Scripture cannot now be seen with our eyes and reason. We hold these realities now by faith, and one day we will see them with our eyes. "Now we look through a mirror into an incomprehensible word, but then face to face" (1 Cor 13:12).[83] And the analogy of faith helps us distinguish God's wisdom from mere human wisdom.

---

[82] Luther notes that all Christians—no matter their nation and culture—interpret Scripture in the same way, because all Christians share the same gospel and Spirit. See Fourth Sermon on Psalm 72 (February 15, 1540), WA 49:34.13–17.

[83] WADB 7:123.

7

The Great Light in Darkness

Reading the Prophets According to the Rule of Faith

LUTHER CONSIDERED LUKE'S USE of Isaiah 9:6 to be the Bible in miniature. "It's a short sermon, but it bears all of Scripture in a pouch."[1] And so it is not surprising that he preached on Isaiah 9:2-6 more than any other Old Testament text. This was largely on account of the lectionary: he often took it as the sermon text for the afternoon sermon on Christmas because of Luke's use of Isaiah 9:6 in the assigned Gospel reading for Christmas (Lk 2:1-14). In his regular Christmas sermons on Luke 2, he would also draw attention to Isaiah 9. And he lectured twice on Isaiah 9—once as part of a lecture series on the entire book and once just on this chapter. Throughout his career Luther read Isaiah 9 according to the analogy of faith. He focused on how Isaiah 9 shows that this King is like no other king and his kingdom is like no other kingdom. He listens to what Scripture says about Scripture: he considers Paul's words in 1 Corinthians 15:55-57 and Colossians 2:13-15 as the best interpretation of Isaiah 9; he also unpacks Isaiah 9 through a typological reading of Judges 6–7. And so Luther chiefly uses the second and third articles of the Apostles' Creed to interpret Isaiah 9.

To show Luther's use of the analogy of faith in Isaiah 9, this chapter will focus on three issues: (1) how the second article illumines the Bible,

---

[1] Afternoon Sermon on the Feast of Christ's Birth (December 25, 1533), WA 37:237.33–34. Luther briefly explains all that "this short sermon" includes, for example, in Sermon on the Sunday After the Feast of the Circumcision (January 4, 1545), WA 49:662.7–663.5.

(2) how Luther uses the rule to form typology or to reason with Scripture according to Scripture, and (3) how Luther explains Christ's relationship to his church. Luther is emphatic: God's word is not dark or obscure; it is as bright as the sun. What seems to be the word's darkness or obscurity is actually human darkness or obscurity.[2] But by the light of the catechism and the Holy Spirit, humans are able to read the Bible. The catechism's light illumines what seems to be a subtle typology: Gideon as a type of Christ and Midian as a type of Christ's enemies. The catechism provides the framework for faithful typology. It also reveals Christ's upside-down relationship to his people. Unlike temporal rulers, who stand on their people's shoulders, Christ holds his people on his shoulders, giving them his adornment and beauty. Luther places the catechism and Bible in dynamic relationship—the Bible isn't just facts and stories about and for someone else; these words are *for us*.

THE RADIANT LIGHT OF THE SECOND ARTICLE

Isaiah removes the distinction between Jews and Gentiles.[3] "The people who walk in darkness see a great light, and over those who dwell in the dark country it shines brightly" (Is 9:2).[4] There are not two groups of people: one group that walks in darkness and one group that walks in light. Everyone dwells in darkness under the tyranny of sin, death, and the law. Luther underscores that if the Jews—who have God's law!—walk in darkness, how much more so the Gentiles.[5] The Jews with the Ten Commandments, the pope with his decretals, the Muslims with their Qur'an, and the philosophers with their reason, all think that they have great lights.[6] But human

---

[2]Luther's dispute with Erasmus is fundamentally about this question. See *Luther and Erasmus: Salvation and Free Will*. See also Erasmus's response to Luther's response, *Hyperaspistes Diatribae* (1526–1527); complete English translation in *Collected Works of Erasmus*, 86 vols. planned (Toronto: University of Toronto Press, 1969–), 76–77; selections in *Erasmus and Luther: The Battle Over Free Will*, trans. Clarence H. Miller and Peter Macardle (Indianapolis: Hackett, 2012). Their debate may also be an example of two warring medieval interpretive traditions, see Stock, *Listening for the Text*, 39–40.
[3]*Die Epistel des Propheten Jesaia* (1526), WA 19:134.19–34.
[4]WADB 11,1:47.
[5]*Die Epistel des Propheten Jesaia* (1526), WA 19:134.6, 13–34; Lectures on Isaiah 9 (1528), WA 25:121.7–12; Lectures on Isaiah 9 (1528), WA 31,2:68.18–21; Commentary on Isaiah Chapter 9 (1543–1544), WA 40,3:605.26–27; Afternoon Sermon on the Feast of the Circumcision (January 1, 1541), WA 49:191.12–14, 192.8–10.
[6]Commentary on Isaiah Chapter 9 (1543–1544), WA 40,3:605.18–21.

The Great Light in Darkness

wisdom cannot save us from death and the devil.[7] Humans continue in their idolatry: humans think that their darkness is light, that their foolishness is wisdom, and that their wickedness is virtue.[8] In harmony with the first table of the Ten Commandments, Isaiah teaches that divine intervention is required.

The light needed is Christ himself.[9] "Christ is the light and sun. His rays are the word of God, the Sacrament, Baptism, Absolution, and the wonderful things he has done and does."[10] As the sun's rays communicate the sun's light, warmth, and presence, the sacraments established by Jesus—God's word, Baptism, the Sacrament, and Absolution—communicate Jesus' light, friendship, and presence.[11] Darkness and those in the darkness cannot reach out and seize the light. As the first commandment teaches, God who is light must reveal himself, and he does so through his word. Humans must allow God's own light—his Son and word—to illumine who God is and what he does.[12] To try to seize God's character and activity according to our own thoughts is to seize a false god and a false Christ.[13] That's why the catechism is so necessary: the Ten Commandments, the Apostles' Creed, the Our Father, and the sacraments must order the hearts, minds, and actions of Christians.[14]

Isaiah masterfully depicts God's King: he is fully human and fully divine in the unity of his person. (All the prophets clearly and exactly describe the

---

[7] Commentary on Isaiah Chapter 9 (1543-1544), WA 40,3:608.11-24. While Luther praises Aristotle and Cicero as good and useful, he still says that their wisdom is not eternal.

[8] Afternoon Sermon on the Feast of Christ's Birth (December 25, 1525), WA 17,1:500.21-502.3; *Die Epistel des Propheten Jesaia* (1526), WA 19:134.1-12.

[9] Commentary on Isaiah Chapter 9 (1543-1544), WA 40,3:611.4-37.

[10] Commentary on Isaiah Chapter 9 (1543-1544), WA 40,3:615.2-4.

[11] See also Afternoon Sermon on the Feast of the Circumcision (January 1, 1541), WA 49:192.12-13. Jesus is brighter than the sun (WA 49:198.5-6).

[12] *Die Epistel des Propheten Jesaia* (1526), WA 19:133.25-28, 135.2-3.

[13] Afternoon Sermon on the First Day of Christmas (December 25, 1531), WA 34,2:513.17-514.1. Luther rails against Jewish interpretations of this passage. These interpretations taught that the child born in Isaiah 9 is Hezekiah and that the Messiah will be another king like Solomon, understanding the passage in too physical and temporal a manner. See Commentary on Isaiah Chapter 9 (1543-1544), WA 40,3:600.29-34, 601.6-12, 605.30-33, 606.1-9, 606.34-37, 641.22-26, 641.30-32; Sermon on the Day Before the Feast of Christ's Birth (December 24, 1537), WA 45:341.24-25; Sermon on the Day Before the Feast of the Circumcision (December 31, 1539), WA 47:872.6-15.

[14] Sermon on the Feast of St. John the Evangelist (December 27, 1531), WA 34,2:536.5-10. Luther laments the lack of familiarity with the catechism; instead Christians are focused on pilgrimages and human actions, which allows our hearts, minds, and actions to order Scripture.

Chalcedonian formula!¹⁵) This child is true and natural man, because he is born of a woman, because he is David's son.¹⁶ This child is also true and natural God, because he brings eternal peace, eternal righteousness, and an eternal kingdom—he does what God does.¹⁷ No human can do any of that.¹⁸ "No one is the Lord of peace or is mighty except God alone. No one can help in death but God alone. No one can overcome the devil and every evil but God alone."¹⁹ This child is born, and what is born dies. But this same child rules over the unseen spiritual realm, therefore he must also be an unseen spiritual being. Because he is born and is a spiritual King, he must die and live eternally.²⁰ In harmony with the second article of the Creed, Isaiah proclaims the Messiah's victorious death and resurrection through which he defeats death. And so Mary holds our treasure: this child.²¹ "God—Creator of heaven and earth—has been born of a woman!"²² Isaiah says all this in but a few words: "For us a Child is born; a Son is given to us" (Is 9:6).²³ "Blessed are all those who believe this, for Scripture does not lie to us and it does not deceive us."²⁴

God's King defeats our tyrants: sin, death, and the law.²⁵ "For you have broken to pieces the yoke of their burden and the rod of their shoulders and the scepter of their oppressor" (Is 9:4).²⁶ Luther finds the great Isaiahist Paul to be the best and clearest interpreter of this passage: "Death has been

---

[15] *Die Epistel des Propheten Jesaia* (1526), WA 19:149.26–150.30; Commentary on Isaiah Chapter 9 (1543–1544), WA 40,3:602.18–27.

[16] *Die Epistel des Propheten Jesaia* (1526), WA 19:149.27–150.13; Commentary on Isaiah Chapter 9 (1543–1544), WA 40,3:602.16–17, 656.3–6, 19–20, 657.29–31; Sermon on the Day Before the Feast of the Circumcision (December 31, 1539), WA 47:874.17, 22, 24–25. In the 1526 tract Luther draws attention to the Hebrew word יֶלֶד.

[17] Commentary on Isaiah Chapter 9 (1543–1544), WA 40,3:605.16–17, 22–24.

[18] That is why Isaiah says this child is a Son *given* to us. He comes to defeat death, sin, and the law. And so he is unlike other children, all of whom are weighed down by death, sin, and the law. *Die Epistel des Propheten Jesaia* (1526), WA 19:150.14–30.

[19] *Die Epistel des Propheten Jesaia* (1526), WA 19:163.21–23.

[20] *Die Epistel des Propheten Jesaia* (1526), WA 19:163.1–17.

[21] Sermon on the Day Before the Feast of Christ's Birth (December 24, 1531), WA 34,2:498.11–13.

[22] Sermon on the Day Before the Feast of Christ's Birth (December 24, 1531), WA 34,2:491.6.

[23] WADB 11,1:47. Commentary on Isaiah Chapter 9 (1543–1544), WA 40,3:659.21–28.

[24] *Die Epistel des Propheten Jesaia* (1526), WA 19:163.30–31.

[25] Afternoon Sermon on the Feast of Christ's Birth (December 25, 1531), WA 17,1:503.4–7; Lectures on Isaiah 9 (1528), WA 25:121.24–28; Lectures on Isaiah 9 (1528), WA 31,2:69.3–16, 17–30; Commentary on Isaiah Chapter 9 (1543–1544), WA 40,3: 603.17–29, 30–39, 626.3.

[26] WADB 11,1:47.

swallowed whole in victory. Death, where is your sting? Hell, where is your victory? Now the sting of death is sin, and the power of sin is the law. But thanks be to God who gives us the victory through our Lord Jesus Christ" (1 Cor 15:55-57).[27] Accordingly what Isaiah calls *the yoke of their burden* is death; what he calls *the rod of their shoulders* is sin; and what he calls *the scepter of their oppressor* is the law. Paul clearly lays bare the chain of logic between death, sin, and the law.[28] The law reveals sin. "But I would not have recognized sin except through the law" (Rom 7:7).[29] And sin brings death. "For death is sin's wages" (Rom 6:23).[30] Without the law, therefore, sin and death are present but not felt; however, without sin there is no death.[31] "It's not possible for death to be without sin or sin to be without death. That's why death couldn't remain over Christ—even if it did hold him for a time on account of us. For in Christ there was no sin, except our sin, which he took on himself. So it also can't remain over Christians, because they are now righteous in Christ and have no sin, although it holds them for a time."[32] Only someone—like this child—born under the law but also without sin can break the tyranny of death, sin, and the law over us.[33]

Jesus had to be born of a woman but in a supernatural way (conceived by the Holy Spirit, not by a man). What is born of man and woman is marred with sin, but what is not born of humans cannot be shared with humans. To

---

[27] WADB 7:135. Afternoon Sermon on the Feast of Christ's Birth (December 25, 1531), WA 17,1:502.21-23; *Die Epistel des Propheten Jesaia* (1526), WA 19:139.34-140.2; Commentary on Isaiah Chapter 9 (1543-1544), WA 40,3:626.3-633.28; Sermon on the Day Before the Feast of Christ's Birth (December 24, 1537), WA 45:343.1-4. Luther calls Paul a student of Isaiah and Isaiah a student of David. On Paul as a student of Isaiah, see Commentary on Isaiah Chapter 9 (1543-1544), WA 40,3: 631.9-12, 659.30; WATR 6:202-3, no. 6805; on Isaiah's love of David, see WATR 1:375, no. 793; 6:317, no. 7001.

[28] Afternoon Sermon on the Feast of Christ's Birth (December 25, 1531), WA 17,1:502.21-23; *Die Epistel des Propheten Jesaia* (1526), WA 19:139.34-140.2; Commentary on Isaiah Chapter 9 (1543-1544), WA 40,3:626.3-633.28; Sermon on the Day Before the Feast of Christ's Birth (December 24, 1537), WA 45:343.1-4.

[29] WADB 7:51.

[30] WADB 7:49. The word Luther uses for "wages" is *Sold*, which—like Paul's Greek—is the monetary compensation for enlisted military service. On *Sold*, see DWB 16:1433-36. On ὀψώνιον, see Fitzmyer, *Romans*, 452; Cranfield, *A Critical and Exegetical Commentary on the Epistle to the Romans*, 1:329.

[31] *Die Epistel des Propheten Jesaia* (1526), WA 19:141.8-13, 144.7-8; Sermon on the Day Before the Feast of Christ's Birth (December 24, 1537), WA 45:341.11-12.

[32] *Die Epistel des Propheten Jesaia* (1526), WA 19:141.8-13.

[33] *Die Epistel des Propheten Jesaia* (1526), WA 19:149.31-150.4; Commentary on Isaiah Chapter 9 (1543-1544), WA 40,3:654.6-16.

defeat sin and death he had to be other than flesh and blood, but he also had to be flesh and blood to share this victory with humans.[34] "By his most glorious victory he overcame death."[35] Because all that is his is ours, we clothe ourselves in his holiness.[36]

Therefore, Satan and his allies—death, sin, and the law—have no rights over us.[37] While they afflict us now, they are like an infamous criminal who awaits his trial from his prison cell, knowing that the verdict over him will be death. They still have what can be called a life, but it isn't much of one. Like the imprisoned criminal, they face their certain death: "He lives no longer so that he might rule, but so that he will be condemned and executed."[38] Because Christ is our champion, he shares his victory with us. "He puts us on his shoulders, so that we would be tramplers of the devil and death, etc. and lords over the devil and death, etc."[39] Christ's people should be fearless; their victory is assured because of Christ's victory.[40] Luther follows Paul's lead and encourages his parishioners and students to taunt their enemies who Jesus has defeated. Luther refashions the words with which Jesus was mocked on the cross to mock sin, death, and the devil (compare Mt 27:39–44): "Hey, climb down from the cross! If you're such a gigantic and mighty lord, prove it with your pinkie. There you hang on the cross of Christ—and soon you must die on it. And the one whom you hung on the cross? He has been freed from it with all of us; we all hang on him."[41] In a mysterious exchange, while humans nailed God on the cross, God nailed the debt of humans to the cross (Col 2:13–15). So in suffering and affliction Christians should remind Satan and his minions about this child.[42]

---

[34] *Die Epistel des Propheten Jesaia* (1526), WA 19:150.31–151.15.
[35] Commentary on Isaiah Chapter 9 (1543–1544), WA 40,3:607.16.
[36] *Die Epistel des Propheten Jesaia* (1526), WA 19:150.6–13.
[37] *Die Epistel des Propheten Jesaia* (1526), WA 19:142.1–9, 143.15, 145.4–6; Commentary on Isaiah Chapter 9 (1543–1544), WA 40,3:609.29–38; 659.36–37.
[38] *Die Epistel des Propheten Jesaia* (1526), WA 19:141.17–27, here 26–27.
[39] Commentary on Isaiah Chapter 9 (1543–1544), WA 40,3:659.38–39.
[40] Commentary on Isaiah Chapter 9 (1543–1544), WA 40,3:651.23–29, citing Rom 8:31 and 1 Jn 5:1; Sermon on the Feast of St. John the Evangelist (December 27, 1531), WA 34,2:536.15–20, 536.30–34.
[41] *Die Epistel des Propheten Jesaia* (1526), WA 19:142.29–33. See also Commentary on Isaiah Chapter 9 (1543–1544), WA 40,3:639.34–37, 655.4–13, 660.18–19.
[42] Sermon on the Day Before the Feast of Christ's Birth (December 24, 1531), WA 34,2:499.22–23; Commentary on Isaiah Chapter 9 (1543–1544), WA 40,3:660.18–19.

The Great Light in Darkness

The incarnation and victory of God—taught by the Bible and the Creed—is complete foolishness to the world. According to philosophers a pure God cannot be placed in impurity, and so even if the Creed only said that the Son of God was born, the world would not stop laughing at Christians.[43] But it gets worse. "Victory happens in the world and in every other battle when we find bloody clothes and hack off heads. Christ's victory won't be like that."[44] This King conquers and rules unlike any earthly king—he does so without a sword.[45] This child leads with the word; the word cast into the world is his sword.[46] Although it seems weak according to appearances, the word is the most powerful thunderbolt, even in the mouth of weak humans. It defeats the Romans, their gods, and their wisdom.[47] It also conquers the devil; where Christ and his word are preached, devils flee.[48] "This is a wonderful warrior to me: whoever defeats them with the weak word."[49]

Ruled Typology

The exegetical tradition showed how Isaiah uses Gideon's victory over Midian as a type of this child's victory.[50] Luther expanded on the tradition.[51]

---

[43] Sermon on the Day Before the Feast of Christ's Birth (December 24, 1531), WA 34,2:492.10-11, 494.3-5.
[44] Sermon on the Day Before the Feast of Christ's Birth (December 24, 1537), WA 45:343.26-27.
[45] *Die Epistel des Propheten Jesaia* (1526), WA 19:149.9-11. Jesus is not violent. Luther underscores how careful Isaiah is not to say the king is a man (*vir*) or another David. Isaiah is emphatic: this King is a baby, and yet he is nothing less than Lord and Prince. If you do not believe in this child, he is a terrible judge. But if you believe in this child, there's nothing to fear—he remains a baby. He is not violent. "He doesn't have a sword but his mother's breast; he's an infant; he lies in a trough" (WA 40,3:650.8-9). He has no weapons—he doesn't even have teeth: he's a baby. He remains a baby (and King) for us forever. Commentary on Isaiah Chapter 9 (1543-1544), WA 40,3:649.7-15, 26-35, 649.36-650.2, 650.10-23, 651.10-22, 653.31-32.
[46] Sermon on the Feast of St. John the Evangelist (December 27, 1531), WA 34,2:531.1; Afternoon Sermon on the Feast of the Circumcision (January 1, 1541), WA 49:195.13-14.
[47] Sermon on the Feast of St. John the Evangelist (December 27, 1531), WA 34,2:531.9-12.
[48] Sermon on the Feast of St. John the Evangelist (December 27, 1531), WA 34,2:532.9-11.
[49] Sermon on the Feast of St. John the Evangelist (December 27, 1531), WA 34,2:531.30-532.23.
[50] *Glossa ordinaria*, 4:119-20. In contrast, Jewish interpreters—according to Luther—saw Hezekiah as the fulfillment of Isaiah 9, even in this comparison to Gideon. In addition to the obvious objection that Hezekiah's reign was not eternal and that there was no peace in his time, Luther doesn't see any parallels between Gideon and Hezekiah. See Commentary on Isaiah Chapter 9 (1543-1544), WA 40,3:600.29-34, 601.6-12, 633.30-634.9, 637.15-18; Sermon on the Day Before the Feast of the Circumcision (December 31, 1539), WA 47:872.6-15.
[51] Afternoon Sermon on the Feast of Christ's Birth (December 25, 1525), WA 17,1:503.8-17; *Die Epistel des Propheten Jesaia* (1526), WA 19:145.18-146.30; Lectures on Isaiah 9 (1528), WA 25:121.20-37; Commentary on Isaiah Chapter 9 (1543-1544), WA 40,3:633.30-641.19; Sermon on the Day Before the Feast of Christ's Birth (December 24, 1537),

He claimed that Isaiah would have liked to include all of Judges 6–7, but it was too much to recite—let alone interpret![52] So Isaiah used "as in the time of Midian" (Is 9:4) to refer to the entirety of Gideon's victory.[53] For Luther this use of Scripture interpreting Scripture—which he enriches with reference to the second article of the Creed—illustrates Isaiah's teaching of Christ's nature and benefits.

Luther draws Gideon as a type of Christ.[54] (In his Isaiah 9 lectures, Luther refers to this as allegory rather than typology: "I don't pay much attention to allegories except when necessity compels us. But allegory is quite necessary for this passage."[55]) Gideon and his three hundred attacked the encampment of 120,000 Midianites, Amalekites, and those of the East with nothing more than trumpets and empty jars; the Midianites, Amalekites, and those of the East slaughtered themselves.[56] Gideon's enemies typify Christ's: Gideon holds the field against three peoples, just as Christ holds the field against sin, death, and the law.[57] The nature of Gideon's victory typifies that of Christ's: Gideon wins without human power or even human weapons, just as Christ wins by submitting to human might and violence.[58] "Truly an amazing battle—a battle without a sword!"[59] Just as the Midianites and their allies kill themselves with their own swords, so death and its allies kill themselves by trying to devour Christ. "Christ has risen again, and he has gobbled up death in his death."[60] Here Luther winks at the baited Leviathan metaphor: Satan does not realize that Christ is God, when he rushes to stab Christ (as it were), he instead stabs himself with his

---

[51] WA 45:343.28–344.6. Although in the 1543–1544 lectures Luther refers to this as allegory not typology, he doesn't seem to have neatly delineated the two approaches.

[52] *Die Epistel des Propheten Jesaia* (1526), WA 19:145.25–28. After this comment, Luther summarizes Judges 6–7. See WA 19:145.28–146.7; see also Commentary on Isaiah Chapter 9 (1543–1544), WA 40,3:634.19–635.30.

[53] WADB 11,1:47.

[54] See especially *Die Epistel des Propheten Jesaia* (1526), WA 19:146.8–30.

[55] Commentary on Isaiah Chapter 9 (1543–1544), WA 40,3:637.19–20.

[56] Luther shows the dissimilarity between Hezekiah's defeat of Sennacherib and Gideon's defeat of the Midianites and their allies: Hezekiah won not in human weakness but in angelic power—angels slaughtered Sennacherib's army (2 Kings 19:20–37). And so Luther argues that the Jewish interpreters who tie Isaiah 9 to Hezekiah are wrong. See Commentary on Isaiah Chapter 9 (1543–1544), WA 40,3:636.27–637.1.

[57] *Die Epistel des Propheten Jesaia* (1526), WA 19:146.10–13.

[58] Commentary on Isaiah Chapter 9 (1543–1544), WA 40,3:634.10–18.

[59] Commentary on Isaiah Chapter 9 (1543–1544), WA 40,3:634.26.

[60] *Die Epistel des Propheten Jesaia* (1526), WA 19:146.16–19, quoting 18–19.

own sword.⁶¹ Gideon leads his three hundred into victory, just as Christ leads his Christians into victory.⁶² The three hundred must have been filled with faith—they entered the battlefield only with a trumpet in their right hand and a lamp in their left hand. In the same way, pastors and the apostles are filled with faith; they are armed with the word alone.⁶³ The faith that defeated the Midianites and their allies is the faith that defeats sin, death, and the devil: "When I am powerless, that's when I am the most powerful, for power is made perfect in powerlessness."⁶⁴ With these comparisons, Luther is only just beginning. The rest of the Gideon story as a type of Christ could fill a whole book!⁶⁵

In this typology of Gideon and Christ, Luther focuses on the second article of the Creed and the ministry of the word, but he also applies Confession and Absolution to this passage. He uses the Midianites as a type for repentant sinners. "I have sinned. That's the slaughter or killing that proceeds from the sound of the trumpets and the light of the flames."⁶⁶ By the Spirit the preaching of the word lays sinners low so that, like the Midianites with their own swords, they slay themselves with their own words: "I confess that I have sinned, O Lord, my Shepherd."⁶⁷ Luther explains that those who know the Bible well know that the slaying of enemies represents this spiritual death of Confession accomplished by the ministers of Christ.⁶⁸ These

---

⁶¹Afternoon Sermon on the Feast of Christ's Birth (December 25, 1525), WA 17,1:503.10-12; *Die Epistel des Propheten Jesaia* (1526), WA 19:145.20-24, 146.16-19; Sermon on the Day Before the Feast of Christ's Birth (December 24, 1537), WA 45:344.4-6. On the baited Leviathan metaphor, see chapter 5, "The Riddle of the Resurrection." On Luther's view of atonement, see Matthieu Arnold, "Luther on Christ's Person and Work," in *The Oxford Handbook of Martin Luther's Theology*, ed. Robert Kolb, Irene Dingel, and L'ubomír Batka (New York: Oxford University Press, 2014), 274-93, esp. 283-86; Lienhard, *Luther: Witness to Jesus Christ*, 176-85; Althaus, *Theology of Martin Luther*, 201-23 Veli-Matti Kärkkäinen, *A Constructive Christian Theology for the Pluralistic World*, 5 vols. (Grand Rapids: Eerdmans, 2013-2017), 1:291-323.

⁶²*Die Epistel des Propheten Jesaia* (1526), WA 19:146.13-16.

⁶³Commentary on Isaiah Chapter 9 (1543-1544), WA 40,3:634.31-32, 635.5-18, 637.34-38, 638.7-11; Afternoon Sermon on the Feast of the Circumcision (January 1, 1541), WA 49:192.21-24.

⁶⁴*Die Epistel des Propheten Jesaia* (1526), WA 19:146.5-6, quoting 2 Cor 12:9.

⁶⁵*Die Epistel des Propheten Jesaia* (1526), WA 19:146.27-30.

⁶⁶Commentary on Isaiah Chapter 9 (1543-1544), WA 40,3:639.1-2. Johann Spangenberg (1484-1550), a student and friend of Luther, interprets Peter's dream in Acts 10 in the same way: to kill and eat unclean animals is to preach the word to pagans and to convert them. See RCS NT 6:136.

⁶⁷Commentary on Isaiah Chapter 9 (1543-1544), WA 40,3:638.25.

⁶⁸Commentary on Isaiah Chapter 9 (1543-1544), WA 40,3:638.19-22.

physical battles point to the spiritual battle in every human heart: the struggle against sin, death, and the flesh. As the Israelites slay their enemies, so Christians slay sin, death, and the flesh through Confession, receiving the spoils of Christ's victory: the Absolution of their sins.[69] Absolution is powerful. It brings our heart back to life, and it routs Satan. And all this happens through mere human words! "Yes, these very words are spoken by a human, nevertheless these works are not human works but God's works."[70] So whenever our conscience attacks us, we must turn to a minister of the church or a brother in Christ and seek Absolution, which puts the law, sin, and death to flight.[71] Gideon and his three hundred as well as other stories from Israel's history graphically depict our pursuit of forgiveness. Daily we must die to the old self, which remains under the law, and be born anew by God's word and Spirit.[72]

THE GOVERNMENT OF THE THIRD ARTICLE

Luther also interprets Isaiah 9 with part of the third article of the Creed: "I believe in the holy Christian church." Isaiah's words—particularly "Whose rule is on his shoulder"—reveal the shape and character of Christ's kingdom, the church.[73] Christ's kingdom is unlike any other kingdom. "I have said the coming kingdom of Christ is a most peaceful, son-ly, and childish kingdom."[74] What earthly kingdom can be described this way? The prophets and apostles agree about the nature of Christ's reign: the church is a kingdom turned upside down.[75]

---

[69]Commentary on Isaiah Chapter 9 (1543–1544), WA 40,3:639.3–14, alluding to Is 9:3; Lk 11:21–23. Perhaps the clearest example of this, for Luther, is the exodus through the Red Sea as a type for Baptism. The same waters bring death to the Egyptians and life to the Israelites, just as the waters of Baptism bring death to the old self and life to the new self. See the prayer for consecrating the baptismal waters, known as "the great flood prayer," *The Baptism Booklet in German* (1523), LW 53:97 (WA 12:43.28–34); Peter Leithart structured his little Baptism book on this prayer, *Baptism: A Guide to Life from Death*, Christian Essentials (Bellingham, WA: Lexham Press, 2021). See also the contrast of verses 28 and 29 in Exodus 14, WADB 8:245.

[70]Commentary on Isaiah Chapter 9 (1543–1544), WA 40,3:632.39–633.27, quoting 633.20–21. See also WA 40,3:631.18–36; Sermon on the Day Before the Feast of the Circumcision (December 31, 1539), WA 47:874.31–33.

[71]Commentary on Isaiah Chapter 9 (1543–1544), WA 40,3:632.15–27.

[72]Commentary on Isaiah Chapter 9 (1543–1544), WA 40,3:654.17–655.3, 660.12–14.

[73]WADB 11,1:47.

[74]Commentary on Isaiah Chapter 9 (1543–1544), WA 40,3:653.30.

[75]Commentary on Isaiah Chapter 9 (1543–1544), WA 40,3:617.7–9.

The tradition understood "His rule is on his shoulder" to refer to the cross.[76] Luther agreed that this fits with the faith, but he thought a simpler interpretation is that *we* Christians are the rule on Christ's shoulders.[77] King Jesus carries his people on his shoulders, in contrast to all earthly kings—not just tyrants!—who are carried by their people.[78] "The rule of this Son born to us is upside down: he carries us, we lie on his shoulder. He must be our bearer. Look how Isaiah has turned worldly custom upside down!"[79] This helps us differentiate the temporal and spiritual kingdoms. Each temporal ruler is carried by thousands of people, but the Christ carries an innumerable hoard on his shoulder.[80] As signs of their rule, earthly kings wear crowns on their heads and hold orbs in their hands; in contrast, Christ carries his people on his shoulder.[81] Temporal lords only adorn themselves with glory; they want to be served. But Christ adorns himself with our sin and shame; he wants to serve. "I want to give you everything. All your guilt will lie on my shoulders."[82] The rule of sin that was on *our* shoulders has been transferred to Christ, and accordingly it has been defeated and taken captive.[83] As the good Samaritan carries the half-dead man and as the good shepherd carries the lost sheep, so Jesus daily carries us and our sin (even as he did on the cross!).[84] "In an earthly kingdom the prince or king is free; all the rest

---

[76] *Glossa ordinaria*, 4:121-22. See the inline gloss on *principatus* as well as the comments of Ambrosius, Theophylact, Tertullian, and Nicholas of Lyra. See *Die Epistel des Propheten Jesaia* (1526), WA 19:151.17-20; Lectures on Isaiah 9 (1528), WA 25:123.3-7; Lectures on Isaiah 9 (1528), WA 31,2:70.25-28.

[77] *Die Epistel des Propheten Jesaia* (1526), WA 19:151.25; Lectures on Isaiah 9 (1528), WA 25:123.7-8; Lectures on Isaiah 9 (1528), WA 31,2:70.28-29.

[78] Afternoon Sermon on the Feast of Christ's Birth (December 25, 1520), WA 9:521.19-522.3; Sermon on the Feast of St. Stephen (December 26, 1525), WA 17,1:504.3-19; Lectures on Isaiah 9 (1528), WA 25:123.7-14; Lectures on Isaiah 9 (1528), WA 31,2:70.28-32; Afternoon Sermon on the First Day of Christmas (December 25, 1531), WA 34,2:511.11-14, 512.1-3.

[79] Afternoon Sermon on the First Day of Christmas (December 25, 1531), WA 34,2:512.23-25.

[80] Sermon on the Feast of St. Stephen (December 26, 1531), WA 34,2:517.10-16; see also *Die Epistel des Propheten Jesaia* (1526), WA 19:152.5-27.

[81] Sermon on the Feast of St. Stephen (December 26, 1525), WA 17,1:504.25-31.

[82] Afternoon Sermon on the First Day of Christmas (December 25, 1531), WA 34,2:513.27.

[83] *Die Epistel des Propheten Jesaia* (1526), WA 19:143.16-25.

[84] *Die Epistel des Propheten Jesaia* (1526), WA 19:151.28-152.4, quoting 1 Pet 2:24; Jn 1:29; Lk 10:34; 15:5. Christ says, "Hop on! I want to carry you; all your sins are forgiven," Afternoon Sermon on the First Day of Christmas (December 25, 1531), WA 34,2:514.16-17.

are slaves. But in Christ's kingdom Christ alone is a slave and we are free."[85] In this way too Jesus inverts the relationship between a leader and his people.

The boundary markers of Christ's kingdom transcend time and place. "And everyone—whoever they may be, Isaiah, Peter, Paul, from the greatest to the least—whom I carry is my land, people, and kingdom."[86] Christ's shoulders are the boundary markers. The citizens of this kingdom are the saints who are gathered from every age and every nation and who are borne by Christ. That's why Isaiah says, "You increase the nations" (Is 9:3).[87] Unlike earthly kings, Christ's kingdom is everywhere, because it is wherever he is. The church is not at Rome or Babylon; it is not under Christ's feet—it is on his shoulders![88] "But these are Christians: those who are on his shoulders."[89] He carries his people like a father carries his child and like a shepherd carries his lamb.

Christ's kingdom is a kingdom of mercy, a kingdom of help, of comfort, of forgiveness—it's a kingdom of faith![90] And so Christians must carefully distinguish Christ's kingdom from all temporal kingdoms. Isaiah helps us to do that. The kingdom of Christ is ruled by a baby; temporal kingdoms are ruled by men.[91] The kingdom of Christ is everywhere; temporal kingdoms are restricted to a plot of land.[92] The kingdom of Christ is a kingdom of peace, ruled by the word; temporal kingdoms are filled with war, ruled by

---

[85] Lectures on Isaiah 9 (1528), WA 31,2:70.32-34. See also *Die Epistel des Propheten Jesaia* (1526), WA 19:152.5-27).

[86] Afternoon Sermon on the First Day of Christmas (December 25, 1531), WA 34,2:513.12-15, 28, here quoting 13-15.

[87] WADB 11,1:47; Commentary on Isaiah Chapter 9 (1543-1544), WA 40,3:622.4-11.

[88] *Die Epistel des Propheten Jesaia* (1526), WA 19:152.10-11; Sermon on the Day Before the Feast of Christ's Birth (December 24, 1537), WA 45:345.10-15; Afternoon Sermon on the First Day of Christmas (December 25, 1531), WA 34,2:512.7-18. Luther admits that the strict rules of dialectics wouldn't allow such a definition of the church—she is not restricted to earthly geography, but she is wherever Christ is (WA 34,2:512.14). Again, for Luther, according to the second commandment, God's word must order speech about the church.

[89] Afternoon Sermon on the First Day of Christmas (December 25, 1531), WA 34,2:513.19. Luther admits that the pope and *Schwärmer* have this text and Baptism; nevertheless, a Christian is one who is on Christ's shoulders, that is, one who believes. *Die Epistel des Propheten Jesaia* (1526), WA 19:151.28-152.4; Afternoon Sermon on the First Day of Christmas (December 25, 1531), WA 34,2:513.1-4.

[90] *Die Epistel des Propheten Jesaia* (1526), WA 19:152.28-35.

[91] Commentary on Isaiah Chapter 9 (1543-1544), WA 40,3:649.7-15.

[92] Afternoon Sermon on the First Day of Christmas (December 25, 1531), WA 34,2:512.7-18.

The Great Light in Darkness 129

the sword.[93] The kingdom of Christ is eternal and spiritual; temporal kingdoms are temporary and physical.[94] "He wonderfully leads us out of captivity, gives us life in the midst of death, righteousness in the midst of sin, riches in the midst of poverty. He turns it all upside down."[95] Christ's kingdom is upside down from temporal kingdoms.

The true Christian church—distinguished from worldly power—is heretical before the world. According to Luther, that's how Jews, Papists, and Muslims see the church.[96] The church has no external adornment. It has no external beauty or status or power that would indicate its true beauty, status, and power. "The veil that covers [the church's holiness] is sin, death, the devil, and the world, so that nothing but death is seen. All the world and all wisdom and all reason stand against me."[97] The church's existence is an article of faith, for it is mightily veiled. Its only adornment is the sacraments: Baptism, Holy Communion, Absolution, and the word. "In me there's nothing but sin; in Christ there's nothing but pure righteousness."[98] "Lord Jesus, you are my righteousness, just as I am your sin."[99] But the abomination of desolation commingles Christ's kingdom with the kingdoms of the world, teaching new doctrines and traditions against Christ and his gospel.[100]

For Us—Golden Words Added to All of the Catechism

For Luther, the Bible and catechism mutually illumine one another. So far we have seen how Luther said that the catechism—most often the second article of the Creed—illumines the Bible. But in his preaching and teaching on Isaiah 9,

---

[93]Lectures on Isaiah 9 (1528), WA 25:122.44-45, 123.1-2; Lectures on Isaiah 9 (1528), WA 31,2:70.16-23; Commentary on Isaiah Chapter 9 (1543-1544), WA 40,3:644.25-30. Luther uses Islam and the Qur'an as a counter-example. According to Luther, the sword is part of Islamic doctrine. See WA 40,3:646.3-16. The Weimar editors cite Sura 4, but it seems that Sura 9 fits better.

[94]Sermon on the Feast of St. Stephen (December 26, 1525), WA 17,1:507.15.

[95]Sermon on the Feast of St. Stephen (December 26, 1525), WA 17,1:504.10-12.

[96]Sermon on the Feast of St. Stephen (December 26, 1531), WA 34,2:518.9-12.

[97]Sermon on the Feast of St. Stephen (December 26, 1531), WA 34,2:519.2-4.

[98]Sermon on the Feast of St. Stephen (December 26, 1531), WA 34,2:519.6-7. This paragraph is based on Sermon on the Feast of St. Stephen (December 26, 1531), WA 34,2:518.12-519.11; alternate witness, 518.26-519.22.

[99]To George Spenlein (April 8, 1516), LW 48:12.

[100]Commentary on Isaiah Chapter 9 (1543-1544), WA 40,3:647.1-14; alluding to Mark 13:14; Matt 24:15. Satan loves confusion: he also strives to confuse the three estates of church, society, and family. See Commentary on Isaiah Chapter 9 (1543-1544), WA 40,3:648.8-17.

Luther also shows how the Bible illumines the catechism—unsurprisingly the second article of the Creed in this particular case. Isaiah teaches that we should add "for us" to every part of the Creed.

By the little phrase "for us," Isaiah proclaims that Mary's child is ours. "And he will be called my Son and gift—so certainly, as if he were placed in my own hands!"[101] Once we were all barren women, but now we are mothers. Jesus earns the spoils of salvation according to his humanity (our flesh, bone, and blood!).[102] But if he is not for us, he is of no help to us—even if he were born a thousand times.[103] Christ is our treasure, life, and salvation, therefore, Christians inscribe these five letters—as great as heaven and earth—on their hearts: for us.[104] "The greatest art is to be able to say 'for us.' "[105] Christians should practice this art every time they say the Creed, for it lists our full inheritance in Christ.[106]

And so Isaiah teaches not to read the Bible or to say the Creed coldly. This is not just some history of who killed whom, when, and why. And it's not just for Jesus—it's for us![107] "The Christian faith—from this prophecy—makes history a possession."[108] But we receive this possession as if it were a sip of beer or as if it were someone else's crown or as if it neither feeds nor warms us.[109]

---

[101] Afternoon Sermon on the First Day of Christmas (December 25, 1531), WA 34,2:510.1–16, quoting 12–13. See also Sermon on the Feast of Christ's Birth (December 25, unknown year), WA 45:427.5–8.
[102] *Die Epistel des Propheten Jesaia* (1526), WA 19:149.14–25; Afternoon Sermon on the First Day of Christmas (December 25, 1531), WA 34,2:510.6.
[103] *Die Epistel des Propheten Jesaia* (1526), WA 19:149.22–24. This is related to Luther's comments on the Holy Spirit. Without the ministry of the Holy Spirit, Christ would remain hidden and be of no benefit to us.
[104] Sermon on the Day Before the Feast of Christ's Birth (December 24, 1531), WA 34,2:496.12–13; Sermon on the Day Before the Feast of the Circumcision (December 31, 1539), WA 47:874.39–875.7.
[105] Sermon on the Day Before the Feast of the Circumcision (December 31, 1539), WA 47:874.35–36.
[106] Afternoon Sermon on the First Day of Christmas (December 25, 1531), WA 34,2:509.1–510.2. Luther seems to commingle the wording of the Nicene Creed with the Apostles' Creed here. He says that we always add "for us" to "conceived by the Holy Spirit" etc., but that we should add this phrase to the entire Creed.
[107] Afternoon Sermon on the First Day of Christmas (December 25, 1531), WA 34,2:509.13–14; Afternoon Sermon on the Feast of Christ's Birth (December 25, 1540), WA 49:176.21–177.3.
[108] Sermon on the Day Before the Feast of the Circumcision (December 31, 1539), WA 47:874.38–39.
[109] Sermon on the Day Before the Feast of Christ's Birth (December 24, 1531), WA 34,2:494.12–13, 495.1–7; Afternoon Sermon on the Feast of Christ's Birth (December 25, 1540), WA 49:177.1–3.

We are blind to the immense treasure that is God for us, preferring 10,000 florin to the gift that made a third of heaven fall.[110] In contrast to our ingratitude, look at the joy of the angels and prophets! The angels sing: "Honor be to God in the highest and peace on earth and good will among people" (Lk 2:14).[111] "Our heart should break into a thousand pieces for joy!"[112]

Conclusion

Luther taught that the Prophets—as represented by Isaiah—must be interpreted according to the analogy of faith. Otherwise humans, like the Papists, Jews, and *Schwärmer*, want to read the Prophets as a key for future events. But this confuses the two types of prophecy: special prophecy, which foretells future things, and general prophecy, which interprets Scripture. Only a few have the gift of special prophecy, while every Christian has the gift of general prophecy.[113] Fallen human nature craves prophecy of what is to come. And so humans demand knowledge of future temporal events from the Bible, but God's word is meant to give hope, encouragement, and correction, so that we would hope and trust in God and love our neighbors. "The impious bid [prophecies of Christ] farewell—they expect other prophecies from us about things to come, about the Turks and other contingencies. We only have prophecies about Christ and his word."[114] When Christians read prophecies like Isaiah 9, they must ask what is the passage proclaiming

---

[110] Sermon on the Day Before the Feast of Christ's Birth (December 24, 1531), WA 34,2:499.1–4; Afternoon Sermon on the Feast of Christ's Birth (December 25, 1544), WA 49:632.29–39. Luther says that the incarnation is what made Satan fall, implying that God would have become incarnate even without the fall. Satan could not bear the idea that he must bow to a human. Strikingly Luther here cites the Qur'an, Sura 2. The tradition interpreted Revelation 12:4 about the angels Satan seduced to join him. For example, see William C. Weinrich, ed., *Revelation*, ACCS NT 12 (Downers Grove, IL: InterVarsity Press, 2005), 178–79.

[111] WADB 6:217. See Sermon on the Day Before the Feast of Christ's Birth (December 24, 1531), WA 34,2:494.10–12, 495.5–6.

[112] Evening Sermon on the Feast of Christ's Birth (December 25, 1543), WA 49:281.34–35. See also WA 49:281.20–23.

[113] WATR 1:529, no. 1049. Elsewhere Luther says the two types of prophecy are general prophecy (to interpret Scripture) and special prophecy (to know times, people, and things). For example, see further WATR 1:15–16, no. 45; 1:545–46, no. 1079; 3:177, no. 121; Epistle on the Second Sunday after Epiphany (*Church Postil*, 1525), WA 17,2:38.25–39.4, LW 76:214–15; Afternoon Sermon on the Second Sunday after Epiphany (1531), WA 34,1:104.16–105.1; Sermon on Pentecost Tuesday (1535), WA 41:268.17–22. Compare Hieronymus Weller von Molsdorf's comments on prophecy, RCS OT 5:96–97. See chapter 2, "How Does Luther Understand Prophecy."

[114] Afternoon Sermon on Pentecost Tuesday (1529), WA 29:377.26–28.

about the King and kingdom proclaimed in the Creed. Hezekiah or David or kings like them do not fulfill Isaiah 9, only the child who is God and man does.[115] His character and kingdom are upside down from the character and kingdoms of earthly kings. And so, according to reason, people ridicule God, mocking the preaching of his word as a fable. But, according to faith, there is nothing more precious than the word of this eternal King of peace and righteousness.[116] The Bible and the Creed teach that this child is for us. Those who firmly believe the "for us" of the Bible and the Creed are doctors of doctors, saints of saints, and prophets of prophets.[117] The analogy of faith trains us in this holy school of saints and prophets.

---

[115]Commentary on Isaiah Chapter 9 (1543-1544), WA 40,3:599.31, 600.29-34, 601.6-12, 605.30-33, 606.1-15, 641.22-26, 641.30-32; Sermon on the Day Before the Feast of Christ's Birth (December 24, 1537), WA 45:341.24-25; Sermon on the Day Before the Feast of the Circumcision (December 31, 1539), WA 47:872.6-15.

[116]Commentary on Isaiah Chapter 9 (1543-1544), WA 40,3:616.4-11.

[117]Sermon on the Day Before the Feast of the Circumcision (December 31, 1539), WA 47:875.4-6.

8

The Light of the Word

Reading the New Testament According to the Rule of Faith

LUTHER PREACHED ON LUKE 24:13–49 for Easter Monday and Tuesday from 1521 to 1534. After a week of daily preaching on the resurrection, Luther was self-conscious about these Gospel readings. "I suppose you've heard enough about the resurrection of Christ."¹ Luther soldiers on and preaches about the resurrection anyway, because Jesus commands us to preach the word without ceasing. Thankfully the word of God is generative.² The readings on Easter Monday and Tuesday gave Luther good reason to show how the people of the resurrection read the Bible differently. And so he focused on how Luke 24 shows what Scripture is for: to comfort and strengthen the weak and to forgive sins. Luther expands Luke's terse words—"And he began with Moses and all the Prophets and interpreted to them all the Scriptures which were said of him" (Lk 24:27)—by interpreting Scripture with Scripture.³ Armed with a quiver of passages, Luther especially preaches on Genesis 3:15 and Genesis 22:18. While he does use the second article of

---

¹Sermon on Easter Tuesday (1523), WA 11:87.22 (compare with *Ordenung vnd Bericht wie es furterhin (mit ihenen so das Hochwirdig Sacrament empfahen wollen) gehalten sol werden* [Hagenau: Johann Setzer, 1523], E2v; WA 12:506.4–5). See WA 11:87.22–24 (compare with *Ordenung vnd Bericht*, E2v; WA 12:506.4–8). See also Sermon on Easter Monday (1524), WA 15:523.2–6; Sermon on Easter Monday (1526), WA 20:323.2–7; The Third Sermon on the Gospel for the Easter Festival (*House Postil*, 1544), WA 52:259.30–32.
²On the generative character of God's word, see, for example, WATR 2:407.36–39, no. 2287; A House Sermon on the Articles of the Creed (1537), WA 45:11.5–12.5 (LW 57:243–44).
³WADB 6:323.

the Creed to interpret Luke 24, he chiefly uses the third article of the Creed and the sacraments of Holy Communion and Absolution, undergirded by the first table of the Ten Commandments. Throughout his career Luther read Luke 24 according to the analogy of faith.

To show Luther's use of the analogy of faith in Luke 24, this chapter addresses four matters: (1) how Christ treats the weak, (2) how the word of God illumines the word of God, (3) how Luther finds Absolution in this passage, and (4) how Luther sees Holy Communion in this passage. The Lord Christ is patient with the weak. He does not rush the process of strengthening them; he patiently and constantly directs them to Scripture as the true and faithful witness to God's character and work. The weak need help reading the Bible, lest it seem to be a book of terror and accusation. The catechism is this help. As God's word itself, it gives the pattern for reading Scripture. Luke 24 clearly mentions two of the Lord's sacraments: Absolution and Holy Communion. Luther uses the catechism to reform medieval church teaching on these sacraments. These are God's word and work for his people; in no way are they human works. Like all of God's words, Absolution and Holy Communion are treasures for the Lord's people regardless of their person and status.

Christ Calls the Weak

Christ calls the weak.[4] The gospel proclaims that Jesus Christ is the Savior who died and rose again to take the sin and death of those who believe in him.[5] Luther groups the hearers of the gospel into three categories: those who despise the gospel, those who bear no fruit from the gospel, and those who receive the gospel with fear.[6] The fearful rightly receive the gospel

---

[4] Sermon on Easter Monday (1523), WA 11:83.17–19.
[5] Sermon on Easter Tuesday (1523), WA 11:87.29–88.9; Gospel for Easter Tuesday (*Church Postil*, 1544), LW 77:70–71 (WA 12:507.12–22).
[6] Sermon on Easter Monday (1523), WA 11:82.2–30 (print, WA 12:497.9–398.19); Sermon on Easter Tuesday (1523), WA 11:88.23–29 (print, WA 12:506.9–508.4); Gospel for Easter Tuesday (*Church Postil*, 1544), LW 77:71–72 (WA 21:239; WA 12:507.12–508.4). Luther labels these groups differently. At times he calls those who bear no fruit arrogant or identifies them with the *Schwärmer*—"they can only produce much chatter about it" (WA 11:82.21–25; WA 12:497.13–23; quoting LW 77:71; WA 12:508.2). And in the print edition of Sermon on Easter Monday (1523), he has four categories, because he subdivides those who bear no fruit from the gospel into two groups: those who are indifferent (the seed that falls along the path) and those who preach about what they don't understand (the *Schwärmer*). The other two categories remain the same:

because they understand their need. Such needy, fearful people are typified by the two disciples whom Jesus encounters on the road to Emmaus.

Luther identifies the root of the disciples' fear: unbelief. The disciples acutely feel their sin and death—they would have shuddered at the rustling of leaves.[7] They still do not understand who Jesus is.[8] "But we had hoped that he would redeem Israel." (Lk 24:21).[9] They thought he was the Messiah, but they fundamentally misunderstood the Messiah's office. They believed he was just a human, who would reign over a secular kingdom like any other king.[10] But Christ the King and his kingdom are unlike any other king and kingdom. "Now this is how it happens in the world: when a king is dead, he has lost the kingdom and government as he has lost his person. But this King Christ truly begins his reign after his death."[11] Jesus sets to work to correct their misunderstanding and to strengthen their hearts.

How Jesus handles these fearful, shaken disciples is how God handles all who are weak and fearful. Because Jesus promises to be present where two or three are gathered in his name, he is present with these disciples (Mt 18:20). "He soon shows Himself to them alone, as if He now after His resurrection has nothing else to do."[12] Jesus does not immediately reveal himself to these two—that would have overwhelmed the already fearful disciples! Instead he patiently instructs them in the external means he has ordained: the word, the Sacrament of the Altar, and Absolution. Through patient conversation Jesus opens the eyes of the disciples' heart so that they see him. And this interaction reveals the quality of Jesus' reign: he calls the

---

those who persecute the word, and those who receive the gospel but are weak (WA 12:497.9–498.19). The parable of the sower applies *every* time we hear the word. See John W. Kleinig, *Grace upon Grace: Spirituality for Today* (St. Louis: Concordia, 2008), 113-15, 239-41.

[7] Sermon on Easter Tuesday (1523), WA 11:87.24–88.1; Gospel for Easter Tuesday (*Church Postil*, 1544), LW 77:70 (WA 12:507.5–11); Sermon on Easter Tuesday (1526), WA 20:348.16–349.2.
[8] Sermon on Easter Tuesday (1526), WA 20:349.2–4.
[9] WADB 6:321. Gospel for Easter Monday (*Church Postil*, 1544), LW 77:46–47 (WA 21:225.15–38).
[10] Sermon on Easter Monday (1524), WA 15:524.5–9.
[11] Afternoon Sermon on Easter Monday (1530), WA 32:55.20–22.
[12] Gospel for Easter Monday (*Church Postil*, 1544), LW 77:47 (WA 21:226.10–12). On the promise of Matthew 18:20, see also Sermon on Easter Monday (1524), WA 15:523.7–17; House Sermon on Easter Tuesday (1533), WA 37:32.23–33.1. Luther emphasizes that this promise doesn't apply to vain mention of Jesus' name (like mindless repetition of the Our Father) but to heartfelt, mindful cries. That Luther applies this promise to disciples whom he calls doubting and unbelieving shows how generously he understands Jesus to intend this promise. The doubting and uncertain need the power of Jesus' presence, and he is present in his word.

weak, erring, and foolish and ministers to them until they are strong and joyful. He does not push away the weak and foolish.[13] Jesus can bear our weakness.

Jesus models how to treat the weak in faith. He is the divine King who uses his reign and might to serve; we should use the good gifts he has given us to serve and strengthen the weak. As we care for children and those who are physically frail and infirm, so we should care for the weak in faith: supporting them, feeding them, and tending them. How ridiculous would it be to demand infants to feed themselves or the sick to be healthy!

> It is the kind of reign in which weakness, lack of understanding, and other sinful defects still remain among the Christians who have begun to believe and be holy. Nevertheless, He bears with them and overlooks it, yet in such a way that they will be corrected. We should not dream about a church on earth in which there are no defects or errors in faith.[14]

Between Jesus' death and resurrection, everyone lost faith, except for Mary who remained rooted in and sustained by God's word. Christians cannot rely on people—no matter how saintly—but must rely on his word alone which does not lie.[15]

Because the church is a creature of the word, it is an article of faith.[16] The defects and weakness of Christians hide the church: there is anger—James and John want to burn down a city (Lk 9:51-56); there is discord—Paul and Barnabas separate after the unified decision of the Jerusalem Council (Acts 15:36–41), and Paul rebukes Peter for his wavering (Gal 2:11-14).[17] The world sees these faults and asks, "These are Christians?"[18] Despite all appearances the church exists under this veil of weakness, just as Christ's divine

---

[13]Gospel for Easter Monday (*Church Postil*, 1544), LW 77:47–48 (WA 21:226.1–227.8).
[14]Gospel for Easter Monday (*Church Postil*, 1544), LW 77:48–49 (WA 21:227.29–33).
[15]Gospel for Easter Monday (*Church Postil*, 1544), LW 77:48–49 (WA 21:227.9–228.14).
[16]Sermon on Acts 15 (1524), WA 15:578–602 (compare with RCS NT 6:207, 208–9); Sermon on the Feast of St. Stephen (December 26, 1531), WA 34,2:518.12–519.11, alternate witness: 518.26–519.22; A Sermon on Jesus Christ, Preached at Court in Torgau (1533), WA 37:50.27–39; LW 57:113–14; Seventh Sermon on Psalm 72 (March 7, 1540), WA 49:48.20–23; Lecture on Psalm 72, LW 10:414 (WA 3:471.12–21).
[17]Sermon on Easter Tuesday (1523), WA 11:88.35–89.5; Gospel for Easter Tuesday (*Church Postil*, 1544), LW 77:73 (WA 12:509.16–32). The print version of this sermon omits the example of James and John.
[18]Sermon on Easter Tuesday (1523), WA 11:89.3. See also Gospel for Easter Tuesday (*Church Postil*, 1544), LW 77:73 (WA 12:509.29–30).

power and might were hidden under human flesh and the cross.[19] It is tempting to judge according to our eyes: to name those who stumble hypocrites. But this attitude takes seriously neither the depths of our fallen condition nor the depths of God's mercy nor the depths of God's law. All humans are fallen; none of us are not weak.[20] Christ calls no one on the basis of their name or actions but only on the basis of his name and actions.[21] And the eighth commandment demands that we interpret things in the kindest way—maybe God is still working in that person's life.[22] "When you boldly penetrate through such weakness, you will see that Christ lies hidden under that weak person and at His time will come forth and let Himself be seen."[23] "Christ stands firm in me, is strong in me, conquers death in me. He stands in the midst of those who are terrified—they are weak; he is strong."[24]

Luther holds the weak as his primary audience.[25] As usual Luther comforts and strengthens the weak and terrified with the catechism. "Dear friends, no one should be ashamed of the Our Father, the Ten Commandments, and the Creed! Let us remain among the children and we'll certainly never be lost."[26] The disciples on the road to Emmaus were completely confused about who Jesus was and what he had done, but they still loved to talk

---

[19] Gospel for Easter Tuesday (*Church Postil*, 1544), LW 77:74 (WA 12:509.33–510.13).

[20] Gospel for Easter Tuesday (*Church Postil*, 1544), LW 77:74 (WA 12:510.14–31).

[21] This will be drawn out below in "The Absolution of Sins." For example, see Sermon on Easter Tuesday (April 7, 1523), WA 11:90.33–91.2; Sermon on Easter Tuesday (1523), WA 12:514.25–27;12:514.29–515.28, 516.16–19; Sermon on Easter Tuesday (1524), WA 15:532.11–16; Sermon on Easter Tuesday (1526), WA 20:352.1–21; Another Sermon on the Gospel for Easter Tuesday (*Church Postil*, 1544), LW 77:96 (WA 21:259.1–8); The Third Sermon on the Gospel for the Easter Festival (*House Postil*, 1544), WA 52:265.22–36.

[22] Gospel for Easter Tuesday (*Church Postil*, 1544), LW 77:75 (WA 12:510.32–511.3). On the interpretation of the eighth commandment, see Sermon on the Eighth, Ninth, and Tenth Commandments (March 3, 1523), WA 11:47.4–48.10; Sermons on Exodus 20 (1525), WA 16:519–25; Sermon on May 22, 1528, WA 30,1:8.19–33; Sermon on September 19, 1528, WA 30,1:40.1–42.31; Sermon on December 7, 1528, WA 30,1:81.11–83.11; *Small Catechism* (1529), TAL 4:221 (WA 30,1:288–89; BoC 1959, 343); *Large Catechism* (1529), BoC 1959, 399–404 (WA 30,1:169.3–174.23).

[23] Gospel for Easter Tuesday (*Church Postil*, 1544), LW 77:75 (WA 12:511.1–3; WA 21:239).

[24] Sermon on Easter Tuesday (1523), WA 11:90.16–17. See also Gospel for Easter Tuesday (*Church Postil*, 1544), LW 77:78 (WA 12:513.30–32).

[25] Luther wishes he could ban despisers and chatterers from sermons. But because ministers of the word don't know what soil is good, they must preach publicly, scattering the seed of the gospel on despisers, chatterers, and fearful alike. See Sermon on Easter Monday (1523), WA 12:497.30–498.3; Gospel for Easter Tuesday (*Church Postil*, 1544), LW 77:71 (WA 12:507.25–29).

[26] Afternoon Sermon on Easter Monday (1530), WA 32:65.26–28.

about him.[27] People like these are the true students of Christ.[28] He finds them weak and weary, but he does not leave them weak and weary.[29] He meets them and strengthens them in the word, the Sacrament of the Altar, and the Absolution, because he is present in his word.[30] To understand the Bible according to the catechism is to find Jesus. It matters for the soul.

The highest wisdom is to know the weak Christ. "Now who could see that this Christ was God's Son? Here all reason must fall, yes, even great, righteous saints."[31] Only the Holy Spirit brings this knowledge and wisdom. Few believe the preaching of the word. Luther illustrates this with a historical example: Pentecost. According to Josephus, about 1.1 million people would have heard Peter's sermon on Pentecost, but only three thousand converted.[32]

The Word Illumines the Word

When we approach the word of God with reason, it remains a closed book. At best our vision is distorted; at worst we are blinded.[33] But this hasn't stopped heretics.[34] Heretics have the same Bible as everyone else, but they trample it with their reason so that nothing of the faith remains in it. And truly the faith is ridiculous to human reason. In Baptism can a bit of water really bring eternal life and victory over death?[35] In Holy Communion can

---

[27] Gospel for Easter Monday (*Church Postil*, 1544), LW 77:48 (WA 21:226.38–227.8).
[28] Gospel for Easter Tuesday (*Church Postil*, 1544), LW 77:77 (WA 12:513.10–11).
[29] Sermon on Easter Tuesday (1523), 11:89.37–39, 90.20–23; Gospel for Easter Tuesday (*Church Postil*, 1544), LW 77:75–76, 77–78 (WA 12:511.27–512.10, 12:513.16–40; WA 21:240). See also Sermon on Easter Tuesday (1526), WA 20:348.8–15; Afternoon Sermon on Easter Tuesday (1531), WA 34,1:310.9–311.1.
[30] Sermon on Easter Tuesday (1526), WA 20:348.8–15; Gospel for Easter Monday (*Church Postil*, 1544), LW 77:50 (WA 21:229.1–12); Sermon on Easter Monday (1524), WA 15:523.25–26.
[31] Gospel for Easter Tuesday (*Church Postil*, 1544), WA 12:510.9–11 (LW 77:74). See also Gospel for Easter Tuesday (*Church Postil*, 1544), LW 77:75 (WA 12:511.14–16). Sermon on Easter Tuesday (1523), WA 11:89.23–28.
[32] Sermon on Easter Tuesday (1523), WA 11:88.29–34; Gospel for Easter Tuesday (*Church Postil*, 1544), LW 77:72–73 (WA 12:509.3–15). See Josephus, *The Jewish War* 6.9.3.
[33] Sermon on Easter Monday (1521), WA 9:667.9–15, 668.8–22. See also Nicholas of Lyra's comments in *Glossa ordinaria*, 5:1000n10.
[34] Afternoon Sermon on Easter Monday (1530), WA 32:58.26–59.18; Sermon on Easter Monday (1534), WA 37:364.1–7.
[35] Afternoon Sermon on Easter Monday (1530), WA 32:59.3–10; Sermon on Easter Monday (1534), WA 37:364.12–16. Luther also points out that reason cannot tolerate baptizing infants (WA 32:63.1–3).

the risen and ascended Christ really be present in bread and wine?[36] In Absolution can my sins really be forgiven by a few words?[37] Luther regularly pointed out that such questions separate God's word—the animating power of the sacraments—from the elements or signs of the sacraments.[38] And Luther insists that it is God's word that washes us, forgives us, and saves us. To try to understand the word according to reason is to be lost.[39] How can the Virgin Mary give birth to a child and remain a virgin? How can the Son of God also be God from eternity? And of course how can the dead live again?[40] Our Lord God loves to oppose reason and make it foolish.[41] Reason alone will never understand the word.[42]

Luther is sometimes misunderstood as antirational, because it is overlooked that he distinguishes reason's acceptability according to its domain (temporal or spiritual) and status (unregenerate or regenerate).[43] Luther praises reason, whether unregenerate or regenerate, in temporal matters as well as reason submitted to faith in spiritual matters, but he condemns unregenerate reason in spiritual matters. For Luther, this illumines why Jews and Muslims call Christians idolaters. Is there more than one God?

---

[36]Afternoon Sermon on Easter Monday (1530), WA 32:58.8-15, 63.5-6, 64.10-23. "As I once heard [a *Schwärmer*] say: 'You'll never ever convince me that a piece of bread is the body of Christ' " (WA 32:58.13-15). For Luther this quote reveals the arrogance of the *Schwärmer* and their true *norma normans* and rule of faith. They do the opposite of what he counseled his congregation to do: "If it's God's Word or an article of faith, whoever speaks against it—be it Turk, Emperor, or Pope—I'll act as if I don't hear it. Because such a noise resounds from the word of God, that no bell, no musket—not even thunder!—sounds so violent and powerful!" Sermon on the Thirteenth Sunday after Trinity (1530), WA 32:99.25-28. See also House Sermon on the First Sunday in Advent (1533), WA 37:202.15-16.

[37]Sermon on Easter Tuesday (1523), WA 12:517.1-6; Afternoon Sermon on Easter Tuesday (1531), WA 34,1:307.11-19 (307.24-31). Luther emphasizes the power of the word in all the sacraments, but it is most explicit in Absolution. God's word accomplishes the very thing it says: it puts us to death and raises us to life; it brings Jesus present; it removes all our sin.

[38]For Luther a sacrament is something Christ commanded with his promise of forgiveness and salvation. Luther seems to have accepted a broader definition of a physical sign as ritual (hence Absolution as a sacrament). See Peters, *Commentary on Luther's Catechisms*, 4:49-59; *Against the Thirty-Two Articles of the Louvain Theologians* (1545), LW 34:354-60 (WA 54:425.1-430.18). See also chapter 3, "The Sacraments: 'The Ceremonies of Ceremonies.' "

[39]Sermon on Easter Monday (1534), WA 37:364.1-7; see also Afternoon Sermon on Easter Monday (1530), WA 32:59.10-12, 64.3-10; Gospel for Easter Monday (*Church Postil*, 1544), LW 77:51-52 (WA 21:230.29-231.10).

[40]Sermon on Easter Monday (1534), WA 37:364.16-18.

[41]Sermon on Easter Monday (1534), WA 37:364.18-20.

[42]Sermon on Easter Monday (1523), WA 12:496.21-24.

[43]See above chapter 1, "Faith Kills Reason."

Not according to reason! So how can Christians say Jesus Christ is God? Islam, in particular, makes sense according to reason. But to judge God's character and essence according to reason alone is to reject the framework God gives for understanding his word. "And so according to reason we want to be the Lord our God's master and to teach him what makes sense and what doesn't."[44] Too often, Luther laments, we throw out a passage if it doesn't make sense rather than trusting it as the word of God and patiently listening to the truth that surpasses understanding. "According to reason we're as clever as a cow in these [divine] matters.... We're not in a tavern. We're in the Christian church, so we must believe not what reason thinks right or what pleases you or me, but what the Scripture tells us."[45]

Only Christ by his Spirit illumines our minds so we can know God and understand his word. "That's why we now sing, 'This is the day that the Lord has made; let us rejoice and be glad in it!'"[46] In the same way that the simple benefit from the sun's light and heat to see things and to grow things, the simple accept what the word says, not asking how or why.[47] The how and why are too great for human reason! "Holy Scripture is a river deep enough to drown an elephant and shallow enough for a sheep to cross like a small brook."[48] Even though they did not understand or believe, the disciples on the road to Emmaus still loved to talk about Jesus and his word. And Jesus is true to his promise in Matthew 18:20: "Where two or three are gathered in my name, there I am

---

[44]Afternoon Sermon on Easter Monday (1530), WA 32:62.24-25.
[45]Afternoon Sermon on Easter Monday (1530), WA 32:63.7-11, see the full passage pp. 62.14-63.11.
[46]Sermon on Easter Monday (1521), WA 9:668.21-669.18, here 668.36-37.
[47]Sermon on Easter Monday (1534), WA 37:364.10-11, 367.18-24; Gospel for Easter Monday (*Church Postil*, 1544), LW 77:52 (WA 21:231.1-10). Luther discourages speculation into the hidden things of God. He believes that such speculation enthrones human reason rather than faith, and this prevents us from knowing God and his word. See, for example, WATR 2:585, no. 2656a; 4:73-74, no. 4008; 4:482-86, no. 4774, 4:642-43, no. 5071; 5:218-20, no. 5534; 6:255, no. 6894. It's illuminating to see Luther's advice to those struggling with the question of election, see *Luther: Letters of Spiritual Counsel*, 109-38.
[48]Sermon on Easter Monday (1534), WA 37:366.36-39. Luther is paraphrasing Gregory the Great, *Morals on the Book of Job*, Epistle 4 (PL 75:515). See also Second Lecture on Psalm 21 (1519-1521), WA 5:598.3-4; Preface to the Lectures on Genesis (1535-1545), WA 42:2.6-7; Sermon after the Third Sunday in Easter (Jubilate; May, 1542), WA 49:256.8-9; WATR 5:168.18-19, no. 5468. Like so many of the things of God, Scripture is not meant for the weights and scales of human judgment; it holds humans in its weights and scales.

in their midst."[49] He meets them and helps them to understand the word. Luther's catechetical reasoning teaches Christians that the commands of God are liberating gifts: because God has commanded it, we pray, and we receive Baptism, the Lord's Supper, and Absolution.[50] In the same way, we listen to the Bible and read the Bible, because God has commanded it.[51] Even if we do not immediately understand or see the fruit, Scripture always brings blessing.[52] For example, Monica prayed for nine years that her son, Augustine would be a Christian; Augustine studied the Bible for nine years without understanding (until he said "I believe").[53] The Lord does more than we understand, because we do not understand the depths of our own sighing.[54]

By the inspiration of the Holy Spirit, the disciples—unlearned fishermen—handed down the faith and the way to read the Bible that they had learned from Jesus.[55] "From one passage they can make a book or a sermon which the world cannot understand."[56] The New Testament was built from these riches. Sadly we have lost this art. Because we read the Bible with the veil of reason, we cannot make sense of Luke's description of the conversation on the road to Emmaus: "And he began with Moses and all the Prophets and explained to them all the Scriptures which were spoken about him" (Lk 24:27).[57] According to reason, Moses seems to say nothing about Jesus—his suffering, resurrection, and forgiveness. But Jesus removed the veil from the disciples' eyes so that they might see and

---

[49] WADB 6:83.
[50] On the command to pray, see Sermon on September 22, 1528, WA 47.22-24; Sermon on December 14, 1528, WA 30,1:95.6-11, 96.15-19, 99.7-15; *Large Catechism* (1529), BoC 1959, 420-21, 422 (WA 30,1:193.16-195.21). On the command to receive the sacraments, see chapter 3, "The Sacraments: 'The Ceremonies of Ceremonies.'"
[51] Gospel for Easter Monday (*Church Postil*, 1544), LW 77:49-50 (WA 21:228.15-229.21). See also Sermon on Easter Monday (1523), WA 11:85.6-11; Another Sermon on the Gospel for Easter Tuesday (*Church Postil*, 1544), LW 77:98 (WA 21:260.25-261.3).
[52] Gospel for Easter Monday (*Church Postil*, 1544), LW 77:49 (WA 21:228.15-20).
[53] Sermon on Easter Monday (1523), WA 11:84.16-19 (12:502.9-16); Sermon on Easter Monday (1534), WA 37:366.33-36.
[54] Sermon on Easter Monday (1523), WA 11:84.16-19 (12:501.18-502.3).
[55] Gospel for Easter Monday (*Church Postil*, 1544), LW 77:56 (WA 21:235.5-36). For Luther the Bible is unlike any other book, it cannot be understood simply by reading; the Holy Spirit must reveal the Bible's meaning and core message. See Gospel for Easter Monday (*Church Postil*, 1544), LW 77:51 (WA 21:230.21-23).
[56] Gospel for Easter Monday (*Church Postil*, 1544), LW 77:56 (WA 21:235.7-9).
[57] WADB 6:323.

understand.⁵⁸ If only Luke had recorded all the passages Jesus spoke of!⁵⁹ But to have done that would require a book as large as the Bible. Although we have no transcript of Jesus' explanation, we can get an idea of what he said from the sermons and books of the apostles.⁶⁰ "I would like to take Moses, the Psalms, Isaiah, and also the same Spirit and make as good a New Testament as the apostles wrote. But because we do not have the Spirit as richly and powerfully, we must learn from them and drink from their spring."⁶¹ By the apostles' light we learn the holy art of interpreting Scripture with Scripture.⁶²

The guiding framework of Scripture interpreting Scripture is the analogy of faith. "If we want to understand the Scriptures, it is necessary that we have the same understanding that the prophets who wrote them had."⁶³ This understanding is summarized in the analogy of faith or the catechism. It helps us to see which passages are dark and which are light, so that we can illumine the dark passages with the light passages.⁶⁴ It also helps us to share the same assumptions and understanding that the prophets and apostles had.

Luther focuses on Genesis 3:15 as the fountainhead of prophecy about Jesus.⁶⁵ This choice might surprise modern readers. After all

---

⁵⁸Sermon on Easter Monday (1526), WA 20:323.7-324.3; Sermon on Easter Monday (1534), WA 37:363.8-27; Gospel for Easter Monday (*Church Postil*, 1544), LW 77:51.24-25 (WA 21:230.1-20).

⁵⁹Sermon on Easter Monday (1534), WA 37:363.14-17. Luther was not the only person to marvel at Luke's vagueness here. Johann Eck (1486-1543) makes similar comments, while Desiderius Erasmus narrates the passed over conversation in his Paraphrase on the Gospel of Luke. See RCS NT 3:485-88.

⁶⁰Gospel for Easter Monday (*Church Postil*, 1544), LW 77:56-57.42 (WA 21:235.37-236.14); Afternoon Sermon on Easter Monday (1530), WA 32:60.20-24. In the postil for the Gospel for Easter Monday, Luther teaches that there is no method that will open the Bible—only the Holy Spirit does that! Every passage of the Bible is about Christ. And so we read the Bible according to the Holy Spirit. If we had strong faith we could make an entire New Testament out of any given passage of the Old Testament. In God's mercy he has given us the New Testament.

⁶¹Gospel for Easter Monday (*Church Postil*, 1544), LW 77:56 (WA 21:235.33-36). See also Gospel for Easter Monday (*Church Postil*, 1544), LW 77:53, 56 (WA 21:232.16-19, 235.5-11); Sermon on Easter Monday (1534), WA 37:365.7-9, 366.19-20.

⁶²See Sermon on Easter Monday (1534), WA 37:364.3-5, 367.15-18.

⁶³Afternoon Sermon on Easter Monday (1524), WA 15:526.24-25.

⁶⁴Just as the Bible has light and dark passages, Christ also taught openly and through figures. The histories of the Old Testament taught about Christ's person and work through figural reading (for example, David vs. Goliath, Samson vs. the Philistines). See Sermon on Easter Monday (1526), WA 20:323.9-324.1; Sermon on Easter Tuesday (1526), WA 20:353.3-5.

⁶⁵Luther spends quite a bit of time with Genesis 3:15. He believes that it was the chief passage that Jesus spoke about, especially since the prophets draw their best work from it (for

Genesis 3:15 is not explicitly cited in the New Testament.[66] But Luther identifies Genesis 3:15 as the text out of which the prophets of the Old Testament draw their best work (as seen especially in the Psalms, but also in passages like 2 Samuel 7:12 and Isaiah 7:14 and Isaiah 53), and these passages are what the apostles built entire books out of.[67] The reasoning of faith about Genesis 3:15 teaches how to reason about the Old Testament in general, which teaches that Jesus is true God and true man in the unity of his person, and, relatedly, that he will die and rise again.[68]

The words with which God curses the serpent are incomprehensible miracles according to reason: "And I will place enmity between you and the woman and between your seed and her Seed. He will crush your head. And you will prick his heel" (Gen 3:15).[69] The Spirit teaches the full meaning of these words: the doctrines of the virgin birth, of Chalcedon, and of the resurrection.[70] The phrasing here hints at the virgin birth (later prophets phrase it even more clearly, especially in Isaiah 7:14). The Lord God says "her Seed," but the Bible's custom is to name the father of the child, not the mother.[71] The grammar fits with the underlying logic: the One who crushes the serpent's head cannot be guilty of sin but must be a

---

example, Is 7:14; 53). Gospel for Easter Monday (*Church Postil*, 1544), LW 77:55–56 (WA 21:234.28–235.4).

[66] Afternoon Sermon on Easter Monday (1530), WA 32:60.13–22. Romans 16:20 and Hebrews 2:14 might be seen as allusions to Genesis 3:15. One modern resource identifies possible allusions to Genesis 3:15 in Romans 16:20 and Revelation 12:17; 13:3; 20:2-3; see G. K. Beale and D. A. Carson, eds., *Commentary on the New Testament Use of the Old Testament* (Grand Rapids: Baker Academic; Nottingham, UK: Apollos, 2007), 693, 1126, 1128, 1145, 1146.

[67] See chapter 4, "The Promised Seed and the Second Article."

[68] See Afternoon Sermon on Easter Monday (1524), WA 15:527.8–30; Sermon on Easter Monday (1526), WA 20:324.4–327.28; Sermon on Easter Tuesday (1526), WA 350.24–351.3 (second witness, 350.36–351.27); Sermon on Easter Monday (1534), WA 37:365.28–366.25; Gospel for Easter Monday (*Church Postil*, 1544), LW 77:54–56 (WA 21:233.5–235.36).

[69] WADB 8:45. Luther has two marginal comments on this verse. First, this is the first promise of Christ's victory over sin, death, and hell. And, second, the word *stechen* ("to prick") points to Jesus' crucifixion and martyrdom. See Sermon on Easter Monday (1526), WA 20:324.26–27: "This is beautifully spoken—beyond comparison! But it's dark to those who don't believe."

[70] Sermon on Easter Monday (1526), WA 20:324.4–327.5; Sermon on Easter Monday (1534), WA 37:365.28–366.8; Gospel for Easter Monday (*Church Postil*, 1544), LW 77:54–56 (WA 21:233.5–235.4; Lectures on Genesis 3:15b (1535), LW 1:193–98 (WA 42:144.12–147.39).

[71] Sermon on Easter Monday (1526), WA 20:324.18–21. Luther notes that this obscure phrasing deceives Satan, who thought that the woman would be married. The angel even said as much to Mary: "Satan won't know that you're a virgin" (20:324.23). Of course, Eve also did not understand that the Seed's mother would be a virgin (20:326.13).

natural child.[72] The promised Seed must be a natural child, so that he shares his nature and victory with humans. And the promised Seed must be innocent, so that he is free from Satan's power. To be innocent the child must not be conceived in sin, which points to the child's conception by the Holy Spirit (as the Creed confesses). Even more than that, the promised Seed must also be powerful enough to defeat Satan and lord over him. No mere human has this power, for Satan lords over human beings through the power of sin and death.[73] "No one except God himself can be the Lord over all creatures."[74] If the promised Seed is to crush Satan's head, he must have power over angels and spirits; to have such power he must be God.[75] And so the promised Seed had to be true God and true man. While all humans die according to the body, God is eternal. "Because he was an eternal person, he could not be kept by death."[76] He would certainly rise again. Here Luther hints at the baited Leviathan metaphor: by being swallowed by death Jesus swallows death and its friends (Satan, sin, and hell).[77] Luther emphasizes that this passage is not just about Jesus; it is also about Jesus' people. "We too trample Satan, and he pricks our heel, because Christ has given his victory to us."[78] This victory is our victory.

All of this Luther derives from the tightly worded curse of the serpent in Genesis 3:15. That's the only Scripture the people of God had for a very long time. And the prophets of God mined this passage to make the promise as plain as possible. The gospel became clearer in each generation leading up to Christ. For example, at first Adam and Eve thought the promise could be brought about through any woman (hence Cain's name[79]), but the promise continues to narrow. After Abraham it became clear that she would be

---

[72]Sermon on Easter Monday (1526), WA 20:326.22–327.2. In contrast, Eve was not Adam's daughter but was made out of his rib.
[73]Sermon on Easter Monday (1526), WA 20:325.4–7. See also above chapter 7, "The Radiant Light of the Second Article."
[74]Gospel for Easter Monday (*Church Postil*, 1544), LW 77:55.36 (WA 21:234.12–13).
[75]Sermon on Easter Monday (1526), WA 20:326.17–327.2; Gospel for Easter Monday (*Church Postil*, 1544), LW 77:55.36 (WA 21:234.5–27).
[76]Gospel for Easter Monday (*Church Postil*, 1544), LW 77:55 (WA 21:234.21–22), quoting Acts 2:24.
[77]Sermon on Easter Monday (1526), WA 20:325.16–28; Gospel for Easter Monday (*Church Postil*, 1544), LW 77:55 (WA 21:234.14–27). See chapter 5, "The Riddle of the Resurrection."
[78]Sermon on Easter Monday (1526), WA 20:325.26–27.
[79]See Lectures on Genesis 4:2, LW 1:241–43 (WA 42:179.39–180.34).

Jewish, then it continues to narrow by family—of Isaac's family, of Jacob's, of one of Jacob's twelve sons, of David's.[80]

In these sermons on Luke 24, Luther expands a handful of other passages to reveal this same inner logic of Genesis 3:15. For example, Genesis 22:18 also shows that the Messiah will be fully man and fully God, that he will die and rise again, and that he will conquer death and give gifts to his people.[81] Luther also points to Genesis 49:10-12 and Deuteronomy 18:18.[82]

> The scepter will not be snatched from Judah,
> nor a master from his feet
> until the Hero comes.
> And on the same the peoples will depend.
> He will bind his foal to the grapevine
> and his she-donkey's son on his noble vine shoot.
> He will wash his vestments in wine,
> and his robe in grape's blood.
> His eyes are redder than wine
> and his teeth whiter than milk. (Gen 49:10-12)

> I will raise up for them a prophet, like you, out of their brothers, and I will place my word in his mouth. He will speak to them all that I will command him. (Deut 18:18)

And of course Luther uses a few choice psalms: Psalms 2; 8; 16; 110.[83] He wouldn't limit his reading of Jesus in the Old Testament to just these passages. Given enough time and a patient enough audience, Luther could romp through the entire Psalter and Old Testament to show how Jesus is revealed in his word. Christians must learn to see the depths and riches of the Old Testament. Only by the daylight of life and of the Bible—Jesus—can they do this. God and his word tolerate no other light.[84] "For in you is the source of life, and in your light we see light" (Ps 36:9).[85] If you take the

---

[80]Sermon on Easter Monday (1526), WA 20:327.13-28.
[81]Sermon on Easter Monday (1526), WA 20:336.28-338.9.
[82]On Genesis 49:10-12, see Sermon on Easter Monday (1526), WA 20:338.33-340.11; WADB 8:195; on Deuteronomy 18:18, see WA 20:338.10-32. Deuteronomy 18:18 was printed in bold with the marginal comment "Christ promised, etc."—"Christ" in bold too. WADB 8:617.
[83]See Afternoon Sermon on Easter Monday (1530), WA 32:60.20-64.2.
[84]Sermon on Easter Monday (1521), WA 9:670.5-8.
[85]WADB 10,1:213.

Light of the word and world out of the Scriptures, all you'll be left with is darkness.

While the word of God is for our comfort and consolation (2 Tim 3:16; Rom 15:4), there is no doubt that the Bible is filled with terrifying passages. Luther saw this as a subjective problem. If we fully understood and clung to the light of Scripture, such passages would not be terrifying. Humans are dark; God's word is light.[86] Satan twists our ignorance into fear, emphasizing our unworthiness and God's wrath and justice (severed from Jesus' person and work). Dealing with terrifying passages means first and foremost distinguishing Satan from Christ. Christ might bring pain at first, but he takes it away; he says "Do not be afraid." But Satan brings no pain at first and then presses dread and terror.[87] If you are scared by passages of the Bible, imagine Christ who died on the cross, rose again, ascended, and is seated at the right hand of the Father. But if Satan continues to press you, hold Satan's conqueror before him: "I'm frightened, you hear! You must stop! Yes, these are Christ's words. Christ again and again. He commands me that I should not be frightened of him."[88] It is true that you will be scared of Jesus because of your sins and his holiness (and our human nature!), but Jesus does not want to leave you in fear.[89] Christ says, I am here to comfort you, not to scare you.[90] And that's how we should read the Bible. "I don't apply [terrifying passages] to myself, because I want to have Christ."[91]

The Bible witnesses to Jesus. So much so, in fact, that Jesus points people to the Bible's testimony of himself rather than to the testimony of the women

---

[86] See *On the Bondage of the Will* (1525), LW 33:24-28 (WA 18:1606-9); *Luther and Erasmus*, Library of Christian Classics 17, 109-12.

[87] Afternoon Sermon on Easter Tuesday (1531), WA 34,1:314.32-34; Another Sermon on the Gospel for Easter Tuesday (*Church Postil*, 1544), LW 77:86 (WA 21:248.9-39). Jesus shows his pierced and scarred hands and feet—he died for you! He does not want you to be terrified. In contrast, after Satan comes with sweet and comforting words, he shows his claws of wrath and death. He holds your sin before you, not relenting and hoping that you would despair.

[88] Afternoon Sermon on Easter Tuesday (1531), WA 34,1:314.9-11. For Luther's full treatment, see WA 34,1:313.19-316.11; LW 77:80-86 (WA 21:242.2-248.8).

[89] Another Sermon on the Gospel for Easter Tuesday (*Church Postil*, 1544), LW 77:84 (WA 21:246.3-13). The proper response to fear of Christ is to want the fear to stop. The obstinate resist and oppose the fear of Christ (LW 77:84; WA 21:246.14-24). See also the above section, "Christ Calls the Weak."

[90] Another Sermon on the Gospel for Easter Tuesday (*Church Postil*, 1544), LW 77:84-86; WA 21:246.25-248.8), quoting Mt 12:20; Is 42:3.

[91] Afternoon Sermon on Easter Tuesday (1531), WA 34,1:315.10.

The Light of the Word 147

at the tomb or the angels or the dead—even rather than his own testimony! "Do you read the Prophets and still not believe? It is true: it is paper and ink, but it is also the most excellent sign. Even Christ himself wants to put more trust in it than in his own appearance."[92] The Bible's testimony is enough. There's no easier way to lose the faith than to ignore the word, for it is too great for reason that the undying God should become man, die, and rise again. "All of our articles in the faith are great and hard—no person without the Holy Spirit's grace and inspiration can grasp them."[93] We cannot think about the faith without Scripture. Keep the word, keep the faith.[94] To hear the word is to see Jesus.[95]

THE ABSOLUTION OF SINS

The Reformation was a movement to return the church to what the Bible teaches about the forgiveness of sins. Luther and others saw the medieval church's teaching on the sacrament of Confession and Absolution as fundamentally distorted and harmful.[96] The medieval Catholic Church taught that Confession and Absolution—usually called the sacrament of Penance—required contrition of the heart, confession of the mouth, and satisfaction of works. Medieval doctors squabbled over the details—especially regarding the role of the priest, human ability to love God, and whether the sacrament worked "by the work performed" (*ex opere operato*) or "by the work of the worker" (*ex opere operantis*). But they agreed in the general outline: contrition of heart (including the desire to confess to a priest) was the foundation of the sacrament; confession needed to be as total as possible, so that appropriate satisfaction could be assigned; God remits eternal punishment

---

[92] Afternoon Sermon on Easter Monday (1530), WA 32:57.1-3. Luther emphasizes that Scripture forbids necromancy (Deut 18:10-12; Is 8:19-20; Lk 16:29, 31). See Gospel for Easter Tuesday (*Church Postil*, 1544), LW 77:78-79; WA 21:241.12-25.

[93] Afternoon Sermon on Easter Monday (1530), WA 32:57.14-58.5, here p. 57.16-17. Also: "So pick up an article from the Creed . . . you won't hold fast to a single one, if you grasp it with reason" (57.19, 20-21). "Christ is best understood and recognized in Scripture" (Gospel for Easter Monday [*Church Postil*, 1544], LW 77:50; WA 21:229.12).

[94] Afternoon Sermon on Easter Monday (1530), WA 32:58.6-8.

[95] Another Sermon on the Gospel for Easter Tuesday (*Church Postil*, 1544), LW 77:86, 88.30 (WA 21:247.38-248.8, 250.14-23).

[96] It's telling that the sacrament of Absolution was called the sacrament of Penance, emphasizing the confession of sin and guilt rather than focusing on the liberating word and work of God. Luther sought to reform the doctrine of Absolution accordingly. Luther called this sacrament "the golden treasure of Absolution," Sermon on Easter Tuesday (1531), WA 34,1:307.11-12.

(on account of contrition), but the satisfaction of works are necessary to remit temporal punishment. Any remaining temporal punishment not remitted through works during one's earthly life had to be satisfied in Purgatory. Indulgences were fitted into this system.[97] Luther condemned indulgences as a symptom of what plagued the church's teaching on forgiveness: trust in human ability and merit.[98]

Luther used Luke 24:46-47 to explain Absolution: "And so it is written: Christ must suffer and rise again from the dead on the third day and have preached in his name the repentance and forgiveness of sins among all nations, beginning in Jerusalem."[99] Luther does not distinguish between the sacrament of Absolution and *the forgiveness of sins*. For Luther how Christians should talk about forgiveness is defined by how the Bible talks about forgiveness ("And so it is written"). These words from the Gospel of Luke show what repentance is, what forgiveness is, and who needs to repent and

---

[97] See Tentler, *Sin and Confession*; Thayer, *Penitence, Preaching, and the Coming of the Reformation*; for succinct treatment of medieval Penance, see Steven E. Ozment, *The Reformation in the Cities: The Appeal of Protestantism to Sixteenth-Century Germany and Switzerland* (New Haven, CT: Yale University Press, 1975), 49–56; David C. Steinmetz, *Misericordia Dei: The Theology of Johannes von Staupitz in its Late Medieval Setting* (Leiden: Brill, 1968), 97–104; Peters, *Commentary on Luther's Catechisms*, 5:31–35; Heiko A. Oberman, *The Harvest of Medieval Theology: Gabriel Biel and Late Medieval Nominalism* (Grand Rapids: Baker Academic, 2000), 147–84; Rittgers, *The Reformation of the Keys*, 23–46. The medieval doctors distinguished between remorse for sin motivated by fear of punishment (attrition) and remorse for sin motivated by love for God (contrition). This distinction—added to the need for total confession of all sins and works-based satisfaction—further encouraged penitents' guilty conscience and sense of unworthiness. The Augsburg Confession and its Defense agreed that contrition and confession were necessary but argued that only faith, not the satisfaction of works, received the proclamation of Absolution. See *Augsburg Confession* (1530) XII, BoC 1959, 34–35 (BSELK 106.2–20); *Defense of the Augsburg Confession* (1531) XII, BoC 1959, 182–210 (BSELK 434.2–510.23).

[98] Luther accused medieval Catholic teaching on Confession and Absolution of being Pelagian. He saw the indulgence system not as a good-faith attempt to console sinners but as a way to monetize Christian doctrine (based on gross extrabiblical speculation—who's in Purgatory, how many years of punishment unconfessed sin requires, etc.). See *Schmalkaldic Articles* (1538) III.I–IV, BoC 1959, 302–10 (BSELK 746.17–766.5; WA 50:221.1–241.5).

[99] WADB 6:323–325. Erasmus's New Testament uses the Majority text variant μετάνοιαν καὶ ἄφεσιν ἁμαρτιῶν. While most modern scholars prefer εἰς in place of καὶ (except for the NRSV), they note that Luke uses both μετάνοιαν καὶ ἄφεσιν ἁμαρτιῶν and μετάνοιαν εἰς ἄφεσιν ἁμαρτιῶν in other passages, so the variant does not change the meaning (see Lk 3:3; Acts 5:31). See *Novum Instrumentum omne*, ed. Erasmus, 191; *Novum Testamentum omne*, ed. Erasmus, 186; Joseph A. Fitzmyer, *The Gospel According to Luke (X–XXIV)*, Anchor Bible 28A (New York: Doubleday, 1985), 1584; I. Howard Marshall, *The Gospel of Luke: A Commentary on the Greek Text*, New International Greek Testament Commentary 3 (Grand Rapids: Eerdmans, 1978), 906; Bruce M. Metzger, *A Textual Commentary on the Greek New Testament*, 2nd ed. (Stuttgart: Deutsche Bibelgesellschaft, 1994), 161.

be forgiven. The sacrament of Absolution opens this text up. Once again Luther shows that by the Spirit's guidance we understand the Bible through the lens of the catechism. He reformed the medieval teaching of Penance according to the analogy of faith.

The Christian doctrine of original sin teaches that despite appearances all people need to repent, because all people are tainted by sin. "Through one person sin entered the world—and death through sin—and death took captive all people, because they are all sinners." (Rom 5:12).[100] It is foolishness to the world. "Original sin is such a deep, evil corruption of nature that reason absolutely cannot understand it; instead it must be believed because of Scripture's revelation (Ps 51; Rom 5; Exod 33; Gen 3)."[101] Reason and law measure external actions alone; God according to his word measures our internal actions and motivations. That's why Jesus commands that the repentance and forgiveness of sins be preached "among all nations."[102] Luther paraphrases Jesus' words as, "You are all totally condemned with all that you do and all that you are—no matter what you are and how big, how great, how high, how holy you are."[103] Everyone stands condemned without any way of making things right. Contrary to the teaching about monastic orders and satisfaction of works, humans are unable to make the first step—humans are unable even to acknowledge their own sin without the ministry of the Spirit.[104] And so they must pray: "Lord, I am a sinner. I must improve myself, but I'm not able to."[105]

True repentance rejects the righteousness and wisdom of the world.[106] The world's wisdom and righteousness teach that repentance consists of human actions which earn or cause forgiveness: human actions make the human

---

[100] WADB 7:45.
[101] *Schmalkaldic Articles* (1538) III.I, BSELK 746.27-29 (WA 50:221.24-222.1; compare BoC 1959, 302); citing Ps 51:7; Rom 5:12-14; Ex 33:20; Gen 3:6-19.
[102] Sermon on Easter Tuesday (1524), WA 15:530.18-19, 530.31-531.5; Sermon on Easter Tuesday (1526), WA 20:351.5-15; House Sermon on Easter Tuesday (1533), WA 37:33.19-31; Another Sermon on the Gospel for Easter Tuesday (*Church Postil*, 1544), LW 77:91-94 (WA 21:253.35-256.30); The Third Sermon on the Gospel for the Easter Festival (*House Postil*, 1544), WA 52:263.27-35.
[103] Another Sermon on the Gospel for Easter Tuesday (*Church Postil*, 1544), WA 21:253.39-254.2 (compare with LW 77:91). See also Sermon on Easter Tuesday (1524), WA 15:530.19.
[104] Sermon on Easter Tuesday (1524), WA 15:531.5; House Sermon on Easter Tuesday (1533), WA 37:33.33-36.
[105] House Sermon on Easter Tuesday (1533), WA 37:33.30-31. See also WA 37:34.14-18; The Third Sermon on the Gospel for the Easter Festival (*House Postil*, 1544), WA 52:262.18-35.
[106] Sermon on Easter Tuesday (1524), WA 15:530.15-19.

person worthy. But Luther objects: "How can we call our works good, if the source is wicked and impure?"[107] "No one is able to worthily repent, unless his heart is enlightened by faith."[108] Rote praying and celibacy are nothing in and of themselves, because they come from an unworthy person—a person tainted by sin. If humans were able to do good works, that would mean that the human person is worthy and holy. But then why would Jesus command the preaching of repentance? This command would be unnecessary; humans would already have the power and ability to be holy.[109] "You must first believe that whatever is outside of Christ is condemned to the abyss of hell—whether a Carthusian or angel [should preach it]."[110] True repentance is to confess your need: you are a sinner in need of help. And that help is found in Christ alone.[111] True repentance lasts a lifetime, day in and day out (not just repeating five Our Fathers). It addresses the entirety of a person (not just your works).[112]

In the same way, true Absolution does not just forgive your sins; it forgives you.[113] And that's the difference between indulgences and Absolution. Indulgences leave a remnant of sin hanging on you, for the only sins forgiven are those confessed and those in the past. But Absolution places you into a different status that never ends. "I place you in this status, in which the forgiveness of sin is eternal."[114] God does not just forgive past sin or prebaptismal sin; he forgives all sin.

Luther compares the constancy of God's forgiveness to the sun: just as the sun shines all day (whether you can see it or not), so also forgiveness lasts

---

[107] The Third Sermon on the Gospel for the Easter Festival (*House Postil*, 1544), WA 52:264.12–13. Compare with House Sermon on Easter Tuesday (1533), WA 37:34.21–22.

[108] Sermon on Easter Tuesday (1523), WA 11:91.4–5.

[109] The Third Sermon on the Gospel for the Easter Festival (*House Postil*, 1544), WA 52:263.30–35; see also Sermon on Easter Tuesday (1524), WA 15:531.6–20. Luther accuses the medieval penitential system of a Pelagian anthropology. Relatedly, Augustine clung to the petitions "Forgive us our debts" and "Lead us not into temptation" in his argument against Pelagius (d. c. 420). For example, see *On the Merits and Forgiveness of Sins* 2.2 (NPNF 5:40); *On Nature and Grace* 20 (NPNF 5:127); *Against Two Letters of the Pelagians* 4.27 (NPNF 5:429–30); *On Grace and Free Will* 26 (NPNF 5:454).

[110] Sermon on Easter Tuesday (1531), WA 34,1:305.5–307.4 here 306.3–4; alluding to Gal 1:8.

[111] Sermon on Easter Tuesday (1531), WA 34,1:305.14–306.4.

[112] Sermon on Easter Tuesday (1523), WA 11:90.26–91.38 (12:514.6–517.8); Sermon on Easter Tuesday (1526), WA 20:351.18–19; Another Sermon on the Gospel for Easter Tuesday (*Church Postil*, 1544), LW 77:98–99 (WA 21:260.26–262.30).

[113] Sermon on Easter Tuesday (1523), WA 11:91.24–37 (WA 12:516.16–39); Sermon on Easter Tuesday (1524), WA 15:531.21–532.26.

[114] Sermon on Easter Tuesday (1523), WA 11:91.31–32 (compare with WA 12:516.33–36).

your entire life from the first time you hear the gospel. "This forgiveness lasts as long as you live—from that first time you hear the gospel. It's like the sun: once the sun begins to shine, it does not stop shining but shines the whole day, so that everyone can receive its light. If someone goes into the basement, he's deprived of its light. But when he comes back out of the basement, he has its light again."[115] Underneath this analogy is the principle *as you believe, so you have*. If you think sunlight is darkness, so it is. If you think God cannot forgive a certain sin, it continues to weigh on your conscience (despite its having been nailed to the cross, Col 2:15). The only balm for this is the word of God. All humans are dark, they need the light of God's word.

That's why Luther sought to reform Confession and Absolution as an instruction in faith rather than in sin.[116] Auricular confession is a tool for the care of souls. As Lateran IV puts it, a pastor confessor is "like a skilled physician he may pour wine and oil into the wounds of the injured."[117] A skilled pastor should use the catechism and the Bible to address particular sins that worry the penitent. The goal is not to delete temporal punishment that would have to be paid off in Purgatory; instead, the goal is for the penitent to rest in the consolation of God's promise of forgiveness. As Luther saw it, confession was made for man, not man for confession—as if Confession should squeeze out a full register of sins.[118] Because Absolution addresses the holiness of the person, it therefore makes possible the holiness of works. Good works are impossible apart from union to Christ through his word and by his Spirit (in Baptism, in Communion, in Absolution).[119]

True Absolution—as the catechism teaches—stands on the word, promise, and name of Jesus alone. Luther draws this out from Luke's phrase "in his

---

[115]Sermon on Easter Tuesday (1524), WA 15:531.35–532.16, here p. 531.38–40.

[116]Albrecht Peters highlights this reform of Confession, but he assumes that it made no difference whether the focus was sin or faith because of the obligatory nature of Confession (Peters, *Commentary on Luther's Catechisms*, 5:91). For Luther the danger would not have been obligation (God's commands are freeing!) but rote rehearsal.

[117]Canon 21, *Concilium Lateranense IV* (1215), in *Conciliorum Oecumenicorum Generaliumque Decreta*, 2,1:178.521–22.

[118]See Peters, *Commentary on Luther's Catechisms*, 5:82–102; Kurt Aland, "Die Privatbeichte im Luthertum," in *Kirchengeschichtliche Entwürfe: Alte Kirche; Reformation und Luthertum; Pietismus und Erweckungsbewegung* (Gütersloh: Gerd Mohn, 1960), 452–519. For a summary of how Luther reformed Penance—or undermined, depending on one's theological commitments—see Tentler, *Sin and Confession*, 349–63.

[119]Luther insists that we should do good works only for Christ's name not for our own. The Third Sermon on the Gospel for the Easter Festival (*House Postil*, 1544), WA 52:18–27.

name." Because humans are unholy, they cannot earn forgiveness. So there's no use in obtaining indulgences; that's seeking forgiveness in the pope's name.[120] There's no use in pilgrimages; that's seeking forgiveness in some dead saint's name.[121] There's no use in strict monastic living; that's seeking forgiveness in my own name.[122] "A monk's name, a nun's name, a pope's name, fasting's name, alms' name won't do. Even St. Peter's name and St. Paul's name—the Virgin Mary's name won't do it!"[123] "God doesn't regard your merits but his mercy."[124] To pursue forgiveness apart from Christ's name is to spurn God's mercy and pursue idolatry (breaking the second commandment). "That's forgiveness in the devil's name."[125]

Christ alone is the measure of forgiveness.[126] Whatever Christ gives is a gift, because he gives without considering merit. His office is to be merciful.[127] "What's forgiven has been gifted, thus we're made righteous out of pure grace."[128] "In ourselves we have nothing but sins; in Christ pure mercy."[129] Without Jesus, there is no forgiveness, so fear God and believe that he gave his Son to die for you.[130] When you stand in faith, you stand in Christ's name and person.[131] Absolution rests on the office and work of Christ alone.[132]

---

[120]Sermon on Easter Tuesday (1523), WA 12:516.26-39; Sermon on Easter Tuesday (1526), WA 20:352.1-3, 20-21; House Sermon on Easter Tuesday (1533), WA 37:34.6-7; The Third Sermon on the Gospel for the Easter Festival (*House Postil*, 1544), WA 52:261.36-38.

[121]Afternoon Sermon on Easter Tuesday (1523), WA 11:92.8-10; The Third Sermon on the Gospel for the Easter Festival (*House Postil*, 1544), WA 52:265.39-266.1.

[122]House Sermon on Easter Tuesday (1533), WA 37:33.9-15

[123]The Third Sermon on the Gospel for the Easter Festival (*House Postil*, 1544), WA 52:265.27-28.

[124]Sermon on Easter Tuesday (1524), WA 15:531.18-19. See also Sermon on Easter Tuesday (1526), WA 20:352.38-41, 353.6-8.

[125]Sermon on Easter Tuesday (1523), WA 12:516.32-33. See further WA 11:90.33-91.2 (12:514.29-515.7).

[126]See Afternoon Sermon on Easter Tuesday (1523), WA 11:92.10-29, 11:93.4-8; Sermon on Easter Tuesday (1524), WA 15:532.11-12.

[127]Sermon on Easter Tuesday (1526), WA 20:352.5-12.

[128]House Sermon on Easter Tuesday (1533), WA 37:35.21. See also Sermon on Easter Tuesday (1526), WA 20:352.10.

[129]Sermon on Easter Tuesday (1531), WA 34,1:308.11.

[130]Sermon on Easter Tuesday (1526), WA 20:352.5-12; Sermon on Easter Tuesday (1531), WA 34,1:309.2-4.

[131]The Third Sermon on the Gospel for the Easter Festival (*House Postil*, 1544), WA 52:265.3-6, 21-22.

[132]Confession and Absolution belong together; they're distinguishable but inseparable (Sermon on Easter Tuesday [1531], WA 34,1:308.4-9). For Luther, that's why Jesus says "repentance *and* forgiveness." Frightened consciences receive comfort in Absolution; the gospel would be of no savor to those who do not perceive their sin and death (Gospel for Easter Tuesday [*Church*

Luther revised Confession and Absolution according to the analogy of faith—from contrition of the heart, confession of the mouth, and satisfaction of works to contrition of the heart and faith in Jesus' word and promise.[133] Luther saw the most fitting summary of this teaching in the Apostles' Creed. He put it this way in the *House Postil*: "As we pray and proclaim in our Creed: I believe in the forgiveness or remission of sins."[134]

THE REVELATION OF HOLY COMMUNION

Luther had no trouble convincing his congregation that Jesus is present in the Sacrament of the Altar. But he struggled to show them that Jesus was present for their comfort and benefit.[135] Medieval Catholics knew that to be in the presence of the holy God is terrifying. This terror was underscored by medieval Catholic liturgical customs: only ordained men could touch the host, lay people were not to receive with their hands; only ordained men received the bread *and* the wine (*sub utraque specie*), lay people only received the host; good works and the sacrament of Confession prepared a person for reception.[136] And so, many lay people avoided receiving

---

Postil, 1544], LW 77:70-71; WA 21:239; WA 12:507.12-25; Another Sermon on the Gospel for Easter Tuesday [*Church Postil*, 1544], LW 77:95-96; WA 21:257.35-258.17). The devil apes God but turns God's word and work upside down, scaring the scared and comforting the self-satisfied. The devil comes with sweet words and leaves a stench; the Spirit comes with bitter words and leaves a sweet smell (Another Sermon on the Gospel for Easter Tuesday [*Church Postil*, 1544], LW 77:80-81.3, 81.5; WA 21:242.22-36, 243.13-23). Christ is present when forgiveness is preached, and where Christ is present the devil can't remain long (House Sermon on Easter Tuesday [1533], WA 37:34.30-31; The Third Sermon on the Gospel for the Easter Festival [*House Postil*, 1544], WA 52:261.7-8).

[133]Luther did not object to the word *satisfaction* (unlike *attrition*) but wanted to reframe it solely as the satisfying work Jesus accomplished in his cross and resurrection. See Sermon on Easter Tuesday (1524), WA 15:531.23-25; Another Sermon on the Gospel for Easter Tuesday (*Church Postil*, 1544), LW 77:99 (WA 21:262.7-11).

[134]The Third Sermon on the Gospel for the Easter Festival (*House Postil*, 1544), WA 52:266.13-14. Compare with House Sermon on Easter Tuesday (1533), WA 37:35.22-24. "That is what we pray: 'I believe in the forgiveness of sins.' Where Christ teaches, there is a kingdom, there all our sins in the whole world are forgiven. God grant that we learn it! Amen." Christ commands repentance and forgiveness to be received and preached. People shouldn't think about their unworthiness but about God's command! Another Sermon on the Gospel for Easter Tuesday (*Church Postil*, 1544), LW 77:98.60; WA 21:260.26-261.3.

[135]As Luther sees it, there's a common thread in his opponents' views of Baptism, the Sacrament, and Absolution: they have confused law with gospel, and they have confused God's action with human action.

[136]Luther saw these customs in direct contradiction to Jesus' command as well as the sacrament of Baptism. These customs created two classes of baptized Christians, as if the ordained were somehow closer to God than lay people. It was this idea (not the setting aside of some for the

Communion. The problem grew so great that Lateran IV (1215) mandated Confession of sins and reception of the Eucharist at least on Easter.[137] Sadly in Luther's time things were not much different. As late as 1528, Luther complains that many women and children do not receive—some had not received in five years![138] Luther addressed his congregants' fears about the Sacrament of the Altar with Luke 24:30-31: "And it happened that when he sat at table with them, took the bread, gave thanks, broke it, and gave it to them, their eyes were opened, and they recognized him."[139] In this encounter with two weak and fearful disciples, we see the true character of the Sacrament and its worthy preparation and reception. As we have seen, through the ministry of the Holy Spirit it is the catechism and analogy of faith—here the Sacrament of the Altar—that uncovers the inner logic of this passage.

Holy Communion is fundamentally for our benefit. "And Christ established the Sacrament of the Altar not as poison but as medicine."[140] Just as Christ is present with and strengthens these frightened disciples, in the Sacrament he is also present with and strengthens you. Jesus is friendly; he is not a tyrant.[141] He offers his body and blood in bread and wine for the strengthening of his people.[142] Jesus does not wait until you are perfectly

---

office of the word) that Luther opposed with the priesthood of all believers. See David J. Luy, "Luther and the General Priesthood: An Embedded Account," in *The Reformation and the Irrepressible Word of God: Interpretation, Theology, and Practice*, ed. Scott M. Manetsch (Downers Grove, IL: IVP Academic, 2019), 168-89. For Luther's argument for receiving the bread and the wine, see *Receiving Both Kinds in the Sacrament* (1522), LW 36:237-67 (WA 10,2:11-41).

[137] Canon 21, *Concilium Lateranense IV* (1215), in *Conciliorum Oecumenicorum Generaliumque Decreta*, 7 vols. projected, ed. Giuseppe Alberigo, Alberto Melloni, and Frederick Lauritzen (Turnhout: Brepols, 2007-2017), 2,1:178.510-31.

[138] Sermon on December 19, 1528, WA 30,1:119.20-21, 120.17-18 (LW 51:191). Luther patiently encouraged parishioners to commune. This is in stark contrast to Karlstadt's approach on Christmas of 1520. Karlstadt demanded parishioners to receive the host in their hand; it was dropped twice (one man was too scared to pick it up). See Nikolaus Müller, *Die Wittenberger Bewegung 1521 und 1522: Die Vorgänge in und um Wittenberg während Luthers Wartburgaufenthalt* (Leipzig: Heinsius, 1911), 132; Amy Nelson Burnett, *Karlstadt and the Origins of the Eucharistic Controversy*, 27-28; Roland H. Bainton, *Here I Stand: A Life of Martin Luther* (New York: Mentor Books, 1950), ch. 12.

[139] WADB 6:323. See Sermon on Easter Monday (1521), WA 9:516.4-5; Sermon on Easter Monday (1523), 11:85.20-21; WATR 1:315, no. 667. In one sermon he says he'll leave open the question whether this is the Sacrament of the Altar, see Sermon on Easter Monday (1521), WA 9:669.20-21.

[140] Sermon on Easter Monday (1523), WA 11:83.14-15.

[141] Sermon on Easter Monday (1523), WA 12:498.31-33, 501.18-502.2, 503.1-4.

[142] Sermon on Easter Monday (1523), WA 12:498.20-29.

strong on your own. As he says, "Come to me all of you who are burdened with toil and worry; I will refresh you" (Mt 11:28).[143] So, Luther advises, go to the Sacrament armed with these words of Jesus. Do you think that he thinks these two disciples are strong? His kingdom is full of people like these: sinners made righteous. Are you broken? Go to him! Even the dead are made alive in his wonderful kingdom.[144]

But like Peter, we are tempted to send Jesus away when we see our sin or to ask for some other thing than the blessing Jesus offers ("LOrd, not just my feet but also my hands and head!" Jn 13:9).[145] We want to avoid communing or to wait until we feel good enough or faithful enough, but that only cedes the field to Satan. The longer we wait, the more trials Satan brings.[146] Eventually those who abstain from the Sacrament of the Altar will have no desire at all to receive. "No, my brother; you must not withdraw from [the Sacrament]. You might withdraw for so long, that you walk away from it entirely. The longer we stay away from it, the colder and worse off we become."[147] The longer it is avoided, the less necessary it seems, for something other than God's word begins to form and frame our lives. Satan knows that God's word always bears fruit, and so at all costs he tries to steer Christians away from it.[148]

The Sacrament of the Altar is a gift of God. Christians do not prepare to receive Jesus in the Sacrament by focusing on their power and worth or by doing good works—as if right reception depends on them.[149] Jesus' presence reveals our need for Jesus—for his strength and forgiveness. Christians prepare to receive Jesus by focusing on Jesus and how they need him to strengthen, forgive, and befriend them. Right reception depends on Jesus. Luther advises that before receiving the Sacrament, Christians pray to God, "Lord, I am a weak ass. That's why I come to you! So that you would help me

---

[143] WADB 6:55.
[144] Sermon on Easter Monday (1523), WA 12:499.1–13.
[145] Sermon on Easter Monday (1523), WA 11:84.25-34 (WA 12:496.5-8, 10-16, 502.17-36); WADB 6:381-83.
[146] Sermon on Easter Monday (1523), WA 11:83.29-38 (WA 12:505.5-10).
[147] Sermon on Easter Monday (1523), WA 12:503.24-26 (compare with WA 11:84.35-37). Here Luther is recounting an anecdote from a desert father; the origin of the quote is unclear. See also Sermon on Easter Monday (1523), WA 12:500.21-24.
[148] Sermon on Easter Monday (1523), WA 11:84.1-4 (WA 12:505.5-10).
[149] Sermon on Easter Monday (1523), WA 11:85.10-14; 12:500.15-18, 503.5-18, 504.24-505.18.

and kindle my heart."[150] Christians prepare to receive God's word in the Sacrament of the Altar by hearing, reading, and singing God's word.[151]

> And we have this point in this Gospel reading. They are unbelieving. They do nothing but talk with Christ, and he helps them. If you are sluggish, read the Bible—even if you had already heard it a thousand times! (That's better than repeating the Our Father again and again.) But best of all—even above reading—is to talk with two or three people. At that the devil must flee.... The devil makes us weak and sluggish. If [Christ] appears in a form that you don't recognize, don't be idle; he will break bread and reveal himself to you.[152]

In this episode at Emmaus, Luther explains that we see the character of Holy Communion, how to prepare for it, and how to receive it (as the catechism teaches too). The Sacrament of the Altar is a free gift, given by God for our healing. And so we prepare for it not by trying to be good enough for it but by admitting our need: we are weak and sick; he is strong and full of health. We receive the Sacrament in faith, faithfully confessing our lack of faith and trusting that God will strengthen and grow us as he does for these two disciples. "If there's a time that you go to the Sacrament and you're weak in faith, you shouldn't therefore run away. He won't drive you away. That's the very reason he's here: to strengthen the weak and to comfort the terrified."[153] The more you probe your faith, the more imperfect you will feel. Turn instead to God's word. If you are fearful of receiving because of God's holiness and your sinfulness, hold God's command to receive before him.

Nothing else is necessary but God's command.[154] God's command is an assurance to Christians. Why pray? God commands it. Why receive Baptism? God commands it. Why receive Communion? God commands it. Why receive Absolution? God commands it. "Without any of my preparation and work, God's word comes to me."[155] God doesn't wait for our good works, for our initiative, or for our permission. He comes to us in his word. And so

---

[150]Sermon on Easter Monday (1523), WA 12:500.13-15.

[151]Sermon on Easter Monday (1523), WA 11:82.16-20, 84.1-4, 84.25-34 (12:496.5-8, 10-16); WA 12:500.4-32.

[152]Sermon on Easter Monday (1523), WA 11:85.16-18, 20-21 (WA 12:505.10-23). See also WA 12:496.32-497.8.

[153]Sermon on Easter Monday (1523), WA 12:503.15-18; see also Sermon on Easter Monday (1523), WA 11:82.6-7; 12:503.26-31.

[154]Sermon on Easter Monday (1523), WA 11:85.6-11.

[155]Sermon on Easter Monday (1523), WA 12:497.2-3.

The Light of the Word

when we feel what we think to be God's accusation against us, that we are not worthy or welcome, Luther taught that we should hold God's word before him, following the example of the Canaanite woman in Matthew 15:21-28. "Yes, Lord, it is true. I am a sinner and unworthy of Your grace. Nevertheless, You have promised forgiveness to sinners, and You 'came not to call the righteous' but (as St. Paul says) 'to save sinners.' "[156] We wrestle with God by holding God's own words before him.[157] "Then, by His own judgment, God has to have mercy on us."[158]

Conclusion

Luther taught that the New Testament was simply the Old Testament preached according to the analogy of faith. "Those [apostles] who have written do nothing more than direct us to the Scriptures of the Old Testament."[159] Were we still as strong in the faith and Spirit as the prophets and apostles, we too could and would pen and preach a New Testament. But because we are not so strong, we must drink from the springs of the apostles to learn how to read and interpret the Bible. That's what the analogy of faith is for. It helps Christians trace the crimson thread of the Old Testament. It helps us find Jesus. "Search Scripture! . . . It's what witnesses to me"

---

[156] Gospel for the Second Sunday in Lent (*Church Postil*, 1540), LW 76:381 (WA 17,2:204.2-5; E² 11:126); quoting Mk 2:17; Lk 5:32; 1 Tim 1:15.

[157] For an extended example of this wrestling, see Luther's sermons and postils on Jesus' exchange with the Canaanite woman in Matthew 15:21-28 (Reminiscere or the Second Sunday in Lent), Sermon on Reminiscere Sunday (1523), WA 11:41-44; Sermon on Reminiscere Sunday (1524), WA 15:453-57; Sermon on Reminiscere Sunday (1525), WA 17,1:80-82; Sermon on Reminiscere Sunday (1526), WA 20:280-87; Sermon on Reminiscere Sunday (1528), WA 27:64-68; Sermon on Reminiscere Sunday (1529), WA 29:63-72; Sermon on Reminiscere Sunday (1534), WA 37:313-16; For Reminiscere Sunday in *Conciunculae quaedam D. Martini Lutheri amico cuidam praescriptae* (Wittenberg: Nicolaus Schirlentz, 1537), C4v-C6v (WA 45:431-32); Sermon on Reminiscere Sunday (March 17, 1538), WA 46:207-12; The Gospel for the Second Sunday in Lent (*Church* Postil, 1540), LW 76:378-82 (E² 11:121-27; WA 17,2:200-204); The Gospel on Reminiscere Sunday (*House Postil*, 1544), 177-82; The Gospel on the Second Sunday in Lent (Roth's *Winter Postil*, 1528), WA 21:106-13; A Second Sermon for the Gospel on Reminiscere Sunday (Roth's *Winter Postil*, 1538), 114-20. Note the regular refrain of "as the words sound."

[158] Gospel for the Second Sunday in Lent (*Church Postil*, 1540), LW 76:381 (WA 17,2:204.5-6; E² 11:126).

[159] Gospel for Epiphany (*Church Postil*, 1544), LW 76:111 (WA 10,1.1:626.11-12; E² 10:388; compare with LW 52:206). See further WA 10,1.1:625.12-626.23; E² 10:387-88 (LW 76:111-12; compare with LW 52:205-6).

(Jn 5:39).¹⁶⁰ References to the analogy of faith (and the catechism) litter these sermons on Luke 24. While Luther focused on the sacraments of the Holy Communion and Absolution, he also mentions other parts of the catechism in his interpretation of Luke 24: he mentions or alludes to both tables of the Ten Commandments,¹⁶¹ all the articles of the Apostles' Creed,¹⁶² one petition of the Our Father,¹⁶³ and Baptism.¹⁶⁴ This preponderance of references to the catechism shows Luther's habit of reciting it every morning. "When I wake up in the morning, I pray the Ten Commandments, the Creed, the Our Father with the children, and some psalm too. I do this only for this reason: I want to keep myself there. I won't—as much as I can—let its musk be washed off me."¹⁶⁵ Luther remained in the word of God by remaining in the catechism. To stray from the catechism is to stray from the form and content of the Bible. "No one should be ashamed of the children's catechism."¹⁶⁶

---

¹⁶⁰WADB 6:345. I'm not sure why Luther rendered γραφάς as a singular.

¹⁶¹On the first commandment, see Sermon on Easter Monday (1521), WA 9:670.5-8; on the second commandment, see The Third Sermon on the Gospel for the Easter Festival (*House Postil*, 1544), WA 52:265.30-36; on the third commandment, see Sermon on Easter Tuesday (1524), WA 15:530.34-35; on the first and fourth commandments, see Afternoon Sermon on Easter Monday (1530), WA 32:60.27-31; on the second table, see WA 32:59.22-31.

¹⁶²On the first article, see House Sermon on Easter Tuesday (1533), WA 37:364.26-30; Gospel for Easter Monday (*Church Postil*, 1544), LW 77:52-53 (WA 21:231.31-232.19); on the second article, see Sermon on Easter Monday (1526), WA 20:325.21-28, 326.22-327.5; Afternoon Sermon on Easter Monday (1526), WA 20:337.12-16; Afternoon Sermon on Easter Monday (1530), WA 32:55.18-58.8, 60.1-63.25; Sermon on Easter Tuesday (1531), WA 34,1:305.5-306.15; on the third article: see Sermon on Easter Tuesday (1523), WA 11:88.34-90.10 (12:509.12-513.9); Afternoon Sermon on Easter Monday (1530), WA 32:55.18-24); Sermon on Easter Tuesday (1524), WA 15:531.6-16; House Sermon on Easter Tuesday (1533), WA 37:35.22-24; The Third Sermon on the Gospel for the Easter Festival (*House Postil*, 1544), WA 52:266.13-16.

¹⁶³On the sixth petition, see House Sermon on Easter Tuesday (1533), WA 37:32.21-23.

¹⁶⁴On Baptism, see Sermon on Easter Monday (1521), WA 9:669.34-38; Sermon on Easter Tuesday (1521), WA 9:675.18-21; Afternoon Sermon on Easter Monday (1530), WA 32:55-65; Sermon on Easter Tuesday (1531), WA 34,1:308.2-4; Sermon on Easter Monday (1534), WA 37:364.12-17.

¹⁶⁵Afternoon Sermon on Easter Monday (1530), WA 32:65.3-6.

¹⁶⁶Afternoon Sermon on Easter Monday (1530), WA 32:65.37-38.

9

Scripture According to Scripture

Five Theses on the Rule of Faith

Luther teaches that the catechism holds the entirety of the Christian faith. Even the educated laity and clergy need simple words and short summaries; how much more the simple and uneducated. Actually that's why Luther thinks the simple need the catechism so badly: the educated have lost or abandoned it. Who will teach it?

> Daily I find that there are now only a few preachers who truly and correctly understand the Our Father, the Creed, and the Ten Commandments and who are able to teach them for the poor common people. All the same, they dash into Daniel, Hosea, John's Apocalypse, and other such difficult books. The poor rabble are drawn in, listen to, and gawk at these jesters with great wonder. And when the year's through, they still can recite neither the Our Father nor the Creed nor the Ten Commandments. But it is these things that are the ancient, true Christian catechism or common education for Christians![1]

The essentials of the catechism must not be sacrificed to explore the bizarre material of the Bible. Sadly—in Luther's day as well as our own—it too often is. "No matter how clear and easy the gospel is, it isn't so for common people. To them nothing is more profitably preached than the catechism."[2] The

---

[1] Preface to Commentary on Zechariah (1527), WA 23:485.28–486.1 (LW 20:156). Also: "The holy fathers or apostles arranged [the Ten Commandments, the Apostles' Creed, and the Our Father] this way, so that they would embrace the chief parts of Christian teaching for common people," Sermon on May 18, 1528, WA 30,1:2.21–23.
[2] WATR 2:482.1–3, no. 2482.

catechism is drawn from the Bible as a touchstone or measuring rod of faithful teaching and practice. And that's what Luther used the analogy of faith for.

Five theses summarize Luther's understanding of the analogy of faith.

1. The analogy of faith is biblical.
2. The reading of the Bible is ruled according to the faith.
3. To read the Bible according to the faith is to read the Bible according to the Bible.
4. The faith is master over all tools and resources for reading the Bible.
5. The faith, as summarized in the catechism, is the beginning and end of the Christian life.

Each thesis will be explained and expanded to recapitulate the central argument of this book: Luther read the Bible according to the analogy of faith.

The Analogy of Faith Is Biblical

The analogy of faith contains the entirety of the Bible's message. "Whatever all of Scripture holds, it is simply expressed in these three [that is, the Ten Commandments, the Apostles' Creed, and the Our Father]."[3] But more importantly, for Luther, the analogy of faith comes from the Bible itself. The Ten Commandments, the Apostles' Creed, and the Our Father are either Bible passages or a pastiche of Bible passages. While modern readers might balk at the idea of the Apostles' Creed as a cluster of Bible passages, Luther went further: its composition was the inspired work of the Holy Spirit.

> I believe the Creed's words were arranged by the apostles. Together they made this fine Creed so short and comforting! And it's the work of the Holy Spirit to describe such things with such brevity, with the most powerful and ornate words. I, Doctor Martin, can't admire the composition of the Creed enough. These words should be contemplated diligently.[4]

Luther seems to affirm the tradition reported by Rufinus (c. 345–410), that after receiving the Spirit on Pentecost and before they dispersed among the

---

[3] Sermon on May 18, 1528, WA 30,1:2.20–21. See also Peters, *Commentary on Luther's Catechisms*, 1:24. Luther inconsistently numbers the parts of the catechism as three or four, depending on whether he calls out the sacraments or leaves them implied under the second and third articles of the Apostles' Creed. See above chapter 3, "Conclusion."

[4] WATR 4:230.6–11, no. 4334 (compare with p. 230.14–20).

nations, the apostles drafted the Creed by committee as a summary of their teaching.[5] The Holy Spirit superintended and inspired this work. "The Holy Spirit composed the Creed most exactly."[6] The Creed was gathered from the many flowers of the meadow of Scripture to make the sweetest honey.[7]

Similarly, for Luther, the sacraments are God's word. Each sacrament has a clear command from Jesus as reported by his most trustworthy witness: the Bible.[8] And so the sacraments too are just Bible passages:

- Baptism, Matthew 28:19 and Mark 16:16;
- Communion, 1 Corinthians 11:23-26 (compare with Mt 26:26-28; Mk 14:22-24; Lk 22:19-20);
- Absolution, John 20:22-23 (compare with Mt 18:18).

Modern readers may find this even more disorienting than Luther's claims about the inspiration of the Apostles' Creed. It seems as if Luther claims that the Bible needs no interpretation. To an extent that's true. Luther teaches that it's not the Bible that needs interpretation, but humans. Humans are dark; God's word is light.[9] As light is not impaired by darkness, God's word is in no way changed by humans. It accomplishes what it says. It is eternal and unchanging.[10]

---

[5]Rufinus, *A Commentary on the Apostles' Creed* 2 (ACW 20:29-30; PL 21:337-39). An alternate tradition identifies each article with an apostle. See sixth-century Pseudo-Augustine, Sermon 240.1 (PL 39:2189) and Pirminius (c. 700-753), *De singulis libris canonicis scarapsus*, (PL 89:1034). Their lists differ. For a detailed explanation of this legend, see Lubac, *The Christian Faith*, 32-53.

[6]WATR 3:685.7-9; compare with lines 18-21. Luther here connects the three main parts of the catechism with the three Persons of the Trinity: "God himself gave the Ten Commandments. Christ himself prescribed the form of the Lord's Prayer. The Holy Spirit composed the Creed most exactly."

[7]Sermon on Trinity Sunday (1535), WA 41:275.29-34. Cruciger edited this sermon into a second postil on the Epistle reading for Trinity Sunday; for this passage, see *Church Postil* (1544), LW 78:22-23 (WA 41:275.26-34 with WA 21:523; here WA 21 should report that text was inserted at p. 275.34 not p. 275.36). See also Gospel on Trinity Sunday (*House Postil*, 1544), WA 52:342.8-343.7.

[8]On the requirements of a sacrament, see *Against the Thirty-Two Articles of the Louvain Theologists* (1545), LW 34:354-60 (WA 54:425.1-430.18). On the Bible as Jesus' most trustworthy witness see, for example, Afternoon Sermon on Easter Monday (1530), WA 32:57.1-3, 58.6-8. See also chapter 8, "The Word Illumines the Word."

[9]See *On the Bondage of the Will* (1525), LW 33:24-28 (WA 18:1606-9); *Luther and Erasmus*, Library of Christian Classics 17, 109-12.

[10]For example, WATR 2:315.14-15, no. 2083A: "Your belief should change—not the word or work of God, which remains forever." WATR 2:316.3-5, no. 2083B: "A child didn't believe, therefore

Here Luther distinguishes between the substance of God's word and its use. According to its substance, God's word is what it is and does what it says apart from any human work. Luther affirms the adage *as you believe, so you have*. Humans still must learn to use God's word; the proper use of God's word is faith. Otherwise humans are like people in a basement who claim that the sun is not shining or inheritors of a great fortune who insist they are poor—it is not actually true, but because they refuse to accept these gifts of sunshine or wealth, it is true. The catechism lays bare the Bible's inner logic. It is the Bible's interpretive key for humans: it reveals their sin, inadequacy, and need; it reveals who God is and what he does; it reveals God's forgiveness and life for humans.

THE READING OF THE BIBLE IS RULED ACCORDING TO THE FAITH

A story isn't simply a heap of facts. A story arranges those facts in a certain way. Of course, there are many ways of arranging and emphasizing the parts of a story, but to change the arrangement and emphasis is—almost always—to change the story. And the Bible is such a big and diverse book! How will even the most learned reader understand its unifying story? The wrong unifying story begets heretics. "Just as no one can become a Christian except by Scripture, so also no one can become a heretic but by Scripture."[11]

The difference is the rule with which heretics and Christians read the Bible. Heretics read the Bible according to a rule crafted out of their own reason; Christians read the Bible according to the rule of faith.[12] That's why Paul writes that all Scripture must be measured against the faith (Rom 12:6). "Paul sees that it's not enough to say, 'I have Scripture,' etc. Instead, you, lay

---

is his baptism not efficacious? Similarly I could say: I didn't believe the gospel twenty years ago, therefore it was nothing." See also WATR 2:349–50, no. 2.178; *Large Catechism* (1529), WA 30,1:223.16–17 (BoC 1959, 447).

[11]Gospel for Epiphany (*Church Postil*, 1522, 1544), LW 76:85 (WA 10,1.1:582.13–15; E² 10:352; compare with LW 52:176). "Rightly is it said that the Bible is a book of heresies," Sermon on the Fourth Sunday in Advent (1526), WA 20:588.34. See also Sermons on Exodus 32 (1526), WA 16:624.9.

[12]On heretics and reason, see, for example, Afternoon Sermon on Easter Monday (1530), WA 32:59.10–12; Sermon on Easter Monday (1534), WA 37:364.1–7; Gospel for Easter Monday (*Church Postil*, 1544), LW 77:51–52 (WA 21:230.21–231.10). Luther's reasoning is reminiscent of Irenaeus's lovely analogy of a mosaic and its key, see Irenaeus, *Against Heresies* 1.8.1.

person, look to the Creed and the Lord's Prayer."[13] The rule of faith safeguards the faithful transmission of the Bible.

Some object that it's a logical fallacy to read the Bible according to the analogy of faith.[14] To read this way assumes the conclusion (*petitio principii*). Luther (and the vast majority of the great tradition) would balk at this accusation. Reason is indeed good (God gave it to us), but as part of our fallen nature reason does not naturally submit to the lordship of our God.[15] And so Luther would fling back the accusation of fallacious thinking on his accusers. To bracket out faith from the interpretive process—even if it's brought back at the end as a check—is to assume the conclusion (*petitio principii*). This side of the fall, reason can only do what God meant it to do when it is fully submitted to his lordship. And this requires faith. Faith—in the objective sense and the subjective sense—reveals the inner logic of the Bible as well as the inner logic of creation and redemption. In this sense the old Latin translation of Paul's phrase in Romans 12:6 is most fitting: *secundum rationem fidei*, according to the reasoning of faith. That's how the Bible is to be read: according to the reasoning of faith. This doesn't give the reader stock, cookie-cut answers. It requires wrestling with the Bible according to its own nature—as a book penned by the Holy Spirit.[16]

Luther could not have been clearer that the analogy of faith is the sine qua non of Christian readings of the Bible. And he also demonstrated this approach in his own teaching and preaching. He read the entirety of Scripture according to the faith. In practice, he more strongly emphasized certain parts of the faith, in particular, the second and third articles, the first commandment, and the sacraments. In my sampling he uses the Our Father rarely. But in theory Luther wants to use all of the catechism for reading the Bible. "The catechism—the Ten Commandments, the Creed, the Lord's Prayer—should be master."[17]

---

[13]Sermon on the Second Sunday after Epiphany (1536), WA 41:511.28–29.
[14]For example, see Kaiser, "Evangelical Hermeneutics," 176–77; Carson, "Unity and Diversity," 90–93; Marschler, "*Analogia fidei*," 228–36.
[15]See Gerrish, *Grace and Reason*, esp. 10–27.
[16]Ironically Vatican II's *Dei Verbum* may represent Luther better than many modern Protestant exegetes: "Holy Scripture must be read and interpreted in the sacred Spirit in which it was written" (12.3).
[17]WATR 1:489.22–23, no. 966.

TO READ THE BIBLE ACCORDING TO THE FAITH
IS TO READ THE BIBLE ACCORDING TO THE BIBLE

Reading the Bible according to the catechism is not to deny Scripture's sufficiency and clarity, as if the Bible needs another authority to be understandable. As usual, here Luther opposes those whom he mocks as "Papists" (those devoted to the Roman Church) and "*Schwärmer*" (a catchall term that includes the Radicals and Reformed).[18] Papists like Erasmus argue that another authority is required to interpret the Bible: the Magisterium. *Schwärmer* also agree that biblical interpretation needs another authority, but they disagree about what that authority is: some, like the heavenly prophets, say the special revelation of dreams; others, like Zwingli—while saying that they are just reading the Bible on its terms—require the authority of grammar and human reason. Luther ultimately sees the Papist and *Schwärmer* positions as the same. Both positions try to unseat God's word as master, hoisting human reason to the judgment seat and throne.

Popular perception fixates on Luther's ridicule of reason: it's "the devil's whore."[19] But this misses Luther's underlying understanding of reason. He doesn't reject philosophy's role in theology; he only bids it to come and die, so that it would be resurrected as a servant under the faith's lordship.[20] Luther distinguishes reason by its domain, temporal or spiritual, and by its state, unregenerate or regenerate. He praises reason when it stays in its place (that is, unregenerate—or regenerate for that matter—reason in temporal matters) or when it submits to the Lord our God (that is, regenerate reason in spiritual matters). He curses reason when it tries to discover and discern spiritual matters. In this way he distinguishes the use of reason from its abuse. Reason within its proper domain (the temporal realm) or submitted to faith is a beautiful gift of God. But to judge God's character and essence according to reason alone is to reject the framework God gives for

---

[18]Modern historians restrict "fanatics" to the Radicals, but Luther makes no such distinction between the Radicals and the Reformed. Carl R. Trueman points this out in "Remembering the Reformation But Celebrating What?," *First Things* (web edition, September 29, 2016): https://www.firstthings.com/blogs/firstthoughts/2016/09/remembering-the-reformation-but-celebrating-what. See further Burnett, "Luther and the *Schwärmer*," 511-13, 521.

[19]*Against the Heavenly Prophets* (1525), LW 40:175 (WA 18:164.25-26). On faith and reason in Luther, see chapter 1, "Faith Kills Reason."

[20]WATR 3:104.24-38, 105.1-10, no. 2938a; see also WATR 3:105.11-29, 106.1-10 (macaronic witness), 106.11-40, 107.1-15 (German witness), no. 2938b.

understanding his word. As Luther puts it: "According to reason we want to be our Lord God's master and to teach him."[21]

But God cannot be understood apart from his word—nor can his creation. By speaking God calls forth what was not and accomplishes his purposes (Rom 4:17). Contrary to what we may think, see, and feel, God's word describes and defines reality. "When you are in death and experience hell, cling to Christ and his word."[22] "Whoever knows [the Ten Commandments, the Apostles' Creed, and the Our Father] is a doctor of Scripture."[23] Such doctors interpret the Bible according to the catechism, asking the following questions:

- What is the Bible saying about how you should love? (the Ten Commandments)
- What is the Bible saying about God's works? (the Apostles' Creed)
- What is the Bible saying about your spiritual and temporal needs? (the Our Father)
- What is the Bible saying about your status with God? (the sacraments)
- And do these interpretations square with the Ten Commandments, the Apostles' Creed, the Our Father, and the sacraments?

With the analogy of faith Luther appears to have reframed the Quadriga.[24] Luther concretizes and personalizes the four senses of Scripture. The catechism doesn't offer abstract ideas of faith, hope, and love. It defines them by God's word: the faith confessed in the Apostles' Creed, the hope prayed for in the Our Father, and the love commanded in the Ten Commandments. Medieval theologians (as well as modern advocates of the Quadriga) would whole heartedly agree, but the Quadriga tends to be presented with this connection assumed rather than stated—so that at first blush its famous lyric reads as unnormed and subjective.

The letter teaches what happened;
the allegory, what you should believe;

---

[21] See Afternoon Sermon on Easter Monday (1530), WA 32:62.24–25.
[22] Sermon on Reminiscere Sunday (1523), WA 11:44.29.
[23] Sermon on the Ave Maria (March 11, 1523), WA 11:60.1.
[24] Ratzinger acknowledges the resonance between the catechism and the Quadriga (or the four senses) too. See Joseph Ratzinger, "Handing on the Faith and the Sources of Faith," in *Handing on the Faith in an Age of Disbelief*, trans. Michael J. Miller (San Francisco: Ignatius, 2006), 32–33.

the moral, how you should act;
the anagogy, whither you should strive.[25]

In contrast, Luther moored the senses of Scripture to Scripture itself and to Jesus Christ the Lord of Scripture. In so doing he moved the three non-literal senses from allegory to literal. All four senses are literal, because, for Luther, the literal sense is defined according to grammar, literary form, historical context, *and* Jesus Christ, the substance of Scripture. Luther also allowed a far freer use of the catechism. Any passage of Scripture could be interpreted with all of the catechism, but he usually kept to using a few choice parts, as we've seen, the second and third articles, the first commandment, and the sacraments.

The analogy of faith is a special case of Scripture interpreting Scripture. God's word is light; humans are darkness. And so for Luther it is sheer folly to try to read the Bible in any other way than by the light of God's word. Because all of the catechism is God's word, to read the Bible according to the analogy of faith is to read light by light. "In your light we see light" (Ps 36:9).[26] But to read the Bible only by grammar and human history is to read light by darkness.[27]

The catechism illumines dark passages and indicates which passages are light. Without the catechism and the Holy Spirit, how does one determine the light by which the Bible is seen? "And this you should know first of all: no prophecy in the Scriptures happens out of one's own interpretation. For there's never been any prophecy produced out of human will, but rather the holy men of God have spoken, moved by the Holy Spirit." (2 Pet 1:20-21).[28]

---

[25] The famous Latin lines are: "Littera gesta docet, quid credas allegoria, moralis quid agas, quo tendas anagogia."

[26] WADB 10,1:213.

[27] As Johnny Cash writes, "I discovered that the Bible can shed a lot of light on commentaries." *Man In White: A Novel* (San Francisco: Harper & Row, 1986), 5.

[28] WADB 7:319. Luther's base text is different here than that of modern English versions. For the end of verse 21, Erasmus has οἱ ἅγιοι θεοῦ ἄνθρωποι rather than ἀπὸ θεοῦ ἄνθρωποι. See *Novum Instrumentum omne*, ed. Erasmus, 172; *Novum Testamentum omne*, ed. Erasmus, 512.

The Faith Is Master over All Tools and Resources for Reading the Bible

Luther taught that the analogy of faith gives the true content of Scripture and the true posture of its interpreter. And he also gladly used critical reference tools! Luther used critical resources: the latest critical editions of the Bible, Hebrew grammars, and technical biblical commentaries, including rabbinic exegesis.[29] Luther had more than a working knowledge of rabbinic sources and Josephus (AD 37–100), although he accessed these sources mostly through compendia.[30] He also consulted books like Pliny the Elder's (AD 23–79) *Natural History* to identify animals and their behavior.[31] Nevertheless, Luther almost never cites his source—unless he disagrees.[32]

He was adamant that these critical tools are only aids to interpretation, not lords over interpretation.[33] For example, when a Hebraist told the Old Testament translation team at Wittenberg that the rabbis understood a certain verse differently than how these Germans had translated it, Luther asked: "Could you make it so that in grammar and pointing, it fits with the new testament?"[34] The substance determines the meaning; grammar only

---

[29]See *Novum Instrumentum omne*, ed. Erasmus; *Novum Testamentum omne*, ed. Erasmus; *Biblia Hebraica* (Brescia: Gershom Soncino, 1494); *Biblia Hebraica*, 2 vols. (Venice: Daniel Bomberg, 1511, 1518); Reuchlin, *De Rudimentis Hebraicis*; Münster, *Miqdaš YHWH*; *Biblia Sacra cum Glossa ordinaria*. See also Luther's letter to Georg Spalatin (January 18, 1518) on resources for Bible reading, *Luther: Letters of Spiritual Counsel*, 111–13 (WABr 2:132–34). Luther said if he could relearn Hebrew all over again, he would only use the best grammarians, David Kimchi and Moses Kimchi, see WATR 1:525.37–39, no. 1040.

[30]Kolb, *Martin Luther and the Enduring Word of God*, 139.

[31]For example, see Luther's gloss on the superscription to Psalm 22 (1513–1516), WA 3:134.24–31 (RCS OT 7:168n7).

[32]On Luther's resources, Kolb, *Martin Luther and the Enduring Word of God*, 136–43; Erik Herrmann, "Luther's Absorption of Medieval Biblical Interpretation and His Use of the Church Fathers," in *The Oxford Handbook of Martin Luther's Theology*, ed. Robert Kolb, Irene Dingel, and L'ubomír Batka (New York: Oxford University Press, 2014); Wood, *Captive to the Word*, 80–82. For more on Hebraic resources in the Reformation, see Stephen G. Burnett, "Reassessing the 'Basel-Wittenberg Conflict' "; Stephen G. Burnett, "The Strange Career of the *Biblia Rabbinica* Among Christian Hebraists."

[33]Mattox, "Luther's Interpretation of Scripture," esp. 46–47; Thompson, *A Sure Ground on Which to Stand*, 116–17; Kolb, *Martin Luther and the Enduring Word of God*, 89–91.

[34]WATR 5:218.26–27, no. 5533 (1542–1543); for an example, of such a case, see Luther's comments on Ps 22:16, WA 5:633–34 (compare with RCS OT 7:177–78). By *das neue testament* Luther does not always mean merely the books of the New Testament; he can also mean "new covenant" and "the Sacrament of the Altar"—even Jesus Christ ("We Christians have the meaning and import of the Bible because we have the New Testament, that is, Jesus Christ," *Last Words of David*, 1543, LW 15:268; WA 54:29.3–4). On this episode, see Bornkamm, *Luther und das Alte*

restricts the possibilities of expression.³⁵ Luther held critical aspects of interpretation—grammar, literary form and context, history, and culture—captive to the whole of Scripture: Christ for us.³⁶ And so he was pleased to use these various tools when they were helpful.³⁷

Luther did not have a set method for reading the Bible. Asking for Luther's method is like asking for someone's method for making friends. This isn't a mechanical process that can be separated from the character of the interpreter and the character of the Bible. Just like making friends, reading the Bible requires a different sequence and combination of tools and approaches. Sometimes Luther begins reading a passage with critical tools: grammar, history, and culture; these critical readings always lead to a catechetical reading. Other times Luther expands or supports a catechetical reading with critical readings. Luther also knew that the critical tools could not be discarded. For example, the loss of Hebrew and Greek might well cause the loss of the gospel: "We shall have a hard time preserving the gospel without the languages. The languages are the sheath in which this sword of the Spirit is contained."³⁸ So the Bible requires a knowledge of grammar and history.

But if one is to have one without the other, better to have history (that is, the Creed!) without grammar than grammar without history. Luther uses Augustine and Jerome as examples. Augustine didn't know Hebrew but his interpretations of the Old Testament remained within the rule of faith. Jerome knew Hebrew well but his interpretation of the Old Testament

---

Testament, 185-208. Bornkamm thinks Luther's manner of "christianizing" Scripture is unconscionable today (pp. 222-27).

³⁵WATR 3:619.28-30, no. 3794 (1538); quoted in RCS OT 7:119. "Indeed grammar is necessary for declining words, conjugating verbs, and construing syntax, but for the proclamation of the meaning and the consideration of the subject matter, grammar is not needed. For grammar should not reign over the meaning."

³⁶See Hains, "Career as Preacher in Wittenberg," 106.

³⁷Robert Kolb calls this the "pick-and-choose approach" inherited from Luther's teachers. Kolb, *Martin Luther and the Enduring Word of God*, 143. Kolb highlights four stages of Luther's interpretation of a passage: doctrinal, critical, narratival, and typological. Kolb, *Martin Luther and the Enduring Word of God*, 153-67.

³⁸*To the Councilmen of All Cities in Germany That They Establish and Maintain Christian Schools* (1524), WA 15:38.7-9 (*What Luther Says*, 2:731, no. 2273; compare with LW 45:360). See also *The Adoration of the Sacrament* (1523), WA 11:455.27-456.3 (LW 36:304); WATR 3:243, no. 3271a.

strayed outside the rule of faith.[39] Luther is clear: all readings of the Bible must be according to the faith for the benefit of God's people.

The Faith, as Summarized in the Catechism, Is the Beginning and End of the Christian Life

Christian teaching and life begin with instruction in the catechism. "Every day a new church grows up, and they need the basics. And so we should diligently present the catechism and dole out milk."[40] As a mother's milk nourishes her children, so the catechism nourishes the children of God.[41] But the children of God can never be weaned from the milk of the catechism. "These three are the greatest sermons: the Our Father, the Creed, and the Ten Commandments. Yes, although children know them and pray them daily, nevertheless we can't ever be done learning them."[42] There is more than enough in the catechism for a lifetime.[43] One may have mastered the very words of the catechism, but still the catechism has more to teach when one is confronted by difficulties and deep truths of the Bible: If even the disciples doubted Jesus' resurrection, how does the church still exist? How is the Old Testament useful and profitable for Christians? What are ghosts?[44] The same old catechism shines new light on new questions. That's why Luther said so often that he might be an old, learned doctor of the Bible, but all the same daily he must humble himself and pray the catechism side-by-side with the little children.[45]

---

[39] See "Prohoemium in lectionem Esaiae Prophetae" (1534), WA 25:87.37–88.42.
[40] WATR 3:310.6–8, no. 3421.
[41] Luther explicitly connects preachers and mothers. He compares preaching to breastfeeding (WATR 3:310.5–6, no. 3421; Sermon on the Passion of the Lord [March 29, 1521], WA 9:649.29–650.2), and he claims that hatred for women and hatred for preachers go hand in hand (WATR 3:171.28–172.4, no. 3104a; WATR 6:196.28–33, no. 6797).
[42] A House Sermon on the Articles of the Creed (1537), WA 45:12.7–9 (compare with LW 57:244).
[43] Sermon on September 22, 1528, WA 30,1:46.27–29; Sermon on September 24, 1528, WA 30,1:51.15; *Large Catechism* (1529), BoC 1959, 441–42 (WA 30,1:216.15–19); A Sermon on Jesus Christ, Preached at Court in Torgau (1533), WA 37:47.11–14 (LW 57:109); A House Sermon on the Articles of the Creed (1537), WA 45:17.16 (LW 57:247).
[44] For a brief article on this question, see Todd R. Hains, "Martin Luther Is Not Afraid of Ghosts," *Bible Study Magazine* 11, no. 6 (September–October 2019): 8–10.
[45] For example, Sermon on the Eighteenth Sunday after Trinity (1530), WA 32:131.5–15; Afternoon Sermon on First Sunday in Advent (1530), WA 32:209.36–38, 210.13–18; Sermon on First Sunday in Advent (1531), WA 34,2:449.20–30; A Sermon on Jesus Christ, Preached at Court in Torgau (1533), WA 37:47.22–25 (LW 57:109); WATR 1:30.26–31.2, no. 81; WATR 3:685.4–23, no. 3883.

This should not be surprising. For Luther, the catechism is nothing other than the Bible itself. And the Bible is like a mysterious body of water, which sheep can wade into and drink but an elephant can drown in.[46] The Bible might look like any other book, but it cannot be read like any other book. Any other book can eventually be mastered—all of its knowledge and secrets mapped and categorized. But not the Bible! "Christians understand the word of God—they can even talk about it, but they can never be done learning it."[47] As the psalmist says: "His wisdom is not to be measured" (Ps 147:5).[48] Luther used an analogy of the Schoolmen to make this point. "God's word is like a sphere or round ball which lies on the table. It only touches the table at a single point or tiny pinpoint, and nevertheless the entire table holds the ball."[49] The Bible and the catechism confront human life and concerns, and so they can be learned by humans. But the Bible and catechism cannot be fully grasped, for they address realities that humans cannot access through reason and the senses. Humans must believe the witness of others about these realities. "Yes, I have studied it diligently, and yet I still haven't fully understood one word from all of Scripture! That's why I haven't yet left the childish teaching. Indeed daily I think about it—I turn it over in my mind and I seek to understand the Ten Commandments and the Creed."[50] The word of God cannot be mastered; it is the beginning, middle, and end of the Christian life.

LUTHER THE CATHOLIC

Luther is almost always depicted as a father of a movement or era. Although not everyone agrees what new thing Luther fathered, he surely fathered something,

---

[46]Sermon on Easter Monday (1534), WA 37:366.36-39. "Holy Scripture is water, in which an elephant drowns and a sheep crosses as through a shallow brook." Luther is paraphrasing Gregory the Great, *Morals on the Book of Job*, Epistle 4 (PL 75:515). Luther was fond of this saying, see also Second Lecture on Psalm 21 (1519–1521), WA 5:598.3-4; Preface to the Lectures on Genesis (1535–1545), WA 42:2.6-7; Sermon after the Third Sunday in Easter (Jubilate; May, 1542), WA 49:256.8-9; WATR 5:168.18-19, no. 5468.

[47]WATR 2:303.1-2, no. 2047. Compare with WATR 1:28.25-27, no. 76; 1:30.22-24, no. 81. I have rendered *sancti* as "Christians," because Luther means saints here in the sense of the communion of saints, not just special dead saints.

[48]WATR 1:28.24; compare with WADB 10,1:580-81.

[49]WATR 1:28.25-30 (here 28-30), no. 76. Compare with WATR 1:30.22-26, no. 81; WATR 2:303.1-4, no. 2047. Edwin A. Abbott anthropomorphizes communion between higher order and lower order things in *Flatland: A Romance of Many Dimensions* (London: Seeley & Co., 1884); Abbott published *Flatland* pseudonymously under "A Square."

[50]WATR 2:303.5-8, no. 2047.

right? Some suggest modernity. Others suggest democracy, capitalism, socialism, modern patriarchy, secularism, Lutheranism, and Protestantism. This insistence that Luther brought about something new likely says more about our own time and culture than Luther and his time and culture. New is best. And so in Luther we see an innovator—how else could he be a creative genius?

But Luther abhors innovation in theology.[51] "If anyone brings up a new teaching against the old teaching—even if it could raise the dead—it must not be believed."[52] The ancient ministry of the word Satan cannot stand. That's why he always tries to mix something new and exciting into the church's witness. "Something new now! We've heard enough about the resurrection!"[53] This desire for something new distorts human expectations of prophecy: "It's not new, therefore isn't it not prophecy?" But prophecy isn't saying something new, it's proclaiming God's word. And God's word never changes. Luther says that if prophecy has to be new, "it follows that Isaiah wasn't a prophet—he prophesied the words of Moses; John wasn't a prophet—he used Isaiah's words."[54] Christian preaching isn't new. The words may change but the substance is always the same.[55] "The catechism is the most perfect teaching."[56] "We do not invent any new understanding, but we adhere to the analogy of holy Scripture and the faith."[57]

Luther saw himself as a lot of things, but never as an innovator. This is the man who sent his questions about indulgences to his bishop.[58] This is the man who had invited his accusers at the Diet of Worms (1521) to show him how he was misunderstanding the Bible (or admit he was right).[59] This is the

---

[51] See his discussion of "new song" in Psalm 33:3, Lecture on Psalm 33, LW 10:154 (WA 3:182.24–183.2).
[52] Sermon on the Second Day of Christmas (1528), WA 27:511.8–9.
[53] Afternoon Sermon on the First Feast Day of Easter (April 1, 1526), WA 20:317.27–28.
[54] Afternoon Sermon on Pentecost Tuesday (1529), WA 29:377.20–378.2, here p. 377.28–31.
[55] WATR 1:488.26–27, no. 965; WATR 2:438.1–6, no. 2378a (compare with WATR 2:438.8–10).
[56] WATR 1:504.24, no. 1002. See also WATR 2:522, no. 2554a-b.
[57] Lectures on Genesis 6:3, LW 2:16 (WA 42:272.1–2).
[58] See Brecht, *Martin Luther*, 1:200–202; Erwin Iserloh, *The Theses Were Not Posted: Luther Between Reform and Reformation*, trans. Jared Wicks (Boston: Beacon Press, 1968); Heiko A. Oberman, *Masters of the Reformation: The Emegence of a New Intellectual Climate in Europe* (Cambridge: Cambridge University Press, 1981), 148–50n88.
[59] Brecht, *Martin Luther*, 1:246–65; Heiko A. Oberman, *Luther: Man Between God and the Devil*, trans. Eileen Walliser-Schwarzbart (New Haven, CT: Yale University Press, 2006), 195–97; Todd R. Hains, "Luther and Bound Conscience in His German Church Postils," (MA thesis, Trinity Evangelical Divinity School, 2011), 120–21.

man who reluctantly had pastors ordained by Johannes Bugenhagen—not because he was unwilling to have new candidates for the ministry ordained by Roman Catholic bishops, but because Roman Catholic bishops were unwilling to ordain new candidates for the ministry from Wittenberg.[60] He challenged the abuse and distortion of church teaching, not the church itself.

Luther was a Catholic. Over the course of his career he harped on the catechism of the Ten Commandments, the Apostles' Creed, the Our Father, and the sacraments. He taught that the most Catholic way to read the Bible was to read it according to the analogy of faith, the most Catholic way to hear preaching was to hear it according to the analogy of faith, and the most Catholic way to obey the Catholic Church was to obey it according to the analogy of faith. Ultimately the Roman Magisterium saw the fruits of this as too radical a way to read the Bible, hear preaching, and obey the church.

Luther subordinated person, office, and authority to God's word and the analogy of faith. The chief question was always whether what someone said and did fit the analogy of faith—no matter how important, holy, or powerful they might be. And so Luther wanted simple children and common, unlearned men and women to carefully test their pastor's teaching against the catechism. Does it fit? "If not, say: 'That the devil preached!' "[61] If it's not according to the analogy of faith, it doesn't matter if the preacher is Peter, Mary, or even Jesus himself, it's Satan speaking. "The Holy Spirit says that he reveals himself this way: that it fits with the faith.' "[62] On the other hand, if it is according to the analogy of faith, it doesn't matter if the preacher is Judas or Caiaphas, it's God speaking. The Spirit by the faith and word makes good readers and interpreters of the Bible.[63]

This is true for the youngest child to the oldest grandparent, for the most learned scholar to the simplest peasant. As Luther impressed on his students, "They are wise who know the rule and analogy of faith."[64]

---

[60] See Haile, *Luther*, 28–29.
[61] Sermon on the Second Sunday after Epiphany (1531), WA 34,1:107.8-9.
[62] Sermon on the Second Sunday after Epiphany (1531), WA 34,1:107.9-10.
[63] "Whoever wants to be a master of interpreting Scripture [must interpret according to the analogy of the faith]." Afternoon Sermon on Cantate Sunday (May 7, 1531), WA 34,1:374.10.
[64] Lectures on Isaiah 29:11 (1527–1530), WA 31,2:178.23-24 (compare LW 16:246).

10

This Is Most Certainly True

A Conclusion

Twenty years after Staupitz had told Luther of his commission to preach and teach the Bible under the pear tree at the Black Cloister, Luther stood under the same pear tree with a student who had doubts of incompetence and weakness.[1]

A great deal had changed. The Black Cloister was no longer the house for the observant Augustinian order; it was now the Luther family residence (with rooms for visitors and student renters). Luther had been released of his vows of obedience by the vicar general of his order, excommunicated by the pope, and placed under imperial ban by the emperor. And Luther could offer comfort better than so what if the ministry of the word kills you? "Dear friend, that's how it was with me too."[2]

"You should preach to God not considering human judgments. If someone can do it better, he should. You should just preach Christ and the catechism. This wisdom will lift you above all judgments, for the word of God is wiser than humans."[3]

Luther pointed the young preacher back to Jesus and the catechism. "Know that you are called. Christ must be yours, so that you may help praise him. In this stand firm."[4]

---

[1] WATR 3:187.27-29, 188.1-27 (macaronic witness), 188.30-42, 189.1-18 (German witness), no. 3143b. See also WATR 3:187.4-25, no. 3143a.
[2] WATR 3:188.1, no.3143b.
[3] WATR 3:188.6-9, no. 3143b (compare lines 39-41).
[4] WATR 3:188.12-13, no. 3143b.

Christ must be yours. This is the simple piety of Luther. He commends it to clergy and laity alike.

And that's why Luther never left the simplicity and depth of the ancient catechism of the Ten Commandments, the Apostles' Creed, and the Our Father. The catechism unfolds the inner logic of the Bible. To know the catechism and to read the Bible by it is to read the Bible by its own light. "By your light we see light" (Ps 36:9).[5]

The catechism is like the ABCs of the Bible. It's brief and accessible for young or old, learned or unlearned, and it can't be replaced. You can never move on from the ABCs without losing the ability to read and write. In the same way, you can never move on from the catechism without losing the ability to read and hear God's word. If you want to read and write, learn the ABCs. If you want to hear God's word, learn the catechism.

And yet, as tends to be the case with common things, the catechism is despised. "Many regard the catechism as a simple, silly teaching which they can absorb and master at one reading. After reading it once they toss the book into a corner as if they are ashamed to read it again."[6] Luther complained that folks were more interested in the apocalyptic of the Bible, the fables of the saints, and the dreams of the eccentric than in the simple, concrete, and personal words of the Ten Commandments, the Apostles' Creed, and the Our Father. That remains the case (though we might add historical criticism, archaeology, and the Enneagram to Luther's list of apocalyptic, fables, and dreams).

The challenge and lesson of Luther's analogy of faith is this: set aside the sweets and junk food of modern biblical studies and theology, and learn the Ten Commandments, the Apostles' Creed, and the Our Father. "The longer they work with the catechism, the less they know of it and the more they have to learn. Only then, hungry and thirsty, will they truly relish what now they cannot bear to smell because they are so bloated and surfeited."[7] Ponder and pray the Ten Commandments, the Apostles' Creed, and the Our Father in your heart day in and day out; let these three great sermons shape you and let them form how you read and pray the Bible.

---

[5] WADB 10,1:213.
[6] Preface to *The Large Catechism* (1529), BoC 1959, 359 (WA 30,1:120.5–8).
[7] Preface to *The Large Catechism* (1529) BoC 1959, 361 (WA 30,1:129.7–10).

As a pastor and fellow Christian, Luther's calling is to point to Jesus. That's what the Bible is all about. See that man on the cross and that God in the manger? He is for you! He forgives your sin and gives you true life. Will you believe it? Will you trust his word and promise for you?

Luther recounts how he directed a downcast woman to Jesus Christ by pointing her back to the catechism. "Dear Mr. Doctor," she told him, "I think I'm lost and can't be saved, because I can't believe!"

He responded: "Do you believe, dear woman, that it's true what you pray in your Creed?" Luther remembers fondly how she received this question with joy. "She clasped her hands together: 'Oh, that I believe! That's certainly true.'" Luther comforted her. "Well, dear woman, then go forth in the name of God! You believe more and better than I!"[8]

---

[8] WATR 5:242.6–24, no. 5662, quoting lines 11–17.

Table of Sources

CHAPTER 2. THE ANCIENT CATECHISM

Twenty-three sermons on the Second Sunday of Epiphany are extant from 1522 to 1546. In the earlier years, Luther preached the Gospel reading, strongly affirming God's blessing of and pleasure in marriage. In the later years, Luther shifted to preaching the Epistle reading or Baptism. Five sermons explicitly handle the Epistle reading (Rom 12:3-8); seven the Gospel reading (Jn 2:1-12). Seven are part of St. Mary's regular Baptism series during Epiphany. The remaining four are part of other sermon series: Matthew 8; John 1; 1 Corinthians 15; Psalm 5.

No sermons are extant for 1522–1523, 1526–1527, 1530, 1540, 1542–1543. Luther indeed preached some of these years, but such sermons are missing from the historical record. However, some of these years he did not preach this Sunday because he was away from Wittenberg (for example, hiding at the Wartburg in 1522), because he refused to preach (for example, in 1530, during one of his preaching strikes), and because he was ill (for example, 1543). Here are the five sermons and one postil on Romans 12:3-8:

1. Afternoon Sermon on the Second Sunday after Epiphany (1531), WA 34,1:99–107
2. Sermon on the Second Sunday after Epiphany (1536), WA 41:507–11.
3. Sermon on the Second Sunday after Epiphany (1537), WA 45:1–5
4. Sermon on the Second Sunday after Epiphany (1538), WA 46:145–51
5. Sermon on the Second Sunday after Epiphany (1545), WA 49:681–86
6. Epistle on the Second Sunday after Epiphany (*Church Postil*, 1525), WA 17,2:32–60, LW 76:214–15

Chapter 3. The Childish Doctrine

In each of the three series of catechism sermons of 1528, Luther preached through the Ten Commandments, the Apostles' Creed, the Our Father, and the sacraments of Baptism and Eucharist. For the Pentecost sermon series, see WA 30,1:2–27; for the Holy Cross sermon series, see WA 30,1:27–57; for the Advent sermon series, see WA 30,1:57–122.

Luther also preached through the Ten Commandments, the Apostles' Creed, the Our Father, and the Ave Maria during Lent of 1523, see WA 11:30-62.

The following four tables, group the sources I used on the parts of the catechism.

THE TEN COMMANDMENTS	
For a detailed examination of Luther's interpretation of the first table, see Peters, *Commentary on Luther's Catechisms*, 1:103–84; Asendorf, *Theologie Martin Luthers*, 305–14 (just the first commandment). For a detailed examination of Luther's interpretation of the second table, see Peters, *Commentary on Luther's Catechisms*, 1:185–316.	
COMMANDMENT	
On the first commandment	Sermon on the First and Second Commandments (February 26, 1523), WA 11:36.2–28 Sermons on Exodus 20 (1525), WA 16:422–64 Sermon on May 18, 1528, WA 30,1:2.32–4.13 Sermon on September 14, 1528, WA 30,1:27.26–29.34 Sermon on November 30, 1528, WA 30,1:58.18–61.22 Sermon on December 7, 1528, WA 30,1:85.5–16 *Small Catechism* (1529), TAL 4:217 (WA 30,1:282–85; BoC 1959, 342) *Large Catechism* (1529), BoC 1959, 365–71, 407–11 (WA 30,1:132.33–139.12, 180.3–182.15) Sermons on Deuteronomy 5 (1529), WA 28:595–61
On the second commandment	Sermon on the First and Second Commandments (February 26, 1523), WA 11:36.29–38.3 Sermons on Exodus 20 (1525), WA 16:464–77 Sermon on May 19, 1528, WA 30,1:4.26–5.15 Sermon on September 15, 1528, WA 30,1:30.9–31.36 Sermon on December 1, 1528, WA 30,1:62.7–64.9 *Small Catechism* (1529), TAL 4:218 (WA 30,1:284–85; BoC 1959, 342) *Large Catechism* (1529), BoC 1959, 371–75 (WA 30,1:139.15–143.14)
On the third commandment	Sermon on the Third Commandment (February 27, 1523), WA 11:38.5–39.30 Sermons on Exodus 20 (1525), WA 16:477–85 Sermon on May 19, 1528, WA 30,1:5.17–27 Sermon on September 15, 1528, WA 30,1:31.37–33.10 Sermon on December 1, 1528, WA 30,1:64.10–66.11 *Small Catechism* (1529), TAL 4:218 (WA 30,1:284–85; BoC 1959, 342) *Large Catechism* (1529), BoC 1959, 375–79 (WA 30,1:143.17–147.3)
On the fourth commandment	Sermon on the Fourth, Fifth, and Sixth Commandments (February 28, 1523), WA 11:40.1–41.12 Sermons on Exodus 20 (1525), WA 16:485–506 Sermon on May 20, 1528, WA 30,1:6.2–7.3 Sermon on September 17, 1528, WA 30,1:33.16–36.16 Sermon on December 3, 1528, WA 30,1:67.1–72.4 Sermon on December 4, 1528, WA 30,1:72.10–74.7 *Small Catechism* (1529), TAL 4: 219 (WA 30,1:286–87; BoC 1959, 343) *Large Catechism* (1529), BoC 1959, 379–89 (WA 30,1:147.5–157.11)

On the fifth commandment	Sermon on the Fourth, Fifth, and Sixth Commandments (February 28, 1523), WA 11:41.14–21 Sermons on Exodus 20 (1525), WA 16:506–10 Sermon on May 20, 1528, WA 30,1:7.5–30 Sermon on September 18, 1528, WA 30,1:36.22–37.13 Sermon on December 4, 1528, WA 30,1:74.8–75.21 *Small Catechism* (1529), TAL 4:219 (WA 30,1:286–87; BoC 1959, 343) *Large Catechism* (1529), BoC 1959, 389–92 (WA 30,1:157.14–160.22)
On the sixth commandment	Sermon on the Fourth, Fifth, and Sixth Commandments (February 28, 1523), WA 11:41.23–30 Sermons on Exodus 20 (1525), WA 16:510–13 Sermon on May 22, 1528, WA 30,1:7.32–8.4 Sermon on September 18, 1528, WA 30,1:37.16–30 Sermon on December 4, 1528, WA 30,1:75.22–77.6 *Small Catechism* (1529), TAL 4:220 (WA 30,1:286–87; BoC 1959, 343) *Large Catechism* (1529), BoC 1959, 392–95 (WA 30,1:160.25–163.25)
On the seventh commandment	Sermon on the Seventh Commandment (March 2, 1523), WA 11:45.2–46.34 Sermons on Exodus 20 (1525), WA 16:513–19 Sermon on May 22, 1528, WA 30,1:8.6–17 Sermon on September 18, 1528, WA 30,1:37.31–39.33 Sermon on December 7, 1528, WA 30,1:77.18–81.10 *Small Catechism* (1529), TAL 4:220 (WA 30,1:286–89; BoC 1959, 343) *Large Catechism* (1529), BoC 1959, 395–99 (WA 30,1:163.28–168.37)
On the eighth commandment	Sermon on the Eighth, Ninth, and Tenth Commandments (March 3, 1523), WA 11:47.4–48.10 Sermons on Exodus 20 (1525), WA 16:519–25 Sermon on May 22, 1528, WA 30,1:8.19–33 Sermon on September 19, 1528, WA 30,1:40.1–42.31 Sermon on December 7, 1528, WA 30,1:81.11–83.11 *Small Catechism* (1529), TAL 4:221 (WA 30,1:288–89; BoC 1959, 343) *Large Catechism* (1529), BoC 1959, 399–404 (WA 30,1:169.3–174.23)
On the ninth and tenth commandments	Sermon on the Eighth, Ninth, and Tenth Commandments (March 3, 1523), WA 11:48.11–15 Sermons on Exodus 20 (1525), WA 16:525–28 Sermon on May 22, 1528, WA 30,1:9.2–14 Sermon on September 19, 1528, WA 30,1:42.32–43.11 Sermon on December 7, 1528, WA 30,1:83.12–85.5 *Small Catechism* (1529), TAL 4:221–22 (WA 30,1:288–91; BoC 1959, 343–44) *Large Catechism* (1529), BoC 1959, 404–7 (WA 30,1:174.28–178.21)

THE APOSTLES' CREED

For a detailed examination of Luther's interpretation of the first article, see Peters, *Commentary on Luther's Catechisms*, 2:59–104; Bayer, *Martin Luther's Theology*, 163–74; Asendorf, *Theologie Martin Luthers*, 47–60. For a detailed examination of Luther's interpretation of the second article, see Peters, *Commentary on Luther's Catechisms*, 2:105–207; Bayer, *Martin Luther's Theology*, 230–34; Asendorf, *Theologie Martin Luthers*, 61–202. For a detailed examination of Luther's interpretation of the third article, see Peters, *Commentary on Luther's Catechisms*, 2:209–306; Bayer, *Martin Luther's Theology*, 239–48; Asendorf, *Theologie Martin Luthers*, 203–66; Prenter, *Spiritus Creator*.

ARTICLE	
On the first article	Sermon on the Creed (March 4, 1523), WA 11:49.7–50.36 Sermon on May 23, 1528, WA 30,1:9.18–30 Sermon on September 21, 1528, WA 30,1:44.32–36 Sermon on December 10, 1528, WA 30,1:87.4–88.14 *Small Catechism* (1529), TAL 4:223 (WA 30,1:292–95; BoC 1959, 344–45) *Large Catechism* (1529), BoC 1959, 411–13 (WA 30,1:183.15–185.28) Afternoon Sermon for the Seventh Sunday after Trinity (July 11, 1529), WA 29:472.30–473.31 A House Sermon on the Articles of the Creed (1537), WA 45:12.16–17.12 (LW 57:244–47) A Sermon on Jesus Christ, Preached at Court in Torgau (1533), WA 37:36.3–17 (LW 57:95)

On the second article	Sermon on the Creed (March 5, 1523), WA 11:51.3–53.4 Sermon on May 23, 1528, WA 30,1:9.31–10.30 Sermon on September 21, 1528, WA 30,1:44.37–45.8 Sermon on December 11, 1528, WA 30,1:88.16–90.24 *Small Catechism* (1529), TAL 4:224 (WA 30,1:294–97; BoC 1959, 345) *Large Catechism* (1529), BoC 1959, 413–15 (WA 30,1:186.1–187.16) A House Sermon on the Articles of the Creed (1537), WA 45:17.16–22.2 (LW 57:247–50) A Sermon on Jesus Christ, Preached at Court in Torgau (1533), WA 37:36.39–72.11 (LW 57:96–138)
	Luther handles the second article tersely in the catechetical sermons, because the church year is framed by this article, so preachers have no shortage of opportunities to preach on it.[1] See further the postils for the feasts of Christmas, Holy Week, the Triduum, and Ascension: LW 75–79. Luther also preached on the second article during the Marian feasts, particularly Candlemas (February 2) and the Annunciation (March 25).
On the third article	Sermon on the Creed (March 6, 1523), WA 11:53.6–54.36 Sermon on May 23, 1528, WA 30,1:10.31–11.7 Sermon on September 21, 1528, WA 30,1:45.9–19 Sermon on December 11, 1528, WA 30,1:91.2–94.13 *Small Catechism* (1529), TAL 4:225 (WA 30,1:296–99; BoC 1959, 345) *Large Catechism* (1529), BoC 1959, 415–19 (WA 30,1:187.21–192.34) A House Sermon on the Articles of the Creed (1537), WA 45:22.6–24.20 (LW 57:250–52) A Sermon on Jesus Christ, Preached at Court in Torgau (1533), WA 37:36.18–38 (LW 57:95–96)

THE OUR FATHER	
For a detailed examination of Luther's interpretation of the first three petitions, see Peters, *Commentary on Luther's Catechisms*, 3:39–115. For a detailed examination of Luther's interpretation of the last four petitions, see Peters, *Commentary on Luther's Catechisms*, 3:117–207.	
On the Our Father in general	Sermon on the Our Father (March 9, 1523), WA 11:55.2–57.19 Sermon on December 14, 1528, WA 30,1:95.5–98.17 Sermon on December 15, 1528, WA 30,1:108.13–109.2 *Large Catechism* (1529), BoC 1959, 420–25 (WA 30,1:193.3–198.2) Sermons on Matthew 5–7 (1532), WA 32:419.37–422.18
On the first petition	Sermon on the Our Father (March 9, 1523), WA 11:56.32–57.19 Sermon on May 25, 1528, WA 30,1:12.2–35 Sermon on September 22, 1528, WA 30,1:46.31–47.25 Sermon on December 14, 1528, WA 30,1:98.19–100.3 *Small Catechism* (1529), TAL 4:225–26 (WA 30,1:298–301; BoC 1959, 346) *Large Catechism* (1529), BoC 1959, 425–26 (WA 30,1:198.5–199.30)
On the second petition	Sermon on the Our Father (March 10, 1523), WA 11:57.25–58.15 Sermon on May 25, 1528, WA 30,1:13.2–31 Sermon on September 22, 1528, WA 30,1:47.27–48.2 Sermon on December 14, 1528, WA 30,1:100.5–101.6 *Small Catechism* (1529), TAL 4:227 (WA 30,1:300–302; BoC 1959, 346) *Large Catechism* (1529), BoC 1959, 426–28 (WA 30,1:199.33–201.25)
On the third petition	Sermon on the Our Father (March 10, 1523), WA 11:58.15–28 Sermon on May 26, 1528, WA 30,1:13.33–14.20 Sermon on September 22, 1528, WA 30,1:48.4–23 Sermon on December 14, 1528, WA 30,1:101.8–102.18 *Small Catechism* (1529), TAL 4:227 (WA 30,1:301–3; BoC 1959, 347) *Large Catechism* (1529), BoC 1959, 428–29 (WA 30,1:201.28–203.27) WATR 4:846, no. 4853

---

[1]Sermon on September 21, 1528, WA 30,1:45.20–23, 46.4–5; Sermon on December 10, 1528, WA 30,1:89.14–15; *Large Catechism* (1529), BoC 1959, 414–15; WA 30,1:187.10–14.

On the fourth petition	Sermon on the Our Father (March 10, 1523), WA 11:58.29–59.5 Sermon on May 26, 1528, WA 30,1:14.22–15.11 Sermon on September 22/23, 1528, WA 30,1:48.25–49.17 Sermon on December 15, 1528, WA 30,1:103.13–104.22 *Small Catechism* (1529), TAL 4:228 (WA 30,1:302–5; BoC 1959, 347) *Large Catechism* (1529), BoC 1959, 430–32 (WA 30,1:203.30–206.8)
On the fifth petition	Sermon on the Our Father (March 10, 1523), WA 11:59.5–13 Sermon on May 26, 1528, WA 30,1:15.13–16.8 Sermon on September 22/23, 1528, WA 30,1:49.17–22 Sermon on December 15, 1528, WA 30,1:105.2–106.14 *Small Catechism* (1529), TAL 4:229 (WA 30,1:304–7; BoC 1959, 347) *Large Catechism* (1529), BoC 1959, 432–33 (WA 30,1:206.12–208.12).
On the sixth petition	Sermon on the Our Father (March 10, 1523), WA 11:59.13–24 Sermon on May 27, 1528, WA 30,1:16.10–17.37 Sermon on September 22/23, 1528, WA 30,1:49.24–50.10 Sermon on December 15, 1528, WA 30,1:106.16–107.20 *Small Catechism* (1529), TAL 4:229 (WA 30,1:306–7; BoC 1959, 347–48) *Large Catechism* (1529), BoC 1959, 433–35 (WA 30,1:208.15–210.14)
On the seventh petition	Sermon on the Our Father (March 10, 1523), WA 11:59.24–30 Sermon on May 27, 1528, WA 30,1:18.2–15 Sermon on September 22/23, 1528, WA 30,1:50.12–26 Sermon on December 15, 1528, WA 30,1:108.2–12 *Small Catechism* (1529), TAL 4:230 (WA 30,1:306–9; BoC 1959, 348) *Large Catechism* (1529), BoC 1959, 435–36 (WA 30,1:210.17–211.33)

THE SACRAMENT OF BAPTISM

On Luther and Baptism, see Peters, *Commentary on Luther's Catechisms*, 4:73–146; Althaus, *Theology of Martin Luther*, 353–74; Trigg, "Luther on Baptism and Penance," 310–17, 320–21; Trigg, *Baptism in the Theology of Martin Luther* (Leiden: Brill, 1994); Asendorf, *Theologie Martin Luthers*, 286–96; Dorothea Wendebourg, "Taufe und Abendmahl," in *Luther Handbuch*, ed. Albrecht Beutel (Tübingen: Mohr Siebeck, 2005), 414–23.

On Baptism's definition	Sermon on May 28, 1528, WA 30,1:19.25–27, 21.3–4 Sermon on September 24, 1528, WA 30,1:50.30–37, 51.36–38 Sermon on December 17, 1528, WA 30,1:110.18–19, 111.1–2, 112.3–6, 18–26 *Small Catechism* (1529), TAL 4:231 (WA 30,1:308.17–22; BoC 1959, 348) *Large Catechism* (1529), BoC 1959, 438 (WA 30,1:213.28–33)
On Baptism's foundational Bible passages	Sermon on May 28, 1528, WA 30,1:18.21–23 Sermon on September 24, 1528, WA 30,1:51.1–6 Sermon on December 17, 1528, WA 30,1:109.27–110.15 *Small Catechism* (1529), TAL 231 (WA 30,1:308.23–26, 310.1–3; BoC 1959, 348) *Large Catechism* (1529), BoC 1959, 437 (WA 30,1:212.13–21) WATR 2:301, no. 2041
On Baptism's benefits	Sermon on May 28, 1528, WA 30,1:20.7–14, 21.15–16 Sermon on May 29, 1528, WA 30,1:23.9–15 Sermon on May 30, 1528, WA 30,1:25:4–5 Sermon on September 24, 1528, WA 30,1:51.14, 52.2 Sermon on September 25, 1528, WA 30,1:54.30–31 Sermon on December 17, 1528, WA 30,1:112.7–10, 113.2–6, 8–9 *Small Catechism* (1529), TAL 4:231 (WA 30,1:310.4–16; BoC 1959, 348–49) *Large Catechism* (1529), BoC 1959, 439 (WA 30,1:215.3–12)

THE SACRAMENT OF THE ALTAR

On Luther and the Sacrament of the Altar, see Peters, *Commentary on Luther's Catechisms*, 4:149–227; Althaus, *Theology of Martin Luther*, 375–403; Gordon A. Jensen, "Luther and the Lord's Supper," in *The Oxford Handbook of Martin Luther's Theology*, ed. Robert Kolb, Irene Dingel, and L'ubomír Batka (New York: Oxford University Press, 2014), 322–32; Asendorf, *Theologie Martin Luthers*, 296–304; Wendebourg, "Taufe und Abendmahl," 414–23.

On the Sacrament of the Altar's definition	Sermon on May 28, 1528, WA 30,1:19.25–27, 21.3–4 Sermon on September 24, 1528, WA 30,1:50.30–37, 51.36–38 Sermon on December 17, 1528, WA 30,1:110.18–19, 111.1–2, 112.3–6, 18–26 *Small Catechism* (1529), TAL 4:231 (WA 30,1:308.17–22; BoC 1959, 348) *Large Catechism* (1529), BoC 1959, 438 (WA 30,1:213.28–33)
On the Sacrament of the Altar's foundational Bible passages	Sermon on May 29, 1528, WA 30,1:23.19–25 Sermon on September 25, 1528, WA 30,1:54.5 Sermon on December 19, 1528, WA 30,1:116.17, 117.5–6 *Small Catechism* (1529), TAL 4:235–36 (WA 30,1:314.21–30, 316.1–11; BoC 1959, 351) *Large Catechism* (1529), BoC 1959, 447 (WA 30,1:222.28–223.6)
	Luther usually cites the words of institution from memory, rather than these separate passages. For the words of institution, see *The German Mass and Order of Service* (1526), LW 53:80–81 (WA 19:97–99).
On the Sacrament of the Altar's benefits	Sermon on May 30, 1528, WA 30,1:25.1–4,6–22, 26.7–12, 16–17, 27.6–7 Sermon on September 25, 1528, WA 30,1:52.39–53.1, 53.6–7, 54.33–34, 55.3–12 Sermon on December 19, 1528, WA 30,1:118.15–17, 119.16–18, 120.12–14, 121.12–17, 122.11–13 *Small Catechism* (1529), TAL 4:236 (WA 30,1:316.12–21; BoC 1959, 352) *Large Catechism* (1529), BoC 1959, 449 (WA 30,1:224.32–225.6)
	Peters highlights that on account of his polemics with the Reformed and the Radicals, Luther underemphasizes the unity brought through the Sacrament (Peters, *Commentary on Luther's Catechisms*, 4:43–48); still see *Blessed Sacrament of the Body of Christ* (1519), LW 35:51–52, 59–60 (WA 2:743.20–744.7, 748.27–749.22); Sermon on Sermon on May 30, 1528, WA 30,1:26.22–25, 27.17–18; WATR 4:27–28, no. 3947; 5:259–60, no. 5579.

ON THE SACRAMENT OF ABSOLUTION

On Luther and Absolution, see Peters, *Commentary on Luther's Catechisms*, 5:1–105; Trigg, "Luther on Baptism and Penance," 317–20; Rittgers, "Confession (Private) and the Confessional," 157–59; Rittgers, "Penance, Penitence, and Repentance," in *Dictionary of Luther and the Lutheran Traditions*, ed. Timothy J. Wengert (Grand Rapids: Baker Academic, 2017), 585–88.

On Absolution's definition	*The Sacrament of Penance* (1519), LW 35:10–11, 22 (WA 2:715.10–20, 722.36–723.2) Sermon on December 15, 1528, WA 30,1:105.21–106.14 *Large Catechism* (1529), BoC 1959, 433 (WA 30,1:207.24–208.12) Epistle for the Sunday after Easter (*Church Postil*, 1544), LW 77:132–33, 133–45 (WA 49:144.29–32, 145.17–153.42) WATR 6:174, no. 6765 See Peters, *Commentary on Luther's Catechisms*, 5:48–50.
On Absolution's benefits	Luther does not systematically list the obvious benefits of Absolution—particularly, forgiveness—but here are some passages where he talks about the grace and mercy of receiving Absolution: *Large Catechism* (1529), BoC 1959, 457–61 (WA 30,1:233.20–238.15) WATR 4:260–61, no. 4362; 4:694, no. 5175; 5:281, no. 5632 See Ewald M. Plass, ed., *What Luther Says*, 3 vols. (St. Louis: Concordia, 1959), 1–9; Peters, *Commentary on Luther's Catechisms*, 4:65–60.

CHAPTER 4. THE RESURRECTION OF THE DEAD

Luther preached on the vast majority of the Torah (Genesis twice): Genesis 8–9, 11–12, 15, 23–31 (1519–1521), see WA 9, compare with WA 22:xlii–xliii; all of Genesis (1523–1525), see WA 14:97–488; print, WA 24:1–710; Exodus (1524–1527), see WA 16:1–646; Leviticus 9–19, 23, 25, 27 (1527), see WA 25:411–36; Numbers 6, 11–14, 16–17, 19–25, 30–31 (1527–1528), see WA 25:436–517; Deuteronomy 1–9 (1529), see WA 28:509–763. But he lectured on only two books of the Torah: Genesis and Deuteronomy. For the Genesis lectures (1535–1545), see LW 1–8 (WA 42–44). For the Deuteronomy lectures (1523–1524; print, 1525), see LW 9 (Luther's translation of Deuteronomy, WA 14:497–544, annotations and glosses, WA 14:545–744).

CHAPTER 5. THE SPOILS OF DEATH'S DEATH

Luther only preached and lectured on one of the Historical Books: Judges. There is one sermon from early in his career, Sermon on the Character of Christ's Resurrection (March 1516), WA 1:58-60, and one incomplete lecture series from early in his career, Lecture on the Book of Judges (1516-1518), WA 4:529-86.

In 1883 Georg Buchwald discovered the only extant notes of the lectures. These fragmentary notes are likely the work of Georg Rörer, working off someone else's notes. They were not published until 1884. See WA 4:527–29; Julius Köstlin, "Vorwort," in *Dr. Martin Luthers Vorlesung über das Buch der Richter: Aus einer in der Zwickauer Ratsschulbibliothek befindlichen Handschrift*, ed. Georg Buchwald (Leipzig: Julius Drescher, 1884), V–IX; Georg Buchwald, "Einleitung," in *Luthers Vorlesung über das Buch der Richter*, 1–14. At first Buchwald thought the lecture series was given from 1528 to 1529, despite Köstlin contradicting him in the foreword, see *Luthers Vorlesung über das Buch der Richter*, VI–VIII, 10.

CHAPTER 6. THE UPSIDE-DOWN KING

Luther lectured on most of the Wisdom books: three times on the Psalms, although only the first lecture series covers the entire Psalter (1513–1515, 1519–1521, 1532–1535), once on Ecclesiastes (1526), once on Song of Songs (1530–1532). But he only preached out of one of the Wisdom books:

the Psalms. See the relevant portion of the Weimar editors' catalog of Luther's sermons by text, WA 22:XLIII–XLIV.

The sources used in this chapter are: *Summarien vber die Psalmen, Und vrsachen des dolmetschens* (Wittenberg: Hans Lufft, 1531–1533), WA 38:9.2–69.17; Sermon on Psalm 72 (May 28, 1533), WA 37:83.2–87.8; seven-part sermon series on Psalm 72 of 1540, WA 49:11.25–49.34; and Lectures on Psalm 72, LW 10:403–14 (WA 3:461.20–471.21, for the glossa, which are not translated in LW 3, WA 3:458.15–461.18).

Chapter 7. The Great Light in Darkness

Out of the three Major Prophets—Isaiah, Jeremiah, and Ezekiel—Luther only lectured on Isaiah. There are two records of the first lectures on Isaiah, see WA 25:121–26; WA 31,2:68–75. See his extensive commentary on Isaiah 9, WA 40,3:597–682. He lectured on the Minor Prophets from 1524 to 1526.

Isaiah was also the only prophetic book Luther preached extensively, and most of those sermons were on Isaiah 9. He also preached two sermons on Jeremiah, one on Ezekiel, one on Zechariah, and one on Malachi. See the relevant portion of the Weimar editors' catalog of Luther's sermons by text, WA 22:XLIV–XLV. The editors mistakenly list the text for Afternoon Sermon on the Feast of the Annunciation to Mary (March 18, 1540) as Zechariah 9:9; it's actually Isaiah 7:14. (Also the date for that sermon should be March 25.) The next sermon—Afternoon Sermon on Palm Sunday (March 21, 1540)—is on Zechariah 9:9; see WA 49:62–66.

Luther preached on Isaiah 9:2-6 at least thirteen times.

1. Afternoon Sermon on the Feast of Christ's Birth (December 25, 1525), WA 17,1:500–504
2. Sermon on the Feast of St. Stephen (December 26, 1525), WA 17,1:504–7
3. Sermon on the Day Before the Feast of Christ's Birth (December 24, 1531), WA 34,2:490–500
4. Afternoon Sermon on the First Day of Christmas (December 25, 1531), WA 34,2:508–14
5. Sermon on the Feast of St. Stephen (December 26, 1531), WA 34,2:515–23

6. Afternoon Sermon on the Feast of St. Stephen (December 26, 1531), WA 34,2:523–30
7. Sermon on the Feast of St. John the Evangelist (December 27, 1531), WA 34,2:530–36
8. Sermon on the Day Before the Feast of Christ's Birth (December 24, 1537), WA 45:341–45
9. Sermon on the Feast of Christ's Birth (December 25, unknown year), WA 45:426–27
10. Sermon on the Day Before the Feast of the Circumcision (December 31, 1539), WA 47:871–75
11. Afternoon Sermon on the Feast of the Circumcision (January 1, 1541), WA 49:191–96
12. Sermon on Day Before the Feast of Epiphany (January 5, 1541), WA 49:196–200
13. Sermon on the Sunday after the Feast of the Circumcision (January 4, 1545), WA 49:660–67

He also adapted two sermons—Afternoon Sermon on the Feast of Christ's Birth (December 25, 1525) and Sermon on the Feast of St. Stephen (December 26, 1526)—for publication: *Die Epistel des Propheten Jesaia, so man in der Christmesse lieset* (1526), WA 19:131-68.

Luther preached on Luke 2 thirty-one times (two sermon transcripts are not extant—December 25, 1526 and December 31, 1526, see WA 20:211).

1. Sermon on the Feast of Christ's Birth (December 25, 1520), WA 9:498–99, 516–20
2. Afternoon Sermon on the Feast of Christ's Birth (December 25, 1520), WA 9:521–25
3. Sermon on the First Sunday after the Feast of Christ's Birth (December 30, 1520), WA 9:499–500, 530–35
4. Sermon on the Feast of St. Stephen (December 26, 1523), WA 11:220–24
5. Sermon on the Feast of Christ's Birth (December 25, 1524), WA 15:780–88
6. Sermon on the Feast of Christ's Birth (December 25, 1525), WA 17,1: 496–500
7. Afternoon Sermon on the First Day of Christmas (December 25, 1527), WA 23:729–33

8. Sermon on the Third Day of Christmas (December 27, 1527), WA 23:742–46
9. Sermon on the First Day of Christmas (December 25, 1528), WA 27:486–96
10. Afternoon Sermon on the First Day of Christmas (December 25, 1528), WA 27:497–509
11. Sermon on the Feast of Christ's Birth (December 25, 1529), WA 29:642–46
12. Afternoon Sermon on the First Day of Christmas (December 25, 1529), WA 29: 657–69
13. Sermon on the First Day of Christmas (December 25, 1530), WA 32:251–61
14. Afternoon Sermon on the First Day of Christmas (December 25, 1530), WA 32:261–70
15. Sermon on the First Day of Christmas (December 25, 1531), WA 34,2:501–8
16. Sermon on Sermon on the Feast of Christ's Birth (December 25, 1532), WA 36:391–94
17. Afternoon Sermon on the Feast of Christ's Birth (December 25, 1532), WA 36:395–98
18. Sermon on the Feast of St. Stephen (December 26, 1532), WA 36:399–402
19. Afternoon Sermon on the Feast of St. Stephen (December 26, 1532), WA 36:402–6
20. House Sermon on the Feast of Christ's Birth (December 25, 1533), WA 37:230–32
21. Afternoon Sermon on the Feast of Christ's Birth (December 25, 1533), WA 37:232–38
22. Sermon on the Feast of Christ's Birth (December 25, 1534), WA 37:621–26
23. Sermon on Afternoon Sermon on Christmas Day (December 25, 1523), WA 41:483–87
24. Sermon on the Feast of Christ's Birth (December 25, 1537), WA 45:346–50
25. Afternoon Sermon on the Feast of Christ's Birth (December 25, 1538), WA 46:516–24

26. Afternoon Sermon on the Feast of Christ's Birth (December 25, 1540), WA 49:176–80
27. Evening Sermon on the Feast of Christ's Birth (December 25, 1543), WA 49:279–85
28. Afternoon Sermon on the Feast of St. Stephen (December 26, 1543), WA 49:286–93
29. Afternoon Sermon on the Feast of Christ's Birth (December 25, 1544), WA 49:631–38.

There are also three postils on Luke 2:

1. Gospel for Christmas Day (*Church Postil*, 1540), LW 75:209–29 (WA 10,1.1:58–95; LW 52:7–31)
2. Gospel for the Night of Christmas (Roth's *Festival Postil*), WA 17,2:298–309
3. Second Sermon on the Gospel for Holy Christmas Day (*House Postil*, 1544), WA 52:41–49.

CHAPTER 8. THE LIGHT OF THE WORD

Because Luther continued to follow the lectionary, almost all of his Sunday and festival preaching was on New Testament texts—the Gospels in particular. The lectionary only had four assigned Old Testament readings: for Epiphany (January 6), the Presentation (February 2), the Annunciation (March 25), and the Feast of John the Baptist (June 24); it also had one reading from the Apocrypha: for the Feast of St. John the Evangelist (December 27). For the lectionary readings, see WADB 7:536–44.

But during the week Luther carried on small and large *lectio continua* sermon series throughout his career: small portions of Acts (1524), 1–2 Corinthians (1525, 1532–1533, 1535), 1 Thessalonians (1538), 1 Timothy (1525, 1538), Titus (1537), 1 John (1532); large portions of Matthew (1525, 1528, 1530–1532, 1537–1540), Luke (1532), and John (1528–1529, 1530–1532, 1537–1540); and all of 1 Peter (1522), 2 Peter (1523), and Jude (1523). For the planned schedule of Wittenberg preaching, see Hains, "Career as Preacher at Wittenberg," 105.

Luther preached sermons on every book of the New Testament but four: 2 Timothy, Philemon, and 2–3 John. In contrast, Luther only lectured on seven books of the New Testament: Romans (1515–1516), Galatians (twice,

1515–1516, 1531), Hebrews (1517–1518), 1 John (1526–1527), Titus (1527), Philemon (1527), 1 Timothy (1528). He also dictated notes on the Gospel of Matthew: *Annotationes D. Mart. Lvth. in Aliqvot cap. Matthaei* (Wittenberg: Johann Luft, 1538); WA 38:447–667; LW 67. On the origin of this work, see WA 38:443–46.

Luther preached on Luke 24 for Easter Monday and Tuesday from 1521 to 1534. From 1536 to his death, either Luther picked a different text on Easter Monday and Easter Tuesday (1538, 1540, 1544), or we have no record that he preached (1536–1537, 1539, 1541–1543, 1545)—many of these years correspond to Luther's ongoing bouts of illness. He preached an Easter Monday sermon on March 29, 1535, but we don't know what passage he took. See WA 41:XIV.

He preached on Luke 24 twenty times (three sermon transcripts are not extant).

1. Sermon on Easter Monday (April 1, 1521), WA 9:515–16; compare with WA 9:665-72
2. Sermon on Easter Tuesday (April 2, 1521), WA 9:672–76
3. Sermon on Easter Monday (April 6, 1523), WA 11:82–85, which was published in *Ordenung vnd Bericht wie es furterhin (mit ihenen so das Hochwirdig Sacrament empfahen wollen) gehalten sol werden* (Hagenau: Johann Setzer, 1523), C2v–E2v (WA 12:494–505)
4. Afternoon Sermon on Easter Monday (April 6, 1523), WA 11:85–87
5. Sermon on Easter Tuesday (April 7, 1523), WA 11:87–91, which was published in *Ordenung vnd Bericht*, E2v–H6r (WA 12:506–17)
6. Afternoon Sermon on Easter Tuesday (April 7, 1523), WA 11:92–94
7. Sermon on Easter Monday (March 28, 1524), WA 15:523–26
8. Afternoon Sermon on Easter Monday (March 28, 1524), WA 15:526–29
9. Sermon on Easter Tuesday (March 29, 1524), WA 15:529–33
10. Sermon on Easter Monday (April 2, 1526), WA 20:323–27, which was published in free adaptation in 1552, WA 20:328–36
11. Afternoon Sermon on Easter Monday (April 2, 1526), WA 20:336–40, which was published in free adaptation in 1552, WA 20:340–48
12. Sermon on Easter Tuesday (April 3, 1526), WA 20:348–53
13. Afternoon Sermon on Easter Monday (April 18, 1530), WA 32:55–65
14. Sermon on Easter Tuesday (April 11, 1531), WA 34,1:301–10
15. Afternoon Sermon on Easter Tuesday (April 12, 1531), WA 34,1:310–18

Table of Sources

16. House Sermon on Easter Tuesday (April 15, 1533), WA 37:32–35
17. Sermon on Easter Monday (April 6, 1534), WA 37:363–67

The text of three sermons is missing:

1. Sermon on Easter Monday (April 17, 1525), WA 17,1:XVI
2. Sermon on Easter Tuesday (April 18, 1525), WA 17,1:XVI.
3. Sermon on Easter Monday (April 22, 1527), WA 23:670–71

There are also four postils:

1. Gospel for Easter Monday (*Church Postil*, 1544), LW 77:44–57 (WA 21:221–36), for Luther's own draft of this postil, see WA 22:434–37; compare with Sermon on Easter Monday (April 6, 1534), WA 37:363–67.
2. Gospel for Easter Tuesday (*Church Postil*, 1544), LW 77:70–79 (WA 21:238–41), which is a revised version of *Ordenung vnd Bericht*, E2v–H6r
3. Another Sermon on the Gospel for Easter Tuesday (*Church Postil*, 1544), LW 77:80–102 (WA 21:242–64), which is based on Sermon on Easter Tuesday (April 11, 1531), WA 34,1:301–10 and Afternoon Sermon on Easter Tuesday (April 12, 1531), WA 34,1:310–18
4. The Third Sermon on the Gospel for the Easter Festival (*House Postil*, 1544), WA 52:259–66, compare with House Sermon on Easter Tuesday (April 15, 1533), WA 37:32–35

Stephen Roth also included two lightly edited versions of previously printed sermons in his *Summer Postil* (1526):

1. Gospel for Easter Monday, WA 10,1.2:225–27, compare with *Ordenung vnd Bericht*, C2v–E2v (WA 12:494–505)
2. Gospel for Easter Tuesday, WA 10,1.2:227–28, compare with *Ordenung vnd Bericht*, E2v–H6r (WA 12:506–17)—this was one of the three postils Caspar Cruciger simply reused to complete the *Church Postil* (1540–1544).

On Stephen Roth's editions of the postils and Luther's opinion of them, see Todd R. Hains, "Church Postil," in *Encyclopedia of Martin Luther and the Reformation*, ed. Mark A. Lamport (Lanham, MD: Rowman & Littlefield, 2017), 141.

Bibliographies

Primary Sources

Biblia Hebraica. Brescia: Gershom Soncino 1494.
Biblia Hebraica. Venice: Daniel Bomberg, 1511, 1518.
Biblia Sacra cum Glossa ordinaria, novisque additionibus. 6 vols. Venice: Magna Societas, 1603.
Bucanus, Gulielmus. *Institutiones Theologicae, seu Locorum Communium Christianae Religionis*. Bern: Le Preux, 1605. English translation, *Institutions of Christian Religion*, trans. Robert Hill (London: Snowdon, 1606).
Calov, Abraham. *Biblia Novi Testamenti Illustrata*. 2 vols. Dresden and Leipzig: Zimmerman, 1719.
Conciliorum Oecumenicorum Generaliumque Decreta. 7 vols. Edited by Giuseppe Alberigo, Alberto Melloni, and Frederick Lauritzen. Turnhout: Brepols, 2007–2017.
Flacius Illyricus, Matthias. *Clavis Scripturae Sacrae*. 2 vols. Frankfurt and Leipzig: Paulus, 1719. First published in 1567.
Gerhard, Johann. *Loci Theologici*. 9 vols. Edited by Eduard Preuss. Berlin: Schlawitz; Leipzig: Hinrichs, 1863–1876. First published in 1610–1625.
Glassius, Salomo. *Philologia Sacra*. Leipzig: Gleditsch, 1713.
Lefèvre d'Étaples, Jacques. *Contenta: Epistola ad Rhomanos, Epistola prima ad Corinthios, Epistola secunda ad Corinthios, Epistola ad Galatas, Epistola ad Ephesios, Epistola ad Philippenses, Epistola ad Colossenses, Epistola prima ad Thessalonica, Epistola secunda ad Thessalonic, Epistola prima ad Timotheum, Epistola secunda ad Timotheum, Epistola ad Titum, Epistola ad Philemonem, Epistola ad Hebraeos*. Paris: H. Stephanus, 1515.
Luther, Martin. *Ordenung vnd Bericht wie es furterhin (mit ihenen so das Hochwirdig Sacrament empfahen wollen) gehalten sol werden*. Hagenau: Johann Setzer, 1523.
———. *Conciunculae quaedam D. Martini Lutheri amico cuidam praescriptae*. Wittenberg: Nicolaus Schirlentz, 1537.
———. *Ein Betbuchlin/ mit eim Calender und Passional/ hübsch zu gericht*. Wittenberg: Hans Lufft, 1538.
———. *Dr. Martin Luthers Vorlesung über das Buch der Richter: Aus einer in der Zwickauer Ratsschulbibliothek befindlichen Handschrift*. Edited by Georg Buchwald Leipzig: Julius Drescher, 1884.
———. *Summarien vber die Psalmen/ Und des ursachen des dolmetschens*. Wittenberg: Hans Lufft, 1531–1533.
Melanchthon, Philipp. *Philippi Melanthonis Opera quae supersunt omnia*. 28 vols. Corpus Reformatorum 1–28. Edited by C. G. Bretschneider. Halle: C. A. Schwetschke, 1834–1860.
Menius, Justus. *In Samuelis Librum Priorem enarratio*. Wittenberg: Johannes Lufft, 1532.

Mentzer, Balthasar. *Disputationes Theologicae et Scholasticae XIV*. Marburg: Egenolphus, 1606.

Müller, Nikolaus. *Die Wittenberger Bewegung 1521 und 1522: Die Vorgänge in und um Wittenberg während Luthers Wartburgaufenthalt*. Leipzig: Heinsius, 1911.

Münster, Sebastian. *Miqdaš YHWH*. 2 vols. Basel: Michael Isinginius and Henricus Petrus, 1534–1535, 1546.

Müntzer, Thomas. "Von dem getichten glawben." In *Schriften und Briefe: Kritische Gesamtausgabe*, edited by Paul Kirn and Günther Franz, 218–24. Gütersloh: Gütersloher Verlagshaus Gerd Mohn, 1968.

Novum Instrumentum omne. Edited by Desiderius Erasmus. Basel: Froben, 1516.

Novum Testamentum omne. Edited by Desiderius Erasmus. 2nd ed. Basel: Froben, 1519.

Pirminius. *De singulis libris canonicis scarapsus*. In PL 89:1029–50.

Pseudo-Augustine. Sermon 240. In PL 39:2188–90.

Reuchlin, Johannes. *De Rudimentis Hebraicis*. Pforzheim: Thomas Anselm, 1506.

Sehling, Emil. *Die Evangelischen Kirchenordnungen des XVI. Jahrhunderts*. 19 vols. Leipzig: Reisland, 1902–2010.

William of Saint-Thierry. *Expositio in Epistolam ad Romanos* (1137). In PL 180:547–694.

Translated Primary Sources

Athanasius. *On the Incarnation*. Translated by John Behr. PPS 44B. Crestwood, NY: St. Vladimir's Seminary Press, 2011.

Augustine. *Faith, Hope, and Love*. Translated by Louis A. Arand. ACW 3. New York: Newman Press, 1947.

———. *Commentary on the Lord's Sermon on the Mount with Seventeen Related Sermons*. Translated by Denis J. Kavanagh. FC 11. Washington, DC: Catholic University of America Press, 1948.

———. Sermon 56. In *Commentary on the Lord's Sermon on the Mount with Seventeen Related Sermons*. Translated by Denis J. Kavanagh. FC 11:239–57. Washington, DC: Catholic University of America Press, 1948.

———. *On the Merits and Forgiveness of Sins*. In NPNF 5:15–78.

———. *On Nature and Grace*. In NPNF 5:121–51.

———. *Against Two Letters of the Pelagians*. In NPNF 5:377–434.

———. *On Grace and Free Will*. In NPNF 5:443–65.

Bray, Gerald, ed. *Romans*. ACCS NT 6. Downers Grove, IL: InterVarsity Press, 1998.

"The Chalcedonian Definition of the Faith." In *Creeds, Councils and Controversies: Documents Illustrating the History of the Church, AD 337–461*, edited by J. Stevenson and W. H. C. Frend, 351–53. London: SPCK, 1989

Chung-Kim, Esther and Todd R. Hains, eds. *Acts*. RCS NT 6. Downers Grove, IL: IVP Academic, 2014.

Cooper, Derek and Martin J. Lohrmann, eds. *1–2 Samuel, 1–2 Kings, 1–2 Chronicles*. RCS OT 5. Downers Grove, IL: IVP Academic, 2016.

Cyprian. *On the Lord's Prayer*. In *On the Lord's Prayer*. Translated by Alistair Stewart-Sykes. PPS 29:65–93. Crestwood, NY: St. Vladimir's Seminary Press, 2004.

Erasmus, Desiderius. *Collected Works of Erasmus*. 86 vols. planned. Toronto: University of Toronto Press, 1969–.

Erasmus, Desiderius and Martin Luther. *Erasmus and Luther: The Battle Over Free Will*. Translated by Clarence H. Miller and Peter Macardle. Indianapolis: Hackett, 2012.

———. *Luther and Erasmus: Salvation and Free Will*. Translated and edited by E. Gordon Rupp and Philip S. Watson. Library of Christian Classics 17. Philadelphia: The Westminster Press, 1969.
Farmer, John, ed. *John 1–12*. RCS NT 4. Downers Grove, IL: IVP Academic, 2014.
Ginzberg, Louis. *The Legends of the Jews*. 2 vols. Translated by Henrietta Szold and Paul Radin. 2nd ed. Philadelphia: The Jewish Publication Society, 2003.
Gregory of Nyssa. *Catechetical Discourse: A Handbook for Catechists*. Translated by Ignatius Green. PPS 60. Crestwood, NY: St. Vladimir's Seminary Press, 2019
Kreitzer, Beth, ed. *Luke*. RCS NT 3. Downers Grove, IL: IVP Academic, 2015.
Krey, Philip D. W. and Peter D. S. Krey, eds. *Romans 9–16*. RCS NT 8. Downers Grove, IL: IVP Academic, 2016.
Luther, Martin. *What Luther Says*. 3 vols. Edited by Ewald Plass. St. Louis: Concordia, 1959.
———. *Martin Luther on Holy Baptism: Sermons to the People (1525–39)*. Edited by Benjamin T. G. Mayes. St. Louis: Concordia, 2018.
———. *Luther: Letters of Spiritual Counsel*. Translated and edited by Theodore G. Tappert. Library of Christian Classics 18. Philadelphia: The Westminster Press, 1960. Reprint, Vancouver, BC: Regent College Publishing, 2003.
Manetsch, Scott M., ed. *1 Corinthians*. RCS NT 9a. Downers Grove, IL: IVP Academic, 2017.
Origen. *On Prayer*. In *On the Lord's Prayer*. Translated by Alistair Stewart-Sykes. PPS 29:111–214. Crestwood, NY: St. Vladimir's Seminary Press, 2004.
———. *Commentary on the Epistle to the Romans*. 2 vols. Translated by Thomas P. Scheck. FC 103–104. Washington, DC: The Catholic University of America Press, 2002.
Rufinus. *A Commentary on the Apostles' Creed*. Translated by J. N. D. Kelly. ACW 20. Mahwah, NJ: Paulist Press, 1954.
Selderhuis, Herman J, ed. *Psalms 1–72*. RCS OT 7. Downers Grove, IL: IVP Academic, 2015.
Tertullian. *On Prayer*. In *On the Lord's Prayer*. Translated by Alistair Stewart-Sykes. PPS 29:41–64. Crestwood, NY: St. Vladimir's Seminary Press, 2004.
Turretin, Francis. *Institutes of Elenctic Theology*. 3 vols. Translated by George Musgrave Giger. Edited by James T. Dennison Jr. Phillipsburg, NJ: P&R Publishing, 1992–1997.
Weinrich, William C. *Revelation*. ACCS NT 12. Downers Grove, IL: InterVarsity Press, 2005.

Secondary Sources

Abbott, Edwin A. *Flatland: A Romance of Many Dimensions*. London: Seeley & Co., 1884.
Aland, Kurt. *Hilfsbuch zum Luther Studium*. 3rd ed. Wittenberg: Luther-Verlag, 1970.
———. "Martin Luther als Schriftausleger." In *Kirchengeschichtliche Entwürfe: Alte Kirche; Reformation und Luthertum; Pietismus und Erweckungsbewegung*, Kurt Aland, 395–419. Gütersloh: Gerd Mohn, 1960.
———. "Die Privatbeichte im Luthertum." In *Kirchengeschichtliche Entwürfe: Alte Kirche; Reformation und Luthertum; Pietismus und Erweckungsbewegung*, Kurt Aland, 452–519. Gütersloh: Gerd Mohn, 1960.
Arnold, Matthieu. "Luther on Christ's Person and Work." In *The Oxford Handbook of Martin Luther's Theology*, edited by Robert Kolb, Irene Dingel, and L'ubomír Batka, 274–93. New York: Oxford University Press, 2014.
Assel, Heinrich. "Gottesnamen und Kernstellen in Luthers Bibelübersetzung 1545: Eine systematisch-theologische Perspektive." In *"Was Dolmetschen für Kunst und Arbeit sei": Die Lutherbibel und andere deutsche Bibelübersetzungen*, edited by Melanie Lange and Martin Rösel, 107–35. Leipzig: Deutsche Bibelgesellschaft und Evangelische Verlagsanstalt, 2014.

Althaus, Paul. *The Theology of Martin Luther*. Translated by Robert C. Schultz. Philadelphia: Fortress Press, 1966.

———. *The Ethics of Martin Luther*. Translated by Robert C. Schultz. Philadelphia: Fortress Press, 1972.

———. "Luther auf der Kanzel: Beobachtungen über die Form seiner Predigt." *Luther: Mitteilungen der Luther-Gesellschaft* 3 (1921): 17–24.

Arndt, William F. "Hermeneutics." In *Lutheran Cyclopedia*, edited by Erwin L. Lueker, 463–64. St. Louis: Concordia, 1954.

Asendorf, Ulrich. *Die Theologie Martin Luthers nach seinen Predigten*. Göttingen: Vandenhoeck & Ruprecht, 1988.

———. "Martin Luther als Prediger: Anmerkungen zur Bedeutung seiner Predigten im Rahmen seiner gesamten Theologie." In *Kirche in der Schule Luthers: Festschrift für D. Joachim Heubach*, edited by Bengt Hägglund and Gehard Müller, 11–22. Erlangen: Martin-Luther-Verlag, 1995.

Ayres, Lewis and Stephen E. Fowl. "(Mis)reading the Face of God: The Interpretation of the Bible in the Church." *Theological Studies* 60, no. 3 (1999): 513–28.

Bainton, Roland H. *Here I Stand: A Life of Martin Luther*. New York: Mentor Books, 1950.

Bast, Robert James. *Honor Your Fathers: Catechisms and the Emergence of a Patriarchal Ideology in Germany, 1400–1600*. Leiden: Brill, 1997.

Bayer, Oswald. *Martin Luther's Theology: A Contemporary Interpretation*. Translated by Thomas H. Trapp. Grand Rapids: Eerdmans, 2008.

Berman, Nina. "Imperial Violence and the Limits of Tolerance: Reading Luther with Las Casas." In *Early Modern Constructions of Europe: Literature, Culture, History*, edited by Florian Kläger and Gerd Bayer, 139–61. New York: Routledge, 2016.

Beutel, Albrecht, ed. *Luther Handbuch*. Tübingen: Mohr Siebeck, 2005.

Beutel, Albrecht. "Theologie als Schriftauslegung." In *Luther Handbuch*, edited by Albrecht Beutel, 444–49. Tübingen: Mohr Siebeck, 2005.

———. "Erfahrene Bibel: Verständnis und Gebrauch des verbum dei scriptum bei Luther." In *Protestantische Konkretionen: Studien zur Kirchengeschichte*, edited by Albrecht Beutel, 66–103. Tübingen: Mohr Siebeck, 1998.

Blocher, Henri. "The 'Analogy of Faith' in the Study of Scripture: In Search of Justification and Guidelines." *Scottish Bulletin of Evangelical Theology* 5 (1987): 17–38.

Bluhm, Heinz. *Martin Luther: Creative Translator*. St. Louis: Concordia, 1965,

Bornkamm, Heinrich. *Luther und das Alte Testament*. Tübingen: Mohr Siebeck, 1948.

Bowald, Mark. *Rendering the Word in Theological Hermeneutics: Mapping Divine and Human Agency*. Bellingham, WA: Lexham Press, 2015.

Brecht, Martin. *Martin Luther*. 3 vols. Translated by James L. Schaaf. Minneapolis: Fortress Press, 1985–1993.

Brewer, Brian C. *Martin Luther and the Seven Sacraments: A Contemporary Protestant Reappraisal*. Grand Rapids: Baker Academic, 2017.

———. "Sacramental Theology." In *Encyclopedia of Martin Luther and the Reformation*, edited by Mark A. Lamport, 669–72. Lanham, MD: Rowman & Littlefield, 2017.

Brown, Christopher Boyd. *Singing the Gospel: Lutheran Hymns and the Success of the Reformation*. Cambridge, MA: Harvard University Press, 2005.

Burnett, Amy Nelson. "Luther and the *Schwärmer*." In *The Oxford Handbook of Martin Luther's Theology*, edited by Robert Kolb, Irene Dingel, and Ľubomír Batka, 511–24. New York: Oxford University Press, 2014.

———. *Karlstadt and the Origins of the Eucharistic Controversy: A Study in the Circulation of Ideas*. New York: Oxford University Press, 2011.

Burnett, Stephen G. "Luthers hebräische Bibel (Brescia, 1494)—Ihre Bedeutung für die Reformation." In *Meilensteine der Reformation: Schlüsseldokumente der frühen Wirksamkeit Martin Luthers*, edited by Irene Dingel and Henning P. Jürgens, 62–69. Gütersloh: Gütersloher Verlagshaus, 2014.

———. "The Strange Career of the *Biblia Rabbinica* Among Christian Hebraists, 1517–1620." In *Shaping the Bible in the Reformation: Books, Scholars and Their Readers in the Sixteenth Century*, edited by Bruce Gordon and Matthew McLean, 63–84. Leiden: Brill, 2012.

———. "Reassessing the 'Basel-Wittenberg Conflict': Dimensions of the Reformation-Era Discussion of Hebrew Scholarship." In *Hebraica Veritas?: Christian Hebraists and the Study of Judaism in Early Modern Europe*, edited by Allison Coudert and Jeffrey S. Shoulson, 181–201. Philadelphia: University of Pennsylvania Press, 2004.

Carson, D. A. "Unity and Diversity in the New Testament: The Possibility of Systematic Theology." In *Scripture and Truth*, edited by D. A. Carson and John D. Woodbridge, 65–95. Grand Rapids: Baker, 1983.

———. "Theological Interpretation of Scripture: Yes, but . . . ." In *Theological Commentary: Evangelical Perspectives*, edited by R. Michael Allen, 187–207. London: T&T Clark, 2011.

Cary, Phillip. *The Meaning of Protestant Theology: Luther, Augustine, and the Gospel That Gives Us Christ*. Grand Rapids: Baker Academic, 2019.

———. *Good News for Anxious Christians: 10 Practical Things You Don't Have to Do*. Grand Rapids: Brazos, 2010.

Cash, Johnny. *Man In White: A Novel*. San Francisco: Harper & Row, 1986.

Catholic Church. *Catechism of the Catholic Church: Revised in Accordance with the Official Latin Text Promulgated by Pope John Paul II* (1993). Accessible online via www.vatican.va

Chung-Kim, Esther and Todd R. Hains. "Introduction to Acts." In *Acts*, edited by Esther Chung-Kim and Todd R. Hains, xliii–lxiii. RCS NT 6. Downers Grove, IL: IVP Academic, 2014.

Cohrs, Ferdinand. *Die Evangelischen Katechismusversuche vor Luthers Enchiridion*. 5 vols. Berlin: A. Hofmann, 1900–1907.

Combs, William W. "Erasmus and the Textus Receptus." *Detroit Baptist Seminary Journal* 1, no. 1 (1996): 35–53.

Cooper, Derek. "The Analogy of Faith in Puritan Exegesis: Scope and Salvation in James 2:14–26." *Stone-Campbell Journal* 12, no. 2 (2009): 235–50.

Cross, Richard. "Luther's Christology and the *Communicatio Idiomatum*." In *The Medieval Luther*, edited by Christine Helmer, 27–46. Tübingen: Mohr Siebeck, 2019.

Cruel, Rudolf. *Geschichte der Deutschen Predigt im Mittelalter*. Hildesheim: G. Olms, 1966.

Dragseth, Jennifer Hockenberry, ed. *The Devil's Whore: Reason and Philosophy in the Lutheran Tradition*. Minneapolis: Fortress Press, 2011.

Dykema, Peter A. "Handbooks for Pastors: Late Medieval Manuals for Parish Priests and Conrad Porta's *Pastorale Lutheri* (1582)." In *Continuity and Change: The Harvest of Late Medieval and Reformation History: Essays presented to Heiko A. Oberman on his 70th Birthday*, edited by Robert J. Bast and Andrew C. Gow, 143–62. Leiden: Brill, 2000.

Ebeling, Gerhard. *Evangelische Evangelienauslegung: Eine Untersuchung zu Luthers Hermeneutik*. Munich: Albert Lempp, 1942; rev. ed. Darmstadt: Wissenschaftliche Buchgesellschaft, 1962.

———. *Luthers Seelsorge: Theologie in der Vielfalt der Lebenssituationen an seinen Briefen dargestellt*. Tübingen: Mohr Siebeck, 1997.

———. *Luther: Einführung in sein Denken*. Tübingen: Mohr Siebeck, 2006.

Edwards, Mark U., Jr. "Luther's Polemical Controversies." In *The Cambridge Companion to Martin Luther*, edited by Donald K. McKim, 192–205.

Elert, Werner. *Morphologie des Luthertums*. 2 vols. Munich: C. H. Beck, 1952.

———. *The Structure of Lutheranism*. 2 vols. Translated by Walter A. Hansen. St. Louis: Concordia Publishing House, 1962.

Ellwein, Eduard. *Summus Evangelista: Die Botschaft des Johannesevangeliums in der Auslegung Luthers*. Munich: Kaiser, 1960.

Emerson, Matthew Y. *"He Descended to the Dead": An Evangelical Theology of Holy Saturday*. Downers Grove, IL: IVP Academic, 2019.

Erickson, Millard. *Christian Theology*. 2nd ed. Grand Rapids: Baker Academic, 1998.

Eyjólfsson, Sigurjón Árni. "Überblick über die Bewertung von Luthers Predigten in der Forschung." In *Luther Between Present and Past: Studies in Luther and Lutheranism*, edited by Ulrik Nissen, Anna Vind, Bo Holm, and Olli-Pekka Vainio, 17–39. Helsinki: Luther-Agricola-Society, 2004.

Fennell, Robert C. *The Rule of Faith and Biblical Interpretation: Reform, Resistance, and Renewal*. Eugene, OR: Cascade, 2018.

Ferguson, Everett. *The Rule of Faith: A Guide*. Eugene, OR: Cascade, 2015.

Ferry, Patrick. "Martin Luther on Preaching: Promises and Problems of the Sermon as a Source of Reformation History and as an Instrument of the Reformation." *Concordia Theological Quarterly* 54, no. 4 (1990): 265–80.

Flor, Martin W. "The Free Conferences of 1903–1906 and the Concept of *Analogia Fidei*." *Concordia Theological Monthly* 40, no. 4 (1969): 218–27.

Frick, Robert. "Luther als Prediger dargestellt auf Grund der Predigten über 1. Kor. 15 (1532/33)." *Lutherjahrbuch* 21 (1939): 28–71.

Frymire, John M. *The Primacy of the Postils: Catholics, Protestants, and the Dissemination of Ideas in Early Modern Germany*. Leiden: Brill, 2010.

Fuller, Daniel P. "Biblical Theology and the Analogy of Faith." In *Unity and Diversity in New Testament Theology: Essays in Honor of George E. Ladd*, edited by R. A. Guelich, 195–213. Grand Rapids: Eerdmans, 1978.

German, Brian T. *Psalms of the Faithful: Luther's Early Reading of the Psalter in Canonical Context*. Bellingham, WA: Lexham Press, 2017.

Gerrish, B. A. *Grace and Reason: A Study in the Theology of Luther*. Oxford: Oxford University Press, 1962.

Gertz, Bernhard. *Glaubenswelt als Analogia: Die theologische Analogie-Lehre Erich Przywaras und ihr Ort in der Auseinandersetzung um die analogia fidei*. Düsseldorf: Patmos, 1969.

———. "Was ist *analogia fidei*?: Klarstellungen zu einem Kontrovers-Thema." *Catholica* 26, no. 4 (1972): 309–24.

Goertz, Hans-Jürgen. "Martin Luther und die Täufer: Versuch einer nachträglichen Annäherung." *Luther* 88, no. 2 (2017): 81–90.

Green, Lowell C. "Justification in Luther's Preaching on Luke 18:9–14." *Concordia Theological Monthly* 43, no. 11 (1972): 732–47.

———. "The 'Third Use of the Law' and Elert's Position." *Logia* 22, no. 2 (2013): 27–33.

Greene-McCreight, Kathryn. *Feminist Reconstructions of Christian Doctrine: Narrative Analysis and Appraisal*. New York: Oxford University Press, 2000.

———. "Literal Sense." In *Dictionary for Theological Interpretation of the Bible*, edited by Kevin J. Vanhoozer, 455–56. Grand Rapids: Baker Academic; London: SPCK, 2005.

———. "Rule of Faith." In *Dictionary for Theological Interpretation of the Bible*, edited by Kevin J. Vanhoozer, 703–4. Grand Rapids: Baker Academic; London: SPCK, 2005.

Gregory, Brad S. *The Unintended Reformation: How a Religious Revolution Secularized Society*. Cambridge, MA: Belknap Press, 2012.

Grimm, Harold J. *Luther as a Preacher*. Columbus, OH: Lutheran Book Concern, 1929.

———. "The Human Element in Luther's Sermons." *Archiv für Reformationsgeschichte* 49, no. 1 (1958): 50–60.

Hacker, Paul. *Faith in Luther: Martin Luther and the Origin of Anthropocentric Religion*. Chicago: Franciscan Herald Press, 1970. Reprint, Steubenville, OH: Emmaus Academic, 2017.

Haemig, Mary Jane. "The Influence of the Genres of Exegetical Instruction, Preaching and Catechesis on Luther." In *The Oxford Handbook of Martin Luther's Theology*, edited by Robert Kolb, Irene Dingel, and L'ubomír Batka, 449–61. New York: Oxford University Press, 2014.

———. "Laypeople as Overseers of the Faith: A Reformation Proposal." *Trinity Seminary Review* 27, no. 1. (2006): 21–27.

———. "The Living Voice of the Catechism: German Lutheran Catechetical Preaching, 1530–1580." PhD diss., Harvard University, 1996.

———. "Introduction to Little Prayer Book (1522)." In *Pastoral Writings*, edited by Mary Jane Haemig, 159-65. Minneapolis: Fortress Press, 2016.

Hägglund, Bengt. "Die Bedeutung der *Regula fidei* als Grundlage theologischer Aussagen." *Studia theologica* 12, no.1 (1958): 1–44.

Haile, H. G. *Luther: An Experiment in Biography*. Garden City, NY: Doubleday, 1979.

Hains, Todd R. "Luther and Bound Conscience in His German Church Postils." MA thesis, Trinity Evangelical Divinity School, 2011.

———. "Career as Preacher at Wittenberg." In *Encyclopedia of Martin Luther and the Reformation*, edited by Mark A. Lamport, 105–107. Lanham, MD: Rowman & Littlefield, 2017.

———. "Church Postil." In *Encyclopedia of Martin Luther and the Reformation*, edited by Mark A. Lamport, 140–42. Lanham, MD: Rowman & Littlefield, 2017.

———. "Martin Luther Is Not Afraid of Ghosts." *Bible Study Magazine* 11, no. 6 (September-October 2019): 8–10.

Headley, John M. *Luther's View of Church History*. New Haven, CT: Yale University Press, 1963.

Helmer, Christine. "Luther's Trinitarian Hermeneutic and the Old Testament." *Modern Theology* 18, no. 1 (2002): 49–73.

———. *The Trinity and Martin Luther*. Rev. ed. Bellingham, WA: Lexham Press, 2017.

———. *How Luther Became the Reformer*. Louisville: Westminster John Knox, 2019.

Hendrix, Scott H. *Ecclesia in via: Ecclesiological Developments in the Medieval Psalms Exegesis and the Dictata Super Psalterium (1513–1515) of Martin Luther*. Leiden: Brill, 1974.

Heppe, Heinrich. *Reformed Dogmatics*. Edited by Ernst Bizer. Translated by George Thomas Thomson. London: George Allen & Unwin, 1950. Reprint, Eugene, OR: Wipf & Stock, 2007.

Herrmann, Erik. "Luther's Absorption of Medieval Biblical Interpretation and His Use of the Church Fathers." In *The Oxford Handbook of Martin Luther's Theology*, edited by Robert Kolb, Irene Dingel, and L'ubomír Batka, 71–90. New York: Oxford University Press, 2014.

Hill, Wesley. *The Lord's Prayer: A Guide to Praying to Our Father*. Christian Essentials. Bellingham, WA: Lexham Press, 2019.

Hof, Otto. "Luther's Exegetical Principle of the Analogy of Faith." *Concordia Theological Monthly* 38, no. 4 (1967): 242–57.
Imberg, Rune. *Bibelläsaren som förändrade världen: Om Martin Luther som bibelteolog— bibelöversättare—bibelutgivare*. Församlingsfakultetens småskrifter 5. Gothenburg: Församlingsförlaget, 2017.
Iserloh, Erwin. *The Theses Were Not Posted: Luther Between Reform and Reformation*. Translated by Jared Wicks. Boston: Beacon Press, 1968.
Jensen, Gordon A. "Luther and the Lord's Supper." In *The Oxford Handbook of Martin Luther's Theology*, edited by Robert Kolb, Irene Dingel, and L'ubomír Batka, 322–32. New York: Oxford University Press, 2014.
Johnson, H. Wayne. "The 'Analogy of Faith' and Exegetical Methodology: A Preliminary Discussion on Relationships." *Journal of the Evangelical Theological Society* 31, no. 1 (1988): 69–80.
Johnson, John F. "*Analogia Fidei* as Hermeneutical Principle." *Springfielder* 36, no. 4 (1973): 249–59.
Juntunen, Katja. *Der Prediger vom "weißen Berg": Zur Rezeption der "besseren Gerechtigkeit" aus Mt 5 in Martin Luthers Predigtüberlieferung, 1522–1546*. Helsinki: Helsinki University Print, 2008.
Kaiser, Walter C., Jr., "Evangelical Hermeneutics: Restatement, Advance or Retreat from the Reformation." *Concordia Theological Quarterly* 46, no. 2–3 (1982): 167–80.
———. *Toward an Exegetical Theology: Biblical Exegesis for Preaching and Teaching*. Grand Rapids: Baker Academic, 1981.
Karant-Nunn, Susan. *Luther's Pastors: The Reformation in the Ernestine Countryside*. Philadelphia: The American Philosophical Society, 1979.
———. "Preaching the Word in Early Modern Germany." In *Preachers and People in the Reformations and Early Modern Period*, edited by Larissa Taylor, 193–219. Leiden: Brill, 2001.
Kärkkäinen, Veli-Matti. *A Constructive Christian Theology for the Pluralistic World*. 5 vols. Grand Rapids: Eerdmans, 2013–2017.
Kattenbusch, Ferdinand. *Luthers Stellung zu den oecumenischen Symbolen*. Giessen: Wenzel, 1883.
Kaufmann, Thomas. *Luther's Jews: A Journey into Anti-Semitism*. Translated by Lesley Sharpe and Jeremy Noakes. Oxford: Oxford University Press, 2017.
Kennedy, Natasha and Ben Myers. *The Apostles' Creed: For All God's Children*. A FatCat Book. Bellingham, WA: Lexham Press, 2022.
Kiessling, Elmer Carl. *The Early Sermons of Luther and Their Relation to the Pre-Reformation Sermon*. Grand Rapids: Zondervan, 1935. Reprint, New York: AMS, 1971.
Kilcrease, Jack D. *Justification by the Word: Restoring Sola Fide*. Bellingham, WA: Lexham Press, 2022.
Kittelson, James M. "Successes and Failures in the German Reformation: The Report from Strasbourg." *Archiv für Reformationsgeschichte* 73 (1982): 153–74.
Kleinig, John. *God's Word: A Guide to Holy Scripture*. Christian Essentials. Bellingham, WA: Lexham Press, 2022.
———. *Grace upon Grace: Spirituality for Today*. St. Louis: Concordia, 2008.
Knapp, Henry M. "Protestant Biblical Interpretation." In *Dictionary for Theological Interpretation of the Bible*, edited by Kevin J. Vanhoozer, 633–38. Grand Rapids: Baker Academic; London: SPCK, 2005.
Koehler, J. P. "The Analogy of Faith." In *The Wauwatosa Theology*, 3 vols., edited by Curtis A. John, 1:221–68. Milwaukee: Northwestern Publishing House, 1997.

Kolb, Robert. *Martin Luther as Prophet, Teacher, and Hero: Images of the Reformer, 1520–1620.* Grand Rapids: Baker, 1999.

———. *Martin Luther and the Enduring Word of God: The Wittenberg School and Its Scripture-Centered Proclamation.* Grand Rapids: Baker Academic, 2016.

———. " 'What Benefit Does the Soul Receive from a Handful of Water?': Luther's Preaching on Baptism, 1528–1539." *Concordia Journal* 25 (1999): 346–63.

———. "Luther's Hermeneutics of Distinctions: Law and Gosepl, Two Kinds of Righteousness, Two Realms, Freedom and Bondage." In *The Oxford Handbook of Martin Luther's Theology*, edited by Robert Kolb, Irene Dingel, and L'ubomír Batka, 168–84. New York: Oxford University Press, 2014.

Kooiman, Willem Jan. *Luther and the Bible.* Translated by John Schmidt. Muhlenberg Press, 1961.

Korsch, Dietrich. "Glaube und Rechtfertigung." In *Luther Handbuch*, edited by Albrecht Beutel, 372–81. Tübingen: Mohr Siebeck, 2005.

Kraft, Heinrich, ed. *Luther als Prediger.* Erlangen: Martin-Luther-Verlag, 1986.

Kreitzer, Beth. "The Lutheran Sermon." In *Preachers and People in the Reformations and Early Modern Period*, edited by Larissa Taylor, 35–64. Leiden: Brill, 2001.

Krodel, Gottfried G. "Luther's Work on the Catechism in the Context of Late Medieval Catechetical Literature." *Concordia Journal* 25, no. 4 (1999): 364–404.

Kwon, Jin Ho. *Christus Pro Nobis: Eine Untersuchung zu Luthers Passions- und Osterpredigtens bis zum Jahr 1530.* Münster: LIT Verlag, 2008.

Leaver, Robin A. *Luther's Liturgical Music: Principles and Implications.* Minneapolis: Fortress Press, 2007.

Legaspi, Michael C. *The Death of Scripture and the Rise of Biblical Studies.* Oxford: Oxford University Press, 2010.

Leithart, Peter J. *Baptism: A Guide to Life from Death.* Christian Essentials. Bellingham, WA: Lexham Press, 2021.

———. *The Ten Commandments: A Guide to the Perfect Law of Liberty.* Christian Essentials. Bellingham, WA: Lexham Press, 2020.

———. *Deep Exegesis: The Mystery of Reading Scripture.* Waco, TX: Baylor University Press, 2009.

Leroux, Neil R. *Luther's Rhetoric: Strategies and Style from the Invocavit Sermons.* St. Louis: Concordia Academic Press, 2002.

Lienhard, Marc. *Luther: Witness to Jesus Christ.* Translated by Edwin H. Robertson Minneapolis: Augsburg, 1982.

Lischer, Richard. "Luther and Contemporary Preaching: Narrative and Anthropology." *Scottish Journal of Theology* 36, no. 4 (1983): 487–504.

Löfstedt, Bengt. "Notizen eines Latinisten zu Luthers Predigten." *Vetenskapssocieteten i Lund: Årsbok* (1985): 24–42.

Lohse, Bernhard. *Martin Luther: An Introduction to his Life and Work.* Translated by Robert C. Schulz. Minneapolis: Fortress Press, 1986.

———. *Martin Luther's Theology: Its Historical and Systematic Development.* Translated and edited by Roy A. Harrisville. Minneapolis: Fortress Press, 2006.

Lubac, Henri de. *Medieval Exegesis: The Four Senses of Scripture.* 3 vols. Translated by Mark Sebanc and E. M. Macierowski. Grand Rapids, MI: Eerdmans, 1998–2009.

———. *The Christian Faith: An Essay on the Structure and Use of the Apostles' Creed.* Translated by Richard Arnandez. San Francisco: Ignatius, 1969.

Lutheran Service Book. St. Louis: Concordia, 2006.

Luy, David J. *Dominus Mortis: Martin Luther on the Incorruptibility of God in Christ.* Minneapolis: Fortress, 2014.

———. "Luther and the General Priesthood: An Embedded Account." In *The Reformation and the Irrepressible Word of God: Interpretation, Theology, and Practice*, edited by Scott M. Manetsch, 168–89. Downers Grove, IL: IVP Academic, 2019.

MacKinnon, James. *Luther and the Reformation.* 4 vols. London: Longmans, Green, and Co., 1925–1930.

Manetsch, Scott M. *Calvin's Company of Pastors: Pastoral Care and the Emerging Reformed Church, 1536–1609.* New York: Oxford University Press, 2012.

Mannermaa, Tuomo. *Two Kinds of Love: Martin Luther's Religious World.* Translated and edited by Kirsi I. Stjerna. Minneapolis: Fortress Press, 2010.

———. *Christ Present in Faith: Luther's View of Justification.* Translated and edited by Kirsi Stjerna. Minneapolis: Fortress Press, 2005.

Marschler, Thomas. "*Analogia fidei*: Anmerkungen zu einem Grundprinzip theologischer Schrifthermeneutik." *Theologie und Philosophie* 87, no. 2 (2012): 208–36.

Marsh, William M. *Martin Luther on Reading the Bible as Christian Scripture: The Messiah in Luther's Biblical Hermeneutic and Theology.* Eugene, OR: Pickwick, 2017.

Mattes, Mark. "Luther on Justification as Forensic and Effective." In *The Oxford Handbook of Martin Luther's Theology*, edited by Robert Kolb, Irene Dingel, and L'ubomír Batka, 264–73. New York: Oxford University Press, 2014.

Mattox, Mickey L. "Luther." In *The Blackwell Companion to Paul*, edited by Stephen Westerholm, 375–90. Malden, MA: Wiley-Blackwell, 2011.

———. "Luther's Interpretation of Scripture: Biblical Understanding in Trinitarian Shape." In *The Substance of Faith: Luther's Doctrinal Theology for Today*, edited by Paul R. Hinlicky, 11–57. Minneapolis: Fortress Press, 2008.

———. "Martin Luther." In *Christian Theologies of Scripture: A Comparative Introduction*, edited by Justin S. Holcomb, 94–113. New York: New York University Press, 2006.

———. "Luther, Martin." In *Dictionary for Theological Interpretation of the Bible*, edited by Kevin J. Vanhoozer, 471–73. Grand Rapids: Baker Academic, 2005.

Menke, Karl-Heinz. "Analogia fidei." In *Lexikon für Theologie und Kirche*, 11 vols., 3rd ed., edited by Michael Buchberger, Walter Kasper, and Konrad Baumgartner, 1:574–77. Freiburg: Herder, 1993–2001.

Menzel, Michael. "Predigt und Predigtorganisation im Mittelalter." *Historisches Jahrbuch* 111 (1991): 337–84.

Meuser, Fred W. *Luther the Preacher.* Minneapolis: Augsburg, 1983.

———. "Luther as Preacher of the Word of God." In *The Cambridge Companion to Martin Luther*, edited by Donald K. McKim, 136–48. Cambridge: Cambridge University Press, 2003.

Mostert, Walter. "Scriptura sui ipsius interpres: Bemerkungen zum Verständnis der Heiligen Schrift durch Luther." *Lutherjahrbuch* 46 (1979): 60–96.

Müller, Nikolaus. *Die Wittenberger Bewegung 1521 und 1522: Die Vorgäng in und um Wittenberg während Luthers Wartburgaufenthalt.* Leipzig: Heinsius, 1911.

Muller, Richard A. *Post-Reformation Reformed Dogmatics: The Rise and Development of Reformed Orthodoxy, ca. 1520 to ca. 1725.* 4 vols. 2nd ed. Grand Rapids: Baker Academic, 2003.

———. *Dictionary of Latin and Greek Theological Terms: Drawn Principally from Protestant Scholastic Theology.* 2nd ed. Grand Rapids: Baker Academic, 2017.

Mülhaupt, Erwin. "Luthers Weihnachtspredigt" (1954). In *Luther im 20. Jahrhundert: Aufsätze*, edited by Erwin Mülhaupt, 25–35. Göttingen: Vandenhoeck & Ruprecht, 1982.

———. "Martin Luther, der Prediger" (1967). In *Luther im 20. Jahrhundert: Aufsätze*, edited by Erwin Mülhaupt, 246–50. Göttingen: Vandenhoeck & Ruprecht, 1982.

Mumme, Jonathan. *Die Präsenz Christi im Amt: Am Beispiel ausgewählter Predigten Martin Luthers, 1535–1546*. Göttingen: Vandenhoeck & Ruprecht, 2015.

Myers, Ben. *The Apostles' Creed: A Guide to the Ancient Catechism*. Christian Essentials. Bellingham, WA: Lexham Press, 2018.

Neebe, Gudrun. *Apostolische Kirche: Grundunterscheidungen an Luthers Kirchenbegriff unter besonderer Berücksichtigung seiner Lehre von den notae ecclesiae*. Berlin: De Gruyter, 1997.

Nembach, Ulrich. *Predigt des Evangeliums: Luther als Prediger, Pädagoge und Rhetor*. Neukirchen-Vluyn: Neukirchener Verlag, 1972.

———. "Martin Luther als Begleiter auf den Weg von der Exegese zur Predigt." In *Luther als Prediger*, edited by Heinrich Kraft, 42–52. Erlangen: Martin-Luther-Verlag, 1986.

Ngien, Dennis. *Luther as a Spiritual Adviser: The Interface of Theology and Piety in Luther's Devotional Writings*. Milton Keynes, UK: Paternoster, 2007.

Oberman, Heiko A. *Luther: Man Between God and the Devil*. Translated by Eileen Walliser-Schwarzbart. New Haven, CT: Yale University Press, 2006.

———. *The Harvest of Medieval Theology: Gabriel Biel and Late Medieval Nominalism*. Grand Rapids: Baker, 2000.

———. *Masters of the Reformation: The Emergence of a New Intellectual Climate in Europe*. Cambridge: Cambridge University Press, 1981.

Oberman, Heiko A., ed. *The Forerunners of the Reformation: The Shape of Late Medieval Thought Illustrated by Key Documents*. Translated by Paul L. Nyhus. New York: Holt, Rinehart, Winston, 1966.

Ocker, Christopher. *Biblical Poetics Before Humanism and Reformation*. New York: Cambridge University Press, 2002.

O'Malley, John W. "Luther the Preacher." *Michigan Germanic Studies* 10 (1984): 3–16.

Opitz, Peter. *Calvins theologische Hermeneutik*. Neukirchener-Vluyn: Neukirchener, 1994.

Osborne, Grant R. *Hermeneutical Spiral: A Comprehensive Introduction to Biblical Interpretation*. Rev. ed. Downers Grove, IL: IVP Academic, 2006.

———. "New Testament Theology." In *Evangelical Dictionary of Theology*, 3rd ed., edited by Daniel J. Treier and Walter A. Elwell, 591–95. Grand Rapids: Baker Academic, 2017.

Ozment, Steven E. *Age of Reform, 1250–1550: An Intellectual and Religious History of Late Medieval and Reformation Europe*. New Haven, CT: Yale University Press, 1980.

———. *Reformation in the Cities: The Appeal of Protestantism to Sixteenth-Century Germany and Switzerland*. New Haven, CT: Yale University Press, 1975.

Pabst, Vera Christina. " '. . . quia habeo optiora exempla': Eine Analyse von Martin Luthers Auseinandersetzung mit dem Mönchtum in seinen Predigten des ersten Jahres nach seiner Rückkehr von der Wartburg, 1522–1523." PhD diss., Universität Hamburg, 2005.

Pak, Sujin. "Scripture, the Priesthood of All Believers, and Applications of 1 Corinthians 14." In *The People's Book: The Reformation and the Bible*, edited by Jennifer Powell McNutt and David Lauber, 33–51. Downers Grove, IL: IVP Academic, 2017.

———. "The Protestant Reformers and the *Analogia Fidei*." In *The Medieval Luther*, edited by Christine Helmer, 227–45. Tübingen: Mohr Siebeck, 2020.

Pelikan, Jaroslav. *Luther the Expositor: Introduction to the Reformer's Exegetical Writings*. St. Louis: Concordia, 1959.

Peters, Albrecht. *Commentary on Luther's Catechisms*. Translated by Holger K. Sonntag, Thomas H. Trapp, and Daniel Thies. 5 vols. St. Louis: Concordia, 2009–2013.

Pieper, Francis. *Christian Dogmatics*. 4 vols. Translated by unnamed translator. St. Louis: Concordia, 1950–1957. German text was published 1917–1924.

Pless, John T. "Sacraments." In *Dictionary of Luther and the Lutheran Traditions*, edited by Timothy J. Wengert, 653–56. Grand Rapids: Baker Academic, 2017.

Posset, Franz. *The Front-Runner of the Catholic Reformation: The Life and Works of Johann von Staupitz*. Aldershot, UK: Ashgate, 2003.

———. "Sola Scriptura—Martin Luther's Invention? Commemorating the 500th Anniversary of the Printed Edition of the Constitutions of the Order of St. Augustine in Nuremberg in 1504–1506." *Augustiniana* 56 (2006): 123–27.

Prenter, Regin. *Spiritus Creator: Luther's Concept of the Holy Spirit*. Translated by John M. Jensen. Philadelphia: Muhlenberg Press, 1953.

Preus, James Samuel. *From Shadow to Promise: Old Testament Interpretation from Augustine to the Young Luther*. Cambridge, MA: Harvard University Press, 1969.

Preus, Robert D. *The Theology of Post-Reformation Lutheranism: A Study of Theological Prolegomena*. St. Louis: Concordia, 1970.

Provan, Iain. *The Reformation and the Right Reading of Scripture*. Waco, TX: Baylor University Press, 2017.

Ratzinger, Joseph. *The Transforming Power of Faith*. Translated by L'Osservatore Romano. San Francisco: Ignatius, 2013.

———. *God's Word: Scripture—Tradition—Office*. Edited by Peter Hünermann and Thomas Söding. Translated by Henry Taylor. San Francisco: Ignatius, 2008.

———. "Foreword." In *Jesus of Nazareth: From the Baptism in the Jordan to the Transfiguration* by Joseph Ratzinger, xi–xxiv. Translated by Adrian J. Walker. New York: Doubleday, 2007.

———. "Handing on the Faith and the Sources of Faith." In *Handing on the Faith in an Age of Disbelief*, by Joseph Ratzinger et al., 13–40. Translated by Michael J. Miller. San Francisco: Ignatius, 2006.

———. *Introduction to Christianity*. Rev. ed. Translated by J. R. Foster. San Francisco: Ignatius, 2004.

———. "Biblical Interpretation in Crisis: On the Question of the Foundations and Approaches of Exegesis Today." In *Biblical Interpretation in Crisis: The Ratzinger Conference on Bible and Church*, edited by Richard John Neuhaus, 1–23. Grand Rapids: Eerdmans, 1989.

Reu, Johann Michael. *Luther's German Bible: An Historical Presentation Together with a Collection of Sources*. Columbus, OH: The Lutheran Book Concern, 1934. Reprint, St. Louis: Concordia, 1984.

Rieske-Braun, Uwe. *Duellum mirabile: Studien zum Kampfmotiv in Martin Luthers Theologie*. Göttingen: Vandenhoeck & Ruprecht, 1999.

Rittgers, Ronald K. "Confession (Private) and the Confessional." In *Dictionary of Luther and the Lutheran Traditions*, edited by Timothy J. Wengert, 157–59. Grand Rapids: Baker Academic, 2017.

———. "Penance, Penitence, and Repentance." In *Dictionary of Luther and the Lutheran Traditions*, edited by Timothy J. Wengert, 585–88. Grand Rapids: Baker Academic, 2017.

———. *The Reformation of the Keys: Confession, Conscience, and Authority in Sixteenth-Century Germany*. Cambridge, MA: Harvard University Press, 2004.

Roberts, Phyllis. "The Ars Praedicandi and the Medieval Sermon." In *Preacher, Sermon and Audience in the Middle Ages*, edited by Carolyn Muessig, 41–62. Leiden: Brill, 2002.

Ryken, Leland. *Worldly Saints: The Puritans as They Really Were*. Grand Rapids: Zondervan, 2010.

Saarinen, Risto. "Justification by Faith: The View of the Mannermaa School." In *The Oxford Handbook of Martin Luther's Theology*, edited by Robert Kolb, Irene Dingel, and L'ubomír Batka, 254–63. New York: Oxford University Press, 2014.

Scaer, David P. "The Theology of Robert David Preus and His Person: Making a Difference." *Concordia Theological Quaterly* 74, no. 1 (2010): 75–91.

Schäfer, Ernst. *Luther als Kirchenhistoriker: Ein Beitrag zur Geschichte der Wissenschaft*. Gütersloh: Bertelsmann, 1897.

Schilling, Johannes. "Katechismen." In *Luther Handbuch*, edited by Albrecht Beutel, 305–12. Tübingen: Mohr Siebeck, 2005.

Schleiff, A. "Theologisch-exegetische Einleitung." In WADB 9:ix–xxxvii.

Schwiebert, E. G. *Luther and his Times: The Reformation from a New Perspective*. St. Louis: Concordia, 1950.

Selderhuis, Herman J. "Introduction to the Psalms." In *Psalms 1–72*, edited by Herman J. Selderhuis, xlv–lvii. RCS OT 7. Downers Grove, IL: IVP Academic, 2015.

Senkbeil, Harold L. *The Care of Souls: Cultivating a Pastor's Heart*. Bellingham, WA: Lexham Press, 2019.

Silcock, Jeffrey G. "Luther on the Holy Spirit and His Use of God's Word." In *The Oxford Handbook of Martin Luther's Theology*, edited by Robert Kolb, Irene Dingel, and L'ubomír Batka, 294–309. New York: Oxford University Press, 2014.

Slenczka, Notger. "Luther's Anthropology." In *The Oxford Handbook of Martin Luther's Theology*, edited by Robert Kolb, Irene Dingel, and L'ubomír Batka, 212–32. New York: Oxford University Press, 2014.

Söhngen, Gottlieb. "The Analogy of Faith: Likeness to God from Faith Alone?" Translated by Kenneth Oakes. *Pro Ecclesia* 21, no. 1 (2012): 56–76.

Starling, David. "The Analogy of Faith in the Theology of Luther and Calvin." *Reformed Theological Review* 72, no. 1 (2013): 5–19.

Steiger, Johann Anselm. "Martin Luthers allegorisch-figürliche Auslegung der Heiligen Schrift." *Zeitschrift für Kirchengeschichte* 110, no. 3 (1999): 331–51.

Steinmetz, David C. *Luther in Context*. 2nd ed. Grand Rapids: Baker Academic, 2002.

———. *Luther and Staupitz: An Essay in the Intellectual Origins of the Protestant Reformation*. Durham, NC: Duke University Press, 1980.

———. *Misericordia Dei: The Theology of Johannes von Staupitz in its Late Medieval Setting*. Leiden: Brill, 1968.

Stephens, W. P. *The Theology of Huldrych Zwingli*. Oxford: Clarendon Press, 1986.

Stock, Brian. *Listening for the Text: On the Uses of the Past*. Baltimore: The Johns Hopkins University Press, 1990.

Stolt, Birgit. *Martin Luthers Rhetorik des Herzens*. Tübingen: Mohr Siebeck, 2000.

———. "*Docere, delectare* und *movere* bei Luther." In *Wortkampf: Frühneuhochdeutsche Beispiele zur rhetorischen Praxis*, edited by Birgit Stolt, 31–77. Frankfurt am Main: Athenäum-Verlag, 1974.

Strauss, Gerald. *Luther's House of Learning: Indoctrination of the Young in the German Reformation*. Baltimore: The Johns Hopkins University Press, 1978.

Tappeiner, Daniel A. "Hermeneutics, the Analogy of Faith and New Testament Sacramental Realism." *The Evangelical Quarterly* 49, no. 1 (1977): 40–52.

Tavard, George H. *Holy Writ or Holy Church: The Crisis of the Protestant Reformation*. New York: Harper and Brothers, 1959.

Tentler, Thomas N. *Sin and Confession on the Eve of the Reformation*. Princeton, NJ: Princeton University Press, 1977.

Thayer, Anne T. *Penitence, Preaching, and the Coming of the Reformation*. Aldershot, UK: Ashgate, 2002.

The 1662 Book of Common Prayer: International Edition. Edited by Samuel L. Bray and Drew Nathaniel Keane. Downers Grove, IL: IVP Academic, 2021.

Thiele, Ernst, ed. *Luthers Sprichwörtersammlung: Nach Seiner Handschrift*. Weimar: Hermann Böhlaus Nachfolger, 1900.

Thompson, Mark D. *A Sure Ground on Which to Stand: The Relation of Authority and Interpretive Method in Luther's Approach to Scripture*. London: Paternoster, 2004.

Treier, Daniel J. "Scripture, Unity of." In *Dictionary for Theological Interpretation of the Bible*, edited by Kevin J. Vanhoozer, 731–34. Grand Rapids: Baker Academic; London: SPCK, 2005.

——— . *Introducing Theological Interpretation of Scripture: Recovering a Christian Practice*. Grand Rapids: Baker Academic, 2008.

Trigg, Jonathan D. "Luther on Baptism and Penance." *The Oxford Handbook of Martin Luther's Theology*, edited by Robert Kolb, Irene Dingel, and L'ubomír Batka, 310–21. New York: Oxford University Press, 2014.

——— . *Baptism in the Theology of Martin Luther*. Leiden: Brill, 1994.

Vanhoozer, Kevin J. "Expounding the Word of the Lord: Joseph Ratzinger on Revelation, Tradition, and Biblical Interpretation." In *The Theology of Benedict XVI: A Protestant Appreciation*, edited by Tim Perry, 66–86. Bellingham, WA: Lexham Press, 2019.

——— . *Hearers and Doers: A Pastor's Guide to Making Disciples Through Scripture and Doctrine*. Bellingham, WA: Lexham Press, 2019.

——— . *Biblical Authority After Babel: Retrieving the Solas in the Spirit of Mere Protestant Christianity*. Grand Rapids: Brazos, 2016.

Vatican Council. *Dei Verbum: Dogmatic Constitution on Divine Revelation*. Promulgated by Pope Paul VI on November 18, 1965. Accessible online via www.vatican.va

Vogelsang, Erich. "Zur Datierung der frühesten Lutherpredigten." *Zeitschrift für Kirchengeschichte* 50 (1931): 112–45.

Voss, Hank. "From 'Grammatical-historical Exegesis' to 'Theological Exegesis': Five Essential Practices." *Evangelical Review of Theology* 37, no. 2 (2013): 140–52.

Wallmann, Johannes. "Prolegomena zur Erforschung der Predigt im Zeitalter der lutherischen Orthodoxie." *Zeitschrift für Theologie und Kirche* 106, no. 3 (2009): 284–304.

Wendebourg, Dorothea. "Taufe und Abendmahl." In *Luther Handbuch*, edited by Albrecht Beutel, 414–23. Tübingen: Mohr Siebeck, 2005.

Wengert, Timothy J. "Wittenberg's Earliest Catechism." *Lutheran Quarterly* 7, no. 3 (1993): 247–60.

Wenzel, Siegfried. *Medieval Artes Praedicandi: A Synthesis of Scholastic Sermon Structure*. Toronto: University of Toronto Press, 2015.

Werdermann, Hermann. *Luthers Wittenberger Gemeinde wiederhergestellt aus seinen Predigten: Zugleich ein Beitrag zu Luthers Homiletik und zur Gemeindepredigt der Gegenwart*. Gütersloh: Bertelsmann, 1929.

White, Graham. *Luther as Nominalist: A Study of the Logical Methods Used in Martin Luther's Disputations in the Light of Their Medieval Background.* Helsinki: Luther-Agricola-Society, 1994.

Wieden, Susanne Bei der. *Luthers Predigten des Jahres 1522: Untersuchungen zu ihrer Überlieferung.* Cologne: Böhlau Verlag, 1999.

Wiemer, Axel. *"Mein Trost, Kampf und Sieg ist Christus": Martin Luthers eschatologische Theologie nach seinen Reihenpredigten über 1. Kor 15 (1532/33).* Berlin: Walter de Gruyter, 2003.

Williams, George H. *The Radical Reformation.* 3rd ed. Kirksville, MO: Sixteenth Century Journal Publishers, 1992.

Wilson, H. S. "Luther on Preaching as God Speaking." *Lutheran Quarterly* 19, no. 1 (2005): 63–76.

Winkler, Eberhard. "Luther als Seelsorger und Prediger." In *Leben und Werk Martin Luthers von 1526 bis 1546: Festgabe zu seinem 500. Geburtstag*, edited by Helmar Junghans, 225–39. Göttingen: Vandenhoeck & Ruprecht, 1983.

Witvliet, John D. "The Interplay of Catechesis and Liturgy in the Sixteenth Century: Examples from the Lutheran and Reformed Traditions." In *The People's Book: The Reformation and the Bible*, edited by Jennifer Powell McNutt and David Lauber, 110–31. Downers Grove, IL: IVP Academic, 2017.

Wood, A. Skevington. *Captive to the Word: Martin Luther; Doctor of Sacred Scripture.* Grand Rapids: Eerdmans, 1969.

Worcester, Thomas. "Catholic Sermons." In *Preachers and People in the Reformations and Early Modern Period*, edited by Larissa Taylor, 4–33. Leiden: Brill, 2001.

Zschoch, Helmut. "Predigten." In *Luther Handbuch*, edited by Albrecht Beutel, 315–21. Tübingen: Mohr Siebeck, 2005.

Modern Biblical Studies Resources

Allen, David L. *Hebrews.* New American Commentary 35. Nashville: B&H, 2010.

Beale, G. K., and D. A. Carson, eds. *Commentary on the New Testament Use of the Old Testament.* Grand Rapids: Baker Academic; Nottingham, UK: Apollos, 2007.

Block, Daniel I. *Judges, Ruth.* New American Commentary 6. Nashville: B&H, 1999.

Carbajosa, Ignacio. *Faith, the Fount of Exegesis: The Interpretation of Scripture in Light of the History of Old Testament Research.* Translated by Paul Stevenson. San Francisco: Ignatius, 2013.

Carpenter, Eugene. *Exodus 19–40.* Evangelical Exegetical Commentary. Bellingham, WA: Lexham Press, 2016.

Cranfield, C. E. B. *A Critical and Exegetical Commentary on the Epistle to the Romans.* 2 vols. International Critical Commentary. Edinburgh: T&T Clark, 1985.

Crenshaw, James L. "Riddles." In *The Anchor Bible Dictionary*, 6 vols., edited by David Noel Freedman, 5:721–23. New York: Doubleday, 1992.

———. *Samson: A Secret Betrayed, A Vow Ignored.* Atlanta: John Knox Press, 1978.

Fitzmyer, Joseph A. *Romans: A New Translation with Commentary.* Anchor Bible 33. New York: Doubleday, 1993.

———. *The Gospel According to Luke (X–XXIV).* Anchor Bible 28A. New York: Doubleday, 1985.

France, R. T. *The Gospel of Matthew.* New International Commentary on the New Testament. Grand Rapids: Eerdmans, 2007.

Hamilton, Victor P. *The Book of Genesis: Chapters 18–50.* New International Commentary on the Old Testament. Grand Rapids: Eerdmans, 1995.

Käsemann, Ernst. *Commentary on Romans*. Translated by Geoffrey W. Bromiley. Grand Rapids: Eerdmans, 1980.

Koehler, Ludwig and Walter Baumgartner, eds. *The Hebrew and Aramaic Lexicon of the Old Testament*. 4 vols. Translated and edited by M. E. J. Richardson. Leiden: Brill, 1994–.

Luz, Ulrich. *Matthew 1–7: A Commentary on Matthew 1–7*. Translated by James E. Crouch. Hermeneia. Minneapolis: Fortress, 2007.

Kittel, Gerhard. "ἀναλογία." In *Theological Dictionary of the New Testament*, 10 vols., edited by Gerhard Kittel, translated by Geoffrey W. Bromiley, 1:347–48. Grand Rapids: Eerdmans, 1964–1976.

Marshall, I. Howard. *The Gospel of Luke: A Commentary on the Greek Text*. New International Greek Testament Commentary 3. Grand Rapids: Eerdmans, 1978.

Metzger, Bruce M. *A Textual Commentary on the Greek New Testament*. 2nd ed. Stuttgart: Deutsche Bibelgesellschaft, 1994.

Moo, Douglas J. *The Epistle to the Romans*. New International Commentary on the New Testament. Grand Rapids: Eerdmans, 1996.

Niditch, Susan. *Judges: A Commentary*. Old Testament Library. Louisville: Westminster John Knox, 2008.

Propp, William H. C. *Exodus 19–40*. Anchor Bible 2A. New York: Doubleday, 2006.

Rad, Gerhard von. *Genesis: A Commentary*. Translated by John H. Marks. Revised edition. Philadelphia: The Westminster Press, 1972.

Sarna, Nahum M. *Genesis*. The JPS Torah Commentary. Philadelphia: The Jewish Publication Society, 1989.

Tate, Marvin E. *Psalms 51–100*. Word Biblical Commentary 20. Dallas: Word, 1998.

Webb, Barry G. *The Book of Judges*. New International Commentary on the Old Testament. Grand Rapids: Eerdmans, 2012.

Westermann, Claus. *Genesis 12–36: A Contintental Commentary*. Translated by John J. Scullion. Minneapolis: Fortress, 1995.

Name Index

Agricola, Johann, 39-40, 97
Alcuin, 82
Ambrosiaster, 12
Ambrosius, 127
Aristotle, 3, 119
Asendorf, Ulrich, 6-7
Athanasius, 110
Augsburg Confession, 148
    Defense, 148
Augustine, 34, 50, 69, 73, 100, 141, 150, 168-69
Bachmann, E. Theodore, 72
Basil of Caesarea, 12
Bornkamm, Heinrich, 8-9, 167-68
Brewer, Brian C., 71-72
Brown, Christopher Boyd, 59
Bucanus, Gulielmus, 12
Bugenhagen, Johannes, 37-38, 172
Burnett, Amy Nelson, 26-27
Calov, Abraham, 17
Calvin, John, 17, 19
Carson, D. A., 15
Cary, Phillip, 36, 41
Center for Baptist Renewal, 12
Cicero, 3, 119
Cooper, Derek, 17, 28
Cruciger, Caspar, 52, 161
Cyprian, 69
Cyril of Jerusalem, 97
Dietrich, Veit, 112
Ebeling, Gerhard, 7, 59
Emerson, Matthew Y., 86
Erasmus, Desiderius, 4, 9, 10, 11, 12, 15-16, 26, 42, 68-69, 118, 142, 148, 164, 166
FatCat, 198
Fennell, Robert C., 16
Flacius, Matthias Illyricus, 17
Formula of Concord, 59, 88, 100

Fuller, Daniel P., 12
Gerhard, Johann, 17
Gerrish, B. A., 24
Gertz, Bernhard, 15-16
Glassius, Salomo, 17
Glossa ordinaria, 9, 23, 86, 92, 93, 112, 127
Greene-McKreight, Kathryn, 9, 56
Gregory of Nyssa, 97
Haemig, Mary Jane, 19, 36
Hägglund, Bengt, 12, 19
Hill, Wesley, 70
Hof, Otto, 18-19
Hugh of St. Victor, 72-73
Hutter, Leonhard, 17
Iserloh, Erwin, 171
Jerome, 100, 168-69
John Chrysostom, 12
Josephus, 82, 87, 138, 167
Kaiser, Walter C., Jr., 12-13, 14, 15
Käsemann, Ernst, 13
Kimchi, David, 9, 167
Kimchi, Moses, 9, 167
Kleinig, John W., 12, 135
Knapp, Henry M., 15
Koehler, J. P., 14
Kolb, Robert, 168
Kolde, Dietrich, 35-36
Krodel, Gottfried G., 35
Lateran IV, 35, 151, 153-54
Lefèvre, Jacques d'Étaples, 15, 96-97
Leithart, Peter J., 12, 58, 126
Löfstedt, Bengt, 21, 32
Luther, Martin
    on allegory, 8, 24
    anti-Judaism, 72
    call to the office of the word, 1-3, 20
    Castle Coburg, 112
    church visitations, 24-25, 40

"an inept allegorist", 7
literal sense, 7-9, 164-66
prayed the catechism with the children, 32, 40, 44, 49, 55, 78, 137, 158, 170
preaching career, 20-21
recording of sermons, 20-22, 32
recording of table talk, 98
Marschler, Thomas, 15
Mattox, Mickey L., 19
Melanchthon, Philipp, 16, 17, 73, 75
Menius, Justus, 100, 112
Menke, Karl-Heinz, 12
Mentzer, Balthasar, 17
Meuser, Fred W., 21
Muller, Richard A., 16, 19
Münster, Sebastian, 9, 82, 86, 93, 97, 105, 106, 109
Müntzer, Thomas, 46-47
Myers, Ben, 50
Nicholas of Lyra, 9, 82, 86, 90, 92, 96, 127
Oecolampadius, Johannes, 39-40
Origen, 12-13, 58, 69, 82, 90, 97, 100
Pak, Sujin, 17, 28, 30
Paul of Burgos, 8, 90, 92-93
Pelikan, Jaroslav, 8, 10, 41, 99
Peter Lombard, 72-73
Peters, Albrecht, 34, 58, 68-69, 73, 74, 76, 151
Pieper, Francis, 14
Pirminius, 61, 161
Pliny the Elder, 97, 98, 167
Poach, Andreas, 22
Preus, Robert D., 16
Psuedo-Augustine, 61, 161
Psuedo-Constantinius, 12
Ratzinger, Joseph, 15, 18, 165
Reuchlin, Johannes, 9, 104
Rörer, Georg, 21-22, 32
Rufinus, 61, 66, 97, 160-61
Selderhuis, Herman J., 8-9
Senkbeil, Harold L., 59
Silcock, Jeffrey G., 59
Starling, David, 18-19, 30
Staupitz, Johann, 1, 20, 173
Stjerna, Kirsi I., 56
Stolz, Johann, 21
Tertullian, 69, 127
Theophylact, 127
Treier, Daniel, 12
Turretin, Francis, 16
Vanhoozer, Kevin J., 12, 18
Vatican II, 18, 163
Weller von Molsdorf, Hieronymus, 30, 131
William of St. Thierry, 15
Zwingli, Huldrych, 7, 12, 39-40, 48, 88, 164

Subject Index

Abraham, 80-94
    as allegory for faith, 91-92
    reasons according to the faith, 81-85
    resurrection of the dead, 85-88, 90-91
Absolution, 44-45, 56, 72-73, 147-53
    allegory of, 125-26
    commanded by God, 141, 156-57
    efficacious word, 73, 108-9, 119, 134, 138
    gives Jesus, 119, 138
    God's act, 108-9, 119, 134, 138
    scriptural command and definition, 52, 75, 161
    See also Confession, forgiveness, Penance, repentance
allegory, 7, 8, 24, 80, 165-66
    according to the faith, 89-93
    of Genesis, 22, 89-93
    of Isaiah, 9:2-6, 124-26
    of Judges, 14:14, 96-99
    not distinguished from typology and figural interpretation, 8, 124
    of Psalm, 72, 109
    See also figural reading, typology
Anabaptists, 47-48, 103
    on the term "rebaptizer," 26
    See also Radicals, Schwärmer
analogy of faith (*analogia fidei*), 12-20, 27, 33-40, 28-54, 55-79, 168-69
analogy of Scripture (*analogia scripturae*), 14-15, 16, 29
Apostles' Creed, 27, 32, 57, 61-68, 160-62, 165
    apostolic origin, 61, 160-61
    articles of faith, 3, 25
    division of, 58, 61-62
    first article, 62-63, 107, 112, 158
    and history, 10-11, 99-101, 168-69
    inspired by the Holy Spirit, 160-61
    second article, 63-65, 79, 85-88, 96-99, 103-7, 118-23, 123-26, 129-31, 158
    third article, 65-67, 78-79, 107-11, 126-29, 147-53, 153-57, 158
Ave Maria, 35, 38
Baited Leviathan metaphor, 96-99, 110, 124-25, 144
Baptism, 34, 38-39, 45, 56, 62, 66, 71-77, 158
    commanded by God, 34, 141, 156-57
    efficacious word, 73, 108-9, 119, 134, 138
    gives Jesus, 119, 138
    God's act, 108-9, 119, 138-39
    infant, 71-72, 161-62
    scriptural command and definition, 52, 75, 161
Bees, 52, 98, 161
Book of Common Prayer, 33
Caiaphas, 44, 172
catechism, 32-40, 55-79, 129-31, 159-72
    as lay Bible, 29, 49-53
    definition of, 19-20, 29, 33-34, 55-57, 74, 78-79, 160
    order of, 34
    quarterly sermons, 22, 37-38, 55
Chalcedon, 4, 64-65, 86-87, 89-90, 98, 102-3, 105-7, 119-20, 142-45
    Its content in different words, 87, 90
Christ, 5-12, 61-68, 68-71, 71-77 96-99, 118-23, 134-38
    allegory of, 89-93, 123-26
    as light, 118-23
    as the promised Seed, 85-88, 142-45
    ascension, 48, 64, 88, 146
    communication idiomatum (communication of attributes), 88
    descent, 86, 89, 99
    king, 103-7, 107-11, 119-23, 126-29, 135
    office, 135, 152

unity of his person. *See* Chalcedon
church, 107-11, 126-29
    allegory of, 92-93, 97-98, 111
    as creature of the word, 41-42, 66-67, 98, 136-37
    catholica as Christian, 66
    Christendom, 33, 56
    external offices, 65-67
Confession, 6, 34-35, 56, 125-26, 147-53, 153-54
    See also Absolution, forgiveness, Penance, repentance
conscience, 37, 76, 91-93, 99, 126, 148, 150-51
contrition, 147, 148, 153
creation, 5, 57, 61-63, 100, 163, 165
Creed. *See* Apostles' Creed, faith
David, 86, 106, 113, 121, 131, 142
death's defeat, 110, 120-21, 122, 124-25, 126, 137, 144-45
    See also Baited Leviathan metaphor
devil, *see* Satan
dialectic, 7, 8, 24, 25, 89
Emmaus, 133-58
Enneagram, 174
Eucharist, *see* Sacrament of the Altar
ex opere operato (by the work performed), 72, 147
ex opere operantis (by the work of the worker), 72, 147
experience, 46-49
faith
    fides qua creditor (the faith by which it is believed), 12-13, 18-19, 67, 163
    fides quae creditor (the faith which is believed), 12-13, 18-19, 67, 163
    and history, 10-11, 99-101
    hope, and love, 57, 165-66
    and love, 111
    and reason, 81-85, 123-26, 138-47, 162-63, 164-66
    "as the words sound," 67-68, 73-74, 76-77, 157
    "as you believe, so you have," 150-51, 162
fanatics, 103, 164
    See also Radicals, Sacramentarians, Schwärmer
figural reading, 8, 10, 99-101, 142
    See also allegory, typology

forgiveness, 36-37, 45, 50, 69-70, 71-77, 147-53, 157
    See also Absolution, sacrament(s)
Freedom, 57, 71, 75-76, 92, 126-29, 151
Gideon, 109, 118, 123-26
God the Father, 43, 61-62, 62-63, 67, 71, 105, 107, 111, 119, 152
God's command, 68, 84, 93-94, 139, 141, 151, 153, 156-57
    See also Absolution, Baptism, Sacrament of the Altar, sacrament(s), Ten Commandments
God's word, 3-5, 10-12, 30-33, 41-49, 138-47, 159-72
    Comfort of, 134-38, 146, 152-53, 154-57
    does what it says, 73-77, 106-7, 108-9, 139, 161-62, 165
    hearing of, 4, 60, 74, 147, 150-51, 156, 172, 174
    Jesus is present in, 57, 69, 74-76, 88, 135-38, 153-57
    reasoning according to, 81-85, 123-26, 138-47, 162-63, 164-66
    See also Absolution, Baptism, catechism, preaching, Sacrament of the Altar, sacrament(s), Scripture
good works, 23, 36-37, 45, 58, 92, 100, 150, 151, 153-57
    See also sanctification, Ten Commandments, works righteousness
gospel, 4, 5-7, 11, 15-17, 19, 42, 47, 50, 59, 63-65, 67-68, 72, 80, 85-88, 91-92, 96-99, 116, 129-31, 134-38, 138-47, 150-51, 152, 153, 159, 161-62, 168
grammar, 9-10, 86, 88, 99, 143, 164, 166, 167-69
Great Exchange, 122
    See also Chalcedon
heresy, 4, 19, 138-39, 148, 150, 162-63
historical criticism, 8, 10-11, 17-18, 99, 174
history, 10-11, 32, 36, 61-68, 88, 95, 99-101, 130, 166, 167-69
holiness, 29, 36, 37, 65, 66, 68, 69, 70, 71, 103, 107, 122, 129, 132, 136, 146, 149-50, 151, 156, 171
Holy Communion, *see* Sacrament of the Altar
Holy Spirit, 65-67

Subject Index

as author of the Apostles' Creed, 52, 160-61
as author of Scripture, 56, 88, 163
gives faith (*fides qua creditur* and *fides quae creditur*), 11, 20, 107, 109, 130, 138, 149
opens Scripture, 2, 4, 5-6, 10-11, 30-33, 70, 82-83, 116, 118, 140-43, 154, 166, 168, 172
and the sacraments, 71-72
speaks in God's word, 4-5, 44, 60, 71, 125-26, 153, 157, 172
works through the church, 65-66
Indulgences, 148, 150, 152, 171
Isaac, 80-94, 98
Isaiah, 11, 86, 118-19, 119-20, 121, 123-24, 127, 128, 129-30, 142, 171
Islam, *see Muslims*
James and John, 136
Jesus, *see* Christ
Jews, 67, 72, 103-5, 108, 109, 114, 118, 129, 131, 139-40
John, 92, 171
Judas, 44, 72
justification, 6, 15-16, 19, 28, 39, 66, 85
See also Apostles' Creed
kingdom of God, 91, 103-11, 126-29
kingdoms of the world, 108, 128-29, 132
law, 100, 137, 149
natural, 82-83
uses, 59-60
See also Ten Commandments
law and gospel, 6-7, 15, 36-37, 91-92, 96-97, 153
light v. darkness, 3-5, 10-11, 118-23, 138-47, 150-51, 160-62, 164-66, 174
literal sense, 7-9, 164-66
liturgy, 33
Lord's Prayer, *see* Our Father
Luke, 142, 148
Luther, Hans, 55
Luther, Lena (Magdalena), 55
Magisterium, 2, 41-42, 164, 172
marriage, 72-73
Mary (Virgin), 35, 65, 86-87, 105, 109, 120, 130, 136, 139, 143-44, 152, 172
ministry of the word, *see* pastors
Muslims, 30, 67, 103, 104, 108, 110, 118, 128-29, 131, 139-40
Nicene Creed, 27, 32, 130

nomina sacra, 25, 51, 105-6
office, 59, 172
of the word, *see* pastors
opera trinitatis ad extra indivisa sunt (the external works of the Trinity are undivided), 57, 62
Our Father, 40, 52, 57, 68-71, 141, 163, 165
division of, 68-69
doxology, 68-69
fifth petition, 69-70
first petition, 69, 114, 115
fourth petition, 69-70, 113-14, 115
rote repetition, 70, 150, 151, 135, 156
second petition, 69, 114, 115
seventh petition, 69-70, 114, 115
sixth petition, 69-70, 158
third petition, 69, 107, 114, 115
Papists, 26, 45, 48, 85, 103-4, 108, 129, 131, 164
pastors, 1, 5, 41-49, 53, 91-92, 100-101, 123-26, 153-54, 171
Paul, 5, 12-13, 28, 44, 57, 80, 86, 101, 120-21, 128, 136, 157, 162
Penance, 45, 48, 147-53
Peter, 44, 92, 128, 136, 155, 172
Philosophy, 3-5
pope, 2, 26, 31, 41-42, 45-46, 66, 114, 118-19, 128, 139
and the catechism, 35, 49-53, 169
preaching
allegory of, 125
and the catechism, 4-5, 28-54, 169, 173-75
as the greatest good, 69, 132
and Jesus, 5-6
and the law, 60
as a sacrament, 41, 65-66, 72-75, 91
true v. false, 27, 36
priesthood of all believers, 153-54
promise
of Jesus' presence, 135, 140-41
of a sacrament, 71-75, 139, 151
of the Seed, 81-88, 93, 143, 144-45
prophecy, 30-33, 166, 171
in the Bible, 86, 130, 142-45
definition of, 18-19, 53
false, 45-47
general and special, 29, 30, 131
gift of, 5, 28
psalm of, 115

Purgatory, 16, 45, 147-48, 151
Qu'ran, 118, 129, 131
Quadriga or the four senses, 165-66
Radicals, 5, 26-27, 31, 45-47, 48-49, 76, 77, 164
    Kingdom of Münster, 103
    See also fanatics, Schwärmer
reason, 3-5, 17-18, 24, 43, 47-49, 65, 76-77, 80, 81-85, 90, 93, 103-7, 107-11, 116, 118, 123-26, 129, 132, 138-47, 149, 162-63, 164-66, 170
redemption, 41, 57, 61-68, 74-75, 85-88, 96-99, 103-7, 118-23, 134-38, 163
    See also Apostles' Creed, gospel, sacrament(s), salvation
Reformed, 5, 17, 26-27, 28, 58, 76, 164
    See also Sacramentarians, Schwärmer
repentance, 56, 147-53
    See also Absolution, Confession, forgiveness, Penance
res et verba (the substance and the words), 20, 31-33, 70-71, 87, 90
rhetoric, 8, 24, 25, 39, 50, 89
righteousness, 74, 103-7, 120, 121, 128-29, 132, 152, 154-55
rule of faith (*regula fidei*), see analogy of faith
Sacrament of the Altar, 27, 38-39, 45, 52, 67, 71-77, 112, 119, 134, 138-39, 153-57, 158, 167
    commanded by God, 141, 156-57
    God's act, 108-9, 119, 134, 138
    gives Jesus, 119, 138
    efficacious word, 73, 108-9, 119, 134, 138
    scriptural command and definition, 52, 75, 161
    Zwinglian view, 48
sacrament(s), 19, 27, 45, 57, 67, 71-77, 108-9, 119, 129, 141, 151
    according to reason, 108-9, 138-39
    and God's word, 73, 76-77, 139, 161
    and the catechism, 19, 20, 29, 33-34, 38-39, 49, 52, 53, 55-56, 78-79, 160, 163, 165, 166, 172
    definition of, 72-74, 139, 161
    distorted into a human work, 44-45, 47-48, 153
    number of, 74-75
    physical sign and rite, 72-73

Sacramentarians, 45, 47-49
    See also Radical, Reformed, Schwärmer
saints, 107, 132, 138
    communion of, 33, 43, 66, 107-8, 128, 170
    example and faith of, 84-85, 110, 112-13
    prayer to, 35, 45
salvation, 129-31
    See also Absolution, Apostles' Creed, Baptism, God's word, preaching, redemption, Sacrament of the Altar, sacrament(s)
Samson, 95-101, 142
Sanctification, 57, 61, 65-67, 111, 136
Satan, 46, 63, 67-68, 70-71, 96-98, 108, 110, 122, 124-26, 128, 143, 144, 156
    allies of (sin, death, and hell; sin, death, and the law), 64, 71, 76, 88, 97-98, 107, 109, 111, 114, 118-19, 120-23, 124-25, 129, 143, 144
    distorts Scripture, 2-3, 4, 5, 32, 44, 48, 64, 112, 152-53, 155, 171, 172
    fall of, 130-31
    how to talk back to, 45, 146
Schwärmer, 26-27, 30, 46-49, 58, 76-77, 85, 128, 131, 134, 139, 164
    See also fanatics, Radical, Reformed, Sacramentarians
Scripture, 14-16, 17-18, 32, 62, 159-72
    as law and gospel, 6-7
    is about Christ, 5-12
    Scripture against Scripture, 1-3
    See also God's word, Scripture interpreting Scripture
Scripture interpreting Scripture (*scriptura sui ipsius interpres*), 8, 28-29, 78, 124, 133-34, 138-47, 164-66
    See also analogy of faith, analogy of Scripture
Sin, 34-37, 42, 59-60, 69-70, 92, 97, 104-7, 120-22, 127, 129, 143-44, 146, 150, 151, 152, 155, 162
    original sin, 86, 149
    See also Absolution, Confession, forgiveness, Penance
St. Agatha, 110
St. Agnes, 110
St. Lucia, 110

Ten Commandments, 17, 24, 34, 37, 38, 39, 40, 57-61, 82, 111-15, 118-19, 161, 165
  division of, 57-58
  eighth commandment, 137
  fifth commandment, 82, 84
  first commandment, 7, 60, 79, 95, 106-7, 114-15, 119, 158, 163, 166
  first table, 58-59, 80, 81, 82, 84-85, 102, 111, 112, 113-15, 119, 134
  fourth commandment, 47, 158
  as natural law, 82
  ninth and tenth commandments, 58
  second commandment, 56, 68, 85, 114-15, 128, 152, 158
  second table, 58, 59, 111, 112, 158
  sixth commandment, 59-60
  third commandment, 114-15, 158
Tetragrammaton, 25, 51, 105-6

three estates, 108, 129
Trinity, 6-7, 32, 34, 57, 61-68, 100, 105, 106-7, 139-40, 161
  See also Apostles' Creed, Chalcedon
Turks, *see* Muslims
two kingdoms, 3, 24, 108, 111, 126-29, 139, 164
typology, 8, 10, 80, 89-90, 95, 99, 106, 117-18, 123-26, 168
  See also allegory, figural reading
Vocation, 1, 43, 59, 108, 172
  See also office
Weimar edition, 20-21, 25-26, 51, 96, 98, 129
Wittenberg, 37, 55, 68, 96, 167, 172
works righteousness, 36-37, 44-49, 58, 84-85, 91-92, 147-48, 149-50, 153

Scripture Index

OLD TESTAMENT

Genesis
3:6-19, *149*
3:15, *142, 143*
4:2, *144*
6:3, *171*
8–9, *183*
11–12, *183*
12–36, *93*
12:1, *81*
15, *183*
22, *23, 80, 85, 86, 89, 98*
22:2, *92*
22:3, *92*
22:9, *87*
22:12, *32*
22:14, *92*
22:18, *80, 81, 85, 88, 93, 133, 145*
24:7, *51*
42:28, *37*
49:10-12, *145*
49:16, *95*
49:16-18, *95*

Exodus
1, *80*
14, *126*
20, *11, 58, 59, 60, 61, 82, 85, 137, 178, 179*
32, *56, 58, 64, 162*
32:5, *64*
33:20, *149*

Leviticus
9–19, *183*
18:21, *84, 85*
26:36, *37*

Numbers
6, *183*
11–14, *183*
12:6, *31*
16–17, *183*
19–25, *183*

Deuteronomy
1–9, *183*
5, *58, 60, 178*
13:1-3, *83*
18:10-12, *147*
18:18, *145*
32:13, *96*

Judges
6, *109*
6–7, *109, 117, 124*
14, *96, 98*
14:8, *98*
14:14, *23, 95, 96, 97, 100*
15:19, *96*

1 Samuel
2:6, *95, 98*
19:11-12, *112, 113*

2 Samuel
7:12, *86, 143*

1 Kings
1, *83*

2 Kings
19:20-37, *124*
21:6, *85*

2 Chronicles
3:1, *93*

Job
41:1, *97, 110*
41:5, *110*

Psalms
1–72, *8*
2, *145*
2:2, *104*
3, *114, 115*
4, *114, 115*
5, *177*
7, *102*
8, *145*
13, *114, 115*
16, *145*
19, *114, 115*
21, *140, 170*
22, *167*
22:16, *10, 167*
22:21, *91*

24, *114*, *115*
33, *171*
33:3, *171*
51, *149*
51–100, *109*
51:7, *149*
60–150, *103*
68, *78*
72, *23*, *102*, *103*, *104*, *105*, *106*, *107*, *108*, *109*, *110*, *111*, *112*, *113*, *114*, *115*, *116*, *136*, *184*
72:1, *107*
72:4, *107*
72:6, *109*
72:14, *110*
72:17, *105*
104, *62*, *73*
110, *107*, *145*
119:12, *74*
119:81-82, *73*
147:5, *170*

Isaiah
2:2, *93*
5, *51*, *143*
7:14, *86*, *143*, *184*
8:19-20, *147*
9, *117*, *118*, *119*, *120*, *123*, *124*, *126*, *127*, *128*, *129*, *131*, *184*
9:2, *118*
9:2-6, *117*
9:2-7, *23*
9:2-6, *184*
9:3, *126*
9:4, *120*, *124*
9:6, *11*, *117*, *120*
29:11, *172*
37:31, *10*
42:3, *146*
42:8, *106*, *107*
53, *143*

Joel
2:28-29, *31*

Zechariah
9:9, *184*

Malachi
3:6, *83*

NEW TESTAMENT

Matthew
1–7, *69*
5–7, *68*, *69*, *70*, *71*, *180*
7:15, *2*
7:24, *42*
8, *177*
11:28, *155*
12:20, *146*
12:42, *105*
15:21-28, *157*
16:2, *4*
16:19, *75*
18:18, *52*, *161*
18:18-19, *75*
18:20, *135*, *140*
19, *47*
19:29, *47*
26:26, *48*
26:26-28, *52*, *75*, *161*
27, *122*
28:18-20, *34*
28:19, *52*, *75*, *161*

Mark
2:17, *157*
13:14, *129*
14:22-24, *52*, *75*, *161*
16:16, *52*, *75*, *161*

Luke
2, *117*, *185*, *187*
2:1-14, *117*
2:11, *51*
2:14, *131*
3:3, *148*
5:32, *157*
9:51-56, *136*

10:34, *127*
11:21-23, *126*
15:5, *51*, *127*
16:29, *147*
16:31, *147*
22:19-20, *52*, *75*, *161*
24, *133*, *134*, *145*, *154*, *158*, *188*
24:1, *23*
24:21, *135*
24:27, *133*, *141*
24:46-47, *148*

John
1, *155*, *177*
1–12, *52*
1:29, *127*
2:1-12, *177*
2:24, *3*, *25*, *41*
5, *158*
14:9, *64*
15:26, *65*
20:22-23, *52*, *75*, *161*

Acts
2:17-18, *31*
2:24, *144*
5:31, *148*
10, *125*
15, *66*, *136*

Romans
1, *59*
1:16, *42*, *91*
1:17, *2*
2:5, *25*
2:11, *25*, *43*
2:17, *25*
4, *12*
4:17, *73*, *165*
5, *149*
5:5, *107*
5:12, *149*
5:12-14, *149*
6, *4*

6:2, *121*
7:7, *121*
8:24-26, *57*
8:31, *122*
9–16, *29*
10:17, *4*
12, *28, 177*
12:3, *23, 28*
12:6, *12, 15, 16, 17, 18, 22, 23, 27, 28, 30, 53, 101, 162, 163*
15:4, *146*
16:20, *143*

1 Corinthians
1, *116*
8:1, *101*
11:2, *52, 75, 161*
12, *42*
12:11, *44*
13, *57*
13:13, *34, 57*
14, *17, 28, 30*
14:2, *80*
14:5, *23, 28*
15, *177*
15:28, *111*
15:55-57, *117, 121*

2 Corinthians
12:9, *125*

Galatians
1:8, *23, 28, 84, 94, 150*
2:11-14, *136*
3:6, *3, 4*
4:21-31, *8*

Ephesians
5:15, *60*

Colossians
1:16, *73*
1:17, *100*
2:1, *117, 122*
2:15, *151*
2:17, *36*

1 Thessalonians
5:21, *23, 44, 59*

1 Timothy
1:15, *157*
4:5, *33*
6:20, *101*

2 Timothy
4, *30*

Hebrews
2:14, *95, 143*
2:14-15, *97*
11:19, *87*
12:1, *81*

1 Peter
2:24, *127*

2 Peter
1:16-21, *23, 28*
1:20-21, *166*

1 John
4:1, *23, 28*
5:1, *122*

Revelation
12:4, *131*
12:17, *143*
13:3, *143*
20:2-3, *143*

New Explorations in Theology Series

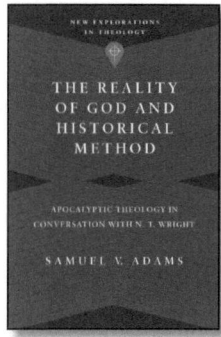

*The Reality of God
and Historical Method*
978-0-8308-4914-7

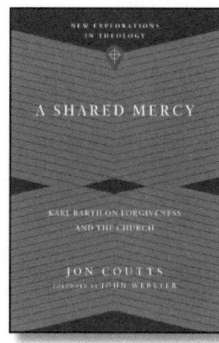

A Shared Mercy
978-0-8308-4915-4

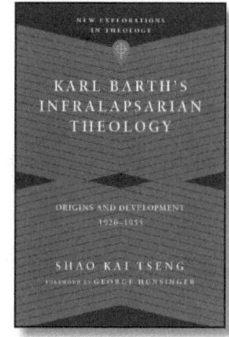

*Karl Barth's Infralapsarian
Theology*
978-0-8308-5132-4

Chrysostom's Devil
978-0-8308-4917-8

*The Making of
Stanley Hauerwas*
978-0-8308-4916-1

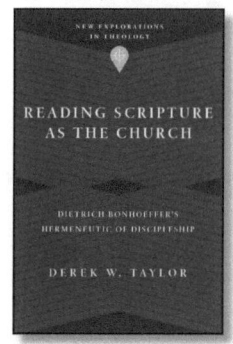

Reading Scripture as the Church
978-0-8308-4918-5

*T. F. Torrance
as Missional Theologian*
978-0-8308-4920-8

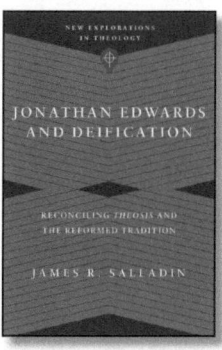

*Jonathan Edwards
and Deification*
978-1-5140-0046-5